Mathematics for Economics and Business

Second Edition

r. Lewins@ic.ac.uk

Mathematics for Economics and Business

Second Edition

Ian Jacques
Coventry University

ADDISON-WESLEY

Harlow, England · Reading, Massachusetts · Menlo Park, California
New York · Don Mills, Ontario · Amsterdam · Bonn · Sydney
Singapore · Tokyo · Madrid · San Juan · Milan · Mexico City
Seoul · Taipei

Addison-Wesley Longman Limited
Edinburgh Gate
Harlow
Essex
CM20 2JE
England
and Associated Companies throughout the world.

Many of the designations used by manufacturers and sellers to distinguish their products are
claimed as trademarks. Addison-Wesley has made every attempt to supply trademark information
about manufacturers and their products mentioned in this book.

Cover design by Viva Design Ltd, Henley-on-Thames
Produced by Addison Wesley Longman China Limited, Hong Kong
NPCC/05

First edition published 1991. Reprinted 1992 and 1993 (twice)
Second edition printed 1994. Reprinted 1996 (twice) and 1998

ISBN 0-201-42769-9

British Library Cataloguing in Publication Data
A catalogue record for this book is available from the British Library.

Library of Congress Cataloging in Publication Data applied for.

To my wife Victoria

Preface to the Second Edition

I would like to express my sincere thanks to the many anonymous reviewers for their constructive suggestions. Their kind and encouraging comments are much appreciated. It is very tempting to put all of these ideas into the new edition. Unfortunately this would increase the length and hence the price of the book, which is something I am reluctant to do. To prevent any significant increase in cost, I have taken the (unusual) step of actually removing one chapter from the first edition to make room for the new material. I apologize to those lecturers who made use of the previous chapter on dynamics. Feedback indicated that this topic is usually taught in the second year of a degree course so is less appropriate for a book at this level.

The new material includes:

- Internal rate of return
- Cramer's rule
- Linear programming

Personally, I would have liked to have put linear programming into the first chapter since I find that this topic is well liked by students and is an ideal vehicle for introducing problem formulation skills. However I recognize that this may not be taught to all first year students, so I have relegated it to the final chapter. This is self-contained and I would like to think that some users will take the opportunity to teach this topic at an early stage of the course.

One final change worth mentioning concerns the treatment of the exponential function. This material has been collected together as a single section, which I hope will enhance students' understanding. It also means that the student's first encounter with differentiation is no longer hindered by the need to grapple with the exponential function at the same time.

Ian Jacques
Coventry, December 1994

Preface to the First Edition

This book is primarily intended for students on economics, business studies and accountancy courses. It assumes very little prerequisite knowledge so it can be read by students who have not undertaken a mathematics course for some time. The style is informal and the book contains a large number of worked examples. Students are encouraged to tackle problems for themselves as they read through each section. Detailed solutions are provided so that all answers can be checked. Consequently, it should be possible to work through this book on a self-study basis. The material is wideranging and varies from elementary topics such as linear and quadratic equations to more sophisticated topics such as constrained optimization of multivariate functions. The book should therefore be suitable for use on both low and high level quantitative methods courses.

I am indebted to the students at Coventry Polytechnic who have been subjected to my lectures during the past six years. It has been an immensely enjoyable and stimulating experience teaching mathematics to a group of students who have an in-built fear of the subject and who need to be constantly persuaded of its utility. Over the years I have experimented with different ways of teaching the material and have tried out numerous examples. These have now converged to the content of this book which I hope is reasonably close to the optimum.

I am extremely grateful to Colin Judd for his painstaking reading of the manuscript. I envy his patience and forbearance in tackling such a difficult task with so little reward.

Ian Jacques
Coventry, June 1991

Contents

Introduction: Getting Started

Notes for students: how to use this book

I am always amazed by the mix of students on first year economics courses. Some have not acquired any mathematical knowledge beyond elementary algebra (and even that can be of a rather dubious nature), some have never studied economics before in their lives, while others have passed preliminary courses in both. Whatever category you are in I hope that you will find this book of value. The chapters covering algebraic manipulation, simple calculus, finance and matrices should also benefit students on business studies and accountancy courses.

The first few chapters are specifically aimed at complete beginners and students who have not taken mathematics courses for some time. I would like to think that these students once enjoyed mathematics, and had every intention of continuing their studies in this area, but somehow never found the time to fit it into an already overcrowded academic timetable. However, I suspect that reality is rather different. Possibly they hated the subject, could not understand it and dropped it at the earliest opportunity. If you find yourself in this position you are probably horrified to discover that you must embark on a quantitative methods course with an examination looming on the horizon. However, there is no need to worry. My experience is that every student, no matter how innumerate, is capable of passing a mathematics examination. All that is required is a commitment to study and a willingness to suspend any prejudices about the subject gained at school. The fact that you have bothered to buy this book at all suggests that you are prepared to do both.

To help you get the most out of this book let me compare the working practices of economics and engineering students. The former rarely bother to read individual books in any great depth. They tend to visit college libraries (usually several days after an essay was due to be handed in) and to skim through a large number of books picking out the relevant information. Indeed, the ability to read selectively and to compare various sources of information is an important skill that all arts and social science students must acquire. Engineering students, on the other hand, are more likely to read just a few books in any one year. They read each of these cover to cover and attempt virtually every problem en route. Even though you are most definitely not an engineer, it is the engineering approach that you need to adopt while studying mathematics. There are several reasons for this. Firstly, a mathematics book can never be described, even by its most ardent admirers, as a good bedtime read. It can take an hour or two of concentrated effort to understand just a few pages of a mathematics text. You are therefore recommended to work through this book systematically in short bursts rather than to attempt to read whole chapters. Each section is designed to

1

take between one and two hours to complete and this is quite sufficient for a single session. Secondly, it is a hierarchical subject in which one topic follows on from the next. A construction firm building an office block is hardly likely to erect the 50th storey without making sure that the intermediate floors and foundations are securely in place. Likewise, you cannot 'dip' into the middle of a mathematics book and expect to follow it unless you have satisfied the prerequisites for that topic. Finally, you actually need to do mathematics yourself before you can understand it. No matter how wonderful your lecturer is, and no matter how many problems are discussed in class, it is only by solving problems yourself that you are ever going to become confident in using and applying mathematical techniques. For this reason several problems are interspersed within the text and you are encouraged to tackle these as you go along. You will require writing paper, graph paper, pens and a calculator for this. There is no need to buy an expensive calculator unless you are feeling particularly wealthy at the moment. A bottom of the range **scientific** calculator should be good enough. Detailed solutions are provided at the end of each chapter so that you can check your answers. However, please avoid the temptation to look at them until you have made an honest attempt at each one. Remember that in the future you may well have to sit down in an uncomfortable chair, in front of a blank sheet of paper and be expected to produce solutions to examination questions of a similar type.

At the end of each section there are some further practice problems to try. You may prefer not to bother with these and to work through them later as part of your revision. Ironically it is those students who really ought to try more problems who are most likely to miss them out. Human psychology is such that if students do not first succeed in solving problems then they are deterred from trying additional problems. However, it is precisely these people who need more practice.

The chapter dependence is shown in Figure I.1. If you have studied some advanced mathematics before then you will discover that parts of Chapters 1, 2 and 4 are familiar. However, you may find that the sections on economic applications contain new material.

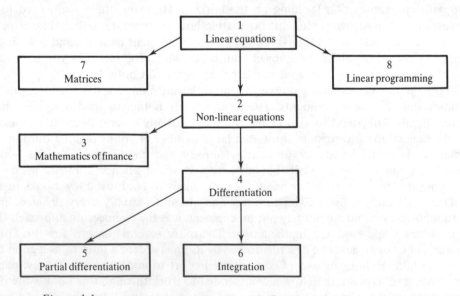

Figure 1.1

You are best advised to test yourself by attempting a selection of problems in each section to see if you need to read through it as part of a refresher course. Economics students in a desperate hurry to experience the delights of calculus can miss out Chapter 3 without any loss of continuity and move straight on to Chapter 4. The mathematics of finance is probably more relevant to business and accountancy students although you can always read it later if it is part of your economics syllabus.

I hope that this book helps you to succeed in your mathematics course. You never know, you might even enjoy it. Remember to wear your engineer's hat while reading the book. I have done my best to make the material as accessible as possible. The rest is up to you!

Notes for tutors: an author's apology

It may seem strange to begin a textbook with an apology. However, apologize I must because there may be some lecturers who will be disappointed, infuriated or upset by this book. Students are given doses of mathematics in many different ways. Some economics and business studies students are expected to go to classes on algebra and calculus which are also attended by students of other disciplines such as physics. Under these circumstances it is impossible to teach any relevant applications and it is not surprising that these students regard mathematics as a bogey subject which it most certainly is not. At the other extreme, mathematics is sometimes taught in-house and is discussed as and when it arises in an economics lecture. The danger of this approach is that it is taught unsystematically and students get lost amidst a flurry of unfamiliar algebraic manipulation. Also, students often fail to make the connection between a piece of mathematics taught in, say, a macroeconomics lecture and the same topic taught in a microeconomics class. This is a great pity because it is precisely the generality of mathematics which makes it so useful. This book falls into neither camp and I apologize to those of you who strongly adhere to either philosophy. In this text mathematics is used to lead the discussion but a large number of applications are introduced once the mathematical ideas have sunk in.

The approach that I have adopted is entirely informal. No attempt is made to dot all of the 'i's or to cross all of the 't's. Please accept my apologies for any inaccuracies that result. For example, I am aware that the integral of the reciprocal function, $1/x$, should really be $\ln|x|$ rather than $\ln x$. However, to spend time pointing out such niceties is an unnecessary distraction to students who are anxious to push ahead and to see the applicability of integration. Also, I apologize for any mistakes or lack of subtlety in describing economics in this book. I have tried to introduce economic concepts and theories in the most elementary way I can with a view to showing students the relevance of mathematics as quickly and as painlessly as possible.

Many students have little or no understanding of basic algebra. Some cannot even multiply negative numbers or add fractions. Consequently, it is essential that weaker students are given an early opportunity to study these topics. However, to bombard them with a crash course on algebra at the very beginning is offputting to say the least. I have tried to smuggle bits of arithmetic and algebra throughout the first two chapters to spread the load. My hope is that students will see the importance and relevance of these skills as they meet them.

As you might expect, calculus is a substantial part of this book. I have used pictures to explain the basic ideas and have shied away from using limits. To kick off a discussion of calculus with formal definitions and proofs seems misguided. Students can always be referred to more advanced books which adopt a rigorous approach. I always promise myself that I will revisit calculus towards the end of a lecture course and show students how it can all be done properly but in practice I just don't seem to have the time!

Finally, I apologize for the ordering of the material. I am aware, for example, that the topics of matrices and linear programming considered in Chapters 7 and 8 are much easier than, say, the topic of partial differentiation in Chapter 5. The former are more or less free-standing topics which could be taught at any time after Chapter 1. The advantage of leaving these to the end is that it enables a lecturer to reach the dizzy heights of multivariate calculus as fast as possible and it is always comforting to know that there are two choice 'plums' left over to teach at the end!

1 *Linear Equations*

The main aim of this chapter is to introduce the mathematics of linear equations. This is an obvious first choice in an introductory text since it is an easy topic which has many applications. There are five sections which are intended to be read in the order that they appear.

Sections 1.1, 1.2 and 1.4 are devoted to mathematical methods. They serve to revise the rules of arithmetic and algebra which you probably met at school but may have forgotten. In particular, the properties of negative numbers and fractions are considered. A reminder is given on how to multiply out brackets and how to manipulate mathematical expressions. You are also shown how to solve simultaneous linear equations. Systems of two equations in two unknowns can be solved using graphs which are described in Section 1.1. However, the preferred method uses elimination which is considered in Section 1.2. This algebraic approach has the advantage that it always gives an exact solution and it extends readily to larger systems of equations.

The remaining two sections are reserved for applications in microeconomics and macroeconomics. You may be pleasantly surprised by how much economic theory you can analyse using just the basic mathematical tools considered here. Section 1.3 introduces the fundamental concept of an economic function and describes how to calculate equilibrium prices and quantities in supply and demand theory. Section 1.5 deals with national income determination in simple macroeconomic models.

The first four sections underpin the rest of the book and are essential reading. The final section is not quite as important and can be omitted if desired.

1.1   Graphs of linear equations

Objectives   At the end of this section you should be able to:

- plot points on graph paper given their coordinates,

- add, subtract, multiply and divide negative numbers,

- sketch a line by finding the coordinates of two points on the line,

- solve simultaneous linear equations graphically,

- sketch a line by using its slope and intercept.

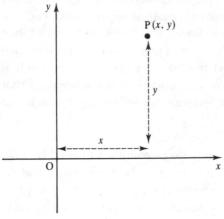

Figure 1.1

Consider the two straight lines shown in Figure 1.1. The horizontal line is referred to as the **x axis** and the vertical line is referred to as the **y axis**. The point where these lines intersect is known as the **origin** and is denoted by the letter O. These lines enable us to identify uniquely any point, P, in terms of its **coordinates**, (x, y). The first number, x, denotes the horizontal distance along the x axis and the second number, y, denotes the vertical distance along the y axis. The arrows on the axes indicate the positive direction in each case.

A point A with coordinates $(2, 3)$ is obtained by starting at the origin, moving 2 units to the right and then moving 3 units vertically upwards. Similarly, a point B with coordinates $(-1, 4)$ is located 1 unit to the left of O (because the x coordinate is negative) and 4 units up. These points, together with C $(-3, -1)$, D $(3, -2)$ and E $(5, 0)$ are plotted in Figure 1.2.

Note that the point C lies in the bottom left-hand quadrant since its x and y coordinates are both negative. It is also worth noticing that E actually lies on the x axis since its y coordinate is zero. Likewise, a point with coordinates of the form $(0, y)$ for some number y would lie somewhere on the y axis. Of course, the point with coordinates $(0, 0)$ is the origin, O.

PROBLEM

1   Plot the following points on graph paper. What do you observe?

$(2, 5), (1, 3), (0, 1), (-2, -3), (-3, -5)$

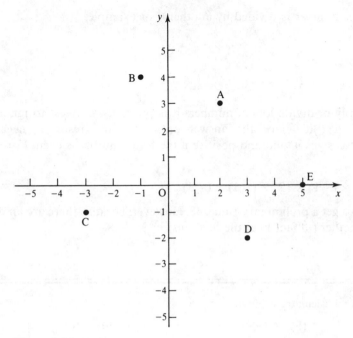

Figure 1.2

Before we can continue the discussion of graphs it is worthwhile revising the properties of negative numbers. The rules for the multiplication of negative numbers are

| negative | × | negative | = | positive |

| negative | × | positive | = | negative |

It does not matter in which order two numbers are multiplied so

| positive | × | negative | = | negative |

These rules produce

$$(-2) \times (-3) = 6$$
$$(-4) \times 5 = -20$$
$$7 \times (-5) = -35$$

respectively. Also, because division is the same sort of operation as multiplication (it just undoes the result of multiplication and takes you back to where you started) exactly the same rules apply when one number is divided by another. For example,

$$(-15) \div (-3) = 5$$
$$(-16) \div 2 = -8$$
$$2 \div (-4) = -1/2$$

In general, to multiply or divide lots of numbers it is probably simplest to ignore the signs to begin with and just to work the answer out. The final result is negative if the total number of minus signs is odd and positive if the total number is even. For example, to evaluate

$$(-2) \times (-4) \times (-1) \times (2) \times (-1) \times (-3)$$

we ignore the signs to get a preliminary value, 48. However, because there are an odd number of minus signs altogether (in fact five) the final answer is -48.

PROBLEM

2 (1) Without using a calculator evaluate

(a) $5 \times (-6)$ **(b)** $(-1) \times (-2)$ **(c)** $(-50) \div 10$

(d) $(-5) \div (-1)$ **(e)** $2 \times (-1) \times (-3) \times 6$ **(f)** $\dfrac{2 \times (-1) \times (-3) \times 6}{(-2) \times 3 \times 6}$

(2) Confirm your answer to part (1) using a calculator.

To add or subtract negative numbers it helps to think in terms of a picture of the x axis:

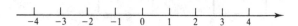

If b is a positive number then

$$a - b$$

can be thought of as an instruction to start at a and to move b units to the left. For example,

$$1 - 3 = -2$$

because if you start at 1 and move 3 units to the left you end up at -2:

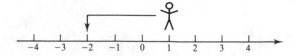

Similarly,

$$-2 - 1 = -3$$

because one unit to the left of -2 is -3.

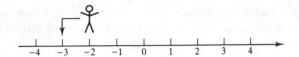

On the other hand,

$$a - (-b)$$

is taken to be $a + b$. This follows from the rule for multiplying two negative numbers since

$$-(-b) = (-1) \times (-b) = b$$

Consequently, to evaluate

$$a - (-b)$$

you start at a and move b units to the right (that is, in the positive direction). For example,

$$-2 - (-5) = -2 + 5 = 3$$

because if you start at -2 and move 5 units to the right you end up at 3.

PROBLEM

3 **(1)** Without using a calculator evaluate

    (a) $1 - 2$ **(b)** $-3 - 4$ **(c)** $1 - (-4)$

    (d) $-1 - (-1)$ **(e)** $-72 - 19$ **(f)** $-53 - (-48)$

(2) Confirm your answer to part (1) using a calculator.

We now return to the problem of graphs. In economics we need to do rather more than just to plot individual points on graph paper. We would like to be able to sketch curves represented by equations and to deduce information from such a picture. Incidentally, it is sometimes more appropriate to label axes using letters other than x and y. For example, in the analysis of supply and demand the variables involved are the quantity and price of a good. It is then convenient to use Q and P instead of x and y. This helps us to remember which variable we have used on which axis. However, in this section, only the letters x and y are used. Also, we restrict our attention to those equations whose graphs are straight lines, deferring consideration of more general curve sketching until Chapter 2.

In Problem 1 you will have noticed that the five points $(2, 5)$, $(1, 3)$, $(0, 1)$, $(-2, -3)$ and $(-3, -5)$ all lie on a straight line. In fact, the equation of this line is

$$-2x + y = 1$$

Any point lies on this line if its x and y coordinates satisfy this equation. For example, $(2, 5)$ lies on the line because when the values $x = 2$ and $y = 5$ are substituted into the left-hand side of the equation we obtain

$$-2(2) + 5 = -4 + 5 = 1$$

which is the right-hand side of the equation. The other points can be checked similarly.

Point	Check	
$(1, 3)$	$-2(1) + 3 = -2 + 3 = 1$	✓
$(0, 1)$	$-2(0) + 1 = 0 + 1 = 1$	✓
$(-2, -3)$	$-2(-2) - 3 = 4 - 3 = 1$	✓
$(-3, -5)$	$-2(-3) - 5 = 6 - 5 = 1$	✓

Notice how the rules for manipulating negative numbers have been used in the calculations.

The general equation of a straight line takes the form

$$\boxed{\begin{array}{c}\text{a multiple}\\\text{of } x\end{array}} \quad + \quad \boxed{\begin{array}{c}\text{a multiple}\\\text{of } y\end{array}} \quad = \quad \boxed{\begin{array}{c}\text{a}\\\text{number}\end{array}}$$

that is

$$dx + ey = f$$

for some given numbers d, e and f. Consequently, such an equation is called a **linear equation**.

The numbers d and e are referred to as the **coefficients**. The coefficients of the linear equation,

$$-2x + y = 1$$

are -2 and 1 (the coefficient of y is 1 because y can be thought of as $1 \times y$).

PROBLEM

4 Check that the points

$$(-1, 2), (-4, 4), (5, -2), (2, 0)$$

all lie on the line

$$2x + 3y = 4$$

and hence sketch this line on graph paper. Does the point $(3, -1)$ lie on this line? How could you test this algebraically?

In general, to sketch a line from its mathematical equation, it is sufficient to calculate the coordinates of any two distinct points lying on it. These two points can be plotted on graph paper and a ruler used to draw the line passing through them. One way of finding the coordinates of a point on a line is simply to choose a numerical value for x and to substitute it into the equation. The equation can then be used to deduce the corresponding value of y. The whole process can be repeated to find the coordinates of the second point by choosing another value for x.

EXAMPLE

Sketch the line

$$4x + 3y = 11$$

Solution

For the first point, let us choose $x = 5$. Substitution of this number into the equation gives

$$4(5) + 3y = 11$$

$$20 + 3y = 11$$

The problem now is to find the value of y which satisfies this equation. A naïve approach might be to use trial and error, that is we could just keep guessing values of y until we find the one that works. Can you guess what y is in this case? However, a more reliable and systematic approach is actually to solve this equation using the rules of mathematics. In fact, the only rule that we need is this:

> you can apply whatever mathematical operation you like to an equation, *provided that you do the same thing to both sides*

There is only one exception to this rule; you must never divide both sides by zero. This should be obvious because a number such as $11/0$ does not exist. (If you do not believe this try dividing 11 by 0 on your calculator.)

The first obstacle which prevents us from writing down the value of y immediately is the number 20 which is added on to the left-hand side. This can be removed by subtracting 20 from the left-hand side. In order for this to be legal we must also subtract 20 from the right-hand side to get

$$3y = 11 - 20$$

$$3y = -9$$

The second obstacle is the number 3 which is multiplying the y. This can be removed by dividing the left-hand side by 3. Of course, we must also divide the right-hand side by 3 to get

$$y = -9/3 = -3$$

Consequently, the coordinates of one point on the line are $(5, -3)$.

For the second point, let us choose $x = -1$. Substitution of this number into the equation gives

$$4(-1) + 3y = 11$$

$$-4 + 3y = 11$$

This can be solved for y as follows:

$$3y = 11 + 4 = 15 \quad \text{(add 4 to both sides)}$$

$$y = 15/3 = 5 \quad \text{(divide both sides by 3)}$$

Hence $(-1, 5)$ lies on the line which can now be sketched on graph paper as shown in Figure 1.3.

■

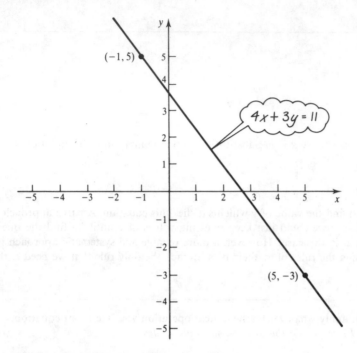

Figure 1.3

PROBLEM

5 Find the coordinates of two points on the line

$$3x - 2y = 4$$

by taking $x = 2$ for the first point and $x = -2$ for the second point. Hence sketch its graph.

In this example we arbitrarily picked two values of x and used the linear equation to work out the corresponding values of y. There is nothing particularly special about the variable x. We could equally well have chosen values for y and solved the resulting equations for x. In fact, the easiest thing to do (in terms of the amount of arithmetic involved) is to put $x = 0$ and find y and then to put $y = 0$ and find x.

EXAMPLE

Sketch the line

$$2x + y = 5$$

Solution

Setting $x = 0$ gives

$$2(0) + y = 5$$

$$0 + y = 5$$

$$y = 5$$

Hence $(0, 5)$ lies on the line.

Setting $y = 0$ gives

$$2x + 0 = 5$$

$$2x = 5$$

$$x = 5/2 \quad \text{(divide both sides by 2)}$$

Hence $(5/2, 0)$ lies on the line.

The line $2x + y = 5$ is sketched in Figure 1.4. Notice how easy the algebra is using this approach. The two points themselves are also slightly more meaningful. They are the points where the line intersects the coordinate axes.

■

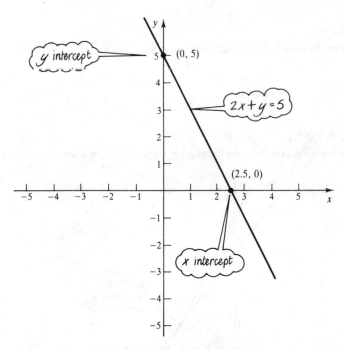

Figure 1.4

PROBLEM

6   Find the coordinates of the points where the line

$$x - 2y = 2$$

intersects the axes. Hence sketch its graph.

In economics it is sometimes necessary to handle more than one equation at the same time. For example, in supply and demand analysis we are interested in two equations, the supply equation and the demand equation. Both involve the same variables Q and P so it makes sense to sketch them on the same diagram. This enables the market equilibrium quantity and price to be determined by finding the point of intersection of the two lines. We shall return to the analysis of supply and demand in Section 1.3. There are many other occasions in economics and business studies when it is necessary to determine the coordinates of points of intersection. The following is a straightforward example which illustrates the general principle.

EXAMPLE

Find the point of intersection of the two lines

$$4x + 3y = 11$$

$$2x + y = 5$$

Solution

We have already seen how to sketch these lines in the previous two examples. We discovered that

$$4x + 3y = 11$$

passes through $(5, -3)$ and $(-1, 5)$, and that

$$2x + y = 5$$

passes through $(0, 5)$ and $(5/2, 0)$.

These two lines are sketched on the same diagram in Figure 1.5 from which the point of intersection is seen to be $(2, 1)$.

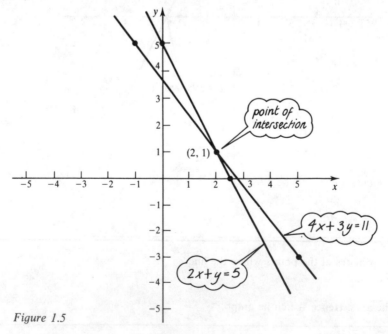

Figure 1.5

It is easy to verify that we have not made any mistakes by checking that $(2, 1)$ lies on both lines. It lies on

$$4x + 3y = 11$$

because

$$4(2) + 3(1) = 8 + 3 = 11 \quad \checkmark$$

and lies on

$$2x + y = 5$$

because

$$2(2) + 1 = 4 + 1 = 5 \quad \checkmark$$

For this reason, we say that $x = 2$, $y = 1$, is the solution of the **simultaneous linear equations**

$$4x + 3y = 11$$
$$2x + y = 5$$

■

PROBLEM

7 Find the point of intersection of

$$3x - 2y = 4$$
$$x - 2y = 2$$

[Hint: you might find your answers to Problems 5 and 6 useful.]

Quite often it is not necessary to produce an accurate plot of an equation. All that may be required is an indication of the general shape together with a few key points or features. It can be shown that provided e is non-zero any equation given by

$$dx + ey = f$$

can be rearranged into the special form

$$y = ax + b$$

An example showing you how to perform such a rearrangement will be considered in a moment. The coefficients a and b have particular significance which we now examine. To be specific, consider

$$y = 2x - 3$$

in which $a = 2$ and $b = -3$.

When x is taken to be zero the value of y is

$$y = 2(0) - 3 = -3$$

The line passes through $(0, -3)$ so the y intercept is -3. This is just the value of b. In other words, the constant term, b, represents the **intercept** on the y axis.

In the same way it is easy to see that, a, the coefficient of x, determines the **slope** of the line. The slope of a straight line is simply the change in the value of y brought about by a one unit increase in the value of x. For the equation

$$y = 2x - 3$$

let us choose $x = 5$ and increase this by a single unit to get $x = 6$. The corresponding values of y are then

$$y = 2(5) - 3 = 10 - 3 = 7$$
$$y = 2(6) - 3 = 12 - 3 = 9$$

respectively. The value of y increases by 2 units when x rises by 1 unit. The slope of the line is therefore 2 which is the value of a. The slope of a line is fixed throughout its length so it is immaterial which two points are taken. The particular choice of $x = 5$ and $x = 6$ was entirely arbitrary. You might like to convince yourself of this by choosing two other points such as $x = 20$ and $x = 21$, say, and repeating the previous calculations.

A graph of the line

$$y = 2x - 3$$

is sketched in Figure 1.6. This is sketched using the information that the intercept is -3 and that for every 1 unit along we go 2 units up. In this example the coefficient of x is positive. This does not have to be the case. If a is negative then for every increase in x there is a corresponding decrease in y, indicating that the line is downhill. If a is zero then the equation is just

$$y = b$$

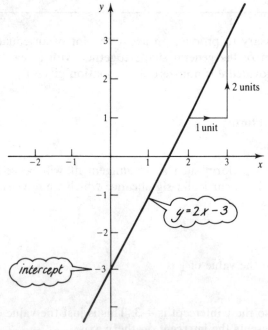

Figure 1.6

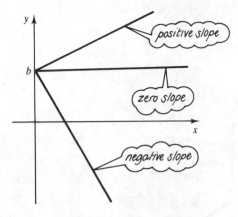

Figure 1.7

indicating that y is fixed at b and the line is horizontal. The three cases are illustrated in Figure 1.7.

It is important to appreciate that in order to use the slope–intercept approach it is necessary for the equation to be written as

$$y = ax + b$$

If a linear equation does not have this form it is usually possible to perform a preliminary rearrangement to isolate the variable y on the left-hand side as the following example demonstrates.

EXAMPLE

Use the slope–intercept approach to sketch the line

$$2x + 3y = 12$$

Solution

We can remove the x term on the left-hand side of

$$2x + 3y = 12$$

by subtracting $2x$. As usual, to balance the equation we must also subtract $2x$ from the right-hand side to get

$$3y = 12 - 2x$$

We now just divide through by 3 to get

$$y = 4 - \tfrac{2}{3}x$$

This is now in the required form with $a = -2/3$ and $b = 4$. The line is sketched in Figure 1.8. A slope of $-2/3$ means that for every 1 unit along we go 2/3 units down (or, equivalently, for every 3 units along we go 2 units down). An intercept of 4 means that it passes through $(0, 4)$.

■

PROBLEM

8   Use the slope–intercept approach to sketch the lines

   (a) $y = x + 2$ **(b)** $4x + 2y = 1$

This completes your first piece of mathematics. I hope that you have not found it quite as bad as you first thought! There now follow a few extra problems to give you more practice. If you have successfully tackled all of the problems given in the text so far you might

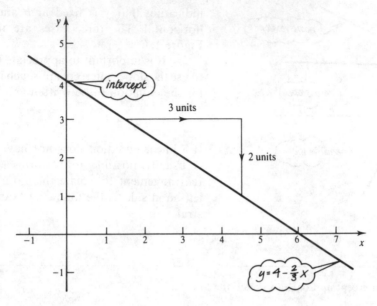

Figure 1.8

prefer to move straight on to the next section. Problems 9–12 can be attempted later as part of your revision. However, if you failed to obtain the correct answers to Problems 1–8 then you should try the practice problems now. Not only will they help to strengthen your mathematical skills but also they should improve your overall confidence.

PRACTICE PROBLEMS

9 Plot the following points on graph paper:

$$P\ (4, 0),\ Q\ (-2, 9),\ R\ (5, 8),\ S\ (-1, -2)$$

Hence find the coordinates of the point of intersection of the line passing through P and Q, and the line passing through R and S.

10 Without using a calculator evaluate

(a) $10 \times (-2)$ (b) $(-1) \times (-3)$ (c) $(-8) \div 2$
(d) $(-5) \div (-5)$ (e) $5 - 6$ (f) $-1 - 2$

(g) $7 - (-4)$ (h) $-9 - (-9)$ (i) $\dfrac{(-3) \times (-6) \times (-1)}{2 - 3}$

11 Solve the following pairs of simultaneous linear equations graphically:

(a) $-2x + y = 2$ (b) $3x + 4y = 12$ (c) $2x + y = 4$ (d) $x + y = 1$
      $2x + y = -6$ $x + 4y = 8$ $4x - 3y = 3$ $6x + 5y = 15$

12 Use the slope–intercept approach to sketch the lines

(a) $y = -x$ (b) $x - 2y = 6$

1.2 Algebraic solution of simultaneous linear equations

Objectives   At the end of this section you should be able to:

- solve a system of two simultaneous linear equations in two unknowns using elimination,

- detect when a system of equations does not have a solution,

- detect when a system of equations has infinitely many solutions,

- solve a system of three simultaneous linear equations in three unknowns using elimination.

In Section 1.1 a graphical method was described for the solution of simultaneous linear equations. Both lines are sketched on the same piece of graph paper and the coordinates of the point of intersection are then simply read off from the diagram. Unfortunately this approach has several drawbacks. It is not always easy to decide on a suitable scale for the axes. Even if the scale allows all four points (two from each line) to fit on the diagram, there is no guarantee that the point of intersection itself also lies on it. You may have encountered this difficulty when solving Problem 11(d) in the previous section. When this happens you have no alternative but to throw away your graph paper and to start again, choosing a smaller scale in the hope that the solution will now fit. The second drawback concerns the accuracy of the graphical solution. All of the problems in Section 1.1 were deliberately chosen so that the answers had nice numbers in them; whole numbers such as -1, 2 and 5 or at worst simple fractions such as $\frac{1}{2}$, $2\frac{1}{2}$ and $-\frac{1}{4}$. In practice, the coefficients of the equations may well involve decimals and we might expect a decimal solution. Indeed, even if the coefficients are whole numbers the solution itself could involve nasty fractions such as $7/8$ or perhaps something like $231/571$. A moment's thought should convince you that in these circumstances it is virtually impossible to obtain the solution graphically, even if we use a really large scale and our sharpest HB pencil in the process! The final drawback concerns the nature of the problem itself. Quite frequently in economics we need to solve three equations in three unknowns or maybe four equations in four unknowns. Unfortunately, the graphical method of solution does not extend to these cases.

In this section an alternative method of solution is described which relies on algebra. It is called the **elimination method** since each stage of the process eliminates one (or more) of the unknowns. This method always produces the exact solution and can be applied to systems of equations larger than just two equations in two unknowns. In order to motivate the method we return to the simple example considered in the previous section:

$$4x + 3y = 11 \quad (1)$$
$$2x + \ y = \ 5 \quad (2)$$

The coefficient of x in equation (1) is 4 and the coefficient of x in equation (2) is 2. If these numbers had turned out to be exactly the same then we could have eliminated the variable x by subtracting one equation from the other. However, we can arrange for this to be the case by multiplying the left-hand side of the second equation by 2. Of course, we must also remember to multiply the right-hand side of the second equation by 2 in order for this operation to be valid. The second equation then becomes

$$4x + 2y = 10 \qquad (3)$$

We may now subtract equation (3) from (1) to get

$$y = 1$$

You may like to think of this in terms of the usual layout for the subtraction of two ordinary numbers, that is

$$4x + 3y = 11$$
$$\underline{4x + 2y = 10} \quad -$$
$$y = 1$$

the x's cancel when you subtract ✓

This number can now be substituted into one of the original equations to deduce x. From equation (1)

$$4x + 3(1) = 11 \qquad \text{(substitute } y = 1)$$
$$4x + 3 = 11$$
$$4x = 8 \qquad \text{(subtract 3 from both sides)}$$
$$x = 2 \qquad \text{(divide both sides by 4)}$$

Hence the solution is $x = 2$, $y = 1$. As a check, substitution of these values into the other original equation (2) gives

$$2(2) + 1 = 5 \qquad \checkmark$$

The method of elimination can be summarized as follows.

Step 1   Add/subtract a multiple of one equation to/from a multiple of the other to eliminate x.

Step 2   Solve the resulting equation for y.

Step 3   Substitute the value of y into one of the original equations to deduce x.

Step 4   Check that no mistakes have been made by substituting both x and y into the other original equation.

Warning   The following example involves fractions. If you have forgotten how to perform calculations with fractions you might like to read through subsection 1.4.3 (p. 50) now since this section contains a review of their basic properties.

EXAMPLE ───

Solve the system of equations

$$3x + 2y = 1 \qquad (1)$$
$$-2x + \ y = 2 \qquad (2)$$

Solution

Step 1 The coefficients of x in equations (1) and (2) are 3 and -2 respectively. We can arrange for these to be the same size (but of opposite sign) by multiplying equation (1) by 2 and multiplying (2) by 3. The new equations will then have x coefficients of 6 and -6 so we can eliminate x this time by adding the equations together. The details are as follows.

Doubling the first equation produces

$$6x + 4y = 2 \qquad (3)$$

Tripling the second equation produces

$$-6x + 3y = 6 \qquad (4)$$

If equation (4) is added to equation (3) then

$$
\begin{aligned}
6x + 4y &= 2 \\
-6x + 3y &= 6 \quad + \\
\hline
7y &= 8 \qquad (5)
\end{aligned}
$$

the x's cancel when you add

Step 2 Equation (5) can be solved by dividing both sides by 7 to get

$$y = 8/7$$

Step 3 If 8/7 is substituted for y in equation (1) then

$$3x + 2\left(\frac{8}{7}\right) = 1$$

$$3x + \frac{16}{7} = 1$$

$$3x = 1 - \frac{16}{7} \qquad \text{(subtract 16/7 from both sides)}$$

$$3x = \frac{7 - 16}{7} \qquad \text{(put over a common denominator)}$$

$$3x = -\frac{9}{7}$$

$$x = \frac{1}{3} \times \left(-\frac{9}{7}\right) \qquad \text{(divide both sides by 3)}$$

$$x = -\frac{3}{7}$$

The solution is therefore $x = -3/7$, $y = 8/7$.

Step 4   As a check, equation (2) gives

$$-2\left(-\frac{3}{7}\right) + \frac{8}{7} = \frac{6}{7} + \frac{8}{7} = \frac{6 + 8}{7} = \frac{14}{7} = 2 \quad \checkmark$$

∎

In the general description of the method we suggested that the variable x is eliminated in step 1. There is nothing special about x. We could equally well eliminate y at this stage and then solve the resulting equation in step 2 for x. You might like to solve the above example using this alternative strategy.

PROBLEM

1 **(1)**   Solve the equations

$$3x - 2y = 4$$
$$x - 2y = 2$$

by eliminating one of the variables.
   (2)   Solve the equations

$$3x + 5y = 19$$
$$-5x + 2y = -11$$

by eliminating one of the variables.

The following examples provide further practice in using the method and illustrate some special cases which may occur.

EXAMPLE

Solve the system of equations

$$x - 2y = 1$$
$$2x - 4y = -3$$

Solution

Step 1   The variable x can be eliminated by doubling the first equation and subtracting the second:

both the x's and the y's cancel !

$$
\begin{array}{r}
2x - 4y = 2 \\
2x - 4y = -3 \\
\hline
0 = 5
\end{array}
\quad -
$$

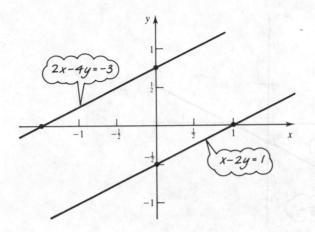

Figure 1.9

The statement '$0 = 5$' is clearly nonsense and something has gone seriously wrong. To understand what is going on here let us try and solve this problem graphically.

The line $x - 2y = 1$ passes through the points $(0, -1/2)$ and $(1, 0)$ (check this). The line $2x - 4y = -3$ passes through the points $(0, 3/4)$ and $(-3/2, 0)$ (check this). Figure 1.9 shows that these lines are parallel and so they do not intersect. It is therefore not surprising that we were unable to find a solution using algebra because this system of equations does not have one. We could have deduced this before when subtracting the equations. The equation which only involves y in step 2 can be written as

$$0y = 5$$

and the problem is to find a value of y for which this equation is true. No such value exists since

$$\boxed{\text{zero}} \quad \times \quad \boxed{\begin{array}{c}\text{any}\\\text{number}\end{array}} \quad = \quad \boxed{\text{zero}}$$

and so the original system of equations does not have a solution. ∎

EXAMPLE

Solve the equations

$$2x - 4y = 1$$
$$5x - 10y = 5/2$$

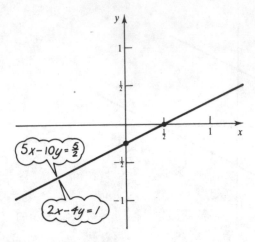

Figure 1.10

Solution

Step 1 The variable x can be eliminated by multiplying the first equation by 5, multiplying the second equation by 2 and subtracting,

$$10x - 20y = 5$$
$$\underline{10x - 20y = 5} \quad -$$
$$0 = 0$$

everything cancels including the right-hand side!

Again, it is easy to explain this using graphs. The line $2x - 4y = 1$ passes through $(0, -1/4)$ and $(1/2, 0)$. The line $5x - 10y = 5/2$ passes through $(0, -1/4)$ and $(1/2, 0)$. Consequently, both equations represent the same line. From Figure 1.10 the lines intersect along the whole of their length and any point on this line is a solution. This particular system of equations has infinitely many solutions. This can also be deduced algebraically. The equation involving y in step 2 is

$$0y = 0$$

which is true for any value of y.

∎

These examples show that a system of equations can possess a unique solution, no solution or infinitely many solutions. Algebraically this can be detected in step 2. If the equation resulting from the elimination of x looks like

$$\boxed{\text{any non-zero number}} \times \boxed{y} = \boxed{\text{any number}}$$

then the equations have a unique solution, or if it looks like

$$\boxed{\text{zero}} \times \boxed{y} = \boxed{\text{any non-zero number}}$$

then the equations have no solution, or if it looks like

$$\boxed{\text{zero}} \quad \times \quad \boxed{y} \quad = \quad \boxed{\text{zero}}$$

then the equations have infinitely many solutions.

It is interesting to notice how the graphical approach 'saved the day' in the previous two examples. They show how useful pictures are as an aid to understanding in mathematics.

PROBLEM

2 Attempt to solve the following systems of equations:

(a) $\begin{aligned} 3x - 6y &= -2 \\ -4x + 8y &= -1 \end{aligned}$ (b) $\begin{aligned} -5x + y &= 4 \\ 10x - 2y &= -8 \end{aligned}$

Comment on the nature of the solution in each case.

We now show how the algebraic method can be used to solve three equations in three unknowns. As you might expect, the details are more complicated than for just two equations, but the principle is the same. We begin with a simple example to motivate the general method. Consider the system

$$x + 3y - z = 4 \qquad (1)$$
$$2x + y + 2z = 10 \qquad (2)$$
$$3x - y + z = 4 \qquad (3)$$

The objective is to find three numbers x, y and z which satisfy these equations simultaneously. Our previous work suggests that we should begin by eliminating x from all but one of the equations.

The variable x can be eliminated from the second equation by multiplying equation (1) by 2 and subtracting equation (2):

$$\begin{aligned} 2x + 6y - 2z &= 8 \\ 2x + y + 2z &= 10 \quad - \\ \hline 5y - 4z &= -2 \qquad (4) \end{aligned}$$

Similarly, we can eliminate x from the third equation by multiplying equation (1) by 3 and subtracting equation (3):

$$\begin{aligned} 3x + 9y - 3z &= 12 \\ 3x - y + z &= 4 \quad - \\ \hline 10y - 4z &= 8 \qquad (5) \end{aligned}$$

At this stage the first equation is unaltered but the second and third equations of the system have changed to equations (4) and (5) respectively, so the current equations are

$$x + 3y - z = 4 \quad (1)$$
$$5y - 4z = -2 \quad (4)$$
$$10y - 4z = 8 \quad (5)$$

Notice that the last two equations constitute a system of just two equations in two unknowns, y and z. This, of course, is precisely the type of problem that we already know how to solve. Once y and z have been calculated the values can be substituted into equation (1) to deduce x.

We can eliminate y in the last equation by multiplying equation (4) by 2 and subtracting equation (5):

$$10y - 8z = -4$$
$$\underline{10y - 4z = 8} \quad -$$
$$-4z = -12 \quad (6)$$

Collecting together the current equations gives

$$x + 3y - z = 4 \quad (1)$$
$$5y - 4z = -2 \quad (4)$$
$$-4z = -12 \quad (6)$$

From the last equation,

$$z = \frac{-12}{-4} = 3 \quad \text{(divide both sides by } -4\text{)}$$

If this is substituted into equation (4) then

$$5y - 4(3) = -2$$
$$5y - 12 = -2$$
$$5y = 10 \quad \text{(add 12 to both sides)}$$
$$y = 2 \quad \text{(divide both sides by 5)}$$

Finally, substituting $y = 2$ and $z = 3$ into equation (1) produces

$$x + 3(2) - 3 = 4$$
$$x + 3 = 4$$
$$x = 1 \quad \text{(subtract 3 from both sides)}$$

Hence the solution is $x = 1$, $y = 2$, $z = 3$.

As usual, it is possible to check the answer by putting these numbers back into the original equations (1), (2) and (3):

$$1 + 3(2) - 3 = 4 \quad \checkmark$$
$$2(1) + 2 + 2(3) = 10 \quad \checkmark$$
$$3(1) - 2 + 3 = 4 \quad \checkmark$$

The general strategy may be summarized as follows. Consider the system

$$?x + ?y + ?z = ?$$
$$?x + ?y + ?z = ?$$
$$?x + ?y + ?z = ?$$

where ? denotes some numerical coefficient.

Step 1 Add/subtract multiples of the first equation to/from multiples of the second and third equations to eliminate x. This produces a new system of the form

$$?x + ?y + ?z = ?$$
$$?y + ?z = ?$$
$$?y + ?z = ?$$

Step 2 Add/subtract a multiple of the second equation to/from a multiple of the third to eliminate y. This produces a new system of the form

$$?x + ?y + ?z = ?$$
$$?y + ?z - ?$$
$$?z = ?$$

Step 3 Solve the last equation for z. Substitute the value of z into the second equation to deduce y. Finally, substitute the values of both y and z into the first equation to deduce x.

Step 4 Check that no mistakes have been made by substituting the values of x, y and z into the original equations.

It is possible to adopt different strategies to that suggested above. For example, it may be more convenient to eliminate z from the last equation in step 2 rather than y. However, it is important to notice that we use the second equation to do this, not the first. Any attempt to use the first equation in step 2 would reintroduce the variable x into the equations which is the last thing we want to do at this stage.

EXAMPLE

Solve the equations

$$4x + y + 3z = 8 \qquad (1)$$
$$-2x + 5y + z = 4 \qquad (2)$$
$$3x + 2y + 4z = 9 \qquad (3)$$

Solution

Step 1 To eliminate x from the second equation we multiply it by 2 and add to equation (1):

$$4x + \quad y + 3z = \quad 8$$
$$\underline{-4x + 10y + 2z = \quad 8} \quad +$$
$$11y + 5z = 16 \qquad (4)$$

To eliminate x from the third equation we multiply equation (1) by 3, multiply equation (3) by 4 and subtract:

$$12x + 3y + \quad 9z = \quad 24$$
$$\underline{12x + 8y + 16z = \quad 36} \quad -$$
$$-5y - \quad 7z = -12 \qquad (5)$$

This produces a new system:

$$4x + \quad y + 3z = \quad 8 \qquad (1)$$
$$11y + 5z = \quad 16 \qquad (4)$$
$$-5y - 7z = -12 \qquad (5)$$

Step 2   To eliminate y from the new third equation (that is, equation (5)) we multiply equation (4) by 5, multiply equation (5) by 11 and add:

$$55y + 25z = \quad 80$$
$$\underline{-55y - 77z = -132} \quad +$$
$$-52z = \quad -52 \qquad (6)$$

This produces a new system:

$$4x + \quad y + \quad 3z = \quad 8 \qquad (1)$$
$$11y + \quad 5z = \quad 16 \qquad (4)$$
$$-52z = -52 \qquad (6)$$

Step 3   The last equation gives

$$z = \frac{-52}{-52} = 1 \quad \text{(divide both sides by } -52)$$

If this is substituted into equation (4) then

$$11y + 5(1) = 16$$
$$11y + 5 = 16$$
$$11y = 11 \quad \text{(subtract 5 from both sides)}$$
$$y = \quad 1 \quad \text{(divide both sides by 11)}$$

Finally, substituting $y = 1$ and $z = 1$ into equation (1) produces

$$4x + 1 + 3(1) = 8$$
$$4x + 4 = 8$$
$$4x = 4 \quad \text{(subtract 4 from both sides)}$$
$$x = 1 \quad \text{(divide both sides by 4)}$$

Hence the solution is $x = 1$, $y = 1$, $z = 1$.

Step 4   As a check the original equations (1), (2) and (3) give

$$4(1) + 1 + 3(1) = 8 \quad \checkmark$$

$$-2(1) + 5(1) + 1 = 4 \quad \checkmark$$

$$3(1) + 2(1) + 4(1) = 9 \quad \checkmark$$

respectively.

■

PROBLEM

3   Solve the following system of equations:

$$2x + 2y - 5z = -5 \quad (1)$$

$$x - y + z = 3 \quad (2)$$

$$-3x + y + 2z = -2 \quad (3)$$

As you might expect, it is possible for three simultaneous linear equations to have either no solution or infinitely many solutions. An illustration of this is given in Problem 6. The method described in this section has an obvious extension to larger systems of equations. However, the calculations are extremely tedious to perform by hand. Fortunately there are many computer packages available which are capable of solving large systems accurately and efficiently (a matter of a few seconds to solve 10 000 equations in 10 000 unknowns!). We shall return to the solution of simultaneous linear equations in Chapter 7 when we describe how matrix theory can be used to solve them.

PRACTICE PROBLEMS

4   Use the method of elimination to solve the systems of equations given in Section 1.1, Problem 11.

5   Solve the following systems of equations:

(**a**) $x - 3y + 4z = 5$ (1)   (**b**) $3x + 2y - 2z = -5$ (1)
     $2x + y + z = 3$ (2) $4x + 3y + 3z = 17$ (2)
     $4x + 3y + 5z = 1$ (3) $2x - y + z = -1$ (3)

6   Attempt to solve the following systems of equations. Comment on the nature of the solution in each case.

(**a**) $x - 2y + z = -2$ (1)   (**b**) $2x + 3y - z = 13$ (1)
      $x + y - 2z = 4$ (2) $x - 2y + 2z = -3$ (2)
    $-2x + y + z = 12$ (3) $3x + y + z = 10$ (3)

1.3   Supply and demand analysis

Objectives   At the end of this section you should be able to:

- use the function notation, $y = f(x)$,

- identify the endogeneous and exogeneous variables in an economic model,

- identify and sketch a linear demand function,

- identify and sketch a linear supply function,

- determine the equilibrium price and quantity for a single-commodity market both graphically and algebraically,

- determine the equilibrium price and quantity for a multicommodity market by solving simultaneous linear equations.

Microeconomics is concerned with the analysis of the economic theory and policy of individual firms and markets. In this section we focus on one particular aspect known as market equilibrium in which the supply and demand balance. We describe how the mathematics introduced in the previous two sections can be used to calculate the equilibrium price and quantity. However, before we do this it is useful to explain the concept of a function. This idea is central to nearly all applications of mathematics in economics.

A **function**, f, is a rule which assigns to each incoming number, x, a uniquely defined outgoing number, y. A function may be thought of as a 'black box' which performs a dedicated arithmetic calculation. As an example, consider the rule 'double and add 3'. The effect of this rule on two specific incoming numbers, 5 and -17, is illustrated in Figure 1.11.

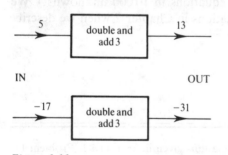

Figure 1.11

Unfortunately, such a representation is rather cumbersome. There are, however, two alternative ways of expressing this rule which are more concise. We can write either

$$y = 2x + 3$$

or

$$f(x) = 2x + 3$$

The first of these is familiar to you from our previous work; corresponding to any incoming number, x, the right-hand side tells you what to do with x to generate the outgoing number, *y*. The second notation is also useful. It has the advantage that it involves the label *f* which is used to name the rule. If, in a piece of economic theory, there are two or more functions we can use different labels to refer to each one. For example, a second function might be

$$g(x) = -3x + 10$$

and we subsequently identify the respective functions simply by referring to them by name, that is as either *f* or *g*.

The new notation also enables the information conveyed in Figure 1.11 to be written

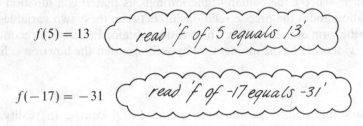

$$f(5) = 13 \qquad read \; 'f \; of \; 5 \; equals \; 13'$$

$$f(-17) = -31 \qquad read \; 'f \; of \; -17 \; equals \; -31'$$

The number inside the brackets is the incoming value, *x*, and the right-hand side is the corresponding outgoing value, *y*.

PROBLEM

1 Evaluate

   (a) $f(25)$ **(b)** $f(1)$ **(c)** $f(17)$ **(d)** $g(0)$ **(e)** $g(48)$ **(f)** $g(16)$

for the two functions

$$f(x) = -2x + 50$$

$$g(x) = -\tfrac{1}{2}x + 25$$

Do you notice any connection between *f* and *g*?

The incoming and outgoing variables are referred to as the **independent** and **dependent** variables respectively. The value of *y* clearly 'depends' on the actual value of *x* that is fed into the function. For example, in microeconomics the quantity demanded, *Q*, of a good depends on the market price, *P*. We might express this as

$$Q = f(P)$$

Such a function is called a **demand** function. Given any particular formula for $f(P)$ it is then a simple matter to produce a picture of the corresponding demand curve on graph paper. There is, however, a difference of opinion between mathematicians and economists on how this should be done. If your quantitative methods lecturer is a mathematician then he or she is likely to plot *Q* on the vertical axis and *P* on the horizontal axis. Economists, on the other hand, normally plot them the other way round with *Q* on the horizontal. In doing so we are merely noting that since *Q* is related to *P* then, conversely, *P* must be related to *Q*, and so

there is a function of the form

$$P = g(Q)$$

The two functions, f and g, are said to be **inverse** functions, that is f is the inverse of g and, equivalently, g is the inverse of f. We adopt the economists' approach in this book. In subsequent chapters we shall investigate other microeconomic functions such as total revenue, average cost and profit. It is conventional to plot each of these against Q (that is, with Q on the horizontal axis) so it makes sense to be consistent and to do the same here.

Written in the form $P = g(Q)$, the demand function tells us that P is a function of Q but it gives us no information about the precise relationship between these two variables. To find this we need to know the form of the function which can be obtained either from economic theory or from empirical evidence. For the moment we hypothesize that the function is linear so that

$$P = aQ + b$$

for some appropriate constants (called **parameters**), a and b. Of course, in reality, the relationship between price and quantity is likely to be much more complicated than this. However, the use of linear functions makes the mathematics nice and easy, and the result of any analysis at least provides a first approximation to the truth. The process of identifying the key features of the real world and making appropriate simplifications and assumptions is known as **modelling**. Models are based on economic laws and help to explain and predict the behaviour of real world situations. Inevitably there is a conflict between mathematical ease and the model's accuracy. The closer the model comes to reality the more complicated the mathematics is likely to be.

A graph of a typical linear demand function is shown in Figure 1.12. Elementary theory shows that demand usually falls as the price of a good rises and so the slope of the line is negative. Mathematically, P is then said to be a **decreasing** function of Q. In symbols we write

$a < 0$

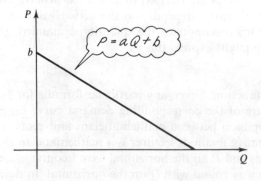

Figure 1.12

It is also apparent from the graph that the intercept, b, is positive, that is

$b > 0$  read 'b is greater than zero'

In fact, it is possible in theory for the demand curve to be horizontal with $a = 0$. This corresponds to perfect competition and we shall return to this special case in Chapter 4.

EXAMPLE

Sketch a graph of the demand function

$P = -2Q + 50$

Hence, or otherwise, determine the value of

(a) P when $Q = 9$
(b) Q when $P = 10$

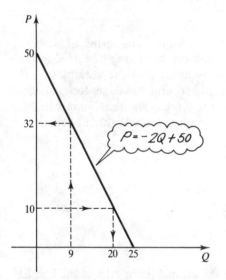

Figure 1.13

Solution

For the demand function

$$P = -2Q + 50$$

$a = -2, b = 50$, so the line has a slope of -2 and an intercept of 50. For every 1 unit along, the line goes down by 2 units so it must cross the horizontal axis when $Q = 25$. (Alternatively, note that when $P = 0$ the equation reads $0 = -2Q + 50$, with solution $Q = 25$.) The graph is sketched in Figure 1.13.

(a) Given any quantity, Q, it is straightforward to use the graph to find the corresponding price, P. A line is drawn vertically upwards until it intersects the demand curve and the value of P is read off from the vertical axis. From Figure 1.13, when $Q = 9$ we see that $P = 32$. This can also be found by substituting $Q = 9$ directly into the demand function to get

$$P = -2(9) + 50 = 32$$

(b) Reversing this process enables us to calculate Q from a given value of P. A line is drawn horizontally until it intersects the demand curve and the value of Q is read off from the horizontal axis. Figure 1.13 indicates that $Q = 20$ when $P = 10$. Again this can be found by calculation. If $P = 10$ then the equation reads

$10 = -2Q + 50$

$-40 = -2Q$ (subtract 50 from both sides)

$20 = Q$ (divide both sides by -2)

∎

---

2 Sketch a graph of the demand function

$$P = -3Q + 75$$

Hence, or otherwise, determine the value of

(a) P when $Q = 23$
(b) Q when $P = 18$

The model of consumer demand given so far is fairly crude in that it assumes that quantity depends solely on the price, P, of the good being considered. In practice Q depends on other factors as well. These include the incomes of consumers, Y, the price of substitutable goods, P_S, the price of complementary goods, P_C, advertising expenditure, A, and consumer's tastes, T. A **substitutable** good is one which could be consumed instead of the good under consideration. For example, in the transport industry, buses and taxis could obviously be substituted for each other in urban areas. A **complementary** good is one which is used in conjunction with other goods. For example, music tapes and hi-fi systems are consumed together. Mathematically, we say that Q is a function of P, Y, P_S, P_C, A and T. This is written

$$Q = f(P, Y, P_S, P_C, A, T)$$

where the variables inside the brackets are separated by commas. In terms of a 'black box' diagram this is represented with six incoming lines and one outgoing line as shown in Figure 1.14. In our previous discussion it was implicitly assumed that the variables Y, P_S, P_C, A and T are held fixed. We describe this situation by calling Q and P **endogenous** variables since they are allowed to vary and are determined within the model. The remaining variables are called **exogenous** since they are constant and are determined outside the model.

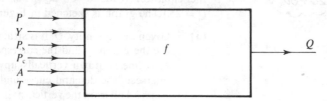

Figure 1.14

Let us return now to the standard demand curve shown in Figure 1.15 as the line EF. This is constructed on the assumption that Y, P_S, P_C, A and T are all constant. Notice that when the price is P^* the quantity demanded is Q_1. Now suppose that income, Y, increases. We would normally expect the demand to rise because the extra income buys more goods at price P^*. The effect is to shift the demand curve to the right because at price P^* consumers can afford the larger number of goods, Q_2. From Figure 1.15 we deduce that if the demand curve is

$$P = aQ + b$$

then a rise in income causes the intercept, b, to increase.

We conclude that if one of the exogenous variables changes the whole demand curve moves, whereas if one of the endogenous variables changes we simply move along the fixed curve.

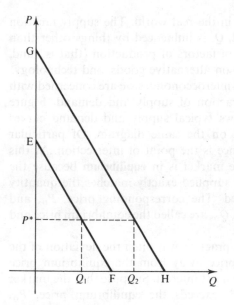

Figure 1.15

Incidentally, it is possible that for some goods an increase in income actually causes the demand curve to shift to the left. In the 1960s and 1970s most western economies saw a decline in the domestic consumption of coal as a result of an increase in income. In this case higher wealth meant that more people were able to install central heating systems which use alternative forms of energy. Under these circumstances the good is referred to as an **inferior** good. On the other hand, a **superior** good is one whose demand rises as income rises. Cars and electrical goods are obvious examples of superior goods. Currently, concern about global warming is also reducing demand for coal. This factor can be incorporated as part of taste although it is difficult to handle mathematically since it is virtually impossible to quantify taste and so to define T numerically.

PROBLEM

3 Describe the effect on the demand curve due to an increase in

 (a) the price of substitutable goods, P_S,
 (b) the price of complementary goods, P_C,
 (c) advertising expenditure, A.

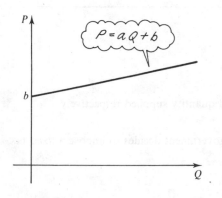

Figure 1.16

The **supply** function is the relation between the quantity, Q, of a good that producers plan to bring to the market and the price, P, of the good. A typical linear supply curve is indicated in Figure 1.16. Economic theory indicates that as the price rises so does the supply. Mathematically, P is then said to be an **increasing** function of Q. A price increase encourages existing producers to raise output and entices new firms to enter the market. The line shown in Figure 1.16 has equation

$$P = aQ + b$$

with slope $a > 0$ and intercept $b > 0$. Note that when the market price is equal to b the supply is zero. It is only when the price exceeds this threshold level that producers decide that it is worth supplying any good whatsoever.

Again this is a simplification of what happens in the real world. The supply function does not have to be linear and the quantity supplied, Q, is influenced by things other than price. These exogenous variables include the prices of factors of production (that is, land, capital, labour and enterprise), the profits obtainable on alternative goods, and technology.

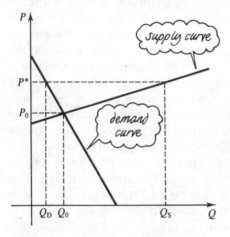

Figure 1.17

In microeconomics we are concerned with the interaction of supply and demand. Figure 1.17 shows typical supply and demand curves sketched on the same diagram. Of particular significance is the point of intersection. At this point the market is in **equilibrium** because the quantity supplied exactly matches the quantity demanded. The corresponding price, P_0, and quantity, Q_0, are called the equilibrium price and quantity.

In practice, it is often the deviation of the market price away from the equilibrium price that is of most interest. Suppose that the market price, P^*, exceeds the equilibrium price, P_0. From Figure 1.17 the quantity supplied, Q_S, is greater than the quantity demanded, Q_D, so there is excess supply. There are stocks of unsold goods which tend to depress prices and cause firms to cut back production. The effect is for 'market forces' to shift the market back down towards equilibrium. Likewise, if the market price falls below equilibrium price then demand exceeds supply. This shortage pushes prices up and encourages firms to produce more goods and so the market drifts back up towards equilibrium.

EXAMPLE _____

The demand and supply functions of a good are given by

$$P = -2Q_D + 50$$
$$P = \tfrac{1}{2}Q_S + 25$$

where P, Q_D and Q_S denote the price, quantity demanded and quantity supplied respectively.

(1)   Determine the equilibrium price and quantity.
(2)   Determine the effect on the market equilibrium if the government decides to impose a fixed tax of \$5 on each good.

Solution

(1)   The demand curve has already been sketched in Figure 1.13. For the supply function,

$$P = \tfrac{1}{2}Q_S + 25$$

we have $a = \tfrac{1}{2}$, $b = 25$, so the line has a slope of $\tfrac{1}{2}$ and an intercept of 25. It therefore passes

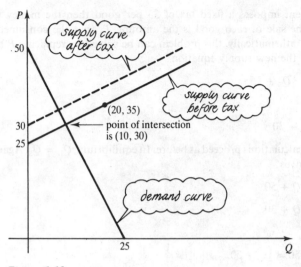

Figure 1.18

through $(0, 25)$. For a second point, let us choose $Q_S = 20$, say. The corresponding value of P is

$$P = \tfrac{1}{2}(20) + 25 = 35$$

so the line also passes through $(20, 35)$. The points $(0, 25)$ and $(20, 35)$ can now be plotted and the supply curve sketched. Figure 1.18 shows both the demand and supply curves sketched on the same diagram. The point of intersection has coordinates $(10, 30)$ so the equilibrium quantity is 10 and the equilibrium price is 30.

It is possible to calculate these values using algebra. In equilibrium, $Q_D = Q_S$. If this common value is denoted by Q then the demand and supply equations become

$$P = -2Q + 50$$
$$P = \tfrac{1}{2}Q + 25$$

This represents a pair of simultaneous equations for the two unknowns P and Q and so could be solved using the elimination method described in the previous section. However, this is not strictly necessary because it follows immediately from the above equations that

$$-2Q + 50 = \tfrac{1}{2}Q + 25$$

since both sides are equal to P. This can be rearranged to calculate Q:

$$-2\tfrac{1}{2}Q + 50 = \quad 25 \qquad \text{(subtract } \tfrac{1}{2}Q \text{ from both sides)}$$

$$-2\tfrac{1}{2}Q = -25 \qquad \text{(subtract 50 from both sides)}$$

$$Q = \quad 10 \qquad \text{(divide both sides by } -2\tfrac{1}{2}\text{)}$$

Finally, P can be found by substituting this value into either of the original equations. The demand equation gives

$$P = -2(10) + 50 = 30$$

As a check, the supply equation gives

$$P = \tfrac{1}{2}(10) + 25 = 30 \qquad \checkmark$$

(2)   If the government imposes a fixed tax of $5 per good then the money that the firm actually receives from the sale of each good is the amount, P, that the consumer pays, less the tax, 5, that is $P - 5$. Mathematically, this problem can be solved by replacing P by $P - 5$ in the supply equation to get the new supply equation

$$P - 5 = \tfrac{1}{2}Q_S + 25$$

that is

$$P = \tfrac{1}{2}Q_S + 30$$

The remaining calculations proceed as before. In equilibrium, $Q_D = Q_S$. Again setting this common value to be Q gives

$$P = -2Q + 50$$
$$P = \tfrac{1}{2}Q + 30$$

Hence

$$-2Q + 50 = \tfrac{1}{2}Q + 30$$

which can be solved as before to give $Q = 8$. Substitution into either of the above equations gives $P = 34$. (Check the details.)

Graphically the introduction of tax shifts the supply curve upwards by 5 units. Obviously the demand curve is unaltered. The dashed line in Figure 1.18 shows the new supply curve from which the new equilibrium quantity is 8 and equilibrium price is 34. Note the effect that government taxation has on the market equilibrium price. This has risen to $34 and so not all of the tax is passed on to the consumer. The consumer pays an additional $4 per good. The remaining $1 of tax must, therefore, be paid by the firm.

■

PROBLEM

4   The demand and supply functions of a good are given by

$$P = -4Q_D + 120$$
$$P = \tfrac{1}{3}Q_S + 29$$

where P, Q_D and Q_S denote the price, quantity demanded and quantity supplied respectively.

(1)   Calculate the equilibrium price and quantity.
(2)   Calculate the new equilibrium price and quantity after the imposition of a fixed tax of $13 per good. Who pays the tax?

We conclude this section by considering a more realistic model of supply and demand by taking into account substitutable and complementary goods. Let us suppose that there are two goods in related markets which we call good 1 and good 2. The demand for either good depends on the prices of both good 1 and good 2. If the corresponding demand functions are linear then

$$Q_{D_1} = a_1 + b_1 P_1 + c_1 P_2$$
$$Q_{D_2} = a_2 + b_2 P_1 + c_2 P_2$$

where P_i and Q_{D_i} denote the price and demand for the ith good and a_i, b_i, c_i are parameters. For the first equation, $a_1 > 0$, because there is a positive demand when the prices of both goods are zero. Also, $b_1 < 0$, because the demand of a good falls as its price rises. The sign of c_1 depends on the nature of the goods. If the goods are substitutable then an increase in the price of good 2 would mean that consumers would switch from good 2 to good 1, causing Q_{D_1} to increase. Substitutable goods are therefore characterized by a positive value of c_1. On the other hand, if the goods are complementary then a rise in the price of either good would see the demand fall so c_1 is negative. Similar results apply to the signs of a_2, b_2 and c_2. The calculation of the equilibrium price and quantity in a two-commodity market model is demonstrated in the following example.

EXAMPLE

The demand and supply functions for two interdependent commodities are given by

$$Q_{D_1} = 10 - 2P_1 + P_2$$
$$Q_{D_2} = 5 + 2P_1 - 2P_2$$
$$Q_{S_1} = -3 + 2P_1$$
$$Q_{S_2} = -2 + 3P_2$$

where Q_{D_i}, Q_{S_i} and P_i denote the quantity demanded, quantity supplied and price of good i respectively. Determine the equilibrium price and quantity for this two-commodity model.

Solution

In equilibrium, we know that the quantity supplied is equal to the quantity demanded for each good, so that

$$Q_{D_1} = Q_{S_1} \quad \text{and} \quad Q_{D_2} = Q_{S_2}$$

Let us write these respective common values as Q_1 and Q_2. The demand and supply equations for good 1 then become

$$Q_1 = 10 - 2P_1 + P_2$$
$$Q_1 = -3 + 2P_1$$

Hence

$$10 - 2P_1 + P_2 = -3 + 2P_1$$

since both sides are equal to Q_1. It makes sense to tidy this equation up a bit by collecting all of the unknowns on the left-hand side and putting the constant terms on to the right-hand side:

$$10 - 4P_1 + P_2 = -3 \quad \text{(subtract } 2P_1 \text{ from both sides)}$$
$$-4P_1 + P_2 = -13 \quad \text{(subtract 10 from both sides)}$$

We can perform a similar process for good 2. The demand and supply equations become

$$Q_2 = 5 + 2P_1 - 2P_2$$
$$Q_2 = -2 + 3P_2$$

because $Q_{D_2} = Q_{S_2} = Q_2$ in equilibrium.

Hence

$$5 + 2P_1 - 2P_2 = -2 + 3P_2$$
$$5 + 2P_1 - 5P_2 = -2 \qquad \text{(subtract } 3P_2 \text{ from both sides)}$$
$$2P_1 - 5P_2 = -7 \qquad \text{(subtract 5 from both sides)}$$

We have therefore shown that the equilibrium prices, P_1 and P_2, satisfy the simultaneous linear equations

$$-4P_1 + P_2 = -13 \qquad (1)$$
$$2P_1 - 5P_2 = -7 \qquad (2)$$

which can be solved by elimination. Following the steps described in Section 1.2 we proceed as follows.

Step 1   Double equation (2) and add to equation (1) to get

$$-4P_1 + P_2 = -13$$
$$\underline{4P_1 - 10P_2 = -14} \quad +$$
$$-9P_2 = -27 \qquad (3)$$

Step 2   Divide both sides of equation (3) by -9 to get $P_2 = 3$.

Step 3   If this is substituted into equation (1) then

$$-4P_1 + 3 = -13$$
$$-4P_1 = -16 \qquad \text{(subtract 3 from both sides)}$$
$$P_1 = 4 \qquad \text{(divide both sides by } -4)$$

Step 4   As a check, equation (2) gives

$$2(4) - 5(3) = -7 \quad \checkmark$$

Hence $P_1 = 4$ and $P_2 = 3$.

Finally, the equilibrium quantities can be deduced by substituting these values back into the original supply equations. For good 1,

$$Q_1 = -3 + 2P_1 = -3 + 2(4) = 5$$

For good 2,

$$Q_2 = -2 + 3P_2 = -2 + 3(3) = 7$$

As a check, the demand equations also give

$$Q_1 = 10 - 2P_1 + P_2 = 10 - 2(4) + 3 = 5 \quad \checkmark$$
$$Q_2 = 5 + 2P_1 - 2P_2 = 5 + 2(4) - 2(3) = 7 \quad \checkmark$$

∎

PROBLEM

5   The demand and supply functions for two interdependent commodities are given by

$$Q_{D_1} = 40 - 5P_1 - P_2$$

$$Q_{D_2} = 50 - 2P_1 - 4P_2$$

$$Q_{S_1} = -3 + 4P_1$$

$$Q_{S_2} = -7 + 3P_2$$

where Q_{D_i}, Q_{S_i} and P_i denote the quantity demanded, quantity supplied and price of good i respectively. Determine the equilibrium price and quantity for this two-commodity model. Are these goods substitutable or complementary?

For a two-commodity market the equilibrium prices and quantities can be found by solving a system of two simultaneous equations. Exactly the same procedure can be applied to a three-commodity market which requires the solution of a system of three simultaneous equations. An example of this can be found in Problem 10. In general, with n goods it is necessary to solve n equations in n unknowns and, as pointed out in Section 1.2, this is best done using a computer package whenever n is large.

PRACTICE PROBLEMS

6   Sketch a graph of the supply function

$$P = \tfrac{1}{3}Q + 7$$

Hence, or otherwise, determine the value of

(a) P when $Q = 12$
(b) Q when $P = 10$
(c) Q when $P = 4$

7   The demand function of a good is

$$Q = 100 - P + 2Y + \tfrac{1}{2}A$$

where Q, P, Y and A denote quantity demanded, price, income and advertising expenditure respectively.

(1)   Calculate the demand when $P = 10$, $Y = 40$ and $A = 6$. Assuming that price and income are fixed, calculate the additional advertising expenditure needed to raise demand to 179 units.
(2)   Is this good inferior or superior?

8   The demand and supply functions of a good are given by

$$P = -5Q_D + 80$$

$$P = 2Q_S + 10$$

where P, Q_D and Q_S denote price, quantity demanded and quantity supplied respectively.

(1)   Find the equilibrium price and quantity

(a) graphically   (b) algebraically

(2)   If the government deducts, as tax, 15% of the market price of each good determine the new equilibrium price and quantity.

9   The demand and supply functions for two interdependent commodities are given by

$$Q_{D_1} = 100 - 2P_1 + P_2$$

$$Q_{D_2} = \quad 5 + 2P_1 - 3P_2$$

$$Q_{S_1} = -10 + P_1$$

$$Q_{S_2} = \quad -5 + 6P_2$$

where Q_{D_i}, Q_{S_i} and P_i denote the quantity demanded, quantity supplied and price of good i respectively. Determine the equilibrium price and quantity for this two-commodity model.

10   The demand and supply functions for three interdependent commodities are

$$Q_{D_1} = \quad 15 - \quad P_1 + 2P_2 + \quad P_3$$

$$Q_{D_2} = \quad 9 + \quad P_1 - \quad P_2 - \quad P_3$$

$$Q_{D_3} = \quad 8 + 2P_1 - \quad P_2 - 4P_3$$

$$Q_{S_1} = -7 + \quad P_1$$

$$Q_{S_2} = -4 + 4P_2$$

$$Q_{S_3} = -5 + 2P_3$$

where Q_{D_i}, Q_{S_i} and P_i denote the quantity demanded, quantity supplied and price of good i respectively. Determine the equilibrium price and quantity for this three-commodity model.

1.4   Algebra

Objectives   At the end of this section you should be able to:

- recognize the symbols $<$, $>$, $\leqslant$ and $\geqslant$,

- manipulate inequalities,

- multiply out brackets,

- add, subtract, multiply and divide numerical fractions,

- add, subtract, multiply and divide algebraic fractions,

- transpose formulae.

ALGEBRA IS BORING

There is no getting away from the fact that algebra *is* boring. Doubtless there are a few enthusiasts who get a kick out of algebraic manipulation but economics students are rarely to be found in this category! Indeed the mere mention of the word algebra is enough to strike fear into the heart of many a first-year student. Unfortunately, you cannot get very far with mathematics unless you have completely mastered this topic. An apposite analogy is the game of chess. Before you can begin to play a game of chess it is necessary to go through the tedium of learning the moves of individual pieces. In the same way it is essential that you learn the rules of algebra before you can enjoy the 'game' of mathematics. Of course, just because you know the rules does not mean that you are going to excel at the game. However, no one is expecting you to become a grandmaster of mathematics, but you should at least be able to follow the mathematics presented in economics books and journals, as well as being able to solve simple problems for yourself.

In the introduction to this book you were advised to attempt all questions in the text. This applies particularly to the material in this section. This section is likely to be heavy going if you have not studied mathematics for some time. To make life easy for you it is split up into four subsections:

(1) Inequalities
(2) Brackets
(3) Fractions
(4) Transposition

You might like to work through these subsections on separate occasions to enable the ideas to sink in. To rush this topic now is likely to lead to only a half-baked understanding which will result in hours of frustration when you study the later chapters of this book.

1.4.1 Inequalities

So far we have repeatedly made use of a picture of the x axis:

Now, although only whole numbers are marked on this diagram, it is implicitly assumed that it can also be used to indicate fractions and decimal numbers as well. To each point on the line there corresponds a particular number. Conversely, every number can be represented by a particular point on the line. For this reason, the line is sometimes referred to as a **number line**. For example, $-2\frac{1}{2}$ lies exactly halfway between -3 and -2. Similarly, $4\frac{7}{8}$ lies $\frac{7}{8}$ths of the way between 4 and 5. In theory, we can even find a point on the line corresponding to a number such as $\sqrt{2}$ although it may be difficult to sketch such a point accurately in practice. My calculator gives the value of $\sqrt{2}$ to be 1.414 213 56 to 8 decimal places. This number therefore lies just less than halfway between 1 and 2.

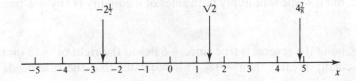

A number line can be used to decide whether or not one number is greater or less than another number. We say that a number a is greater than a number b if a lies to the right of b on the line and write this as

$a > b$

(In Section 1.3 the notation $a > 0$ was used to indicate that a is positive; that is, a is greater than zero.) Likewise, we say that a is less than b if a lies to the left of b and write this as

$a < b$

From the diagram we see that

$-2 > -4$

because -2 lies to the right of -4. This is equivalent to the statement

$-4 < -2$

Similarly,

$0 > -1$ (or equivalently $-1 < 0$)

$2 > -2\frac{1}{2}$ (or equivalently $-2\frac{1}{2} < 2$)

$4\frac{7}{8} > \sqrt{2}$ (or equivalently $\sqrt{2} < 4\frac{7}{8}$)

There are occasions when we would like the letters a and b to stand for mathematical expressions rather than actual numbers. In this situation we sometimes use the symbols $\geqslant$ and $\leqslant$ to mean 'greater than or equal to' and 'less than or equal to' respectively.

We have already seen that we can manipulate equations in any way we like provided that we do the same thing to both sides. An obvious question to ask is whether this rule extends to inequalities. To investigate this consider the inequality

$1 < 3$ (1)

which is clearly true. If we add 4 to both sides then we obtain

$5 < 7$

which is a true statement.

If we add -5 to both sides of inequality (1) then we obtain

$-4 < -2$

which is also true.

If we multiply both sides of inequality (1) by 2 then we obtain

$2 < 6$

which is again true.

So far so good, but if we now multiply both sides of inequality (1) by -6 then we obtain

$-6 < -18$

which is false. In fact, quite the reverse is true since -6 lies to the right of -18 on the number line and so -6 is actually greater than -18. This indicates that the rule needs modifying before we can extend it to inequalities and that we need to be careful when manipulating such things.

PROBLEM

1 Starting with the true statement

$$6 > 3$$

decide which of the following are valid operations when performed on both sides:

(a) add 6   (b) multiply by 2   (c) subtract 3
(d) add -3 (e) divide by 3   (f) multiply by -4
(g) multiply by -1 (h) divide by -3 (i) add -10

These examples show that the usual rule does apply to inequalities with the important proviso that

---

if both sides are multiplied or divided by a negative number then the sense of the inequality is reversed

---

By this we mean that '$>$' changes to '$<$', '$\leq$' changes to '$\geq$' and so on.

EXAMPLE

Simplify the inequality

$$2x + 3 < 4x + 7$$

Solution

The first problem is to decide what is meant by the word 'simplify'. At the moment there are x's on both sides of the inequality sign and it would obviously look neater if these were collected together. We do this by subtracting $4x$ from both sides to get

$$-2x + 3 < 7$$

We can also put all of the constant terms on to the right-hand side by subtracting 3 from both sides to get

$$-2x < 4$$

This is certainly an improvement but we can go further to make the inequality even more meaningful. We may divide both sides by -2 to get

$$x > -2$$

Notice that the sense has been reversed at this stage because we have divided by a negative number. We have therefore shown that any number x satisfies the original inequality provided that it lies to the right of the number -2 on the number line.

■

2 Simplify the inequalities

  (a) $2x < 3x + 7$ (b) $21x - 19 \geqslant 4x + 15$

1.4.2 Brackets

Brackets are used to avoid any misunderstanding about the way an expression is to be evaluated. Suppose that a group of students is asked to find the value of

$$1 - 3 + 5$$

One suspects that the majority of students would say that the answer is 3 which is found by first subtracting 3 from 1 and then adding 5. However, there is a fair chance that some might produce -7, thinking that they should first add 3 and 5 and then subtract the result from 1. (There may be other students who obtain different values entirely but we had better forget about them!) In a sense both answers are correct since, as it stands, the expression is ambiguous. To overcome this, brackets are introduced, using the convention that things inside brackets are evaluated first. Hence we would either write

$$(1 - 3) + 5$$

to indicate that subtraction is performed first or write

$$1 - (3 + 5)$$

to indicate that addition is performed first. In fact, brackets have already been used in Section 1.1 in the context of multiplying negative numbers. For example, on page 8 we wrote

$$(-2) \times (-4) \times (-1) \times (2) \times (-1) \times (-3)$$

which is much easier to interpret than its bracketless counterpart:

$$-2 \times -4 \times -1 \times 2 \times -1 \times -3$$

It is also conventional to suppress the multiplication sign when multiplying brackets together so the above product could be written as

$$(-2)(-4)(-1)(2)(-1)(-3)$$

Similarly, the multiplication sign is implied in

$$(5 - 2)(7 + 1)$$

which is the product of 3 and 8. The following problem gives you an opportunity to try out these conventions for yourself and to use the brackets facility on your calculator.

3 (1) Without using your calculator evaluate

(a) $(1 - 3) + 10$	(b) $1 - (3 + 10)$	(c) $2(3 + 4)$
(d) $(10 \div 5) - 3$	(e) $(15 - 8)(2 + 6)$	(f) $((2 - 3) + 7) \div 6)$

(2) Confirm your answer to part (1) using a calculator.

In mathematics it is necessary to handle expressions in which some of the terms involve letters as well as numbers. It is useful to be able to take an expression containing brackets and to rewrite it as an equivalent expression without brackets and vice versa. The process of removing brackets is called 'expanding the brackets' or 'multiplying out the brackets'. This is based on the **distributive law** which states that for any three numbers a, b and c

$$a(b + c) = ab + ac$$

It is easy to verify this law in simple cases. For example, if $a = 2$, $b = 3$ and $c = 4$ then the left-hand side is

$$2(3 + 4) = 2 \times 7 = 14$$

However,

$$ab = 2 \times 3 = 6 \quad \text{and} \quad ac = 2 \times 4 = 8$$

and so the right-hand side is $6 + 8$ which is also 14.

This law can be used when there are any number of terms inside the brackets. We have

$$a(b + c + d) = ab + ac + ad$$
$$a(b + c + d + e) = ab + ac + ad + ae$$

and so on.

It does not matter in which order two numbers are multiplied so we also have

$$(b + c)a = ba + ca$$
$$(b + c + d)a = ba + ca + da$$
$$(b + c + d + e)a = ba + ca + da + ea$$

EXAMPLE _____

Multiply out the brackets in

(a) $x(x - 2)$
(b) $2(x + y - z) + 3(z + y)$
(c) $x + 3y - (2y + x)$

Solution

(a) The use of the distributive law to multiply out $x(x - 2)$ is straightforward. This gives

$$x(x - 2) = xx - x2$$

It is usual in mathematics to abbreviate xx to x^2. It is also standard practice to put the numerical coefficient in front of the variable so $x2$ is usually written $2x$. Hence

$$x(x - 2) = x^2 - 2x$$

(b)   To expand

$$2(x + y - z) + 3(z + y)$$

we need to apply the distributive law twice. We have

$$2(x + y - z) = 2x + 2y - 2z$$

$$3(z + y) = 3z + 3y$$

Adding together gives

$$2(x + y - z) + 3(z + y) = 2x + 2y - 2z + 3z + 3y$$

We could stop at this point. Note, however, that some of the terms are similar. Towards the beginning of the expression there is a term $2y$ whereas at the end there is a like term $3y$. Obviously these can be collected together to make a total of $5y$. A similar process can be applied to the terms involving z. The expression simplifies to

$$2x + 5y + z$$

(c)   It may not be immediately apparent how to expand

$$x + 3y - (2y + x)$$

However, note that

$$-(2y + x)$$

is the same as

$$(-1)(2y + x)$$

which expands to give

$$(-1)(2y) + (-1)x = -2y - x$$

Hence

$$x + 3y - (2y + x) = x + 3y - 2y - x = y$$

after collecting like terms.

■

In this example the solutions are written out in painstaking detail. This is done to show you precisely how the distributive law is applied. The solutions to all three parts could have been written down in only one or two steps of working. You are, of course, at liberty to compress the working in your own solutions but please do not be tempted to overdo this. You might want to check your answers at a later date and may find it difficult if you have tried to be too clever.

PROBLEM

4 Multiply out the brackets, simplifying your answer as far as possible.

  (a) $(5 - 2z)z$ **(b)** $6(x - y) + 3(y - 2x)$ **(c)** $x - y + z - (x^2 + x - y)$

We conclude our discussion of brackets by describing how to multiply two brackets together. This is based on the result

$$(a + b)(c + d) = ac + ad + bc + bd$$

At first sight this formula might appear to be totally unmemorable. In fact, all you have to do is to multiply each term in the first pair of brackets by each term in the second in all possible combinations, that is

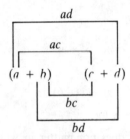

This rule then extends to brackets with more than two terms. For example, to multiply out

$$(a + b)(c + d + e)$$

notice that the first pair of brackets has two terms and the second has three terms. So, to form each individual product, we can pick from one of two terms in the first pair of brackets and from one of three terms in the second. There are then six possibilities in total giving

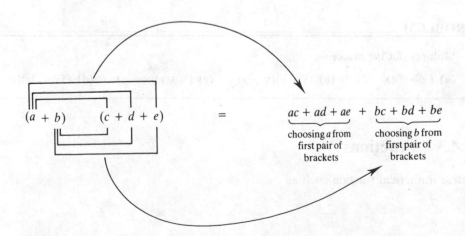

EXAMPLE

Multiply out the brackets

(a) $(x + 1)(x + 2)$
(b) $(2x - y)(x + y - 6)$

simplifying your answer as far as possible.

Solution

(a)

$$(x + 1)(x + 2) = xx + x2 + 1x + (1)(2)$$

If we use the abbreviation x^2 for xx and the convention that numerical coefficients are placed in front of the variable then this can be written as

$$x^2 + 2x + x + 2$$

Finally, collecting like terms gives

$$x^2 + 3x + 2$$

(b)

$$(2x - y)(x + y - 6) = 2xx + 2xy + 2x(-6) - yx - yy - y(-6)$$
$$= 2x^2 + 2xy - 12x - yx - y^2 + 6y$$

It might seem that there are no like terms but since it does not matter in which order two numbers are multiplied yx is the same as xy. The terms $2xy$ and $-yx$ can therefore be combined to give

$$2xy - xy = xy$$

Hence the simplified expression is

$$2x^2 + xy - 12x - y^2 + 6y$$

∎

PROBLEM

5 Multiply out the brackets

   (a) $(x + 3)(x - 2)$ **(b)** $(x + y)(x - y)$ **(c)** $(x + y)(x + y)$ **(d)** $(5x + 2y)(x - y + 1)$

1.4.3 Fractions

For a numerical fraction such as

$$\frac{7}{8}$$

the number, 7, on the top is called the **numerator** and the number, 8, on the bottom is called the **denominator**. In this book we are also interested in the case when the numerator and denominator involve letters as well as numbers. These are referred to as **algebraic fractions**. For example,

$$\frac{1}{x^2 - 2} \quad \text{and} \quad \frac{2x^2 - 1}{y + z}$$

are both algebraic fractions. The letters x, y and z are used to represent numbers so the rules for the manipulation of algebraic fractions are the same as those for ordinary numerical fractions. The rules for multiplication and division are as follows.

> to multiply fractions you multiply their corresponding numerators and denominators

In symbols,

$$\frac{a}{b} \times \frac{c}{d} = \frac{a \times c}{b \times d} = \frac{ac}{bd}$$

> to divide by a fraction you turn it upside down and multiply

In symbols,

$$\frac{a}{b} \div \frac{c}{d} = \frac{a}{b} \times \frac{d}{c}$$

turn the divisor upside down

$$= \frac{ad}{bc}$$

rule for multiplying fractions

EXAMPLE

Calculate

(a) $\quad \dfrac{2}{3} \times \dfrac{5}{4}$

(b) $\quad 2 \times \dfrac{6}{13}$

(c) $\quad \dfrac{6}{7} \div \dfrac{4}{21}$

(d) $\quad \dfrac{1}{2} \div 3$

Solution

(a) The multiplication rule gives

$$\frac{2}{3} \times \frac{5}{4} = \frac{2 \times 5}{3 \times 4} = \frac{10}{12}$$

We could leave the answer like this although it can be simplified by dividing top and bottom by 2 to get $\frac{5}{6}$.

    The two answers are equivalent. If a cake is cut into 6 pieces and you eat 5 of them then you eat just as much as someone who cuts the cake into 12 pieces and eats 10 (although it might appear that you are not such a glutton). It is also valid to 'cancel' by 2 at the very beginning, that is

$$\frac{{}^1\!\cancel{2}}{3} \times \frac{5}{\cancel{4}_2} = \frac{1 \times 5}{3 \times 2} = \frac{5}{6}$$

(b) The whole number 2 is equivalent to the fraction $\frac{2}{1}$ so

$$2 \times \frac{6}{13} = \frac{2}{1} \times \frac{6}{13} = \frac{2 \times 6}{1 \times 13} = \frac{12}{13}$$

(c) To calculate

$$\frac{6}{7} \div \frac{4}{21}$$

the divisor is turned upside down to get $\frac{21}{4}$ and then multiplied to get

$$\frac{6}{7} \div \frac{4}{21} = \frac{{}^3\!\cancel{6}}{{}_1\!\cancel{7}} \times \frac{\cancel{21}^{\,3}}{\cancel{4}_{\,2}} = \frac{3 \times 3}{1 \times 2} = \frac{9}{2}$$

(d) We write 3 as $\frac{3}{1}$ so

$$\frac{1}{2} \div 3 = \frac{1}{2} \div \frac{3}{1} = \frac{1}{2} \times \frac{1}{3} = \frac{1}{6}$$

■

PROBLEM _____

6 (1) Without using a calculator evaluate

    (a) $\dfrac{1}{2} \times \dfrac{3}{4}$ **(b)** $7 \times \dfrac{1}{14}$ **(c)** $\dfrac{2}{3} \div \dfrac{8}{9}$ **(d)** $\dfrac{8}{9} \div 16$

    (2) Confirm your answer to part (1) using a calculator.

The rules for addition and subtraction are as follows.

> to add (or subtract) two fractions you put them over a common denominator and add (or subtract) their numerators

EXAMPLE

Calculate

(a) $\dfrac{1}{5} + \dfrac{2}{5}$ (b) $\dfrac{1}{4} + \dfrac{2}{3}$ (c) $\dfrac{7}{12} - \dfrac{5}{8}$

Solution

(a) The fractions $\frac{1}{5}$ and $\frac{2}{5}$ already have the same denominator so to add them we just add their numerators to get

$$\frac{1}{5} + \frac{2}{5} = \frac{1 + 2}{5} = \frac{3}{5}$$

(b) The fractions $\frac{1}{4}$ and $\frac{2}{3}$ have denominators 4 and 3. One number which is divisible by both 3 and 4 is 12 so we choose this as the common denominator. Now 4 goes into 12 exactly 3 times so

$$\frac{1}{4} = \frac{1 \times 3}{4 \times 3} = \frac{3}{12}$$

multiply top and bottom by 3

and 3 goes into 12 exactly 4 times so

$$\frac{2}{3} = \frac{2 \times 4}{3 \times 4} = \frac{8}{12}$$

multiply top and bottom by 4

Hence

$$\frac{1}{4} + \frac{2}{3} = \frac{3}{12} + \frac{8}{12} = \frac{3 + 8}{12} = \frac{11}{12}$$

(c) The fractions $\frac{7}{12}$ and $\frac{5}{8}$ have denominators 12 and 8. One number which is divisible by both 12 and 8 is 24, so we choose this as the common denominator. Now 12 goes into 24 exactly twice so

$$\frac{7}{12} = \frac{7 \times 2}{24} = \frac{14}{24}$$

and 8 goes into 24 exactly 3 times so

$$\frac{5}{8} = \frac{5 \times 3}{24} = \frac{15}{24}$$

Hence

$$\frac{7}{12} - \frac{5}{8} = \frac{14}{24} - \frac{15}{24} = -\frac{1}{24}$$

It is not essential that the lowest common denominator is used. Any number will do provided that it is divisible by the two original denominators. If you are stuck then you could always multiply the original two denominators together. In part (c) the denominators multiply to give 96 so this can be used instead. Now

$$\frac{7}{12} = \frac{7 \times 8}{96} = \frac{56}{96}$$

and

$$\frac{5}{8} = \frac{5 \times 12}{96} = \frac{60}{96}$$

so

$$\frac{7}{12} - \frac{5}{8} = \frac{56}{96} - \frac{60}{96} = \frac{56 - 60}{96} = \frac{-4^1}{96_{24}} = -\frac{1}{24}$$

as before.

■

PROBLEM

7 (1) Without using a calculator evaluate

(a) $\dfrac{3}{7} - \dfrac{1}{7}$ (b) $\dfrac{1}{3} + \dfrac{2}{5}$ (c) $\dfrac{7}{18} - \dfrac{1}{4}$

(2) Confirm your answer to part (1) using a calculator.

Provided that you can manipulate ordinary fractions there is no reason why you should not be able to manipulate algebraic fractions just as easily since the rules are the same.

EXAMPLE

Find expressions for each of the following:

(a) $\dfrac{x}{x-1} \times \dfrac{2}{x(x+4)}$

(b) $\dfrac{2}{x-1} \div \dfrac{x}{x-1}$

(c) $\dfrac{x+1}{x^2+2} + \dfrac{x-6}{x^2+2}$

(d) $\dfrac{x}{x+2} - \dfrac{1}{x+1}$

Solution

(a) To multiply two fractions we multiply their corresponding numerators and denominators so

$$\frac{x}{x-1} \times \frac{2}{x(x+4)} = \frac{2x}{(x-1)x(x+4)}$$

$$= \frac{2}{(x-1)(x+4)}$$

the x's cancel top and bottom

(b) To divide by

$$\frac{x}{x-1}$$

we turn it upside down and multiply so

$$\frac{2}{x-1} \div \frac{x}{x-1} = \frac{2}{x-1} \times \frac{x-1}{x}$$

$$= \frac{2}{x}$$

the (x−1)'s cancel top and bottom

(c) The fractions

$$\frac{x+1}{x^2+2} \quad \text{and} \quad \frac{x-6}{x^2+2}$$

already have the same denominator so to add them we just add their numerators to get

$$\frac{x+1}{x^2+2} + \frac{x-6}{x^2+2} = \frac{x+1+x-6}{x^2+2}$$

$$= \frac{2x-5}{x^2+2}$$

(d) The fractions

$$\frac{x}{x+2} \quad \text{and} \quad \frac{1}{x+1}$$

have denominators $x+2$ and $x+1$. An obvious common denominator is given by their product, $(x+2)(x+1)$. Now $x+2$ goes into $(x+2)(x+1)$ exactly $x+1$ times so

$$\frac{x}{x+2} = \frac{x(x+1)}{(x+2)(x+1)}$$

multiply top and bottom by (x+1)

Also $x + 1$ goes into $(x + 2)(x + 1)$ exactly $x + 2$ times so

$$\frac{1}{x + 1} = \frac{(x + 2)}{(x + 2)(x + 1)}$$

multiply top and bottom by $(x + 2)$

Hence

$$\frac{x}{x + 2} - \frac{1}{x + 1} = \frac{x(x + 1)}{(x + 2)(x + 1)} - \frac{(x + 2)}{(x + 2)(x + 1)}$$

$$= \frac{x(x + 1) - (x + 2)}{(x + 2)(x + 1)}$$

It is worth multiplying out the brackets on the top to simplify, that is

$$\frac{x^2 + x - x - 2}{(x + 2)(x + 1)} = \frac{x^2 - 2}{(x + 2)(x + 1)}$$

∎

PROBLEM

8 Find expressions for the following algebraic fractions, simplifying your answers as far as possible.

(a) $\dfrac{5}{x - 1} \times \dfrac{x - 1}{x + 2}$ **(b)** $\dfrac{x^2}{x + 10} \div \dfrac{x}{x + 1}$ **(c)** $\dfrac{4}{x + 1} + \dfrac{1}{x + 1}$ **(d)** $\dfrac{2}{x + 1} - \dfrac{1}{x + 2}$

1.4.4 Transposition

Quite frequently in economics it is necessary to rearrange equations. This is called **transposition**. No new mathematical techniques are required. It is simply a matter of applying the rules of algebra that we have already discussed.

EXAMPLE

Transpose the following equations to express x in terms of y:

(a) $ax = bx + cy + d$

(b) $y = \dfrac{x + 1}{x - 2}$

Solution

(a)   In the equation

$$ax = bx + cy + d$$

there are terms involving x on both sides and since we are hoping to rearrange this into the form

$x = $ an expression involving y

it makes sense to collect the x's on the left-hand side. To do this we subtract bx from both sides to get

$ax - bx = cy + d$

Notice that x is a common factor of the left-hand side so the distributive law can be applied 'in reverse' to take the x outside the brackets, that is

$(a - b)x = cy + d$

Finally, both sides are divided by $a - b$ to get

$$x = \frac{cy + d}{a - b}$$

which is of the desired form.

(b)   It is difficult to see where to begin with the equation

$$y = \frac{x + 1}{x - 2}$$

because there is an x in both the numerator and the denominator. Indeed, the thing that is preventing us getting started is precisely the fact that the expression is a fraction. We can, however, remove the fraction simply by multiplying both sides by the denominator to get

$(x - 2)y = x + 1$

and if we multiply out the brackets then

$xy - 2y = x + 1$

We want to rearrange this into the form

$x = $ an expression involving y

so we collect the x's on the left-hand side and put everything else on to the right-hand side. To do this we first add $2y$ to both sides to get

$xy = x + 1 + 2y$

and then subtract x from both sides to get

$xy - x = 1 + 2y$

The distributive law can now be applied 'in reverse' to take out the common factor of x, that is

$(y - 1)x = 1 + 2y$

Finally, dividing through by $y - 1$ gives

$$x = \frac{1 + 2y}{y - 1}$$

∎

This example contains some of the hardest algebraic manipulation seen so far in this book. I hope that you managed to follow the individual steps. However, it all might appear as if we have 'pulled rabbits out of hats'. You may feel that, if left on your own, you are never going to be able to decide what to do at each stage. Unfortunately there is no watertight strategy that always works although the following five-point plan is worth considering if you get stuck. To transpose a given equation of the form

   $y = $ an expression involving x

into an equation of the form

   $x = $ an expression involving y

you proceed as follows:

(1)	remove fractions
(2)	multiply out the brackets
(3)	collect all of the x's on to the left-hand side
(4)	take out a factor of x
(5)	divide by the coefficient of x

You might find it helpful to look back at the previous example in the light of this strategy. In part (b) it is easy to identify each of the five steps. Part (a) also used this strategy starting with the third step.

PROBLEM

9   Transpose the following equations to express x in terms of y:

   (a) $y = ax + b$ **(b)** $x - ay = cx + y$ **(c)** $y = \dfrac{x - 2}{x + 4}$

PRACTICE PROBLEMS

10   Which of the following inequalities are true?

   (a) $-2 < 1$ **(b)** $-6 > -4$ **(c)** $3 < 3$
   (d) $3 \leqslant 3$ **(e)** $-21 \geqslant -22$ **(f)** $4 < \sqrt{25}$

11   Simplify the following inequalities:

   (a) $2x > x + 1$ **(b)** $7x + 3 \leqslant 9 + 5x$ **(c)** $x - 5 \geqslant 4x + 4$ **(d)** $x - 1 < 2x - 3$

12   Multiply out the brackets.

   (a) $7(x - y)$ **(b)** $(5x - 2y)z$ **(c)** $y + 2z - 2(x + 3y - z)$
   (d) $(x - 5)(x - 2)$ **(e)** $x(x - y + 7)$ **(f)** $x(x + 1)(x + 2)$ **(g)** $(x - 1)(x + 1 - y)$

13 **(1)** Without using your calculator evaluate

(a) $\dfrac{4}{5} \times \dfrac{25}{28}$ (b) $\dfrac{2}{7} \times \dfrac{14}{25} \times \dfrac{30}{48}$ (c) $\dfrac{9}{16} \div \dfrac{3}{8}$ (d) $\dfrac{2}{5} \times \dfrac{1}{12} \div \dfrac{8}{25}$

(e) $\dfrac{10}{13} - \dfrac{2}{13}$ (f) $\dfrac{5}{9} + \dfrac{2}{3}$ (g) $2\dfrac{3}{5} + 1\dfrac{3}{7}$ (h) $5\dfrac{9}{10} - \dfrac{1}{2} + 1\dfrac{2}{5}$

(2) Confirm your answer to part (1) using a calculator.

14 Find expressions for the following fractions:

(a) $\dfrac{x^2 + 6x}{x - 2} \times \dfrac{x - 2}{x}$ (b) $\dfrac{1}{x} \div \dfrac{1}{x + 1}$ (c) $\dfrac{2}{xy} + \dfrac{3}{xy}$

(d) $x - \dfrac{2}{x + 1}$ (e) $\dfrac{5}{x(x + 1)} - \dfrac{2}{x} + \dfrac{3}{x + 1}$

15 Transpose the equations

(a) $Q = aP + b$ to express P in terms of Q,

(b) $Y = aY + b + I$ to express Y in terms of I,

(c) $Q = \dfrac{1}{aP + b}$ to express P in terms of Q,

(d) $V = \dfrac{5t + 1}{t - 1}$ to express t in terms of V.

1.5 National income determination

Objectives At the end of this section you should be able to:

- identify and sketch linear consumption functions,

- identify and sketch linear savings functions,

- set up simple macroeconomic models,

- calculate equilibrium national income,

- analyse IS and LM schedules.

Macroeconomics is concerned with the analysis of economic theory and policy at a national level. In this section we focus on one particular aspect known as national income determination. We describe how to set up simple models of the national economy which enable equilibrium levels of income to be calculated. Initially we assume that the economy is divided into two sectors, households and firms. Firms use resources such as land, capital and labour to produce goods and services. These resources are known as **factors of production** and are taken to belong to households. **National income** represents the flow of income from firms to households given as payment for these factors. Households can then spend this money in one of two ways. Income can be used for the consumption of goods produced by firms or it can be put into savings. Consumption, C, and savings, S, are therefore functions of income, Y, that is

$$C = f(Y)$$

$$S = g(Y)$$

for some appropriate consumption function, f, and savings function, g. Moreover, C and S are normally expected to increase as income rises so f and g are both increasing functions.

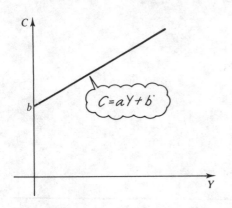

Figure 1.19

We begin by analysing the consumption function. As usual we need to quantify the precise relationship between C and Y. If this relationship is linear then a graph of a typical consumption function is shown in Figure 1.19. It is clear from this graph that if

$$C = aY + b$$

then $a > 0$ and $b > 0$. The intercept b is the level of consumption when there is no income (that is when $Y = 0$) and is known as **autonomous consumption**. The slope, a, is the change in C brought about by a one-unit increase in Y and is known as the **marginal propensity to consume** (MPC). As previously noted, income is used up in consumption and savings so that

$$Y = C + S$$

It follows that only a proportion of the one-unit increase in income is consumed; the rest goes into savings. Hence the slope, a, is generally smaller than 1, that is $a < 1$. It is standard practice in mathematics to collapse the two separate inequalities $a > 0$ and $a < 1$ into the single inequality

$$0 < a < 1$$

The relation

$$Y = C + S$$

enables the precise form of the savings function to be determined from any given consumption function. This is illustrated in the following example.

EXAMPLE

Sketch a graph of the consumption function

$$C = 0.6Y + 10$$

Determine the corresponding savings function and sketch its graph.

Solution

The graph of the consumption function

$$C = 0.6Y + 10$$

has intercept 10 and slope 0.6. It passes through $(0, 10)$. For a second point, let us choose $Y = 40$ which gives $C = 34$. Hence the line also passes through $(40, 34)$. The consumption function is sketched in Figure 1.20.

To find the savings function we use the relation

$$Y = C + S$$

which gives

$S = Y - C$	(subtract C from both sides)
$\quad = Y - (0.6Y + 10)$	(substitute C)
$\quad = Y - 0.6Y - 10$	(multiply out the brackets)
$\quad = 0.4Y - 10$	(collect terms)

The savings function is also linear. Its graph has intercept -10 and slope 0.4. This is sketched in Figure 1.21 using the fact that it passes through $(0, -10)$ and $(25, 0)$. ∎

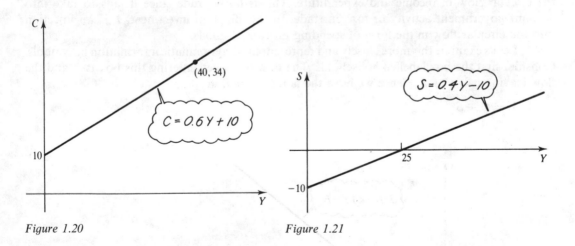

Figure 1.20   Figure 1.21

PROBLEM

1   Determine the savings function which corresponds to the consumption function

$$C = 0.8Y + 25$$

For the general consumption function

$$C = aY + b$$

we have

$$S = Y - C$$
$$= Y - (aY + b) \qquad \text{(substitute } C)$$
$$= Y - aY - b \qquad \text{(multiply out the brackets)}$$
$$= (1 - a)Y - b \qquad \text{(take out a common factor of } Y)$$

The slope of the savings function is called the **marginal propensity to save** (MPS) and is given by $1 - a$, that is

$$\text{MPS} = 1 - a = 1 - \text{MPC}$$

Moreover, since $a < 1$ we see that the slope, $1 - a$, is positive. Figure 1.22 shows the graph of this savings function. One interesting feature, which contrasts with other economic functions considered so far, is that it is allowed to take negative values. In particular, note that **autonomous savings** (that is, the value of S when $Y = 0$) are equal to $-b$, which is negative because $b > 0$. This is to be expected because whenever consumption exceeds income, households must finance the excess expenditure by withdrawing savings.

The simplest model of the national economy is illustrated in Figure 1.23, which shows the circular flow of income and expenditure. This is fairly crude since it fails to take into account government activity or foreign trade. In this diagram **investment**, I, is an injection into the circular flow in the form of spending on capital goods.

Let us examine this more closely and represent the diagrammatic information in symbols. Consider first the box labelled households. The flow of money entering this box is Y and the flow leaving it is $C + S$. Hence we have the familiar relation

$$Y = C + S$$

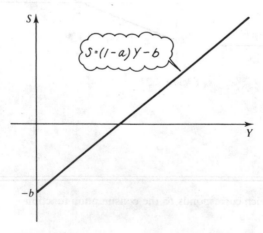

Figure 1.22

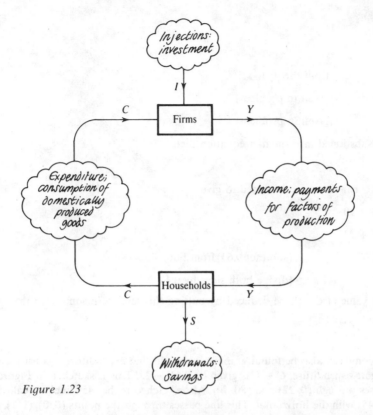

Figure 1.23

For the box labelled firms the flow entering it is $C + I$ and the flow leaving it is Y so

$$Y = C + I$$

Suppose that the level of investment that firms plan to inject into the economy is known to be some fixed value, I^*. If the economy is in equilibrium the flow of income and expenditure balance so that

$$Y = C + I^*$$

From the assumption that the consumption function is

$$C = aY + b$$

for given values of a and b these two equations represent a pair of simultaneous equations for the two unknowns Y and C. In these circumstances C and Y can be regarded as endogenous variables since their precise values are determined within the model, whereas I^* is fixed outside the model and is exogenous.

EXAMPLE _____

Find the equilibrium level of income and consumption if the consumption function is

$$C = 0.6Y + 10$$

and planned investment $I = 12$.

Solution

We know that

$$Y = C + I \qquad \text{(from theory)}$$

$$C = 0.6Y + 10 \qquad \text{(given in problem)}$$

$$I = 12 \qquad \text{(given in problem)}$$

If the value of I is substituted into the first equation then

$$Y = C + 12$$

The expression for C can also be substituted to give

$$Y = 0.6Y + 10 + 12$$

$$Y = 0.6Y + 22$$

$$0.4Y = 22 \qquad \text{(subtract } 0.6Y \text{ from both sides)}$$

$$Y = 55 \qquad \text{(divide both sides by 0.4)}$$

The corresponding value of C can be deduced by putting this level of income into the consumption function to get

$$C = 0.6(55) + 10 = 43$$

The equilibrium income can also be found graphically by plotting expenditure against income. In this example the aggregate expenditure, $C + I$, is given by $0.6Y + 22$. This is sketched in Figure 1.24 using the fact that it passes through $(0, 22)$ and $(80, 70)$. Also sketched is the '45° line', so called because it makes an angle of 45° with the horizontal. This line passes through the points $(0, 0), (1, 1), \ldots, (50, 50)$ and so on. In other words, at any point on this line expenditure and income are in balance. The equilibrium income can therefore be found by inspecting the point of intersection of this line and the aggregate expenditure line, $C + I$. From Figure 1.24 this occurs when $Y = 55$ which is in agreement with the calculated value.

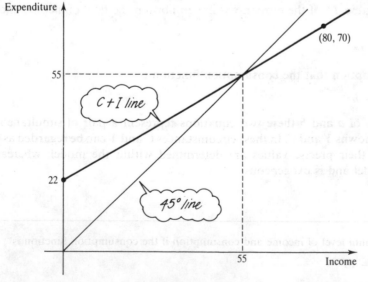

Figure 1.24

PROBLEM

2 Find the equilibrium level of income if the consumption function is

$$C = 0.8Y + 25$$

and planned investment $I = 17$. Calculate the new equilibrium income if planned investment rises by one unit.

To make the model more realistic let us now include **government expenditure**, G, and **taxation**, T, in the model. The injections box in Figure 1.23 now includes government expenditure in addition to investment so

$$Y = C + I + G$$

We assume that planned government expenditure and planned investment are autonomous with fixed values G^* and I^* respectively, so that in equilibrium

$$Y = C + I^* + G^*$$

The withdrawals box in Figure 1.23 now includes taxation. This means that the income that households have to spend on consumer goods is no longer Y but rather $Y - T$ (income less tax) which is called **disposable income**, Y_d. Hence

$$C = aY_d + b$$

with

$$Y_d = Y - T$$

In practice, the tax will either be autonomous ($T = T^*$ for some lump sum T^*) or be a proportion of national income ($T = tY$ for some proportion t), or a combination of both ($T = tY + T^*$).

EXAMPLE

Given that

$$G = 20$$

$$I = 35$$

$$C = 0.9Y_d + 70$$

$$T = 0.2Y + 25$$

calculate the equilibrium level of national income.

Solution

At first sight this problem looks rather forbidding, particularly since there are so many variables. However, all we have to do is to write down the relevant equations and to substitute systematically one equation into another until only Y is left.

We know that

$$Y = C + I + G \quad (1) \quad \text{(from theory)}$$

$$G = 20 \qquad (2) \qquad \text{(given in problem)}$$

$$I = 35 \qquad (3) \qquad \text{(given in problem)}$$

$$C = 0.9Y_\text{d} + 70 \qquad (4) \qquad \text{(given in problem)}$$

$$T = 0.2Y + 25 \qquad (5) \qquad \text{(given in problem)}$$

$$Y_\text{d} = Y - T \qquad (6) \qquad \text{(from theory)}$$

This represents a system of six equations in six unknowns. The obvious thing to do is to put the fixed values of G and I into equation (1) to get

$$Y = C + 35 + 20 = C + 55 \qquad (7)$$

This has at least removed G and I so there are only three more variables (C, Y_d and T) left to eliminate. We can remove T by substituting equation (5) into (6) to get

$$Y_\text{d} = Y - (0.2Y + 25)$$

$$= Y - 0.2Y - 25$$

$$= 0.8Y - 25 \qquad (8)$$

and then remove Y_d by substituting equation (8) into (4) to get

$$C = 0.9(0.8Y - 25) + 70$$

$$= 0.72Y - 22.5 + 70$$

$$= 0.72Y + 47.5 \qquad (9)$$

We can eliminate C by substituting equation (9) into (7) to get

$$Y = C + 55$$

$$= 0.72Y + 47.5 + 55$$

$$= 0.72Y + 102.5$$

Finally solving for Y gives

$$0.28Y = 102.5 \qquad \text{(subtract } 0.72Y \text{ from both sides)}$$

$$Y = 366 \qquad \text{(divide both sides by 0.28)}$$

■

PROBLEM

3 Given that

$$G = 40$$

$$I = 55$$

$$C = 0.8Y_\text{d} + 25$$

$$T = 0.1Y + 10$$

calculate the equilibrium level of national income.

To conclude this section we return to the simple two-sector model,

$$Y = C + I$$

$$C = aY + b$$

Previously, the investment, I, was taken to be constant. It is more realistic to assume that planned investment depends on the rate of interest, r. As the interest rate rises so investment falls and we have a relationship

$$I = cr + d$$

where $c < 0$ and $d > 0$. Unfortunately, this model consists of three equations in the four unknowns Y, C, I and r so we cannot expect it to determine national income uniquely. The best we can do is to eliminate C and I, say, and to set up an equation relating Y and r. This is most easily understood by an example. Suppose that

$$C = 0.8Y + 100$$

$$I = -20r + 1000$$

We know that the commodity market is in equilibrium when

$$Y = C + I$$

Substitution of the given expressions for C and I into this equation gives

$$Y = (0.8Y + 100) + (-20r + 1000)$$

$$= 0.8Y - 20r + 1100$$

which rearranges as

$$0.2Y + 20r = 1100$$

This equation, relating national income, Y, and interest rate, r, is called the **IS schedule**.

We obviously need some additional information before we can pin down the values of Y and r. This can be done by investigating the equilibrium of the money market. The money market is said to be in equilibrium when the supply of money, M_S, matches the demand for money, M_D, that is when

$$M_S = M_D$$

There are many ways of measuring the **money supply**. In simple terms it can be thought of as consisting of the notes and coins in circulation, together with money held in bank deposits. The level of M_S is assumed to be controlled by the central bank and is taken to be autonomous so that

$$M_S = M_S^*$$

for some fixed value M_S^*.

The demand for money comes from three sources: transactions, precautions and speculations. The **transactions demand** is used for the daily exchange of goods and services whereas the **precautionary demand** is used to fund any emergencies requiring unforeseen expenditure. Both are assumed to be proportional to national income. Consequently, we lump these together and write

$$L_1 = k_1 Y$$

where L_1 denotes the aggregate transaction–precautionary demand and k_1 is a positive constant. The **speculative demand** for money is used as a reserve fund in case individuals or firms decide to invest in alternative assets such as government bonds. In Chapter 3 we show that, as interest rates rise, speculative demand falls. We model this by writing

$$L_2 = k_2 r + k_3$$

where L_2 denotes speculative demand, k_2 is a negative constant and k_3 is a positive constant. The total demand, M_D, is the sum of the transaction–precautionary demand and speculative demand, that is

$$M_D = L_1 + L_2$$
$$= k_1 Y + k_2 r + k_3$$

If the money market is in equilibrium then

$$M_S = M_D$$

that is

$$M_S^* = k_1 Y + k_2 r + k_3$$

This equation, relating national income, Y, and interest rate, r, is called the **LM schedule**. If we assume that equilibrium exists in both the commodity and money markets then the IS and LM schedules provide a system of two equations in two unknowns Y and r. These can easily be solved either by elimination or by graphical methods.

EXAMPLE

Determine the equilibrium income and interest rate given the following information about the commodity market:

$$C = 0.8Y + 100$$
$$I = -20r + 1000$$

and the money market:

$$M_S = 2375$$
$$L_1 = 0.1Y$$
$$L_2 = -25r + 2000$$

What effect would a decrease in the money supply have on the equilibrium levels of Y and r?

Solution

The IS schedule for these particular consumption and investment functions has already been obtained in the preceding text. It was shown that the commodity market is in equilibrium when

$$0.2Y + 20r = 1100 \quad (1)$$

For the money market we see that the money supply is

$$M_S = 2375$$

and that the total demand for money (that is, the sum of the transaction–precautionary demand, L_1, and the speculative demand, L_2) is

$$M_D = L_1 + L_2 = 0.1Y - 25r + 2000$$

The money market is in equilibrium when

$$M_S = M_D$$

that is

$$2375 = 0.1Y - 25r + 2000$$

The LM schedule is therefore given by

$$0.1Y - 25r = 375 \qquad (2)$$

Equations (1) and (2) constitute a system of two equations for the two unknowns Y and r. The steps described in Section 1.2 can be used to solve this system:

Step 1 Double equation (2) and subtract from equation (1) to get

$$0.2Y + 20r = 1100$$
$$\underline{0.2Y - 50r = 750} \quad -$$
$$70r = 350 \qquad (3)$$

Step 2 Divide both sides of equation (3) by 70 to get

$$r = 5$$

Step 3 Substitute $r = 5$ into equation (1) to get

$$0.2Y + 100 = 1100$$
$$0.2Y = 1000 \qquad \text{(subtract 100 from both sides)}$$
$$Y = 5000 \qquad \text{(divide both sides by 0.2)}$$

Step 4 As a check, equation (2) gives

$$0.1(5000) - 25(5) = 375 \qquad \checkmark$$

The equilibrium levels of Y and r are therefore 5000 and 5 respectively.

To investigate what happens to Y and r as the money supply falls we could just take a smaller value of M_S such as 2300 and repeat the calculations. However, it is more instructive to perform the investigation graphically. Figure 1.25 shows the IS and LM curves plotted on the same diagram with r on the horizontal axis and Y on the vertical axis. These lines intersect at $(5, 5000)$, confirming the equilibrium levels of interest rate and income obtained by calculation. Any change in the money supply will obviously have no effect on the IS curve. On the other hand, a change in the money supply does affect the LM curve. To see this, let us return to the general LM schedule

$$k_1 Y + k_2 r + k_3 = M_S^*$$

and transpose it to express Y in terms of r:

$$k_1 Y = -k_2 r - k_3 + M_S^* \qquad \text{(subtract } k_2 r + k_3 \text{ from both sides)}$$
$$Y = \left(\frac{-k_2}{k_1}\right) r + \frac{-k_3 + M_S^*}{k_1} \qquad \text{(divide both sides by } k_1 \text{)}$$

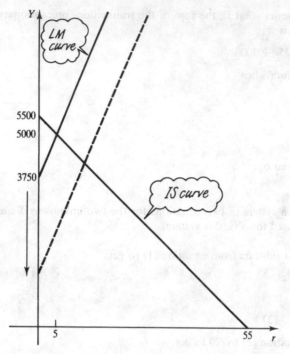

Figure 1.25

Expressed in this form we see that the LM schedule has slope $-k_2/k_1$ and intercept $(-k_3 + M_S^*)/k_1$.

Any decrease in M_S^* therefore decreases the intercept (but not the slope) and the LM curve shifts downwards. This is indicated by the dashed line in Figure 1.25. The point of intersection shifts both downwards and to the right. We deduce that as the money supply falls, interest rates rise and national income decreases (assuming that both the commodity and money markets remain in equilibrium).

∎

PROBLEM

4 Determine the equilibrium income, Y, and interest rate, r, given the following information about the commodity market:

$$C = 0.7Y + 85$$

$$I = -50r + 1200$$

and the money market:

$$M_S = 500$$

$$L_1 = 0.2Y$$

$$L_2 = -40r + 230$$

Sketch the IS and LM curves on the same diagram. What effect would an increase in the value of autonomous investment have on the equilibrium values of Y and r?

PRACTICE PROBLEMS

5   Write down expressions for the savings function given that the consumption function is

(a) $C = 0.9Y + 72$ (b) $C = \dfrac{Y^2 + 500}{Y + 10}$

6   For a closed economy with no government intervention the consumption function is

$$C = 0.6Y + 30$$

and planned investment is

$$I = 100$$

Calculate the equilibrium levels of

(a)   national income
(b)   consumption
(c)   savings

7   An open economy is in equilibrium when

$$Y = C + I + G + X - M$$

where

Y = national income

C = consumption

I = investment

G = government expenditure

X = exports

M = imports

Determine the equilibrium level of income given that

$C = 0.8Y + 80$

$I = 70$

$G = 130$

$X = 100$

$M = 0.2Y + 50$

8   Given that

consumption,	$C = 0.8Y + 60,$
investment,	$I = -30r + 740,$
money supply,	$M_S = 4000,$
transaction–precautionary demand for money,	$L_1 = 0.15Y,$
speculative demand for money,	$L_2 = -20r + 3825,$

determine the values of national income, Y, and interest rate, r, on the assumption that both the commodity and the money markets are in equilibrium.

2 *Non-linear Equations*

The main aim of this chapter is to describe the mathematics of non-linear equations. The approach is similar to that of Chapter 1. There are three sections. Section 2.1 should be read before Section 2.2 although Section 2.3 can be studied at any time.

The first section investigates the simplest non-linear equation, known as a quadratic. A quadratic equation can easily be solved either by factorizing it as the product of two linear factors or by using a special formula. You are also shown how to sketch the graphs of quadratic functions. The techniques are illustrated by finding the equilibrium price and quantity for quadratic supply and demand functions.

Section 2.2 introduces additional functions in microeconomics, including revenue and profit. There is very little new material in this section. It mainly consists of applying the ideas of Section 2.1 to sketch graphs of quadratic revenue and profit functions and to find their maximum values.

Finally, the topic of algebra, which we started in Chapter 1, is completed by investigating the rules of indices and logarithms. This is probably the hardest section and you may find it heavy going. However, the notation and rules of indices are extremely important and are used frequently in subsequent chapters. If you do run into difficulty or are short of time then the material on logarithms could possibly be omitted, particularly if you do not intend to study the next chapter on the mathematics of finance.

2.1 Quadratic functions

Objectives   At the end of this section you should be able

- solve a quadratic equation using 'the formula',

- solve a quadratic equation given its factorization,

- sketch the graph of a quadratic function using a table of function values,

- sketch the graph of a quadratic function by finding the coordinates of the intercepts,

- determine equilibrium price and quantity given a pair of quadratic demand and supply functions.

The first chapter considered the topic of linear mathematics. In particular, we described how to sketch the graph of a linear function and how to solve a linear equation (or system of simultaneous linear equations). It was also pointed out that not all economic functions are of this simple form. In assuming that the demand and supply graphs are straight lines we are certainly making the mathematical analysis easy, but we may well be sacrificing realism. It may be that the demand and supply graphs are curved and, in these circumstances, it is essential to model them using more complicated functions. The simplest non-linear function is known as a **quadratic** and takes the form

$$f(x) = ax^2 + bx + c$$

for some parameters a, b and c. (In fact, even if the demand function is linear, functions derived from it, such as total revenue and profit, turn out to be quadratic. We investigate these functions in the next section.) For the moment we concentrate on the mathematics of quadratics and show how to sketch graphs of quadratic functions and how to solve quadratic equations.

Consider the elementary equation

$$x^2 - 9 = 0$$

It is easy to see that the expression on the left-hand side is a special case of the above with $a = 1$, $b = 0$ and $c = -9$. To solve this equation we add 9 to both sides to get

$$x^2 = 9$$

x^2 is an abbreviation for $x \times x$

so we need to find a number, x, which when multiplied by itself produces the value 9. A moment's thought should convince you that there are exactly two numbers which work, namely 3 and -3 because

$$3 \times 3 = 9 \quad \text{and} \quad (-3) \times (-3) = 9$$

These two solutions are called the **square roots** of 9. The symbol $\sqrt{}$ is reserved for the positive square root so in this notation the solutions are $\sqrt{9}$ and $-\sqrt{9}$. These are usually combined and written $\pm\sqrt{9}$. The equation

$$x^2 - 9 = 0$$

is trivial to solve because the number 9 has obvious square roots. In general, it is necessary to use a calculator to evaluate square roots. For example, the equation

$$x^2 - 2 = 0$$

can be written as

$$x^2 = 2$$

and so has solutions $x = \pm\sqrt{2}$. My calculator gives 1.414 213 56 (correct to 8 decimal places) for the square root of 2, so the above equation has solutions

$$1.414\,213\,56 \quad \text{and} \quad -1.414\,213\,56$$

PROBLEM

1 Solve the following quadratic equations. (Round your solutions to 2 decimal places if necessary.)

(**a**) $x^2 - 100 = 0$ (**b**) $2x^2 - 8 = 0$ (**c**) $x^2 - 3 = 0$ (**d**) $x^2 - 5.72 = 0$
(**e**) $x^2 + 1 = 0$ (**f**) $3x^2 + 6.21 = 0$ (**g**) $x^2 = 0$

All of the equations considered in Problem 1 are of the special form

$$ax^2 + c = 0$$

in which the coefficient of x is zero. To solve more general quadratic equations we use a formula which enables the solutions to be calculated in a few lines of working. It can be shown that

$$ax^2 + bx + c = 0$$

has solutions

$$x = \frac{-b \pm \sqrt{(b^2 - 4ac)}}{2a}$$

The following example describes how to use this formula. It also illustrates the fact (which you have already discovered in Problem 1) that a quadratic equation can have two solutions, one solution or no solutions.

EXAMPLE

Solve the quadratic equations

(a) $2x^2 + 9x + 5 = 0$
(b) $x^2 - 4x + 4 = 0$
(c) $3x^2 - 5x + 6 = 0$

Solution

(a) For the equation

$$2x^2 + 9x + 5 = 0$$

we have $a = 2$, $b = 9$ and $c = 5$. Substituting these values into the formula

$$x = \frac{-b \pm \sqrt{(b^2 - 4ac)}}{2a}$$

gives

$$x = \frac{-9 \pm \sqrt{(9^2 - 4(2)(5))}}{2(2)}$$

$$= \frac{-9 \pm \sqrt{(81 - 40)}}{4}$$

$$= \frac{-9 \pm \sqrt{41}}{4}$$

The two solutions are obtained by taking the $+$ and $-$ signs separately, that is

$$\frac{-9 + \sqrt{41}}{4} = -0.649 \quad \text{(correct to 3 decimal places)}$$

$$\frac{-9 - \sqrt{41}}{4} = -3.851 \quad \text{(correct to 3 decimal places)}$$

It is easy to check that these are solutions by substituting them into the original equation. For example, putting $x = -0.649$ into

$$2x^2 + 9x + 5$$

gives

$$2(-0.649)^2 + 9(-0.649) + 5 = 0.001\,402$$

which is close to zero as required. We cannot expect to produce an exact value of zero because we rounded $\sqrt{41}$ to 3 decimal places. You might like to check for yourself that -3.851 is also a solution.

(b) For the equation

$$x^2 - 4x + 4 = 0$$

we have $a = 1$, $b = -4$ and $c = 4$. Substituting these values into the formula

$$x = \frac{-b \pm \sqrt{(b^2 - 4ac)}}{2a}$$

gives

$$x = \frac{-(-4) \pm \sqrt{((-4)^2 - 4(1)(4))}}{2(1)}$$

$$= \frac{4 \pm \sqrt{(16 - 16)}}{2}$$

$$= \frac{4 \pm \sqrt{0}}{2}$$

$$= \frac{4 \pm 0}{2}$$

Clearly we get the same answer irrespective of whether we take the $+$ or the $-$ sign here. In other words, this equation has only one solution, $x = 2$. As a check, substitution of $x = 2$ into the original equation gives

$$(2)^2 - 4(2) + 4 = 0$$

(c)   For the equation

$$3x^2 - 5x + 6 = 0$$

we have $a = 3$, $b = -5$ and $c = 6$. Substituting these values into the formula

$$x = \frac{-b \pm \sqrt{(b^2 - 4ac)}}{2a}$$

gives

$$x = \frac{-(-5) \pm \sqrt{((-5)^2 - 4(3)(6))}}{2(3)}$$

$$= \frac{5 \pm \sqrt{(25 - 72)}}{6}$$

$$= \frac{5 \pm \sqrt{(-47)}}{6}$$

The number under the square root sign is negative and, as you discovered in Problem 1, it is impossible to find the square root of a negative number. We conclude that the quadratic equation

$$3x^2 - 5x + 6 = 0$$

has no solutions.

■

This example demonstrates the three cases that can occur when solving quadratic equations. The precise number of solutions that an equation can have depends on whether the number under the square root sign is positive, zero or negative.

● If $b^2 - 4ac > 0$ then there are two solutions

$$x = \frac{-b + \sqrt{(b^2 - 4ac)}}{2a} \quad \text{and} \quad x = \frac{-b - \sqrt{(b^2 - 4ac)}}{2a}$$

- If $b^2 - 4ac = 0$ then there is one solution

$$x = \frac{-b \pm \sqrt{0}}{2a} = \frac{-b}{2a}$$

- If $b^2 - 4ac < 0$ then there are no solutions because $\sqrt{(b^2 - 4ac)}$ does not exist.

PROBLEM

2 Solve the following quadratic equations (where possible):

(a) $2x^2 - 19x - 10 = 0$ (b) $4x^2 + 12x + 9 = 0$ (c) $x^2 + x + 1 = 0$
(d) $x^2 - 3x + 10 = 2x + 4$

You may be familiar with another method for solving quadratic equations. This is based on the factorization of a quadratic into the product of two linear factors. Section 1.4 described how to multiply out two pairs of brackets. One of the examples in that section showed that

$$(x + 1)(x + 2) = x^2 + 3x + 2$$

Consequently, the solutions of the equation

$$x^2 + 3x + 2 = 0$$

are the same as those of

$$(x + 1)(x + 2) = 0$$

Now the only way that two numbers can be multiplied together to produce a value of zero is when (at least) one of the numbers is zero.

$$\boxed{\text{if } ab = 0 \text{ then either } a = 0 \text{ or } b = 0 \text{ (or both)}}$$

It follows that either

$$x + 1 = 0 \text{ with solution } x = -1$$

or

$$x + 2 = 0 \text{ with solution } x = -2$$

The quadratic equation

$$x^2 + 3x + 2 = 0$$

therefore has two solutions $x = -1$ and $x = -2$.

The difficulty with this approach is that it is impossible, except in very simple cases, to work out the factorization from any given quadratic so the preferred method is to use the formula. However, if you are lucky enough to be given the factorization, or perhaps clever enough to spot the factorization for yourself, then it does provide a viable alternative.

PROBLEM

3   Write down the solutions to the following quadratic equations. (There is no need to multiply out the brackets.)

(**a**) $(x - 4)(x + 3) = 0$ (**b**) $x(10 - 2x) = 0$ (**c**) $(2x - 6)^2 = 0$

One important feature of linear functions is that their graphs are always straight lines. Obviously the intercept and slope vary from function to function but the shape is always the same. It turns out that a similar property holds for quadratic functions. Now, whenever you are asked to produce a graph of an unfamiliar function it is often a good idea to tabulate the function, to plot these points on graph paper and to join them up with a smooth curve. The precise number of points to be taken depends on the function but, as a general rule, between 5 and 10 points usually produce a good picture. A table of values for the simple square function

$$f(x) = x^2$$

is given by

x	-3	-2	-1	0	1	2	3
$f(x)$	9	4	1	0	1	4	9

The first row of the table gives a selection of 'incoming' numbers, x, while the second row shows the corresponding 'outgoing' numbers, y. Points with coordinates (x, y) are then plotted on graph paper to produce the curve shown in Figure 2.1. For convenience, different scales are used on the x and y axes.

Mathematicians call this curve a **parabola** whereas economists refer to it as **U shaped**. Notice that the graph is symmetric about the y axis with a minimum point at the origin; if

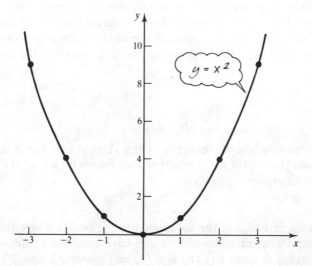

Figure 2.1

a mirror is placed along the y axis then the left-hand part is the image of the right-hand part. The following problem is designed to give you an opportunity to tabulate and sketch graphs of more general quadratic functions.

PROBLEM

4 Complete the following tables of function values and hence sketch a graph of each quadratic function:

(a) $f(x) = 4x^2 - 12x + 5$

x	-1	0	1	2	3	4
$f(x)$						

(b) $f(x) = -x^2 + 6x - 9$

x	0	1	2	3	4	5	6
$f(x)$							

(c) $f(x) = -2x^2 + 4x - 6$

x	-2	-1	0	1	2	3	4
$f(x)$							

The results of Problem 4 suggest that the graph of a quadratic is always parabolic. Furthermore, whenever the coefficient of x^2 is positive the graph bends upwards (U-shape). A selection of U-shaped curves is shown in Figure 2.2. Similarly, when the coefficient of x^2 is negative the graph bends downwards (inverted U-shape). A selection of inverted U-shaped curves is shown in Figure 2.3.

The task of sketching graphs from a table of function values is extremely tedious, particularly if only a rough sketch is required. It is usually more convenient just to determine a few key points on the curve. The obvious points to find are the intercepts with the coordinate axes since these enable us to 'tether' the parabola down in the various positions shown in Figures 2.2 and 2.3. The curve crosses the y axis when $x = 0$. Evaluating the function

$$f(x) = ax^2 + bx + c$$

at $x = 0$ gives

$$f(0) = a(0)^2 + b(0) + c = c$$

so the constant term determines where the curve cuts the vertical axis (as it did for linear functions). The curve crosses the x axis when $y = 0$ or, equivalently, when $f(x) = 0$, so we need to solve the quadratic equation

$$ax^2 + bx + c = 0$$

This can be done using 'the formula' and the solutions are the points where the graph cuts the horizontal axis. In general, a quadratic equation can have two, one or no solutions and these possibilities are illustrated in cases (a), (b) and (c) in Figures 2.2 and 2.3. In case (a) the curve crosses the x axis at A, turns round and crosses it again at B so there are two

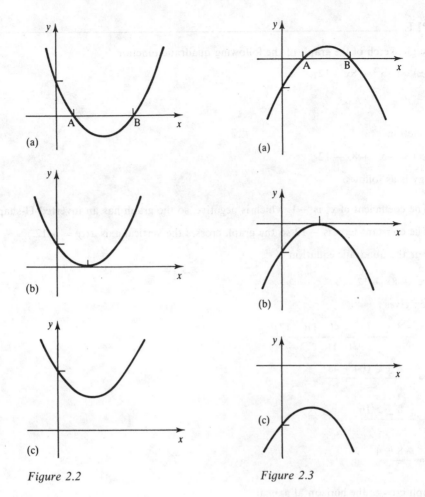

Figure 2.2   Figure 2.3

solutions. In case (b) the curve turns round just as it touches the x axis so there is only one solution. Finally, in case (c) the curve turns round before it has a chance to cross the x axis so there are no solutions.

The strategy for sketching the graph of a quadratic function

$$f(x) = ax^2 + bx + c$$

may now be stated.

Step 1   Determine the basic shape. The graph has a U-shape if $a > 0$ and an inverted U-shape if $a < 0$.

Step 2   Determine the y intercept. This is obtained by substituting $x = 0$ into the function, which gives $y = c$.

Step 3   Determine the x intercepts (if any). These are obtained by solving the quadratic equation

$$ax^2 + bx + c = 0$$

This three-step strategy is illustrated in the following example.

EXAMPLE _____

Give a rough sketch of the graph of the following quadratic function:

$$f(x) = -x^2 + 8x - 12$$

Solution

For the function

$$f(x) = -x^2 + 8x - 12$$

the strategy is as follows.

Step 1   The coefficient of x^2 is -1, which is negative, so the graph has an inverted U-shape.

Step 2   The constant term is -12 so the graph crosses the vertical axis at $y = -12$.

Step 3   For the quadratic equation

$$-x^2 + 8x - 12 = 0$$

the formula gives

$$x = \frac{-8 \pm \sqrt{(8^2 - 4(-1)(-12))}}{2(-1)}$$

$$= \frac{-8 \pm \sqrt{(64 - 48)}}{-2}$$

$$= \frac{-8 \pm \sqrt{16}}{-2}$$

$$= \frac{-8 \pm 4}{-2}$$

so the graph crosses the horizontal axis at

$$x = \frac{-8 + 4}{-2} = 2$$

and

$$x = \frac{-8 - 4}{-2} = 6$$

The information obtained in steps 1–3 is sufficient to produce the sketch shown in Figure 2.4.

   In fact, we can go even further in this case and locate the coordinates of the turning point, that is the maximum point, on the curve. By symmetry, the x coordinate of this point occurs exactly halfway between $x = 2$ and $x = 6$, that is at

$$x = \tfrac{1}{2}(2 + 6) = 4$$

The corresponding y coordinate is found by substituting $x = 4$ into the function to get

$$f(4) = -(4)^2 + 8(4) - 12 = 4$$

The maximum point on the curve therefore has coordinates $(4, 4)$.

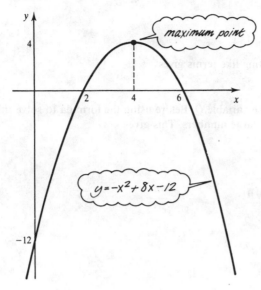

Figure 2.4

■

PROBLEM

5 Use the three-step strategy to produce rough graphs of the following quadratic functions:

   (a) $f(x) = 2x^2 - 11x - 6$ **(b)** $f(x) = x^2 - 6x + 9$

We conclude this section by seeing how to solve a particular problem in microeconomics. In Section 1.3 the concept of market equilibrium was introduced and in each of the problems the supply and demand functions were always given to be linear. The following example shows this to be an unnecessary restriction and indicates that it is almost as easy to manipulate quadratic supply and demand functions.

EXAMPLE

Given the supply and demand functions

$$P = Q_S^2 + 14Q_S + 22$$
$$P = -Q_D^2 - 10Q_D + 150$$

calculate the equilibrium price and quantity.

Solution

In equilibrium, $Q_S = Q_D$, so if we denote this equilibrium quantity by Q the supply and demand functions become

$$P = Q^2 + 14Q + 22$$
$$P = -Q^2 - 10Q + 150$$

Hence

$$Q^2 + 14Q + 22 = -Q^2 - 10Q + 150$$

since both sides are equal to P. Collecting like terms gives

$$2Q^2 + 24Q - 128 = 0$$

which is just a quadratic equation in the variable Q. Before using the formula to solve this it is a good idea to divide both sides by 2 to avoid large numbers. This gives

$$Q^2 + 12Q - 64 = 0$$

and so

$$Q = \frac{-12 \pm \sqrt{((12)^2 - 4(1)(-64))}}{2(1)}$$

$$= \frac{-12 \pm \sqrt{(400)}}{2}$$

$$= \frac{-12 \pm 20}{2}$$

The quadratic equation has solutions $Q = -16$ and $Q = 4$. Now the solution $Q = -16$ can obviously be ignored because a negative quantity does not make sense. The equilibrium quantity is therefore 4. The equilibrium price can be calculated by substituting this value into either the original supply or demand equation.

From the supply equation,

$$P = 4^2 + 14(4) + 22 = 94$$

As a check, the demand equation gives

$$P = -(4)^2 - 10(4) + 150 = 94 \quad \checkmark$$

You might be puzzled by the fact that we actually obtain two possible solutions, one of which does not make economic sense. The supply and demand curves are sketched in Figure 2.5. This shows that

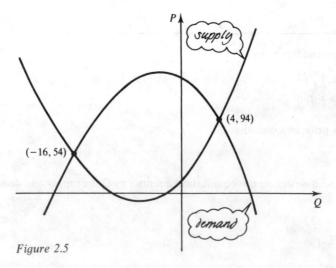

Figure 2.5

there are indeed two points of intersection confirming the mathematical solution. However, in economics the quantity and price are both positive so the functions are only defined in the top right-hand (that is, positive) quadrant. In this region there is just one point of intersection at (4, 94).

∎

PROBLEM

6 Given the supply and demand functions

$$P = 2Q_S^2 + 10Q_S + 10$$
$$P = -Q_D^2 - 5Q_D + 52$$

calculate the equilibrium price and quantity.

PRACTICE PROBLEMS

7 Solve the equation $f(x) = 0$ for each of the following quadratic functions:

(a) $f(x) = x^2 - 16$ (b) $f(x) = x(100 - x)$ (c) $f(x) = -x^2 + 22x - 85$
(d) $f(x) = x^2 - 18x + 81$ (e) $f(x) = 2x^2 + 4x + 3$

8 Sketch the graphs of the quadratic functions given in Problem 7.

9 Given the quadratic supply and demand functions

$$P = Q_S^2 + 2Q_S + 12$$
$$P = -Q_D^2 - 4Q_D + 68$$

determine the equilibrium price and quantity.

2.2 Revenue, cost and profit

Objectives At the end of this section you should be able to:

- sketch the graphs of the total revenue, total cost, average cost and profit functions,

- find the level of output which maximizes total revenue,

- find the level of output which maximizes profit,

- find the break-even levels of output.

The main aim of this section is to investigate one particular function in economics, namely profit. By making reasonable simplifying assumptions, the profit function is shown to be quadratic and so the methods developed in Section 2.1 can be used to analyse its properties. We describe how to find the levels of output required for a firm to break even and to maximize profit. The **profit** function is denoted by the Greek letter π (pronounced 'pie') and is defined to be the difference between total revenue, TR, and total cost, TC, that is

$$\pi = \text{TR} - \text{TC}$$

This definition is entirely sensible because TR is the amount of money received by the firm from the sale of its goods and TC is the amount of money that the firm has to spend to produce these goods. We begin by considering the total revenue and total cost functions in turn.

The **total revenue** received from the sale of Q goods at price P is given by

$$\text{TR} = PQ$$

For example, if the price of each good is \$70 and the firm sells 300 then the revenue is

$$\$70 \times 300 = \$21,000$$

Given any particular demand function, expressing P in terms of Q, it is a simple matter to obtain a formula for TR solely in terms of Q. A graph of TR against Q can then be sketched.

EXAMPLE

Given the demand function

$$P = 100 - 2Q$$

express TR as a function of Q and hence sketch its graph.

(1) For what values of Q is TR zero?
(2) What is the maximum value of TR?

Solution

Total revenue is defined by

$$\text{TR} = PQ$$

and, since $P = 100 - 2Q$, we have

$$\text{TR} = (100 - 2Q)Q$$
$$= 100Q - 2Q^2$$

This function is quadratic and so its graph can be sketched using the strategy described in Section 2.1.

Step 1 The coefficient of Q^2 is negative so the graph has an inverted U-shape.

Step 2 The constant term is zero so the graph crosses the TR axis at the origin.

Step 3 To find where the curve crosses the horizontal axis we could use 'the formula'. However, this is not necessary since it follows immediately from the factorization

$$\text{TR} = (100 - 2Q)Q$$

that TR = 0 when either $100 - 2Q = 0$ or $Q = 0$. In other words, the quadratic equation has two solutions, $Q = 0$ and $Q = 50$.

The total revenue curve is shown in Figure 2.6.

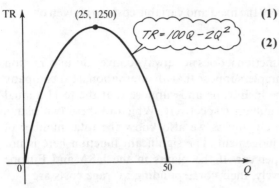

Figure 2.6

(1) From Figure 2.6 the total revenue is zero when $Q = 0$ and $Q = 50$.

(2) By symmetry, the parabola reaches its maximum halfway between 0 and 50, that is at $Q = 25$. The corresponding total revenue is given by

$$TR = 100(25) - 2(25)^2 = 1250$$

■

PROBLEM

1 Given the demand function

$$P = 1000 - Q$$

express TR as a function of Q and hence sketch a graph of TR against Q. What value of Q maximizes total revenue and what is the corresponding price?

In general, given the linear demand function

$$P = aQ + b \qquad (a < 0, \, b > 0)$$

the total revenue function is

$$TR = PQ$$
$$= (aQ + b)Q$$
$$= aQ^2 + bQ$$

This function is quadratic in Q and, since $a < 0$, the TR curve has an inverted U-shape. Moreover, since the constant term is zero, the curve always intersects the vertical axis at the origin. This fact should come as no surprise to you; if no goods are sold the revenue must be zero.

We now turn our attention to the **total cost** function, TC, which relates the production costs to the level of output, Q. As the quantity produced rises, the corresponding cost also rises, so the TC function is increasing. However, in the short run, some of these costs are fixed. **Fixed costs**, FC, include the cost of land, equipment, rent and possibly skilled labour. Obviously, in the long run all costs are variable, but these particular costs take time to vary, so can be thought of as fixed in the short run. **Variable costs**, on the other hand, vary with output and include the cost of raw materials, components, energy and unskilled labour. If VC denotes the variable cost per unit of output then the total variable cost, TVC, in producing Q goods is given by

$$TVC = (VC)Q$$

The total cost is the sum of the contributions from the fixed and variable costs so is given by

$$\text{TC} = \text{FC} + (\text{VC})Q$$

Now although this is an important economic function it does not always convey the information necessary to compare individual firms. For example, suppose that an international car company operates two plants, one in the USA and one in Europe and suppose that the total annual costs are known to be \$200 million and \$45 million respectively. Which of these two plants is regarded as the most efficient? Unfortunately, unless we also know the total number of cars produced it is impossible to make any judgement. The significant function here is not the total cost, but rather the average cost per car. If the plants in the USA and Europe manufacture 80 000 and 15 000 cars, respectively, their corresponding average costs are

$$\frac{200\,000\,000}{80\,000} = 2500$$

and

$$\frac{45\,000\,000}{15\,000} = 3000$$

On the basis of these figures the plant in the USA appears to be the more efficient. In practice, other factors would need to be taken into account before deciding to increase or decrease the scale of operations in either country.

In general, the **average cost** function, AC, is obtained by dividing the total cost by output so that

$$\text{AC} = \frac{\text{TC}}{Q}$$

$$= \frac{\text{FC} + (\text{VC})Q}{Q}$$

$$= \frac{\text{FC}}{Q} + \frac{(\text{VC})\cancel{Q}}{\cancel{Q}}$$

$$= \frac{\text{FC}}{Q} + \text{VC}$$

EXAMPLE

Given that fixed costs are 1000 and that variable costs are 4 per unit, express TC and AC as functions of Q. Hence sketch their graphs.

Solution

We are given that FC = 1000 and VC = 4 so

$$\text{TC} = 1000 + 4Q$$

and

$$AC = \frac{TC}{Q}$$

$$= \frac{1000 + 4Q}{Q}$$

$$= \frac{1000}{Q} + 4$$

The graph of the total cost function is easily sketched. It is a straight line with intercept 1000 and slope 4. It is sketched in Figure 2.7. The average cost function is of a form that we have not met before so we have no prior knowledge about its basic shape. Under these circumstances it is useful to tabulate the function. The tabulated values are then plotted on graph paper and a smooth curve obtained by joining the points together. One particular table of function values is

Q	100	250	500	1000	2000
AC	14	8	6	5	4.5

These values are readily checked. For instance, when $Q = 100$

$$AC = \frac{1000}{100} + 4 = 10 + 4 = 14$$

A graph of the average cost function, based on this table, is sketched in Figure 2.8. This curve is known as a **rectangular hyperbola** and is sometimes referred to by economists as being **L shaped**.

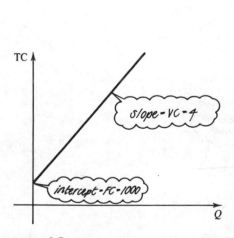

Figure 2.7

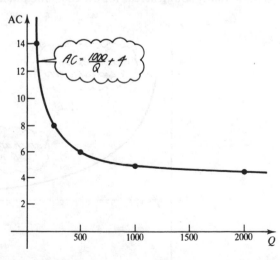

Figure 2.8

PROBLEM

2 Given that fixed costs are 100 and that variable costs are 2 per unit, express TC and AC as functions of Q. Hence sketch their graphs.

In general, whenever the variable cost, VC, is a constant the total cost function,

$$TC = FC + (VC)Q$$

is linear. The intercept is FC and the slope is VC. For the average cost function

$$AC = \frac{FC}{Q} + VC$$

Note that if Q is small, then FC/Q is large so the graph bends sharply upwards as Q approaches zero. As Q increases, FC/Q decreases and eventually tails off to zero for large values of Q. The AC curve therefore flattens off and approaches VC as Q gets larger and larger. This phenomenon is hardly surprising since the fixed costs are shared between more and more goods so have little effect on AC for large Q. The graph of AC therefore has the basic L-shape shown in Figure 2.9. This discussion assumes that VC is a constant. In practice, this may not be the case and VC might depend on Q. The TC graph is then no longer linear and the AC graph becomes U shaped rather than L shaped. An example of this can be found in Problem 6 at the end of this section.

Figure 2.10 shows typical TR and TC graphs sketched on the same diagram. These are drawn on the assumption that the demand function is linear (which leads to a quadratic total revenue function) and that the variable costs are constant (which leads to a linear total cost function). The horizontal axis represents quantity, Q. Strictly speaking the label Q means different things for the two functions. For the revenue function, Q denotes the quantity of goods actually sold whereas for the cost function it denotes the quantity produced. In sketching

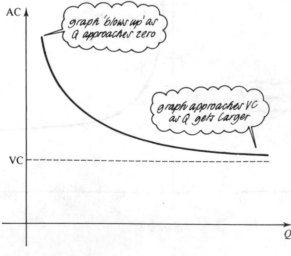

Figure 2.9

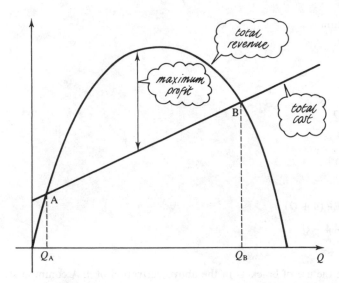

Figure 2.10

both graphs on the same diagram we are implicitly assuming that these two values are the same and that the firm sells all of the goods that it produces.

The two curves intersect at precisely two points, A and B, corresponding to output levels Q_A and Q_B. At these points the cost and revenue are equal and the firm breaks even. If $Q < Q_A$ or $Q > Q_B$ then the TC curve lies above that of TR so cost exceeds revenue. For these levels of output the firm makes a loss. If $Q_A < Q < Q_B$ then revenue exceeds cost and the firm makes a profit which is equal to the vertical distance between the revenue and cost curves. The maximum profit occurs where the gap between them is largest. The easiest way of calculating maximum profit is to obtain a formula for profit directly in terms of Q using the defining equation,

$$\pi = TR - TC$$

EXAMPLE

If fixed costs are 4, variable costs per unit are 1 and the demand function is

$$P = 10 - 2Q$$

obtain an expression for π in terms of Q and hence sketch a graph of π against Q.

(1)   For what values of Q does the firm break even?
(2)   What is the maximum profit?

Solution

We begin by obtaining expressions for the total cost and total revenue. For this problem, FC = 4 and VC = 1 so

$$TC = FC + (VC)Q$$

$$= 4 + Q$$

The given demand function is

$$P = 10 - 2Q$$

so

$$TR = PQ$$
$$= (10 - 2Q)Q$$
$$= 10Q - 2Q^2$$

Hence the profit is given by

$$\pi = TR - TC$$
$$= (10Q - 2Q^2) - (4 + Q)$$
$$= 10Q - 2Q^2 - 4 - Q$$
$$= -2Q^2 + 9Q - 4$$

It is important to notice the use of brackets in the above derivation of π. A common student mistake is to forget to include the brackets and just to write down

$$\pi = TR - TC$$
$$= 10Q - 2Q^2 - 4 + Q$$
$$= -2Q^2 + 11Q - 4$$

This cannot be right since the whole of the total cost needs to be subtracted from the total revenue, not just the fixed costs. You might be surprised to learn that many economics students make this sort of blunder particularly under examination conditions. I hope that if you have carefully worked through Section 1.4 on algebraic manipulation then you will not fall into this category!

To sketch a graph of the profit function we follow the strategy described in Section 2.1.

Step 1 The coefficient of Q^2 is negative so the graph has an inverted U-shape.

Step 2 The constant term is -4 so the graph crosses the vertical axis when $\pi = -4$.

Step 3 The graph crosses the horizontal axis when $\pi = 0$ so we need to solve the quadratic equation

$$-2Q^2 + 9Q - 4 = 0$$

This can be done using 'the formula' to get

$$Q = \frac{-9 \pm \sqrt{(81 - 32)}}{2(-2)}$$
$$= \frac{-9 \pm 7}{-4}$$

so $Q = 0.5$ and $Q = 4$.

The profit curve is sketched in Figure 2.11.

(1) From Figure 2.11 we see that profit is zero when $Q = 0.5$ and $Q = 4$.
(2) By symmetry, the parabola reaches its maximum halfway between 0.5 and 4, that is at

$$Q = \tfrac{1}{2}(0.5 + 4) = 2.25$$

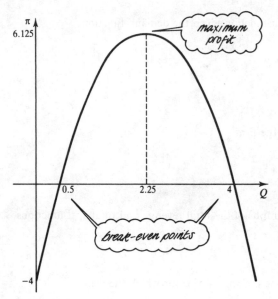

Figure 2.11

The corresponding profit is given by

$$\pi = -2(2.25)^2 + 9(2.25) - 4 = 6.125$$

∎

PROBLEM

3 If fixed costs are 25, variable costs per unit are 2 and the demand function is

$$P = 20 - Q$$

obtain an expression for π in terms of Q and hence sketch its graph.

(1) Find the levels of output which give a profit of 31.

(2) Find the maximum profit and the value of Q at which it is achieved.

PRACTICE PROBLEMS

4 Given the following demand functions, express TR as a function of Q and hence sketch the graphs of TR against Q.

(a) $P = 4$ **(b)** $P = 7/Q$ **(c)** $P = 10 - 4Q$

5 Given that fixed costs are 500 and that variable costs are 10 per unit, express TC and AC as functions of Q. Hence sketch their graphs.

6 Given that fixed costs are 1 and that variable costs are $Q + 1$ per unit, express TC and AC as functions of Q. Hence sketch their graphs.

7 Find an expression for the profit function given the demand function

$$2Q + P = 25$$

and the average cost function

$$\text{AC} = \frac{32}{Q} + 5$$

Find the values of Q for which the firm

(a) breaks even
(b) makes a loss of 432 units
(c) maximizes profit

8 Sketch, on the same diagram, graphs of the total revenue and total cost functions,

$$\text{TR} = -2Q^2 + 14Q$$

$$\text{TC} = 2Q + 10$$

(1) Use your graphs to estimate the values of Q for which the firm

    (a) breaks even   (b) maximizes profit

(2) Confirm your answer to part (1) using algebra.

2.3   Indices and logarithms

Objectives   At the end of this section you should be able to:

- evaluate b^n in the case when n is positive, negative, whole number or fraction,

- simplify algebraic expressions using the rules of indices,

- investigate the returns to scale of a production function,

- evaluate logarithms in simple cases,

- use the rules of logarithms to solve equations in which the unknown occurs as a power.

We have already used b^2 as an abbreviation for $b \times b$. In this section we extend the notation to b^n for any value of n, positive, negative, whole number or fraction. We also describe how this notation is used in one particular application. In general, if

$$M = b^n$$

we say that b^n is the **exponential form of M to base b**. The number n is then referred to as the **index**, **power** or **exponent**. An obvious way of extending

$$b^2 = b \times b$$

to other positive whole number powers, n, is to define

$$b^3 = b \times b \times b$$

$$b^4 = b \times b \times b \times b$$

and, in general,

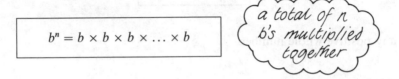

$$b^n = b \times b \times b \times \ldots \times b$$

a total of n b's multiplied together

To include the case of negative powers, consider the following table of values of 2^n.

2^{-3}	2^{-2}	2^{-1}	2^0	2^1	2^2	2^3	2^4
?	?	?	?	2	4	8	16

To work from left to right along the completed part of the table all you have to do is to multiply each number by 2. Equivalently, if you work from right to left you simply divide by 2. It makes sense to continue this pattern beyond $2^1 = 2$. Dividing this by 2 gives

$$2^0 = 2 \div 2 = 1$$

and dividing again by 2 gives

$$2^{-1} = 1 \div 2 = \tfrac{1}{2}$$

and so on. The completed table is then

2^{-3}	2^{-2}	2^{-1}	2^0	2^1	2^2	2^3	2^4
$\tfrac{1}{8}$	$\tfrac{1}{4}$	$\tfrac{1}{2}$	1	2	4	8	16

Notice that

$$2^{-1} = \frac{1}{2} = \frac{1}{2^1}$$

$$2^{-2} = \frac{1}{4} = \frac{1}{2^2}$$

$$2^{-3} = \frac{1}{8} = \frac{1}{2^3}$$

In other words, negative powers are evaluated by taking the reciprocal of the corresponding positive power. Motivated by this particular example we define

$$b^0 = 1$$

and

$$b^{-n} = \frac{1}{b^n}$$

where n is any positive whole number.

EXAMPLE _____

Evaluate

(a) 3^2
(b) 4^3
(c) 7^0
(d) 5^1
(e) 5^{-1}
(f) $(-2)^6$
(g) 3^{-4}
(h) $(-2)^{-3}$
(i) $(1.723)^0$

Solution

Using the definitions

$$b^n = b \times b \times b \times \ldots \times b$$

$$b^0 = 1$$

$$b^{-n} = \frac{1}{b^n}$$

we obtain

(a) $3^2 = 3 \times 3 = 9$
(b) $4^3 = 4 \times 4 \times 4 = 64$
(c) $7^0 = 1$
(d) $5^1 = 5$
(e) $5^{-1} = \dfrac{1}{5^1} = \dfrac{1}{5}$
(f) $(-2)^6 = (-2) \times (-2) \times (-2) \times (-2) \times (-2) \times (-2)$
$$= 64$$
where the answer is positive because there are an even number of minus signs.

(g) $3^{-4} = \dfrac{1}{3^4} = \dfrac{1}{3 \times 3 \times 3 \times 3} = \dfrac{1}{81}$

(h) $(-2)^{-3} = \dfrac{1}{(-2)^3} = \dfrac{1}{(-2) \times (-2) \times (-2)} = -\dfrac{1}{8}$

where the answer is negative because there are an odd number of minus signs.

(i) $(1.723)^0 = 1$

because any number raised to the power of zero equals 1.

∎

PROBLEM

1 **(1)** Without using a calculator evaluate

    (a) 10^2 **(b)** 10^1 **(c)** 10^0 **(d)** 10^{-1} **(e)** 10^{-2} **(f)** $(-1)^{100}$

    (g) $(-1)^{99}$ **(h)** 7^{-3} **(i)** $(-9)^2$ **(j)** $(72\,101)^1$ **(k)** $(2.718)^0$

(2) Confirm your answer to part (1) using a calculator.

We handle fractional powers in two stages. We begin by defining b^m where m is a reciprocal such as $\frac{1}{2}$ or $\frac{1}{8}$ and then consider more general fractions such as $\frac{3}{4}$ or $\frac{3}{8}$ later. Assuming that n is a positive whole number, we define

$$\boxed{b^{1/n} = n\text{th root of } b}$$

By this we mean that $b^{1/n}$ is a number which, when raised to the power n, produces b. In symbols, if $c = b^{1/n}$ then $c^n = b$. Using this definition,

$$9^{1/2} = \text{square root of } 9 \ = 3 \quad (\text{because } 3^2 = 9)$$

$$8^{1/3} = \text{cube root of } 8 \ \ = 2 \quad (\text{because } 2^3 = 8)$$

$$625^{1/4} = \text{fourth root of } 625 = 5 \quad (\text{because } 5^4 = 625)$$

Of course, the nth root of a number may not exist. There is no number c satisfying $c^2 = -4$, for example, and so $(-4)^{1/2}$ is not defined. It is also possible for some numbers to have more than one nth root. For example, there are two values of c which satisfy $c^4 = 16$, namely $c = 2$ and $c = -2$. In these circumstances it is standard practice to take the positive root, so $16^{1/4} = 2$.

We now turn our attention to the case of b^m where m is a general fraction of the form p/q for some whole numbers p and q. What interpretation are we going to put on a number such as $16^{3/4}$? To be consistent with our previous definitions, the numerator, 3, can be thought of as an instruction for us to raise 16 to the power of 3, and the denominator tells us to take the fourth root. In fact, it is immaterial in which order these two operations are carried out.

If we begin by cubing 16 we get

$$16^3 = 16 \times 16 \times 16 = 4096$$

and taking the fourth root of this gives

$$16^{3/4} = (4096)^{1/4} = 8 \qquad (\text{because } 8^4 = 4096)$$

On the other hand, taking the fourth root first gives

$$16^{1/4} = 2 \qquad (\text{because } 2^4 = 16)$$

and cubing this gives

$$16^{3/4} = 2^3 = 8$$

which is the same answer as before. We therefore see that

$$(16^3)^{1/4} = (16^{1/4})^3$$

This result holds for any base b and fraction p/q (provided that q is positive), so we define

$$b^{p/q} = (b^p)^{1/q} = (b^{1/q})^p$$

EXAMPLE

Evaluate

(a) $8^{4/3}$
(b) $25^{-3/2}$

Solution

(a) The number $8^{4/3}$ can be evaluated by raising 8 to the power 4 and taking the cube root. Given that we are allowed to perform these operations in any order, it is perhaps easier to do the cube root first to avoid large numbers so

$$8^{4/3} = (8^{1/3})^4 = 2^4 = 16$$

(b) The number $25^{-3/2}$ can be evaluated by raising 25 to the power -3 and taking the square root. Again it is easier to do the square root first so

$$25^{-3/2} = (25^{1/2})^{-3} = 5^{-3} = \frac{1}{5^3} = \frac{1}{125}$$

For this particular exponential form we have actually carried out three distinct operations. The minus sign tells us to reciprocate, the fraction $\frac{1}{2}$ tells us to take the square root and the 3 tells us to cube. You might like to check for yourself that you get the same answer irrespective of the order in which these three operations are performed.

■

PROBLEM

2 (1) Without using your calculator evaluate

   (a) $16^{1/2}$ **(b)** $27^{1/3}$ **(c)** $4^{5/2}$ **(d)** $8^{-2/3}$ **(e)** $1^{-17/25}$

   (2) Confirm your answer to part (1) using a calculator.

There are two reasons why the exponential form is useful. Firstly, it is a convenient shorthand for what otherwise might be a very lengthy number. The exponential form

$$9^8$$

is much easier to write down than either of the equivalent forms

$$9 \times 9 \times 9 \times 9 \times 9 \times 9 \times 9 \times 9$$

or

43 046 721

Secondly, there are four basic rules of indices which facilitate the manipulation of such numbers. The four rules may be stated as follows:

$$\boxed{\textit{Rule 1} \quad b^m \times b^n = b^{m+n}}$$

$$\boxed{\textit{Rule 2} \quad b^m \div b^n = b^{m-n}}$$

$$\boxed{\textit{Rule 3} \quad (b^m)^n = b^{mn}}$$

$$\boxed{\textit{Rule 4} \quad (ab)^n = a^n b^n}$$

It is certainly not our intention to provide mathematical proofs in this book. However, it might help you to remember these rules if we give you a justification based on some simple examples. We consider each rule in turn.

Rule 1 Suppose we want to multiply together 2^2 and 2^5. Now $2^2 = 2 \times 2$ and $2^5 = 2 \times 2 \times 2 \times 2 \times 2$ so

$$2^2 \times 2^5 = (2 \times 2) \times (2 \times 2 \times 2 \times 2 \times 2)$$

Notice that we are multiplying together a total of seven 2's and so by definition this is just 2^7, that is

$$2^2 \times 2^5 = 2^7 = 2^{2+5}$$

This confirms rule 1 which tells you that if you multiply two numbers all you have to do is to add the indices.

Rule 2   Suppose we want to divide 2^2 by 2^5. This gives

$$\frac{\cancel{2} \times \cancel{2}}{2 \times 2 \times 2 \times \cancel{2} \times \cancel{2}} = \frac{1}{2 \times 2 \times 2} = \frac{1}{2^3}$$

Now, by definition, reciprocals are denoted by negative indices so this is just 2^{-3}, that is

$$2^2 \div 2^5 = 2^{-3} = 2^{2-5}$$

This confirms rule 2 which tells you that if you divide two numbers all you have to do is to subtract the indices.

Rule 3   Suppose we want to raise 10^2 to the power 3. By definition, for any number b,

$$b^3 = b \times b \times b$$

so replacing b by 10^2 we have

$$(10^2)^3 = 10^2 \times 10^2 \times 10^2$$
$$= (10 \times 10) \times (10 \times 10) \times (10 \times 10)$$
$$= 10^6$$

because there are six 10's multiplied together, that is

$$(10^2)^3 = 10^6 = 10^{2 \times 3}$$

This confirms rule 3 which tells you that if you take a 'power of a power' all you have to do is to multiply the indices.

Rule 4   Suppose we want to raise 2×3 to the power 4. By definition,

$$b^4 = b \times b \times b \times b$$

so replacing b by 2×3 gives

$$(2 \times 3)^4 = (2 \times 3) \times (2 \times 3) \times (2 \times 3) \times (2 \times 3)$$

and, because it does not matter in which order numbers are multiplied, this can be written as

$$(2 \times 2 \times 2 \times 2) \times (3 \times 3 \times 3 \times 3)$$

that is

$$(2 \times 3)^4 = 2^4 \times 3^4$$

This confirms rule 4 which tells you that if you take the power of a product of two numbers all you have to do is to take the power of each number separately and multiply.

A word of warning is in order regarding these laws. Notice that in rules 1 and 2 the bases of the numbers involved are the same. These rules do not apply if the bases are different. For example, rule 1 gives no information about

$$2^4 \times 3^5$$

Similarly, please notice that in rule 4 the numbers a and b are multiplied together. For some strange reason some business and economics students seem to think that rule 4 also applies to addition so that

$$(a + b)^n = a^n + b^n$$

This statement is **NOT TRUE**. It would make algebraic manipulation a whole lot easier if it were true but I am afraid to say that it is definitely false! If you need convincing of this, note, for example, that

$$(1 + 2)^3 = 3^3 = 27$$

which is not the same as

$$1^3 + 2^3 = 1 + 8 = 9$$

One variation of rule 4 which is true is the following:

$$\left(\frac{a}{b}\right)^n = \frac{a^n}{b^n} \quad (b \neq 0)$$

This is all right because division (unlike addition or subtraction) is the same sort of operation as multiplication. In fact,

$$\left(\frac{a}{b}\right)^n$$

can be thought of as

$$\left(a \times \frac{1}{b}\right)^n$$

so applying rule 4 to this product gives

$$a^n \times \left(\frac{1}{b}\right)^n = \frac{a^n}{b^n}$$

as required.

Incidentally, there might be occasions (such as in examinations!) when you only half remember a rule or perhaps think that you have discovered a brand new rule for yourself. If you are ever worried about whether some rule is legal or not you should always check it out by trying numbers, just as we did for $(a + b)^n$. Obviously, one numerical example which actually works does not prove that the rule will always work. However, one example which fails is good enough to tell you that your supposed rule is rubbish.

The following example demonstrates how rules 1–4 are used to simplify algebraic expressions.

EXAMPLE

Simplify

(a) $x^{1/4} \times x^{3/4}$

(b) $\dfrac{x^2 y^3}{x^4 y}$

(c) $(x^2 y^{-1/3})^3$

Solution

(a) The expression

$$x^{1/4} \times x^{3/4}$$

represents the product of two numbers in exponential form with the same base. From rule 1 we may add the indices to get

$$x^{1/4} \times x^{3/4} = x^{1/4 + 3/4} = x^1$$

which is just x.

(b) The expression

$$\frac{x^2 y^3}{x^4 y}$$

is more complicated than that in part (a) since it involves numbers in exponential form with two different bases, x and y. From rule 2,

$$\frac{x^2}{x^4}$$

may be simplified by subtracting indices to get

$$x^2 \div x^4 = x^{2-4} = x^{-2}$$

Similarly,

$$\frac{y^3}{y} = y^3 \div y^1 = y^{3-1} = y^2$$

Hence

$$\frac{x^2 y^3}{x^4 y} = x^{-2} y^2$$

It is not possible to simplify this any further because x^{-2} and y^2 have different bases. However, if you prefer, this can be written as

$$\frac{y^2}{x^2}$$

because negative powers denote reciprocals.

(c) An obvious first step in the simplification of

$$(x^2 y^{-1/3})^3$$

is to apply rule 4, treating x^2 as the value of a and $y^{-1/3}$ as b to get

$$(x^2y^{-1/3})^3 = (x^2)^3(y^{-1/3})^3$$

Rule 3 then allows us to write

$$(x^2)^3 = x^{2 \times 3} = x^6$$

$$(y^{-1/3})^3 = y^{(-1/3) \times 3} = y^{-1}$$

Hence

$$(x^2y^{-1/3})^3 = x^6y^{-1}$$

As in part (b), if you think it looks neater, you can write this as

$$\frac{x^6}{y}$$

because negative powers denote reciprocals.

■

PROBLEM

3 Simplify

(a) $(x^{3/4})^8$ (b) $\dfrac{x^2}{x^{3/2}}$ (c) $(x^2y^4)^3$ (d) $\sqrt{x}(x^{5/2} + y^3)$

[Hint: in part (d) note that $\sqrt{x} = x^{1/2}$ and multiply out the brackets.]

There are occasions throughout this book when we use the rules of indices and definitions of b^n. For the moment, we concentrate on one specific application where we see these ideas in action. The output, Q, of any production process depends on a variety of inputs, known as **factors of production**. These include land, capital, labour and enterprise. For simplicity we restrict our attention to capital and labour. **Capital**, K, denotes all man-made aids to production such as buildings, tools and plant machinery. **Labour**, L, denotes all paid work in the production process. The dependence of Q on K and L may be written

$$Q = f(K, L)$$

which is called a **production function**. Once this relationship is made explicit, in the form of a formula, it is straightforward to calculate the level of production from any given combination of inputs. For example, if

$$Q = 100K^{1/3}L^{1/2}$$

then the inputs $K = 27$ and $L = 100$ lead to an output

$$Q = 100(27)^{1/3}(100)^{1/2}$$

$$= 100(3)(10)$$

$$= 3000$$

Of particular interest is the effect on output when inputs are scaled in some way. If capital and labour both double, does the production level also double, does it go up by more than double or does it go up by less than double? For the particular production function,

$$Q = 100K^{1/3}L^{1/2}$$

we see that, when K and L are replaced by $2K$ and $2L$, respectively,

$$Q = 100(2K)^{1/3}(2L)^{1/2}$$

Now, by rule 4,

$$(2K)^{1/3} = 2^{1/3}K^{1/3} \qquad \text{and} \qquad (2L)^{1/2} = 2^{1/2}L^{1/2}$$

so

$$Q = 100(2^{1/3}K^{1/3})(2^{1/2}L^{1/2})$$
$$= (2^{1/3}2^{1/2})(100K^{1/3}L^{1/2})$$

The second term, $100K^{1/3}L^{1/2}$, is just the original value of Q, so we see that the output is multiplied by

$$2^{1/3}2^{1/2}$$

Using rule 1, this number may be simplified by adding the indices to get

$$2^{1/3}2^{1/2} = 2^{5/6}$$

Moreover, because $5/6$ is less than 1, the scale factor is smaller than 2. In fact, my calculator gives

$$2^{5/6} = 1.78 \qquad \text{(to 2 decimal places)}$$

so output goes up by just less than double.

It is important to notice that the above argument does not depend on the particular value, 2, that is taken as the scale factor. Exactly the same procedure can be applied if the inputs, K and L, are scaled by a general number λ (where λ is a Greek letter, pronounced 'lambda'). Replacing K and L by λK and λL respectively in the formula

$$Q = 100K^{1/3}L^{1/2}$$

gives

$$Q = 100(\lambda K)^{1/3}(\lambda L)^{1/2}$$
$$= 100\lambda^{1/3}K^{1/3}\lambda^{1/2}L^{1/2} \qquad \text{(rule 4)}$$
$$= (\lambda^{1/3}\lambda^{1/2})(100K^{1/3}L^{1/2})$$
$$= \lambda^{5/6}(100K^{1/3}L^{1/2}) \qquad \text{(rule 1)}$$

We see that the output gets scaled by $\lambda^{5/6}$ which is smaller than λ since the power, $5/6$, is less than 1. We describe this by saying that the production function exhibits decreasing returns to scale.

In general, a function

$$Q = f(K, L)$$

is said to be **homogeneous** if

$$f(\lambda K, \lambda L) = \lambda^n f(K, L)$$

for some number, n. This means that when both variables K and L are multiplied by λ we can pull out all of the λ's as a common factor, λ^n. The power, n, is called the **degree of homogeneity**. In the previous example we showed that

$$f(\lambda K, \lambda L) = \lambda^{5/6} f(K, L)$$

and so it is homogeneous of degree $5/6$. In general, if the degree of homogeneity, n, satisfies:

- $n < 1$ the function is said to display **decreasing returns to scale**.
- $n = 1$ the function is said to display **constant returns to scale**.
- $n > 1$ the function is said to display **increasing returns to scale**.

EXAMPLE

Show that the following production function is homogeneous and find its degree of homogeneity

$$Q = 2K^{1/2}L^{3/2}$$

Does this function exhibit decreasing returns to scale, constant returns to scale or increasing returns to scale?

Solution

We are given that

$$f(K, L) = 2K^{1/2}L^{3/2}$$

so replacing K by λK and L by λL gives

$$f(\lambda K, \lambda L) = 2(\lambda K)^{1/2}(\lambda L)^{3/2}$$

We can pull out all of the λ's by using rule 4 to get

$$2\lambda^{1/2}K^{1/2}\lambda^{3/2}L^{3/2}$$

and then using rule 1 to get

$$\lambda^2(2K^{1/2}L^{3/2})$$

$$\lambda^{1/2}\,\lambda^{3/2} = \lambda^{1/2 + 3/2} = \lambda^2$$

We have therefore shown that

$$f(\lambda K, \lambda L) = \lambda^2 f(K, L)$$

and so the function is homogeneous of degree 2. Moreover, since $2 > 1$ we deduce that it has increasing returns to scale.

PROBLEM

4 Show that the following production functions are homogeneous and comment on their returns to scale:

(a) $Q = 7KL^2$ (b) $Q = 50K^{1/4}L^{3/4}$

You may well have noticed that all of the production functions considered so far are of the form

$$Q = AK^\alpha L^\beta$$

for some positive constants, A, α and β. (The Greek letters α and β are pronounced 'alpha' and 'beta' respectively.) Such functions are called **Cobb–Douglas** production functions. It is easy to see that they are homogeneous of degree $\alpha + \beta$ because if

$$f(K, L) = AK^\alpha L^\beta$$

then

$$f(\lambda K, \lambda L) = A(\lambda K)^\alpha (\lambda L)^\beta$$
$$= A\lambda^\alpha K^\alpha \lambda^\beta L^\beta \qquad \text{(rule 4)}$$
$$= \lambda^{\alpha+\beta}(AK^\alpha L^\beta) \qquad \text{(rule 1)}$$
$$= \lambda^{\alpha+\beta} f(K, L)$$

Consequently, Cobb–Douglas production functions exhibit

- decreasing returns to scale, if $\alpha + \beta < 1$.
- constant returns to scale, if $\alpha + \beta = 1$.
- increasing returns to scale, if $\alpha + \beta > 1$.

By the way, not all production functions are of this type. Indeed, it is not even necessary for a production function to be homogeneous. Some examples illustrating these cases are given in Problems 9 and 10 at the end of this section. We shall return to the topic of production functions in Chapter 5.

At the beginning of this section we stated that if a number, M, is expressed as

$$M = b^n$$

then b^n is called the exponential form of M to base b. The approach taken so far has simply been to evaluate M from any given values of b and n. In practice, it may be necessary to reverse this process and to find n from known values of M and b. To solve the equation

$$32 = 2^n$$

we need to express 32 as a power of 2. In this case it is easy to work out n by inspection. Simple trial and error easily gives $n = 5$ because

$$2^5 = 32$$

We describe this expression by saying that the logarithm of 32 to base 2 is 5. In symbols we write

$$\log_2 32 = 5$$

Quite generally,

$$\text{if } M = b^n \text{ then } \log_b M = n$$

where n is called the **logarithm of M to base b**.

Students have been known to regard logarithms as something rather abstract and difficult to understand. There is, however, no need to worry about logarithms since they simply provide an alternative way of thinking about numbers such as b^n. Read through the following example and try Problem 5 for yourself. You might discover that they are easier than you expect!

EXAMPLE

Evaluate

(a) $\log_3 9$
(b) $\log_4 2$
(c) $\log_7 \frac{1}{7}$

Solution

(a)   To find the value of $\log_3 9$ we convert the problem into one involving powers. From the definition of a logarithm to base 3 we see that the statement

$$\log_3 9 = n$$

is equivalent to

$$9 = 3^n$$

The problem of finding the logarithm of 9 to base 3 is exactly the same as that of writing 9 as a power of 3. The solution of this equation is clearly $n = 2$ since

$$9 = 3^2$$

Hence $\log_3 9 = 2$.

(b)   Again to evaluate $\log_4 2$ we merely rewrite

$$\log_4 2 = n$$

in exponential form as

$$2 = 4^n$$

The problem of finding the logarithm of 2 to base 4 is exactly the same as that of writing 2 as a power of 4. The value of 2 is obtained from 4 by taking the square root which involves raising 4 to the power of $\frac{1}{2}$, so

$$2 = 4^{1/2}$$

Hence $\log_2 4 = \frac{1}{2}$.

(c) If

$$\log_7 \tfrac{1}{7} = n$$

then

$$\tfrac{1}{7} = 7^n$$

The value of $\tfrac{1}{7}$ is found by taking the reciprocal of 7 which involves raising 7 to the power of -1, that is

$$\tfrac{1}{7} = 7^{-1}$$

Hence $\log_7 \tfrac{1}{7} = -1$. ∎

PROBLEM

5 (1) Write down the values of n which satisfy

    (a) $1000 = 10^n$ **(b)** $100 = 10^n$ **(c)** $10 = 10^n$

    (d) $1 = 10^n$ **(e)** $\dfrac{1}{10} = 10^n$ **(f)** $\dfrac{1}{100} = 10^n$

(2) Use your answer to part (1) to write down the values of

    (a) $\log_{10} 1000$ **(b)** $\log_{10} 100$ **(c)** $\log_{10} 10$

    (d) $\log_{10} 1$ **(e)** $\log_{10} \tfrac{1}{10}$ **(f)** $\log_{10} \tfrac{1}{100}$

(3) Confirm your answer to part (2) using a calculator.

Given the intimate relationship between exponentials and logarithms you should not be too surprised to learn that logarithms satisfy three rules which are comparable with those for indices. The rules of logarithms are as follows.

$$\boxed{\text{Rule 1} \quad \log_b(x \times y) = \log_b x + \log_b y}$$

$$\boxed{\text{Rule 2} \quad \log_b(x \div y) = \log_b x - \log_b y}$$

$$\boxed{\text{Rule 3} \quad \log_b x^m = m \log_b x}$$

A long time ago, before the pocket calculator was invented, people used tables of logarithms to perform complicated arithmetic calculations. It was generally assumed that everyone could add or subtract numbers using pen and paper but that people found it hard to multiply and divide. The first two rules gave a means of converting calculations involving multiplication and division into easier calculations involving addition and subtraction. For example, to work out

$$1.765\,12 \times 25.329\,71$$

we would first look up the logarithms of 1.765 12 and 25.329 71 using tables and then add these logarithms together on paper. According to rule 1 the value obtained is just the logarithm of the answer. Finally, using tables of antilogarithms (which effectively raised the base to an appropriate power), the result of the calculation was obtained. Fortunately for us this is all history and we can now perform arithmetic calculations in a fraction of the time it took our predecessors to multiply or divide two numbers. This might suggest that logarithms are redundant. However, the idea of a logarithm remains an important one. The logarithm function itself, that is

$$f(x) = \log_b(x)$$

is of value and we shall investigate its properties later in the book. For the time being we demonstrate how logarithms can be used to solve algebraic equations in which the unknown appears as a power. This technique will be of particular use in the next chapter when we solve compound interest problems.

EXAMPLE

Find the value of x which satisfies

(a) $200(1.1)^x = 20\,000$
(b) $5^x = 2(3)^x$

Solution

(a)   An obvious first step in the solution of

$$200(1.1)^x = 20\,000$$

is to divide both sides by 200 to get

$$(1.1)^x = 100$$

In Chapter 1 it was pointed out that we can do whatever we like to an equation, provided that we do the same thing to both sides. In particular, we may take logarithms of both sides to get

$$\log(1.1)^x = \log(100)$$

Now by rule 3 we have

$$\log(1.1)^x = x \log(1.1)$$

so the equation becomes

$$x \log(1.1) = \log(100)$$

Notice the effect that rule 3 has on the equation. It brings the unknown down to the same level as the rest of the expression. This is the whole point of taking logarithms since it converts an equation in which the unknown appears as a power into one which can be solved using familiar algebraic methods. Dividing both sides of the equation

$$x \log(1.1) = \log(100)$$

by $\log(1.1)$ gives

$$x = \frac{\log(100)}{\log(1.1)}$$

So far no mention has been made of the base of the logarithm. The above equation for x is true no matter what base is used. It makes sense to use logarithms to base 10 because all scientific calculators have this facility as one of their function keys. In fact most calculators have two different logarithm functions; logarithms to base 10 (possibly indicated by log or $\log_{10}$) and logarithms to base e (possibly indicated by ln or $\log_e$). The letter e actually stands for the number 2.718 281... and logarithms to base e are called **natural logarithms**, which accounts for the abbreviation 'ln'. If you want you can use the ln function instead of the log function on your calculator to find the value of x. It does not matter which base you use provided you are consistent and use the same one to evaluate the top and bottom of the fraction

$$\frac{\log(100)}{\log(1.1)}$$

Using base 10, my calculator gives

$$x = \frac{\log(100)}{\log(1.1)} = \frac{2}{0.041\,392\,685} = 48.32$$

to 2 decimal places.

As a check, if this number is substituted back into the original equation, then

$$200(1.1)^x = 200(1.1)^{48.32} = 20\,004 \qquad \checkmark$$

We cannot expect to obtain the exact answer because we only rounded x to 2 decimal places.

(b)   To solve

$$5^x = 2(3)^x$$

we take logarithms of both sides to get

$$\log(5^x) = \log(2 \times 3^x)$$

The right-hand side is the logarithm of a product and, according to rule 1, can be written as the sum of the logarithms so the equation becomes

$$\log(5^x) = \log(2) + \log(3^x)$$

As in part (a) the key step is to use rule 3 to 'bring down the powers'. If rule 3 is applied to both

$$\log(5^x) \qquad \text{and} \qquad \log(3^x)$$

then the equation becomes

$$x \log(5) = \log(2) + x \log(3)$$

This is now the type of equation that we know how to solve. We collect x's on the left-hand side to get

$$x \log(5) - x \log(3) = \log(2)$$

and then pull out a common factor of x to get

$$x[\log(5) - \log(3)] = \log(2)$$

Now, by rule 2, the difference of two logarithms is the same as the logarithm of their quotient so

$$\log(5) - \log(3) = \log(5 \div 3)$$

Hence the equation becomes

$$x \log\left(\frac{5}{3}\right) = \log(2)$$

so

$$x = \frac{\log(2)}{\log(5/3)}$$

Finally, taking logarithms to base 10 using a calculator gives

$$x = \frac{0.301\,029\,996}{0.221\,848\,750} = 1.36$$

to 2 decimal places.

As a check, the original equation,

$$5^x = 2(3)^x$$

becomes

$$5^{1.36} = 2(3)^{1.36}$$

that is

$$8.92 = 8.91 \qquad \checkmark$$

Again the slight discrepancy is due to rounding errors in the value of x.

∎

PROBLEM

6   Solve the following equations for x:

(a) $3^x = 7$ (b) $5(2)^x = 10^x$

In this section we have met a large number of definitions and rules concerning indices and logarithms. For convenience, we collect these together in the form of a summary. The facts relating to indices are particularly important and you should make every effort to memorize these before proceeding with the rest of this book.

Summary

If n is a positive whole number then

$$b^n = b \times b \times \ldots \times b$$

$$b^0 = 1$$

$$b^{-n} = 1/b^n$$

$$b^{1/n} = n\text{th root of } b$$

Also, if p and q are whole numbers with $q > 0$ then

$$b^{p/q} = (b^p)^{1/q} = (b^{1/q})^p$$

The four rules of indices are

Rule 1 $b^m \times b^n = b^{m+n}$

Rule 2 $b^m \div b^n = b^{m-n}$

Rule 3 $(b^m)^n = b^{mn}$

Rule 4 $(ab)^n = a^n b^n$

Logarithms

If $M = b^n$ then $n = \log_b M$. The three rules of logarithms are

Rule 1 $\log_b(x \times y) = \log_b x + \log_b y$

Rule 2 $\log_b(x \div y) = \log_b x - \log_b y$

Rule 3 $\log_b x^m = m \log_b x$

PRACTICE PROBLEMS

7 **(1)**   Without using your calculator evaluate

    (a) 8^2 **(b)** 2^1 **(c)** 3^{-1} **(d)** 17^0 **(e)** $1^{1/5}$ **(f)** $36^{1/2}$
    (g) $8^{2/3}$ **(h)** $49^{-3/2}$

    (2)   Confirm your answer to part (1) using a calculator.

8 Use the rules of indices to simplify

    (a) $y^{3/2} \times y^{1/2}$

    (b) $\dfrac{x^2 y}{xy^{-1}}$

    (c) $(xy^{1/2})^4$

9 Which of the following production functions are homogeneous? For those functions which are homogeneous write down their degrees of homogeneity and comment on their returns to scale.

    (a) $Q = 500K^{1/3}L^{1/4}$
    (b) $Q = 3LK + L^2$
    (c) $Q = L + 5L^2K^3$

10 Show that the production function

$$Q = A[bK^{\alpha} + (1 - b)L^{\alpha}]^{1/\alpha}$$

is homogeneous and displays constant returns to scale.

11 Write down the value of

(a) $\log_b b^2$ (b) $\log_b b$ (c) $\log_b 1$ (d) $\log_b \sqrt{b}$ (e) $\log_b(1/b)$

12 Solve the following equations:

(a) $10(1.07)^x = 2000$ (b) $10^{x-1} = 3$ (c) $5^{x-2} = 5$ (d) $2(7)^{-x} = 3^x$

3 *Mathematics of Finance*

This chapter provides an understanding of the way in which financial calculations are worked out. There are three sections which should be read in the order that they appear.

Section 3.1 shows how to calculate the future value of a lump sum which is invested to earn interest. This interest can be added to the investment annually, semi-annually, quarterly or even more frequently. A rather strange number, $e = 2.718\,28\ldots$, is introduced to solve problems in which interest is compounded continuously.

A wide variety of applications are considered in Sections 3.2 and 3.3. In Section 3.2 a mathematical object known as a geometric progression is introduced which is used to calculate the future value of a savings plan and the monthly repayments of a loan. Section 3.3 describes the opposite problem of calculating the present value given a future value. The process of working backwards is called discounting. It can be used to decide how much money to invest today in order to achieve a specific target sum in a few years' time. Discounting can be used to appraise different investment projects. On the macroeconomic level, the relationship between interest rates and speculative demand for money is investigated.

The material in this chapter will be of greatest benefit to students on business studies and accountancy courses. The only ideas which are needed in later chapters are the exponential and natural logarithm functions. However, it should be possible to make sense of these functions as and when they arise, so the whole of this chapter can be omitted if desired.

3.1 Compound interest

Objectives At the end of this section you should be able to:

- use percentages in mathematical calculations,
- calculate the future value of a principal under annual compounding,
- calculate the future value of a principal under continuous compounding,
- determine the annual percentage rate of interest given a nominal rate of interest.

Today, businesses and individuals are faced with a bewildering array of loan facilities and investment opportunities. In this chapter we explain how these financial calculations are carried out to enable an informed choice to be made between the various possibilities available. We begin by considering what happens when a single lump sum is invested and show how to calculate the amount accumulated over a period of time. To do this, it is essential that you appreciate what is meant by a percentage. In general, whenever we speak of $r\%$ of something, we simply mean the fraction $(r/100)$ths of it. For example, suppose that the price of a good rises by 20% from its current value of $5,000. Expressed as a fraction, 20% is the same as

$$\frac{20}{100} = \frac{1}{5}$$

so the price rise is

$$\frac{1}{5} \times \$5,000 = \$1,000$$

The new price of the good is therefore

$$\$5,000 + \$1,000 = \$6,000$$

In fact, the new price can be obtained directly by noting that it is just

$$100\% + 20\% = 120\%$$

of $5,000 so it must be

$$\frac{120}{100} \times \$5,000 = \$6,000$$

Here are a few simple problems for you to try for yourself. They are designed to get you back into the groove with percentage calculations. As usual, the answers are provided at the end of the book and you should have a go at them now before continuing.

PROBLEMS

1   A bank is prepared to offer a 90% house loan to first-time buyers. How much will the bank lend to a couple wanting to buy a house worth $300,000?

2   The government imposes a 15% tax on the price of a good. Determine the tax imposed on a good priced by a firm at $1,000. How much does the consumer pay for the good?

3   A firm's annual sales rise from 50 000 to 55 000 goods from one year to the next. Express the rise in sales as a percentage.

Suppose that someone gives you the option of receiving $500 now or $500 in three years' time. Which of these alternatives would you accept? Most people would take the money now, partly because they may have an immediate need for it, but also because they recognize that $500 is worth more today than in three years' time. Even if we ignore the effects of inflation, it is still better to take the money now, since it can be invested and will increase in value over the three-year period. In order to work out this value we need to know the rate of interest and the basis on which it is calculated. Let us begin by assuming that the $500 is invested for three years at 10% interest compounded annually. What exactly do we mean by '10% interest compounded annually'? Well, at the end of each year, the interest is calculated and is added on to the amount currently invested. If the original amount is $500 then after one year the interest is 10% of $500 which is

$$\frac{10}{100} \times \$500 = \frac{1}{10} \times \$500 = \$50$$

so the amount rises by $50 to $550.

What happens to this amount at the end of the second year? Is the interest also $50? This would actually be the case with **simple interest** when the amount of interest received is the same for all years. However, with **compound interest**, we get 'interest on the interest'. Nearly all financial investments use compound rather than simple interest, because investors need to be rewarded for not taking the interest payment out of the fund each year. Under annual compounding the interest obtained at the end of the second year is 10% of the amount invested at the start of that year. This not only consists of the original $500, but also the $50 already received as interest on the first year's investment. Consequently, we get an additional

$$\frac{1}{10} \times \$550 = \$55$$

raising the sum to $605. Finally, at the end of the third year, the interest is

$$\frac{1}{10} \times \$605 = \$60.5$$

so the investment is $665.5. You are therefore $165.5 better off by taking the $500 now and investing it for three years. The calculations are summarized in Table 3.1.

Table 3.1

End of year	Interest	Investment
1	$50	$550
2	$55	$605
3	$60.5	$665.5

PROBLEM

4 Find the value, in 10 years' time, of $1,000 invested at 8% interest compounded annually.

The previous calculations were performed by finding the interest earned each year and adding it on to the amount accumulated at the beginning of the year. As you may have discovered in Problem 4 this can be rather laborious, particularly if the money is invested over a long period of time. What is really needed is a method of calculating the investment after, say, ten years without having to determine the amount for the nine intermediate years. To do this let us return to the problem of investing $500 at 10% interest compounded annually. The original sum of money is called the **principal** and is denoted by P and the final sum is called the **future value** and is denoted by S. At the end of one year the total amount invested is just 100% + 10% of the principal, P, so it is

$$P \times \frac{110}{100} = P(1.1)$$

Here, the 100% reflects the fact that we get the original amount back at the end of the year and the 10% corresponds to the interest which is added on to this amount. This procedure is repeated in subsequent years so at the end of each year the investment gets multiplied by a factor of 1.1. After two years we get

$$P(1.1) \times (1.1) = P(1.1)^2$$

and after three years the future value is

$$S = P(1.1)^2 \times (1.1) = P(1.1)^3$$

Setting $P = 500$ we see that

$$S = 500(1.1)^3 = \$665.5$$

which is, of course, the same as the amount calculated previously.

In general, if the interest rate is $r\%$ compounded annually then at the end of one year a principal, P, becomes 100% + $r\%$ of P which is

$$P\left(\frac{100}{100} + \frac{r}{100}\right) = P\left(1 + \frac{r}{100}\right)$$

In other words, each year the investment gets multiplied by

$$1 + \frac{r}{100}$$

so, after n years,

$$S = P\left(1 + \frac{r}{100}\right)^n$$

Given the values of r, P and n it is trivial to evaluate S using the power key $\boxed{x^y}$ on a calculator.

PROBLEM

5 Use the formula

$$S = P\left(1 + \frac{r}{100}\right)^n$$

to find the value, in 10 years' time, of \$1,000 invested at 8% interest compounded annually. [You might like to compare your answer with that obtained in Problem 4.]

The compound interest formula derived above involves four variables, r, n, P and S. Provided that we know any three of these we can use the formula to determine the remaining variable. This is illustrated in the following example.

EXAMPLE

A principal of \$25,000 is invested at 12% interest compounded annually. After how many years will the investment first exceed \$250,000?

Solution

We want to save a total of \$250,000 starting with an initial investment of \$25,000. The problem is to determine the number of years required for this on the assumption that the interest is fixed at 12% throughout this time. The formula for compound interest is

$$S = P\left(1 + \frac{r}{100}\right)^n$$

We are given that

$$P = 25\,000, \ S = 250\,000, \ r = 12$$

so we need to solve the equation

$$250\,000 = 25\,000\left(1 + \frac{12}{100}\right)^n$$

for n.

One way of doing this would just be to keep on guessing values of n until we find the one that works. However, a more mathematical approach is to use logarithms because we are being asked to solve an equation in which the unknown occurs as a power. Following the method described in Section 2.3 we first divide both sides by $25\,000$ to get

$$10 = (1.12)^n$$

Taking logarithms of both sides gives

$$\log(10) = \log(1.12)^n$$

and if you apply the third rule of logarithms you get

$$\log(10) = n \log(1.12)$$

$\log_b x^m = m \log_b x$

Hence

$$n = \frac{\log(10)}{\log(1.12)}$$

$$= \frac{1}{0.049\,218\,023} \qquad \text{(taking logarithms to base 10)}$$

$$= 20.3 \qquad \text{(to 1 decimal place)}$$

Now we know that n must be a whole number because interest is only added on at the end of each year. We assume that the first interest payment occurs exactly 12 months after the initial investment and every 12 months thereafter. The answer, 20.3, tells us that after only 20 years the amount is less than \$250,000 so we need to wait until 21 years have elapsed before it exceeds this amount. In fact, after 20 years

$$S = \$25,000(1.12)^{20} = \$241,157.33$$

and after 21 years

$$S = \$25,000(1.12)^{21} = \$270,096.21$$

■

In this example we calculated the time taken for \$25,000 to increase by a factor of ten. It can be shown that this time depends only on the interest rate and not on the actual value of the principal. To see this, note that if a general principal, P, increases ten-fold then its future value is $10P$. If the interest rate is 12% then we need to solve

$$10P = P\left(1 + \frac{12}{100}\right)^n$$

for n. The Ps cancel (indicating that the answer is independent of P) to produce the equation

$$10 = (1.12)^n$$

This is identical to the equation obtained in the previous example, and, as we have just seen, has the solution $n = 20.3$.

PROBLEM

6   A firm estimates that its sales will rise by 3% each year and that it needs to sell at least 10 000 goods each year in order to make a profit. Given that its current annual sales are only 9000, how many years will it take before the firm breaks even?

You may have noticed that in all of the previous problems it is assumed that the interest is compounded annually. It is possible for interest to be added to the investment more frequently than this. For example, suppose that a principal of $500 is invested for 3 years at 10% interest compounded quarterly. What do we mean by '10% interest compounded quarterly'? Well, it does *not* mean that we get 10% interest every three months. Instead, the 10% is split into four equal portions, one for each quarter. Every three months the interest accrued is

$$\frac{10\%}{4} = 2.5\%$$

so after the first quarter the investment gets multiplied by 1.025 to give

$500(1.025)$

and after the second quarter it gets multiplied by another 1.025 to give

$500(1.025)^2$

and so on. Moreover, since there are exactly 12 three-month periods in three years we deduce that the future value is

$500(1.025)^{12} = \$672.44$

Notice that this is greater than the sum obtained at the start of this section under annual compounding. (Why is this?)

This example highlights the fact that the compound interest formula

$$S = P\left(1 + \frac{r}{100}\right)^n$$

derived earlier for annual compounding can also be used for other types of compounding. All that is needed is to reinterpret the symbols r and n. The variable r now represents the rate of interest per time period and n represents the total number of periods.

EXAMPLE

A principal of $10 is invested at 12% interest for one year. Determine the future value if the interest is compounded

(a)   annually
(b)   semi-annually
(c)   quarterly
(d)   monthly
(e)   weekly

Solution

The formula for compound interest gives

$$S = 10\left(1 + \frac{r}{100}\right)^n$$

(a) If the interest is compounded annually then $r = 12$, $n = 1$, so

$$S = \$10(1.12)^1 = \$11.20$$

(b) If the interest is compounded semi-annually then an interest of $12/2 = 6\%$ is added on every six months and, since there are two six-month periods in a year,

$$S = \$10(1.06)^2 = \$11.24$$

(c) If the interest is compounded quarterly then an interest of $12/4 = 3\%$ is added on every three months and, since there are four three-month periods in a year,

$$S = \$10(1.03)^4 = \$11.26$$

(d) If the interest is compounded monthly then an interest of $12/12 = 1\%$ is added on every month and, since there are 12 months in a year,

$$S = \$10(1.01)^{12} = \$11.27$$

(e) If the interest is compounded weekly then an interest of $12/52 = 0.23\%$ is added on every week and, since there are 52 weeks in a year,

$$S = \$10(1.0023)^{52} = \$11.27$$

∎

In the above example we see that the future value rises as the frequency of compounding rises. This is to be expected because the basic feature of compound interest is that we get 'interest on the interest'. However, one important observation that you might not have expected is that, although the future values increase, they appear to be approaching a fixed value. It can be shown that this always occurs. The type of compounding in which the interest is added on with increasing frequency is called **continuous compounding**. In theory, we can find the future value of a principal under continuous compounding using the approach taken in the previous example. We work with smaller and smaller time periods until the numbers settle down to a fixed value. However, it turns out that there is a special formula that can be used to compute this directly. The future value, S, of a principal, P, compounded continuously for t years at an annual rate of $r\%$ is

$$S = Pe^{rt/100}$$

The letter e actually stands for a number which is

2.718 281 828 459 045 235 36 to 20 decimal places

It is rare to see the number e used on its own in mathematics. It is normally raised to some power, as in the formula for continuous compounding. Indeed, the reason for denoting this number by e is that it is the first letter of the word 'exponential'. Fortunately for us, all scientific calculators have a special function key $\boxed{e^x}$ which enables us to raise e to any power although it may be necessary first to press the shift key to activate it. To use the formula

$$S = Pe^{rt/100}$$

to calculate S from given values of P, r and t you work as follows. You first multiply the interest rate, r, by the number of years, t, and divide by 100. You then simply press the $\boxed{e^x}$ key and finally multiply by the principal, P. If $r = 12$, $t = 1$ and $P = 10$ then this procedure gives

$$S = \$10e^{12 \times 1/100} = \$10e^{0.12} = \$11.27$$

check this using your own calculator

which is in agreement with the limiting value obtained in the previous example.

EXAMPLE

A principal of \$2,000 is invested at 10% interest compounded continuously. After how many days will the investment first exceed \$2,100?

Solution

We want to save a total of \$2,100 starting with an initial investment of \$2,000. The problem is to determine the number of days required for this on the assumption that the interest rate is 10% compounded continuously. The formula for continuous compounding is

$$S = Pe^{rt/100}$$

We are given that

$$S = 2100, \quad P = 2000, \quad r = 10$$

so we need to solve the equation

$$2100 = 2000e^{10t/100}$$

for t. Dividing through by 2000 gives

$$1.05 = e^{0.1t}$$

The fact that the unknown occurs as a power suggests that we take logarithms in the usual way. Normally we use base 10. However, it is more convenient to use logarithms to base e. As was pointed out in Section 2.3, most calculators have the facility to evaluate logarithms to the base e. These are called natural logarithms and we write $\log_e M$ using the shorthand $\ln M$. By the definition of logarithms given in Section 2.3 we know that if

$$M = b^n \quad \text{then} \quad n = \log_b M$$

so working to base e we deduce that if

$$M = e^n \quad \text{then} \quad n = \ln M$$

If we apply this definition to the equation

$$1.05 = e^{0.1t}$$

with $M = 1.05$ and $n = 0.1t$ then

$$0.1t = \ln(1.05) = 0.048\,790\,2$$

and so $t = 0.488$ to three decimal places.

The variable t which appears in the formula for continuous compounding is measured in years so to convert it to days we multiply by 365 (assuming that there are 365 days in a year). Hence

$$t = 365 \times 0.488 = 178.1 \text{ days}$$

We deduce that the amount invested first exceeds $2,100 some time during the 179th day.

■

PROBLEMS

7 **(1)** A principal, $30, is invested at 6% interest for two years. Determine the future value if the interest is compounded

    (a) annually   **(b)** semi-annually   **(c)** quarterly   **(d)** monthly
    (e) weekly   **(f)** daily

  (2) Use the formula

$$S = Pe^{rt/100}$$

to determine the future value of $30 invested at 6% interest compounded continuously for two years. Confirm that it is in agreement with the results of part (1).

8 Determine the rate of interest required for a principal of $1,000 to produce a future value of $4,000 after ten years compounded continuously.

Given that there are so many ways of calculating compound interest people often find it difficult to appraise different investment opportunities. What is needed is a standard 'benchmark' which enables an individual to compare different forms of savings or credit schemes on an equal basis. The one that is commonly used is annual compounding. All firms offering investment or loan facilities are required to provide the effective annual rate. This is often referred to as the **annual percentage rate** which is abbreviated to APR. The APR is the rate of interest which, when compounded annually, produces the same yield as the nominal (that is, the stated) rate of interest.

EXAMPLE

Determine the annual percentage rate of interest of a deposit account which has a nominal rate of 8% compounded monthly.

Solution

To determine the APR we find expressions for the future value of a principal, P, at the end of one year when the interest rate is

(a) 8% compounded monthly
(b) r% compounded annually

By equating these two expressions the value of r can be deduced.

(a) If the account offers a return of 8% compounded monthly then each month the interest is

$$\frac{8}{12} = \frac{2}{3} = 0.67\%$$

of the amount invested at the beginning of that month. After one year a principal, P, yields

$$P(1.0067)^{12}$$

because there are 12 months in a year.

(b) If the rate of interest is r% compounded annually then after one year the principal, P, yields

$$P\left(1 + \frac{r}{100}\right)$$

If these are to be the same then

$$P\left(1 + \frac{r}{100}\right) = P(1.0067)^{12}$$

The P's cancel to give

$$1 + \frac{r}{100} = (1.0067)^{12} = 1.0834$$

which can easily be solved to get $r = 8.34\%$.

PROBLEM

9 Determine the annual percentage rate of interest if the nominal rate is 12% compounded quarterly.

PRACTICE PROBLEMS

10 The value of an asset, currently priced at $100,000, is expected to increase by 20% a year.

  (1) Find its value in ten years' time.
  (2) After how many years will it be worth $1 million?

11 How long will it take for a sum of money to double if it is invested at 5% interest compounded annually?

12   A piece of machinery depreciates in value by 5% a year. Determine its value in three years' time if its current value is $50,000.

13   A principal, $7,000, is invested at 9% interest for eight years. Determine its future value if the interest is compounded

    (a)   annually
    (b)   semi-annually
    (c)   monthly
    (d)   continuously

14   A department store has its own credit card facilities for which it charges interest at a rate of 2% each month. Explain briefly why this is not the same as an annual rate of 24%. What is the annual percentage rate?

15   Determine the APR if the nominal rate is 7% compounded continuously.

3.2   Geometric series

Objectives   At the end of this section you should be able to:

    ●   recognize a geometric progression,

    ●   evaluate a geometric series,

    ●   calculate the total investment obtained from a regular savings plan,

    ●   calculate the instalments needed to repay a loan.

Consider the following sequence of numbers:

    2, 6, 18, 54, ...   (1)

One obvious question, often asked in intelligence tests, is what is the next term in the sequence? All that is required is for you to spot the pattern so that it can be used to generate the next term. In this case successive numbers are obtained by multiplying by 3, so the fifth term is

    $54 \times 3 = 162$

the sixth term is

    $162 \times 3 = 486$

and so on. Any sequence in which terms are calculated by multiplying their predecessor by a fixed number is called a **geometric progression** and the multiplicative factor itself is called a **geometric ratio**. The sequence on the previous page is a geometric progression with geometric ratio 3. The reason for introducing these sequences is not to help you to answer intelligence tests but rather to analyse compound interest problems. You may well have noticed that all of the problems given in the previous section produced such a sequence. For example, if a principal, \$500, is invested at 10% interest compounded annually, then the future values in successive years are

$$500(1.1), \ 500(1.1)^2, \ 500(1.1)^3, \ldots \qquad (2)$$

which we recognize as a geometric progression with geometric ratio 1.1.

PROBLEM

1   Decide which of the following sequences are geometric progressions. For those sequences which are of this type write down their geometric ratios

(**a**) $3, 6, 12, 24, \ldots$ (**b**) $5, 10, 15, 20, \ldots$ (**c**) $1, -3, 9, -27, \ldots$
(**d**) $8, 4, 2, 1, \frac{1}{2}, \ldots$ (**e**) $500, 500(1.07), 500(1.07)^2, \ldots$

All of the problems considered in Section 3.1 involved a single lump-sum payment into an investment account. The task was simply to determine its future value after a period of time when it is subject to a certain type of compounding. In this section, we extend this to include multiple payments. This situation occurs whenever individuals save regularly or when businesses take out a loan which is paid back using fixed monthly or annual instalments. To tackle these problems we need to be able to sum (that is, to add together) consecutive terms of a geometric progression. Such an expression is called a **geometric series**. Suppose that we want to sum the first six terms of the geometric progression given by sequence (1). The easiest way of doing this is to write down these six numbers and add them together to get

$$2 + 6 + 18 + 54 + 162 + 486 = 728$$

Suppose, however, that you needed to find the sum of the first 25 terms of sequence (2), that is to evaluate the geometric series

$$500(1.1) + 500(1.1)^2 + \ldots + 500(1.1)^{25}$$

This is a much harder task, not only because there are more terms, but also because it is necessary to use a calculator to work out each individual term. Under these circumstances the preferred method is to use a special formula. It can be shown that the sum of the first n terms of a geometric progression is equal to

$$a\left(\frac{r^n - 1}{r - 1}\right) \qquad (r \neq 1)$$

The letter a denotes the first term in the sequence and r denotes the geometric ratio. Use of the symbol r to denote both the interest rate and the geometric ratio is unfortunate but fairly standard. In practice, it is usually clear from the context what this symbol represents so no confusion should arise.

A proof of this formula is given in Problem 9 at the end of this section. As a check, let us use it to determine the sum of the first six terms of sequence (1). In this case the first term $a = 2$, the geometric ratio $r = 3$ and the number of terms $n = 6$, so the geometric series is equal to

$$2\left(\frac{3^6 - 1}{3 - 1}\right) = 3^6 - 1 = 728$$

which agrees with the previous value found by summing the terms longhand. In this case there is no real benefit in using the formula. However, for the series

$$500(1.1) + 500(1.1)^2 + \ldots + 500(1.1)^{25}$$

we have $a = 500(1.1)$, $r = 1.1$, $n = 25$ so the geometric series is equal to

$$500(1.1)\left(\frac{(1.1)^{25} - 1}{1.1 - 1}\right) = 54\,090.88$$

You might like to convince yourself of the utility of the formula by evaluating this series longhand and comparing the computational effort involved!

PROBLEM

2 (1) Write down the next term in the sequence

$$1, 2, 4, 8, \ldots$$

and hence find the sum of the first five terms. Check that this agrees with the value obtained using

$$a\left(\frac{r^n - 1}{r - 1}\right)$$

(2) Evaluate the geometric series

$$100(1.07) + 100(1.07)^2 + \ldots + 100(1.07)^{20}$$

There are two particular applications of geometric series that we now consider, involving savings and loans. We begin by analysing savings plans. In the simplest case an individual decides to invest a regular sum of money into a bank account. This is sometimes referred to as a **sinking fund** and is used to meet some future financial commitment. It is assumed that he or she saves an equal amount and that the money is put into the account at the same time each year (or month). We further assume that the interest rate does not change. The latter may not be an entirely realistic assumption since it can fluctuate wildly in volatile market conditions. Indeed, banks offer a variety of rates of interest depending on the notice required for withdrawal and on the actual amount of money saved. Problem 7 at the end of this section considers what happens when the interest rate rises as the investment goes above certain threshold levels.

EXAMPLE

A person saves \$100 in a bank account at the beginning of each month. The bank offers a return of 12% compounded monthly.

(1) Determine the total amount saved after 12 months.
(2) After how many months does the amount saved first exceed \$2,000?

Solution

(1) During the year a total of 12 regular savings of \$100 are made. Each \$100 is put into an account which gives a return of 12% compounded monthly, or equivalently, a return of 1% each month. However, each payment is invested for a different period of time. For example, the first payment is invested for the full 12 months whereas the final payment is invested for 1 month only. We need to work out the future value of each payment separately and add them together.

The first payment is invested for 12 months, gaining a monthly interest of 1%, so its future value is

$$100(1.01)^{12}$$

The second payment is invested for 11 months so its future value is

$$100(1.01)^{11}$$

Likewise, the third payment yields

$$100(1.01)^{10}$$

and so on. The last payment is invested for one month so its future value is

$$100(1.01)^{1}$$

The total value of the savings at the end of 12 months is then

$$100(1.01)^{12} + 100(1.01)^{11} + \ldots + 100(1.01)^{1}$$

If we rewrite this series in the order of ascending powers we then have the more familiar form

$$100(1.01)^{1} + \ldots + 100(1.01)^{11} + 100(1.01)^{12}$$

This is equal to the sum of the first 12 terms of a geometric progression in which the first term is $100(1.01)$ and the geometric ratio is 1.01. Its value can therefore be found by using

$$a\left(\frac{r^{n} - 1}{r - 1}\right)$$

with $a = 100(1.01)$, $r = 1.01$ and $n = 12$ which gives

$$\$100(1.01)\left(\frac{(1.01)^{12} - 1}{1.01 - 1}\right) = \$1,280.93$$

(2) In part (1) we showed that after 12 months the total amount saved is

$$100(1.01) + 100(1.01)^{2} + \ldots + 100(1.01)^{12}Y$$

Using exactly the same argument it is easy to see that after n months the account contains

$$100(1.01) + 100(1.01)^{2} + \ldots + 100(1.01)^{n}$$

The formula for the sum of the first n terms of a geometric progression shows that this is the same as

$$100(1.01)\left(\frac{1.01^n - 1}{1.01 - 1}\right) = 10\,100(1.01^n - 1)$$

The problem here is to find the number of months needed for total savings to rise to $2,000. Mathematically, this is equivalent to solving the equation

$$10\,100(1.01^n - 1) = 2000$$

for n. Following the strategy described in Section 2.3 gives

$$1.01^n - 1 = 0.198$$

$$1.01^n = 1.198$$

$$\log(1.01)^n = \log(1.198)$$

$$n\log(1.01) = \log(1.198)$$

$$n = \frac{\log(1.198)}{\log(1.01)}$$

$$= 18.2$$

It follows that after 18 months savings are less than $2,000, whereas after 19 months savings exceed this amount. The target figure of $2,000 is therefore reached at the end of the 19th month.

■

PROBLEM

3 An individual saves $1,000 in a bank account at the beginning of each year. The bank offers a return of 8% compounded annually.

(1) Determine the amount saved after 10 years.

(2) After how many years does the amount saved first exceed $20,000?

We now turn our attention to loans. Many businesses finance their expansion by obtaining loans from a bank or other financial institution. Banks are keen to do this provided that they receive interest as a reward for lending money. Businesses pay back loans by monthly or annual repayments. The way in which this repayment is calculated is as follows. Let us suppose that interest is calculated on a monthly basis and that the firm repays the debt by fixed monthly instalments at the end of each month. The bank calculates the interest charged during the first month based on the original loan. At the end of the month this interest is added on to the original loan and the repayment is simultaneously deducted to determine the amount owed. The bank then charges interest in the second month based on this new amount and the process is repeated. Provided that the monthly repayment is greater than the interest charged each month, the amount owed decreases and eventually the debt is cleared. In practice, the period during which the loan is repaid is fixed in advance and the monthly repayments are calculated to achieve this end.

EXAMPLE

Determine the monthly repayments needed to repay a $100,000 loan which is paid back over 25 years when the interest rate is 8% compounded annually.

Solution

In this example the time interval between consecutive repayments is one month whereas the period during which interest is charged is one year. This type of financial calculation typifies the way in which certain types of housing loans are worked out. The interest is compounded annually at 8% so the amount of interest charged during the first year is 8% of the original loan, that is

$$\frac{8}{100} \times 100\,000 = 8000$$

This amount is added on to the outstanding debt at the end of the first year. During this time 12 monthly repayments are made, so if each instalment is x the outstanding debt must decrease by $12x$. Hence, at the end of the first year, the amount owed is

$$100\,000 + 8000 - 12x = 108\,000 - 12x$$

In order to be able to spot a pattern in the annual debt let us write this as

$$100\,000(1.08) - 12x$$

where the first part simply reflects the fact that 8% interest is added on to the original sum of $100,000. At the end of the second year a similar calculation is performed. The amount owed rises by 8% to become

$$[100\,000(1.08) - 12x](1.08) = 100\,000(1.08)^2 - 12x(1.08)$$

and we deduct $12x$ for the repayments to get

$$100\,000(1.08)^2 - 12x(1.08) - 12x$$

This is the amount owed at the end of the second year. Each year we multiply by 1.08 and subtract $12x$ so at the end of the third year we owe

$$[100\,000(1.08)^2 - 12x(1.08) - 12x](1.08) - 12x$$
$$= 100\,000(1.08)^3 - 12x(1.08)^2 - 12x(1.08) - 12x$$

and so on. These results are summarized in Table 3.2. If we continue the pattern we see that after 25 years the amount owed is

$$100\,000(1.08)^{25} - 12x(1.08)^{24} - 12x(1.08)^{23} - \ldots - 12x$$
$$= 100\,000(1.08)^{25} - 12x[1 + 1.08 + (1.08)^2 + \ldots + (1.08)^{24}]$$

where we have taken out a common factor of $12x$ and have rewritten the powers of 1.08 in ascending

Table 3.2

End of year	Outstanding debt
1	$100\,000(1.08)^1 - 12x$
2	$100\,000(1.08)^2 - 12x(1.08)^1 - 12x$
3	$100\,000(1.08)^3 - 12x(1.08)^2 - 12x(1.08)^1 - 12x$

order. The first term is easily evaluated using a calculator to get

$$100\,000(1.08)^{25} = 684\,847.520$$

The geometric series inside the square brackets can be worked out from the formula

$$a\left(\frac{r^n - 1}{r - 1}\right)$$

The first term $a = 1$, the geometric ratio $r = 1.08$ and we are summing the first 25 terms so $n = 25$. (Can you see why there are actually 25 terms in this series rather than 24?) Hence

$$[1 + 1.08 + (1.08)^2 + \ldots + (1.08)^{24}]$$

$$= \frac{1.08^{25} - 1}{1.08 - 1} = 73.106$$

The amount owed at the end of 25 years is therefore

$$684\,847.520 - 12x(73.106)$$

$$= 684\,847.520 - 877.272x$$

In this expression, x denotes the monthly repayment which is chosen so that the debt is completely cleared after 25 years. This will be so if x is the solution of

$$684\,847.520 - 877.272x = 0$$

Hence

$$x = \frac{684\,847.520}{877.272} = \$780.66$$

The monthly repayment on a 25-year loan of $100,000 is $780.66, assuming that the interest rate remains fixed at 8% throughout this period.

It is interesting to substitute this value of x into the expressions for the outstanding debt given in Table 3.2. The results are listed in Table 3.3. What is so depressing about these figures is that the debt only falls by about $1,500 to begin with, in spite of the fact that over $9,000 is being repaid each year!

Table 3.3

End of year	Outstanding debt
1	$98,632.08
2	$97,154.73
3	$95,559.18

∎

PROBLEM

4   A person requests an immediate bank overdraft of $2,000. The bank generously agrees to this but insists that it should be repaid by 12 monthly instalments and charges 1% interest every month on the outstanding debt. Determine the monthly repayment.

PRACTICE PROBLEMS

5 Find the value of the geometric series

$$1000 + 1000(1.03) + 1000(1.03)^2 + \ldots + 1000(1.03)^9$$

6 A regular saving of $500 is made into a sinking fund at the start of each year for 10 years. Determine the value of the fund at the end of the tenth year on the assumption that the rate of interest is

(a) 11% compounded annually   (b) 10% compounded continuously

7 A bank has three different types of account in which the interest rate depends on the amount invested. The 'ordinary' account offers a return of 6% and is available to every customer. The 'extra' account offers 7% and is only available to customers with $5,000 or more to invest. The 'superextra' account offers 8% and is only available to customers with $20,000 or more to invest. In each case interest is compounded annually and is added to the investment at the end of the year.

A person saves $4,000 at the beginning of each year for 25 years. Calculate the total amount saved on the assumption that the money is transferred to a higher interest account at the earliest opportunity.

8 Determine the monthly repayments needed to repay a $50,000 loan which is paid back over 25 years when the interest rate is 9% compounded annually. Calculate the increased monthly repayments needed in the case when

(a) the interest rate rises to 10%   (b) the period of repayment is reduced to 20 years.

9 If

$$S_n = a + ar + ar^2 + \ldots + ar^{n-1}$$

write down an expression for rS_n and deduce that

$$rS_n - S_n = ar^n - a$$

Hence show that the sum of the first n terms of a geometric progression with first term a and geometric ratio r is given by

$$a\left(\frac{r^n - 1}{r - 1}\right)$$

provided that $r \neq 1$.

3.3   Investment appraisal

Objectives   At the end of this section you should be able to:

● calculate present values under discrete and continuous compounding,

● use net present values to appraise investment projects,

- calculate the internal rate of return,

- calculate the present value of an annuity,

- use discounting to compare investment projects,

- calculate the present value of government securities.

In Section 3.1 the following two formulas were used to solve compound interest problems:

$$S = P\left(1 + \frac{r}{100}\right)^t \qquad (1)$$

$$S = Pe^{rt/100} \qquad (2)$$

The first of these can be applied to any type of compounding in which the interest is added on to the investment at the end of discrete time intervals. The second formula is used when the interest is added on continuously. Both formulas involve the variables

P = principal

S = future value

r = interest rate

t = time

In the case of discrete compounding the letter t represents the number of time periods. (In Section 3.1 this was denoted by n.) For continuous compounding t is measured in years. Given any three of these variables it is possible to work out the value of the remaining variable. Various examples were considered in Section 3.1. Of particular interest is the case where S, r and t are given, and P is the unknown to be determined. In this situation we know the future value, and we want to work backwards to calculate the original principal. This process is called **discounting** and the principal, P, is called the **present value**. The rate of interest is sometimes referred to as the **discount rate**. Equations (1) and (2) are easily rearranged to produce explicit formulas for the present value under discrete and continuous compounding:

$$P = \frac{S}{(1 + r/100)^t} = S\left(1 + \frac{r}{100}\right)^{-t}$$

reciprocals are denoted by negative powers

$$P = \frac{S}{e^{rt/100}} = Se^{-rt/100}$$

EXAMPLE

Find the present value of $1,000 in four years' time if the discount rate is 10% compounded

(a)   semi-annually
(b)   continuously

Solution

(a)   The discount formula for discrete compounding is

$$P = S\left(1 + \frac{r}{100}\right)^{-t}$$

If compounding occurs semi-annually then $r = 5$ since the interest rate per six months is $10/2 = 5$, and $t = 8$ since there are eight six-month periods in four years. We are given that the future value is $1,000 so

$$P = \$1,000(1.05)^{-8} = \$676.84$$

(b)   The discount formula for continuous compounding is

$$P = Se^{-rt/100}$$

In this formula, r is the annual discount rate which is 10, and t is measured in years, so is 4. Hence the present value is

$$P = \$1,000e^{-0.4} = \$670.32$$

Notice that the present value in part (b) is smaller than that in part (a). This is to be expected because continuous compounding always produces a higher yield. Consequently, we need to invest a smaller amount under continuous compounding to produce the future value of $1,000 after four years.

■

PROBLEM

1   Find the present value of $100,000 in ten years' time if the discount rate is 6% compounded

(a)   annually
(b)   continuously

Present values are a useful way of appraising investment projects. Suppose that you are invited to invest $600 today in a business venture, which is certain to produce a return of $1,000 in five years' time. If the discount rate is 10% compounded semi-annually then part (a) of the previous example shows that the present value of this return is $676.84. This exceeds the initial outlay of $600 so the venture is regarded as profitable. We quantify this profit by calculating the difference between the present value of the revenue and the present value of the costs, which is known as the **net present value** (NPV). In this example, the net present value is

$$\$676.84 - \$600 = \$76.84$$

Quite generally, a project is considered worthwhile when the NPV is positive. Moreover, if a decision is to be made between two different projects then the one with the higher NPV is the preferred choice.

An alternative way of assessing individual projects is based on the **internal rate of return** (IRR). This is the annual rate which, when applied to the initial outlay, yields the same return as the project after the same number of years. The investment is considered worthwhile provided the IRR exceeds the market rate. Obviously, in practice, other factors such as risk need to be considered before a decision is made.

The following example illutrates both NPV and IRR methods and shows how a value of the IRR itself can be calculated.

EXAMPLE

A project requiring an initial outlay of $15,000 is guaranteed to produce a return of $20,000 in three years' time. Use the

(a) net present value
(b) internal rate of return

methods to decide whether this investment is worthwhile if the prevailing market rate is 5% compounded annually. Would your decision be affected if the interest rate was 12%?

Solution

(a) The present value of $20,000 in three years' time, based on a discount rate of 5%, is found by setting $S = 20,000$, $t = 3$ and $r = 5$ in the formula

$$P = S\left(1 + \frac{r}{100}\right)^{-t}$$

This gives

$$P = \$20,000(1.05)^{-3} = \$17,276.75$$

The NPV is therefore

$$\$17,276.75 - \$15,000 = \$2,276.75$$

The project is to be recommended because this value is positive.

(b) To calculate the IRR we use the formula

$$S = P\left(1 + \frac{r}{100}\right)^{t}$$

We are given $S = 20\,000$, $P = 15\,000$ and $t = 3$ so we need to solve

$$20\,000 = 15\,000\left(1 + \frac{r}{100}\right)^{3}$$

for r. An obvious first step is to divide both sides of this equation by $15\,000$ to get

$$\frac{4}{3} = \left(1 + \frac{r}{100}\right)^{3}$$

The difficulty in solving this equation is that the unknown, r, is trapped inside the brackets, which are raised to the power of 3. This is analogous to the problem of solving an equation such as

$$x^2 = 5.23$$

say, which we would solve by taking square roots of both sides to find x. This suggests that we can extract r by taking cube roots of both sides of

$$\left(1 + \frac{r}{100}\right)^3 = \frac{4}{3}$$

to get

$$1 + \frac{r}{100} = \left(\frac{4}{3}\right)^{1/3} = 1.1$$

Hence

$$\frac{r}{100} = 1.1 - 1 = 0.1$$

and so the IRR is 10%. The project is therefore to be recommended because this value exceeds the market rate of 5%.

For the last part of the problem we are invited to consider whether our advice would be different if the market rate was 12%. Using the NPV method we need to repeat the calculations, replacing 5 by 12. The corresponding net present value is then

$$\$20,000(1.12)^{-3} - \$15,000 = -\$764.40$$

This time the NPV is negative so the project leads to an effective loss and is not to be recommended. The same conclusion can be reached more easily using the IRR method. We have already seen that the internal rate of return is 10% and can deduce immediately that you would be better off investing the $15,000 at the market rate of 12% since this gives the higher yield.

■

PROBLEM

2 An investment project requires an initial outlay of $8,000 and will produce a return of $17,000 at the end of five years. Use the

(a) net present value
(b) internal rate of return

methods to decide whether this is worthwhile if the capital could be invested elsewhere at 15% compounded annually.

This example illustrates the use of two different methods for investment appraisal. It may appear at first sight that the method based on the IRR is the preferred approach, particularly if you wish to consider more than one interest rate. However, this is not usually the case. The IRR method can give wholly misleading advice when *comparing* two or more projects, as the following example demonstrates.

EXAMPLE

Suppose that it is possible to invest in only one of two different projects. Project A requires an initial outlay of $1,000 and yields $1,200 in four years' time. Project B requires an outlay of $30,000 and yields

$35,000 after four years. Which of these projects would you choose to invest in when the market rate is 3% compounded annually?

Solution

Let us first solve this problem using net present values.

For Project A

$$NPV = \$1,200(1.03)^{-4} - \$1,000 = \$66.18$$

For Project B

$$NPV = \$35,000(1.03)^{-4} - \$30,000 = \$1097.05$$

Both projects are viable as they produce positive net present values. Moreover, the second project is preferred since it has the higher value. You can see that this recommendation is correct by considering how you might invest $30,000. If you opt for Project A then the best you can do is to invest $1,000 of this amount to give a return of $1,200 in four years' time. The remaining $29,000 could be invested at the market rate of 3% to yield

$$\$29,000(1.03)^4 = \$32,639.76$$

The total return is then

$$\$1,200 + \$32,639.76 = \$33,839.76$$

On the other hand, if you opt for Project B then the whole of the $30,000 can be invested to yield $35,000. In other words, in four years' time you would be

$$\$35,000 - \$33,639.76 = \$1,160.24$$

better off by choosing Project B, which confirms the advice given by the NPV method.

However, this is contrary to the advice given by the IRR method. For Project A, the internal rate of return, r_A, satisfies

$$1200 = 1000\left(1 + \frac{r_A}{100}\right)^4$$

Dividing by 1000 gives

$$\left(1 + \frac{r_A}{100}\right)^4 = 1.2$$

and if we take fourth roots we get

$$1 + \frac{r_A}{100} = (1.2)^{\frac{1}{4}} = 1.047$$

so $r_A = 4.7\%$.

For Project B the internal rate of return, r_B, satisfies

$$35\,000 = 30\,000\left(1 + \frac{r_B}{100}\right)^4$$

This can be solved as before to get $r_B = 3.9\%$.

Project A gives the higher internal rate of return even though, as we have seen, Project B is the preferred choice.

■

The results of this example show that the IRR method is an unreliable way of comparing investment opportunities when there are significant differences between the amounts involved. This is because the IRR method compares percentages and obviously a large percentage of a small sum could give a smaller profit than a small percentage of a larger sum.

PROBLEM

3   A firm needs to choose between two projects, A and B. Project A involves an initial outlay of $13,500 and yields $18,000 in two years' time. Project B requires an outlay of $9,000 and yields $13,000 after two years. Which of these projects would you advise the firm to invest in if the annual market rate of interest is 7%?

So far in this section we have calculated the present value of a single future value. We now consider the case of a sequence of payments over time. The simplest cash flow of this type is an **annuity**, which is a sequence of regular equal payments. It can be thought of as the opposite of a sinking fund. This time a lump sum is invested and, subsequently, equal amounts of money are withdrawn at fixed time intervals. Provided that the payments themselves exceed the amount of interest gained during the time interval between payments, the fund will decrease and eventually become zero. At this point the payments cease. In practice, we are interested in the value of the original lump sum needed to secure a regular income over a known period of time. This can be done by summing the present values of the individual payments.

EXAMPLE

Find the present value of an annuity which yields an income of $10,000 at the end of each year for ten years, assuming that the interest rate is 7% compounded annually.

Solution

The first payment of $10,000 is made at the end of the first year. Its present value is calculated using the formula

$$P = S\left(1 + \frac{r}{100}\right)^{-t}$$

with $S = 10\,000$, $r = 7$ and $t = 1$, so

$$P = \$10,000(1.07)^{-1} = \$9,345.79$$

This means that if we want to take out $10,000 from the fund in one year's time then we need to invest $9,345.79 today. The second payment of $10,000 is made at the end of the second year so its present value is

$$\$10,000(1.07)^{-2} = \$8,734.39$$

This is the amount of money that needs to be invested now to cover the second payment from the fund. In general, the present value of $10,000 in t years' time is

$$10\,000(1.07)^{-t}$$

so the total present value is

$$10\,000(1.07)^{-1} + 10\,000(1.07)^{-2} + \ldots + 10\,000(1.07)^{-10}$$

This is a geometric series so we may use the formula

$$a\left(\frac{r^n - 1}{r - 1}\right)$$

In this case, $a = 10\,000(1.07)^{-1}$, $r = 1.07^{-1}$ and $n = 10$ so the present value of the annuity is

$$\$10,000(1.07)^{-1}\left(\frac{1.07^{-10} - 1}{1.07^{-1} - 1}\right) = \$70,235.82$$

This represents the amount of money that needs to be invested now so that a regular annual income of $10,000 can be withdrawn from the fund for the next ten years.

■

PROBLEM

4   Find the present value of an annuity which yields an income of $2,000 at the end of each month for ten years, assuming that the interest rate is 6% compounded monthly.

The argument used in the previous example can be used to calculate the net present value. For instance, suppose that a business requires an initial investment of $60,000, which is guaranteed to return a regular payment of $10,000 at the end of each year for the next ten years. If the discount rate is 7% compounded annually then the previous example shows that the present value is $70,235.82. The net present value of the investment is therefore

$$\$70,235.82 - \$60,000 = \$10,235.82$$

A similar procedure can be used when the payments are irregular although it is no longer possible to use the formula for the sum of a geometric progression. Instead the present value of each individual payment is calculated and the values are then summed longhand. Suppose that a small business has $20,000 to invest in one of two projects. As a result of this cash injection the projects will produce different amounts of revenue during the next few years. The firm must decide which of these two projects is likely to give the larger return. To be specific, let us suppose that the cash flows from the two projects are those listed in Table 3.4. Which of these projects would you choose? If we simply add together all of the individual receipts it appears that Project A is to be preferred since the total revenue generated from Project A is $1,000 greater than that from Project B. However, this naïve approach fails to take into account the time distribution. From Table 3.4, we see that both projects yield a single receipt of $10,000. For Project A this occurs at the end of year 3 whereas for Project B this occurs at the end of year 1. This $10,000 is worth more in Project B because it occurs earlier in the revenue stream and, once received, could be invested for longer at the prevailing rate of interest. To compare these projects we need to discount the revenue stream to the present value. The present values obtained

Table 3.4

| End of year | Revenue | |
	Project A	Project B
1	$6,000	$10,000
2	$3,000	$6,000
3	$10,000	$9,000
4	$8,000	$1,000
Total	$27,000	$26,000

depend on the discount rate. Table 3.5 shows the present values based on an assumed rate of 11% compounded annually. These values are calculated using the formula

$$P = S(1.11)^{-t}$$

For example, the present value of the $10,000 revenue in Project A is given by

$$\$10,000(1.11)^{-3} = \$7,311.91$$

The net present values for Project A and Project B are given by

$$\$20,422.67 - \$20,000 = \$422.67$$

and

$$\$21,109.19 - \$20,000 = \$1,109.19$$

respectively. Consequently, if it is only possible to invest in one of these projects, the preferred choice is Project B.

Table 3.5

	Discounted revenue	
End of year	*Project A*	*Project B*
1	$5,405.41	$9,000.01
2	$2.434.87	$4,869.73
3	$7,311.91	$6,580.72
4	$5,269.85	$658.73
Total	$20,422.04	$21,109.19

PROBLEM

5   A firm has a choice of spending $10,000 today on one of two projects. The revenue obtained from these projects is listed in Table 3.6. Assuming that the discount rate is 15% compounded annually, which of these two projects would you advise the company to invest in?

Table 3.6

	Revenue	
End of year	*Project 1*	*Project 2*
1	$2,000	$1,000
2	$2,000	$1,000
3	$3,000	$2,000
4	$3,000	$6,000
5	$3,000	$4,000

It is sometimes useful to find the internal rate of return of a project yielding a sequence of payments over time. However, as the following example demonstrates, this can be difficult to calculate, particularly when there are more than two payments.

EXAMPLE

(1) Calculate the IRR of a project which requires an initial outlay of $20,000 and produces a return of $8,000 at the end of year 1 and $15,000 at the end of year 2.
(2) Calculate the IRR of a project which requires an initial outlay of $5,000 and produces returns of $1,000, $2,000 and $3,000 at the end of years 1, 2 and 3, respectively.

Solution

(1) In the case of a single payment, the IRR is the annual rate of interest, r, which, when applied to the initial outlay, P, yields a known future payment, S. If this payment is made after t years then

$$S = P\left(1 + \frac{r}{100}\right)^t$$

or, equivalently

$$P = S\left(1 + \frac{r}{100}\right)^{-t}$$

Note that the right-hand side of this last equation is just the present value of S. Consequently, the IRR can be thought of as the rate of interest at which the present value of S equals the initial outlay P.

The present value of $8,000 in one year's time is

$$8000\left(1 + \frac{r}{100}\right)^{-1}$$

where r is the annual rate of interest. Similarly, the present value of $15,000 in two year's time is

$$15\,000\left(1 + \frac{r}{100}\right)^{-2}$$

If r is to be the IRR then the sum of these present values must equal the initial investment of $20,000. In other words the IRR is the value of r which satisfies the equation

$$20\,000 = 8000\left(1 + \frac{r}{100}\right)^{-1} + 15\,000\left(1 + \frac{r}{100}\right)^{-2}$$

The simplest way of solving this equation is to multiply both sides by $(1 + r/100)^2$ to remove all negative indices. This gives

$$20\,000\left(1 + \frac{r}{100}\right)^2 = 8000\left(1 + \frac{r}{100}\right) + 15\,000$$

$$b^m \times b^n = b^{m+n}$$
$$b^0 = 1$$

Now

$$\left(1 + \frac{r}{100}\right)^2 = \left(1 + \frac{r}{100}\right)\left(1 + \frac{r}{100}\right) = 1 + \frac{r}{50} + \frac{r^2}{10\,000}$$

so if we multiply out the brackets we obtain

$$20\,000 + 400r + 2r^2 = 8000 + 80r + 15\,000$$

Collecting like terms gives

$$2r^2 + 320r - 3000 = 0$$

This is a quadratic in r so can be solved using the formula described in Section 2.1 to get

$$r = \frac{-320 \pm \sqrt{(320)^2 - 4(2)(-3000)}}{2(2)}$$

$$= \frac{-320 \pm 355.5}{4}$$

$$= 8.9\% \text{ or } -168.9\%$$

We can obviously ignore the negative solution so can conclude that the IRR is 8.9%.

(2)   If an initial outlay of \$5,000 yields \$1,000, \$2,000 and \$3,000 at the end of years 1, 2 and 3, respectively, then the internal rate of return, r, satisfies the equation

$$5000 = 1000\left(1 + \frac{r}{100}\right)^{-1} + 2000\left(1 + \frac{r}{100}\right)^{-2} + 3000\left(1 + \frac{r}{100}\right)^{-3}$$

A sensible thing to do here might be to multiply through by $(1 + r/100)^{-3}$. However, this produces an equation involving r^3 (and lower powers of r), which is no easier to solve than the original. Indeed, a moment's thought should convince you that in general, when dealing with a sequence of payments over n years, the IRR will satisfy an equation involving r^n (and lower powers of r). Under these circumstances it is virtually impossible to obtain the exact solution. The best way of proceeding would be to use a non-linear equation solver routine on a computer, particularly if it is important that an accurate value of r is obtained. However, if all that is needed is a rough approximation then this can be done by systematic trial-and-error. We merely substitute likely solutions into the right-hand side of the equation until we find the one that works. For example, putting $r = 5$ gives

$$\frac{1000}{1.05} + \frac{2000}{(1.05)^2} + \frac{3000}{(1.05)^3} = 5358$$

Other values of the expression

$$1000\left(1 + \frac{r}{100}\right)^{-1} + 2000\left(1 + \frac{r}{100}\right)^{-2} + 3000\left(1 + \frac{r}{100}\right)^{-3}$$

corresponding to $r = 6, 7, \ldots, 10$ are listed in the following table:

r	6	7	8	9	10
value	5242	5130	5022	4917	4816

Given that we are trying to find r so that this value is 5000, this table indicates that r is somewhere between 8% (which produces a value greater than 5000) and 9% (which produces a value less than 5000).

If a more accurate estimate of IRR is required then we simply try further values between 8% and 9%. For example, it is easy to check that putting $r = 8\frac{1}{2}$ gives 4969, indicating that the exact value of r is between 8% and $8\frac{1}{2}$%. We conclude that the IRR is 8% to the nearest percentage.

∎

PROBLEM

6   A project requires an initial investment of $12,000. It has a guaranteed return of $8,000 at the end of year 1 and a return of $2,000 each year at the end of years 2, 3 and 4.

Estimate the IRR to the nearest percentage. Would you recommend that someone invests in this project if the prevailing market rate is 8% compounded annually?

We conclude this section by using the theory of discounting to explain the relationship between interest rates and the speculative demand for money. This was first introduced in Section 1.5 in the analysis of LM schedules. Speculative demand consists of money held in reserve to take advantage of changes in the value of alternative financial assets, such as government bonds. As their name suggests these issues can be bought from the government at a certain price. In return, the government pays out interest on an annual basis for a prescribed number of years. At the end of this period the bond is redeemed and the purchaser is repaid the original sum. For example, suppose the government issues a ten-year bond valued at $5,000 at 9% interest. In return for giving the government $5,000 it pays out $450 interest every year for ten years. At the end of the ten years the bond is redeemed by the government and $5,000 is paid back to the purchaser. Now these bonds can be bought and sold at any point in their lifetime. The person who buys the bond is entitled to all of the future interest payments, together with the final payment of $5,000. The value of existing securities clearly depends on the number of years remaining before redemption, together with the prevailing rate of interest which may well no longer be 9%. Let us suppose that there are just four years left between now and the date of redemption. The future cash flow that is paid on the bond is summarized in the second column of Table 3.7. This is similar to that of an annuity except that in the final year an extra payment of $5,000 is received when the government pays back the original investment. The present value of this income stream is calculated in Table 3.7 using a variety of discount rates ranging from 5% to 13% compounded annually.

Table 3.7

		Present values				
End of year	*Cash flow*	*5%*	*7%*	*9%*	*11%*	*13%*
1	450	429	421	413	405	398
2	450	408	393	379	365	352
3	450	389	367	347	329	312
4	5450	4484	4158	3861	3590	3343
Total present value		5710	5339	5000	4689	4405

The important point to notice from this table is that the value of the bond falls as interest rates rise. This is entirely to be expected since the formula we use to calculate individual present values is

$$P = \frac{S}{(1 + r/100)^t}$$

and larger values of r produce smaller values of P. The effect of this relationship on financial markets can now be analysed. Let us suppose that the interest rate is high at, say, 13%. As you can see from Table 3.7, the price of the bond is relatively low. Moreover, one might reasonably expect that, in the future, interest rates are likely to fall, thereby increasing the present value of the bond. In this situation an investor would be encouraged to buy this bond in the expectation of not only receiving the cash flow from holding the bond, but also receiving a capital gain on its present value. Speculative balances therefore decrease as a result of high interest rates because money is converted into securities. Exactly the opposite happens when interest rates are low. The corresponding present value is relatively high, and, with an expectation of a rise in interest rates and a possible capital loss, investors are reluctant to invest in securities so speculative balances are high.

PROBLEM

7   A ten-year bond is originally offered by the government at $1,000 with an annual return of 7%. Assuming that the bond currently has three years left before redemption and that the prevailing interest rate is 8% compounded annually, calculate its present value.

PRACTICE PROBLEMS

8   Determine the present value of $7,000 in two years' time if the discount rate is 8% compounded

(a) quarterly
(b) continuously

9   A small business promises a profit of $8,000 on an initial investment of $20,000 after five years.

(1) Calculate the internal rate of return.
(2) Would you advise someone to invest in this business if the market rate is 6% compounded annually?

10 You are given the opportunity of investing in one of three projects. Projects A, B and C require initial outlays of $20,000, $30,000 and $100,000 and are guaranteed to return $25,000, $37,000 and $117,000, respectively, in three years' time. Which of these projects would you invest in if the market rate is 5% compounded annually?

11 Determine the present value of an annuity which pays out $100 at the end of each year

(a) for five years
(b) in perpetuity

if the interest rate is 10% compounded annually.

12 A firm decides to invest in a new piece of machinery which is expected to produce an additional revenue of $8,000 at the end of every year for ten years. At the end of this period the firm plans to sell the machinery for scrap for which it expects to receive $5,000. What is the maximum amount that the firm should pay for the machine if it is not to suffer a net loss as a result of this investment? You may assume that the discount rate is 6% compounded annually.

13 During the next three years a business decides to invest $10,000 at the *beginning* of each year. The corresponding revenue that it can expect to receive at the *end* of each year is given in Table 3.8. Calculate the net present value if the discount rate is 4% compounded annually.

Table 3.8

End of year	Revenue
1	$5,000
2	$20,000
3	$50,000

14 A project requires an initial investment of $50,000. It produces a return of $40,000 at the end of year 1 and $30,000 at the end of year 2. Find the exact value of the internal rate of return.

15 A government bond which originally cost $500 with a yield of 6% has five years left before redemption. Determine its present value if the prevailing rate of interest is 15%.

4 *Differentiation*

This chapter provides a simple introduction to the general topic of calculus. In fact, 'calculus' is a Latin word and a literal translation of it is 'stone'. Unfortunately, all too many students interpret this as meaning a heavy millstone that they have to carry around with them! However, as we shall see, the techniques of calculus actually provide us with a quick way of performing calculations. (The process of counting was originally performed using stones a long time ago.)

There are eight sections which should be read in the order that they appear. It should be possible to omit Sections 4.5 and 4.7 at a first reading and Section 4.6 can be read any time after Section 4.3.

Section 4.1 provides a leisurely introduction to the basic idea of differentiation. The material is explained using pictures which will help you to understand the connection between the underlying mathematics and the economic applications in later sections.

There are six rules of differentiation which are evenly split between Sections 4.2 and 4.4. Section 4.2 considers the easy rules which all students will need to know. However, if you are on a business studies or accountancy course, or are on a low level economics route, then the more advanced rules in Section 4.4 may not be of interest and could be ignored. As far as possible, examples given in later sections and chapters are based on the easy rules only so that such students are not disadvantaged. However, the more advanced rules are essential to any proper study of mathematical economics and their use in deriving general results is unavoidable.

Sections 4.3 and 4.5 describe standard economic applications. Marginal functions associated with revenue, cost, production, consumption and savings functions are all discussed in Section 4.3. The important topic of elasticity is described in Section 4.5. The distinction is made between price elasticity along an arc and price elasticity at a point. Familiar results involving general linear demand functions and the relationship between price elasticity of demand and revenue are derived.

Sections 4.6 and 4.7 are devoted to the topic of optimization which is used to find the maximum and minimum values of economic functions. In the first half of Section 4.6 we concentrate on the mathematical technique. The second half contains four examination-type problems, all taken from economics, which are solved in detail. In Section 4.7, mathematics is used to derive general results relating to the optimization of profit and production functions.

The final section considers two important mathematical functions, namely the exponential and natural logarithm functions. We describe how to differentiate these functions and illustrate their use in economic modelling.

This is probably the most important topic in the whole book, and one that we shall continue in Chapters 5 and 6, since it provides the necessary background theory for much of mathematical economics. You are therefore advised to make every effort to attempt the problems given in each section. The prerequisites include an understanding of the concept of a function together with the ability to manipulate algebraic expressions. These are covered in Chapters 1 and 2 and, if you have worked successfully through this material, you should find that you are in good shape to begin calculus.

4.1   The derivative of a function

Objectives   At the end of this section you should be able to:

● find the slope of a straight line given any two points on the line,

● detect whether a line is uphill, downhill or horizontal using the sign of the slope,

● recognize the notation $f'(x)$ and dy/dx for the derivative of a function,

● estimate the derivative of a function by measuring the slope of a tangent,

● differentiate power functions.

This introductory section is designed to get you started with differential calculus in a fairly painless way. There are really only three things that we are going to do. We discuss the basic idea of something called a derived function, give you two equivalent pieces of notation to describe it and finally show you how to write down a formula for the derived function in simple cases.

In Chapter 1 the slope of a straight line was defined to be the change in the value of y brought about by a one unit increase in x. In fact, it is not necessary to restrict the change in x to a one unit increase. More generally, the **slope**, or **gradient**, of a line is taken to be the change in y divided by the corresponding change in x as you move between any two points on the line. It is customary to denote the change in y by Δy where Δ is the Greek letter delta.

Likewise, the change in x is written Δx. In this notation we have

$$\text{slope} = \frac{\Delta y}{\Delta x}$$

EXAMPLE

Find the slope of the straight line passing through

(a) A (1, 2) and B (3, 4)
(b) A (1, 2) and C (4, 1)
(c) A (1, 2) and D (5, 2)

Solution

(a) Points A and B are sketched in Figure 4.1. As we move from A to B the y coordinate changes from 2 to 4 which is an increase of 2 units, and the x coordinate changes from 1 to 3 which is also an increase of 2 units. Hence

$$\text{slope} = \frac{\Delta y}{\Delta x} = \frac{4-2}{3-1} = \frac{2}{2} = 1$$

(b) Points A and C are sketched in Figure 4.2. As we move from A to C the y coordinate changes from 2 to 1 which is a decrease of 1 unit, and the x coordinate changes from 1 to 4 which is an increase of 3 units. Hence

$$\text{slope} = \frac{\Delta y}{\Delta x} = \frac{1-2}{4-1} = \frac{-1}{3}$$

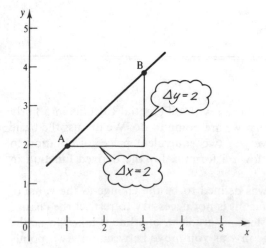

Figure 4.1

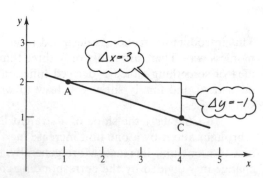

Figure 4.2

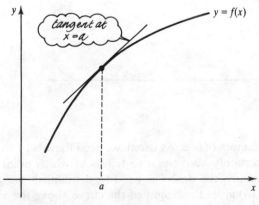

Figure 4.3

(c)   Points A and D are sketched in Figure 4.3. As we move from A to D the y coordinate remains fixed at 2, and the x coordinate changes from 1 to 5 which is an increase of 4 units. Hence

$$\text{slope} = \frac{\Delta y}{\Delta x} = \frac{2 - 2}{5 - 1} = \frac{0}{4} = 0$$

■

PROBLEM

1   Find the slope of the straight line passing through

  (a) E $(-1, 3)$ and F $(3, 11)$ **(b)** E $(-1, 3)$ and G $(4, -2)$ **(c)** E $(-1, 3)$ and H $(49, 3)$

From these examples we see that the gradient is positive if the line is uphill, negative if the line is downhill and zero if the line is horizontal.

Unfortunately, not all functions in economics are linear so it is necessary to extend the definition of slope to include more general curves. To do this we need the idea of a tangent which is illustrated in Figure 4.4.

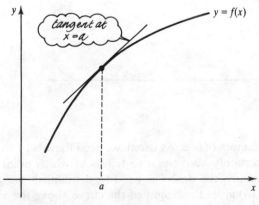

Figure 4.4

A straight line which passes through a point on a curve and which just touches the curve at this point is called a **tangent**. The slope, or gradient, of a curve at $x = a$ is then defined to be that of the tangent at $x = a$. Since we have already seen how to find the slope of a straight line this gives us a precise way of measuring the slope of a curve. A simple curve together with a selection of tangents at various points is shown in Figure 4.5. Notice how each tangent passes through exactly one point on the curve and strikes a glancing blow. In this case, the slopes of the tangents increase as we move from left to right along the curve. This reflects the fact that the curve is flat at $x = 0$ but becomes progressively steeper further away.

This highlights an important difference between the slope of a straight line and the slope of a curve. In the case of a straight line the gradient is fixed throughout its length and it is immaterial which two points on a line are used to find it. For example, in Figure 4.6 all of the ratios $\Delta y / \Delta x$ have the value 1/2. However, as we have just seen, the slope of a curve varies as we move along it. In mathematics we use the symbol

$$f'(a) \qquad \text{read 'f dashed of a'}$$

to represent the slope of the graph of a function f at $x = a$. This notation conveys the maximum

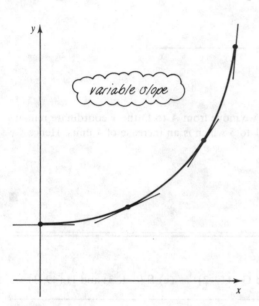

Figure 4.5

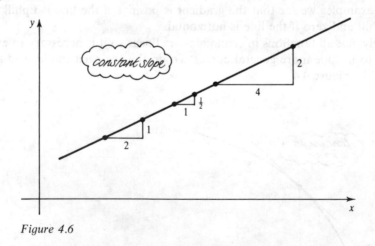

Figure 4.6

amount of information with the minimum of fuss. As usual, we need the label f to denote which function we are considering. We certainly need the a to tell us at which point on the curve the gradient is being measured. Finally, the dash ' is used to distinguish the gradient from the function value. The notation $f(a)$ gives the height of the curve above the x axis at $x = a$ whereas $f'(a)$ gives the gradient of the curve at this point.

The slope of the graph of a function is called the **derivative** of the function. It is interesting to notice that corresponding to each value of x there is a uniquely defined derivative $f'(x)$. In other words, the rule 'find the slope of the graph of f at x' defines a function. This slope function is usually referred to as the **derived function**. An alternative notation for the derived function is

$$\frac{dy}{dx}$$

read 'dee y by dee x'

Historically, this symbol arose from the corresponding notation $\Delta y / \Delta x$ for the gradient of a straight line; the letter d is the English equivalent of the Greek letter Δ. However, it is important to realize that

$$\frac{dy}{dx}$$

does not mean 'dy divided by dx'. It should be thought of as a single symbol representing the derivative of y with respect to x. It is immaterial which notation is used although the context may well suggest which is more appropriate. For example, if we use

$$y = x^2$$

to identify the square function then it is natural to use

$$\frac{dy}{dx}$$

for the derived function. On the other hand, if we use

$$f(x) = x^2$$

then $f'(x)$ seems more appropriate.

EXAMPLE

Complete the following table of function values and hence sketch an accurate graph of $f(x) = x^2$.

x	-2.0	-1.5	-1.0	-0.5	0.0	0.5	1.0	1.5	2.0
$f(x)$									

Draw the tangents to the graph at $x = -1.5$, -0.5, 0, 0.5 and 1.5. Hence estimate the values of $f'(-1.5)$, $f'(-0.5)$, $f'(0)$, $f'(0.5)$ and $f'(1.5)$.

Solution

Using a calculator we obtain

x	-2.0	-1.5	-1.0	-0.5	0.0	0.5	1.0	1.5	2.0
$f(x)$	4	2.25	1	0.25	0	0.25	1	2.25	4

The corresponding graph of the square function is sketched in Figure 4.7. From the graph we see that

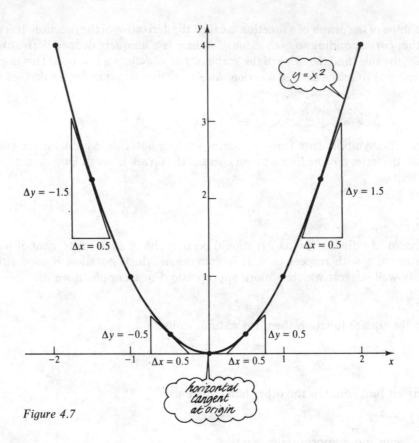

Figure 4.7

the slopes of the tangents are

$$f'(-1.5) = \frac{-1.5}{0.5} = -3$$

$$f'(-0.5) = \frac{-0.5}{0.5} = -1$$

$$f'(0) = 0$$

$$f'(0.5) = \frac{0.5}{0.5} = 1$$

$$f'(1.5) = \frac{1.5}{0.5} = 3$$

The value of $f'(0)$ is zero because the tangent is horizontal at $x = 0$. Notice that

$$f'(-1.5) = -f'(1.5) \qquad \text{and} \qquad f'(-0.5) = -f'(0.5)$$

This is to be expected because the graph is symmetric about the y axis. The slopes of the tangents to the left of the y axis have the same size as those of the corresponding tangents to the right. However, they have opposite signs since the curve slopes downhill on one side and uphill on the other.

■

PROBLEM

2 Complete the following table of function values and hence sketch an accurate graph of $f(x) = x^3$.

x	-1.50	-1.25	-1.00	-0.75	-0.50	-0.25	0.00
$f(x)$		-1.95			-0.13		
x	0.25	0.50	0.75	1.00	1.25	1.50	
$f(x)$		0.13			1.95		

Draw the tangents to the graph at $x = -1, 0$ and 1. Hence estimate the values of $f'(-1)$, $f'(0)$ and $f'(1)$.

Problem 2 should convince you how hard it is in practice to calculate $f'(a)$ exactly using graphs. It is impossible to sketch a perfectly smooth curve using graph paper and pencil, and it is equally difficult to judge, by eye, precisely where the tangent should be. There is also the problem of measuring the vertical and horizontal distances required for the slope of the tangent. These inherent errors may compound to produce quite inaccurate values for $f'(a)$. Fortunately, there is a really simple formula that can be used to find $f'(a)$ when f is a power function. It can be proved that

$$\text{if } f(x) = x^n \qquad \text{then} \qquad f'(x) = nx^{n-1}$$

or, equivalently,

$$\text{if } y = x^n \qquad \text{then} \qquad \frac{dy}{dx} = nx^{n-1}$$

The process of finding the derived function symbolically (rather than using graphs) is known as **differentiation**. In order to differentiate x^n all that needs to be done is to bring the power down to the front and then to subtract one from the power:

x^n differentiates to nx^{n-1}

bring down the power

subtract one from the power

To differentiate the square function we set $n = 2$ in this formula to deduce that

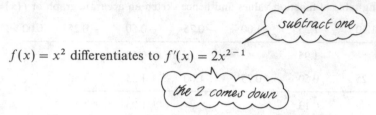

$f(x) = x^2$ differentiates to $f'(x) = 2x^{2-1}$

that is

$$f'(x) = 2x^1 = 2x$$

Using this result we see that

$$f'(-1.5) = 2 \times (-1.5) = -3$$
$$f'(-0.5) = 2 \times (-0.5) = -1$$
$$f'(0) = 2 \times (0) = 0$$
$$f'(0.5) = 2 \times (0.5) = 1$$
$$f'(1.5) = 2 \times (1.5) = 3$$

which are in agreement with the results obtained graphically in the preceding example.

PROBLEM

3   If $f(x) = x^3$ write down a formula for $f'(x)$. Calculate $f'(-1)$, $f'(0)$ and $f'(1)$. Confirm that these are in agreement with your rough estimates obtained in Problem 2.

EXAMPLE

Differentiate

(a) $y = x^4$
(b) $y = x^{10}$
(c) $y = x$
(d) $y = 1$
(e) $y = 1/x^4$
(f) $y = \sqrt{x}$

Solution

(a)   To differentiate $y = x^4$ we bring down the power (that is, 4) to the front and then subtract one from the power (that is, $4 - 1 = 3$) to deduce that

$$\frac{dy}{dx} = 4x^3$$

(b)   Similarly, if

$$y = x^{10} \qquad \text{then} \qquad \frac{dy}{dx} = 10x^9$$

(c)   To use the general formula to differentiate x we first need to express $y = x$ in the form $y = x^n$ for some number n. In this case $n = 1$ because $x^1 = x$ so

$$\frac{dy}{dx} = 1x^0 = 1 \qquad \text{since} \qquad x^0 = 1$$

This result is also obvious from the graph of $y = x$ sketched in Figure 4.8.

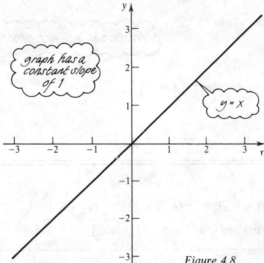

Figure 4.8

(d)   Again, to differentiate 1 we need to express $y = 1$ in the form $y = x^n$. In this case $n = 0$ because $x^0 = 1$ so

$$\frac{dy}{dx} = 0x^{-1} = 0$$

This result is also obvious from the graph of $y = 1$ sketched in Figure 4.9.

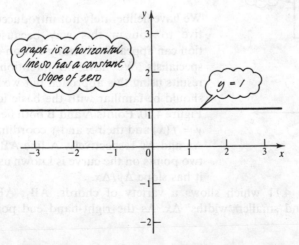

(e) Noting that $1/x^4 = x^{-4}$ it follows that if

$$y = \frac{1}{x^4} \qquad \text{then} \qquad \frac{dy}{dx} = -4x^{-5} = -\frac{4}{x^5}$$

The power has decreased to -5 because $-4 - 1 = -5$.

(f) Noting that $\sqrt{x} = x^{1/2}$ it follows that if

$$y = \sqrt{x} \qquad \text{then} \qquad \frac{dy}{dx} = \frac{1}{2}x^{-1/2}$$

$$= \frac{1}{2x^{1/2}}$$

$$= \frac{1}{2\sqrt{x}}$$

negative powers denote reciprocals

fractional powers denote roots

The power has decreased to $-\frac{1}{2}$ because $\frac{1}{2} - 1 = -\frac{1}{2}$. ∎

PROBLEM

4 Differentiate

(a) $y = x^5$ **(b)** $y = x^6$ **(c)** $y = x^{100}$ **(d)** $y = 1/x$ **(e)** $y = 1/x^2$

[Hint: in parts (d) and (e) note that $1/x = x^{-1}$ and $1/x^2 = x^{-2}$.]

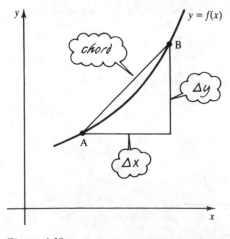

Figure 4.10

In more advanced books on mathematics the derivative is defined via the concept of a limit and is usually written in symbols as

$$\frac{dy}{dx} = \lim_{\Delta x \to 0} \frac{\Delta y}{\Delta x}$$

We have deliberately not introduced the derivative to you in this way because the notation can appear frightening to non-mathematics specialists. We have no intention of proving results using this approach but we feel that you should be familiar with the basic idea. Look at Figure 4.10. Points A and B both lie on the curve $y = f(x)$ and their x and y coordinates differ by Δx and Δy respectively. A line AB which joins two points on the curve is known as a **chord** and it has slope $\Delta y / \Delta x$.

Now look at Figure 4.11 which shows a variety of chords, AB_1, AB_2, $AB_3,\ldots$, corresponding to smaller and smaller 'widths' Δx. As the right-hand end points, B_1, B_2,

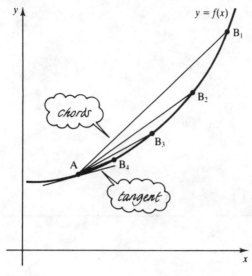

Figure 4.11

$B_3, \ldots,$ get closer to A the 'width', Δx, tends to zero. More significantly, the slope of the chord gets closer to that of the tangent at A. We describe this by saying that in the limit, as Δx tends to zero, the slope of the chord, $\Delta y / \Delta x$, is equal to that of the tangent. This limit is written

$$\lim_{\Delta x \to 0} \frac{\Delta y}{\Delta x}$$

We deduce that the formal definition

$$\frac{dy}{dx} = \lim_{\Delta x \to 0} \frac{\Delta y}{\Delta x}$$

coincides with the idea that dy/dx represents the slope of the tangent which is the approach adopted in this book.

PRACTICE PROBLEMS

5   Verify that the points $(0, 2)$ and $(3, 0)$ lie on the line

$$2x + 3y = 6$$

Hence find the slope of this line. Is the line uphill, downhill or horizontal?

6   Verify that the points $(0, b)$ and $(1, a + b)$ lie on the line

$$y = ax + b$$

Hence show that this line has slope a.

7   Sketch the graph of the function

$$f(x) = 5$$

Explain why it follows from this that

$$f'(x) = 0$$

8 Differentiate the function

$$f(x) = x^7$$

Hence calculate the slope of the graph of

$$y = x^7$$

at the point $x = 2$.

9 Differentiate

(a) $y = x^8$ **(b)** $y = x^{50}$ **(c)** $y = 1/x^3$ **(d)** $y = x^{1/3}$

4.2 Rules of differentiation

Objectives   At the end of this section you should be able to:

- use the constant rule to differentiate a function of the form $cf(x)$,

- use the sum rule to differentiate a function of the form $f(x) + g(x)$,

- use the difference rule to differentiate a function of the form $f(x) - g(x)$,

- evaluate second-order derivatives.

In this section we consider three elementary rules of differentiation. Subsequent sections of this chapter describe various applications to economics. However, before you can tackle these successfully, you must have a thorough grasp of the basic techniques involved. The problems in this section are repetitive in nature. This is deliberate. Although the rules themselves are straightforward it is necessary for you to practise them over and over again before you can become proficient in using them. In fact, you will not be able to get much farther with the rest of this book until you have mastered the rules of this section.

Rule 1: The Constant Rule

If

$$h(x) = cf(x) \qquad \text{then} \qquad h'(x) = cf'(x)$$

for any constant c.

This rule tells you how to find the derivative of a constant multiple of a function:

$$\boxed{\text{differentiate the function and multiply by the constant}}$$

EXAMPLE

Differentiate

(a) $y = 2x^4$
(b) $y = 10x$

Solution

(a) To differentiate $2x^4$ we first differentiate x^4 to get $4x^3$ and then multiply by 2. Hence if

$$y = 2x^4 \qquad \text{then} \qquad \frac{dy}{dx} = 2(4x^3) = 8x^3$$

(b) To differentiate $10x$ we first differentiate x to get 1 and then multiply by 10. Hence if

$$y = 10x \qquad \text{then} \qquad \frac{dy}{dx} = 10(1) = 10$$

∎

PROBLEM

1 Differentiate

(a) $y = 4x^3$ **(b)** $y = 2/x$

This rule can be used to show that

$$\boxed{\text{constants differentiate to zero}}$$

To see this note that the equation

$$y = c$$

is the same as

$$y = cx^0$$

because $x^0 = 1$. By the constant rule we first differentiate x^0 to get $0x^{-1}$ and then multiply by c. Hence if

$$y = c \qquad \text{then} \qquad \frac{dy}{dx} = c(0x^{-1}) = 0$$

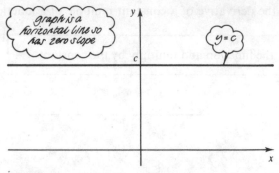

Figure 4.12

This result is also apparent from the graph of $y = c$, sketched in Figure 4.12, which is a horizontal line c units away from the x axis. It is an important result and explains why lone constants lurking in mathematical expressions disappear when differentiated.

Rule 2: The Sum Rule

If

$$h(x) = f(x) + g(x) \quad \text{then} \quad h'(x) = f'(x) + g'(x)$$

This rule tells you how to find the derivative of the sum of two functions:

> differentiate each function separately and add

EXAMPLE

Differentiate

(a) $y = x^2 + x^{50}$

(b) $y = x^3 + 3$

Solution

(a) To differentiate $x^2 + x^{50}$ we need to differentiate x^2 and x^{50} separately and to add. Now

x^2 differentiates to $2x$

and

x^{50} differentiates to $50x^{49}$

so if

$$y = x^2 + x^{50} \quad \text{then} \quad \frac{dy}{dx} = 2x + 50x^{49}$$

(b)   To differentiate $x^3 + 3$ we need to differentiate x^3 and 3 separately and to add. Now

x^3 differentiates to $3x^2$

and

3 differentiates to 0

so if

$$y = x^3 + 3 \qquad \text{then} \qquad \frac{dy}{dx} = 3x^2 + 0 = 3x^2$$

constants differentiate to zero

∎

PROBLEM

2   Differentiate

(a) $y = x^5 + x$ (b) $y = x^2 + 5$

Rule 3: The Difference Rule

If

$$h(x) = f(x) - g(x) \qquad \text{then} \qquad h'(x) = f'(x) - g'(x)$$

This rule tells you how to find the derivative of the difference of two functions:

differentiate each function separately and subtract

EXAMPLE

Differentiate

(a) $y = x^5 - x^2$

(b) $y = x - \dfrac{1}{x^2}$

Solution

(a)   To differentiate $x^5 - x^2$ we need to differentiate x^5 and x^2 separately and to subtract. Now

x^5 differentiates to $5x^4$

and

x^2 differentiates to $2x$

so if

$$y = x^5 - x^2 \qquad \text{then} \qquad \frac{dy}{dx} = 5x^4 - 2x$$

(b) To differentiate $x - 1/x^2$ we need to differentiate x and $1/x^2$ separately and subtract. Now

x differentiates to 1

and

$\dfrac{1}{x^2}$ differentiates to $-\dfrac{2}{x^3}$

so if

$$y = x - \frac{1}{x^2} \qquad \text{then} \qquad \frac{dy}{dx} = 1 - \left(-\frac{2}{x^3}\right) = 1 + \frac{2}{x^3}$$

PROBLEM

3 Differentiate

    (a) $y = x^2 - x^3$ **(b)** $y = 50 - \dfrac{1}{x^3}$

It is possible to combine these three rules and so to find the derivative of more involved functions as the following example demonstrates.

EXAMPLE

Differentiate

(a) $y = 3x^5 + 2x^3$
(b) $y = x^3 + 7x^2 - 2x + 10$
(c) $y = 2\sqrt{x} + \dfrac{3}{x}$

Solution

(a) The sum rule shows that to differentiate $3x^5 + 2x^3$ we need to differentiate $3x^5$ and $2x^3$ separately and to add. By the constant rule

$3x^5$ differentiates to $3(5x^4) = 15x^4$

and

$2x^3$ differentiates to $2(3x^2) = 6x^2$

so if

$$y = 3x^5 + 2x^3 \qquad \text{then} \qquad \frac{dy}{dx} = 15x^4 + 6x^2$$

With practice you will soon find that you can just write the derivative down in a single line of working by differentiating term by term. For the function

$$y = 3x^5 + 2x^3$$

we could just write

$$\frac{dy}{dx} = 3(5x^4) + 2(3x^2) = 15x^4 + 6x^2$$

(b) So far we have only considered expressions comprising at most two terms. However, the sum and difference rules still apply to lengthier expressions so we can differentiate term by term as before. For the function

$$y = x^3 + 7x^2 - 2x + 10$$

we get

$$\frac{dy}{dx} = 3x^2 + 7(2x) - 2(1) + 0 = 3x^2 + 14x - 2$$

(c) To differentiate

$$y = 2\sqrt{x} + \frac{3}{x}$$

we first rewrite it using the notation of indices as

$$y = 2x^{1/2} + 3x^{-1}$$

Differentiating term by term then gives

$$\frac{dy}{dx} = 2\left(\frac{1}{2}\right)x^{-1/2} + 3(-1)x^{-2} = x^{-1/2} - 3x^{-2}$$

which can be written in the more familiar form

$$= \frac{1}{\sqrt{x}} - \frac{3}{x^2}$$

■

PROBLEM

4 Differentiate

(a) $y = 9x^5 + 2x^2$ **(b)** $y = 5x^8 - \dfrac{3}{x}$

(c) $y = x^2 + 6x + 3$ **(d)** $y = 2x^4 + 12x^3 - 4x^2 + 7x - 400$

Whenever a function is differentiated the thing that you end up with is itself a function. This suggests the possibility of differentiating a second time to get the 'slope of the slope function'. This is written as

$$f''(x)$$

read 'f double dashed of x'

or

$$\frac{\mathrm{d}^2 y}{\mathrm{d}x^2}$$

read 'dee two y by dee x squared'

For example, if

$$f(x) = 5x^2 - 7x + 12$$

then differentiating once gives

$$f'(x) = 10x - 7$$

and if we now differentiate $f'(x)$ we get

$$f''(x) = 10$$

The function $f'(x)$ is called the **first-order derivative** and $f''(x)$ is called the **second-order derivative**.

EXAMPLE

Evaluate $f''(1)$ where

$$f(x) = x^7 + \frac{1}{x}$$

Solution

To find $f''(1)$ we need to differentiate

$$f(x) = x^7 + x^{-1}$$

twice and to put $x = 1$ into the end result. Differentiating once gives

$$f'(x) = 7x^6 + (-1)x^{-2} = 7x^6 - x^{-2}$$

and differentiating a second time gives

$$f''(x) = 7(6x^5) - (-2)x^{-3} = 42x^5 + 2x^{-3}$$

Finally, substituting $x = 1$ into

$$f''(x) = 42x^5 + \frac{2}{x^3}$$

gives

$$f''(1) = 42 + 2 = 44$$

■

PROBLEM

5   Evaluate $f''(6)$ where

$$f(x) = 4x^3 - 5x^2$$

Throughout this section the functions have all been of the form $y = f(x)$ where the letters x and y denote the variables involved. In economic functions different symbols are used. It should be obvious, however, that we can still differentiate such functions by applying the rules of this section. For example, if a supply function is given by

$$Q = P^2 + 3P + 1$$

and we need to find the derivative of Q with respect to P then we can apply the sum and difference rules to obtain

$$\frac{dQ}{dP} = 2P + 3$$

Differentiation is a purely mechanical process which depends on the layout of the function and not on the labels used to identify the variables. Problem 8 contains some additional examples involving a variety of symbols. It is designed to boost your confidence before you work through the applications described in the next section.

PRACTICE PROBLEMS

6 Differentiate

(a) $y = 5x^2$

(b) $y = \dfrac{3}{x}$

(c) $y = 2x + 3$

(d) $y = x^2 + x + 1$

(e) $y = x^2 - 3x + 2$

(f) $y = 3x - \dfrac{7}{x}$

(g) $y = 2x^3 - 6x^2 + 49x - 54$

(h) $y = ax + b$

(i) $y = ax^2 + bx + c$

(j) $y = 4\sqrt{x} - \dfrac{3}{x} + \dfrac{7}{x^2}$

7 Find expressions for d^2y/dx^2 in the case when

(a) $y = 7x^2 - x$

(b) $y = \dfrac{1}{x^2}$

(c) $y = ax + b$

8 Find expressions for

(a) $\dfrac{dQ}{dP}$ for the supply function $Q = P^2 + P + 1$

(b) $\dfrac{d(TR)}{dQ}$ for the total revenue function $TR = 50Q - 3Q^2$

(c) $\dfrac{d(AC)}{dQ}$ for the average cost function $AC = \dfrac{30}{Q} + 10$

(d) $\dfrac{dC}{dY}$ for the consumption function $C = 3Y + 7$

(e) $\dfrac{dQ}{dL}$ for the production function $Q = 10\sqrt{L}$

(f) $\dfrac{d\pi}{dQ}$ for the profit function $\pi = -2Q^3 + 15Q^2 - 24Q - 3$

4.3 Marginal functions

Objectives At the end of this section you should be able to:

- calculate marginal revenue and marginal cost,

- derive the relationship between marginal and average revenue for both a monopoly and perfect competition,

- calculate marginal product of labour,

- state the law of diminishing marginal productivity using the notation of calculus,

- calculate marginal propensity to consume and marginal propensity to save.

At this stage you may be wondering what on earth differentiation has got to do with economics. In fact, we cannot get very far with economic theory without making use of calculus. In this section we concentrate on three main areas which illustrate its applicability:

(1)   Revenue and cost
(2)   Production
(3)   Consumption and savings.

We consider each of these in turn.

4.3.1   Revenue and cost

In Chapter 2 we investigated the basic properties of the revenue function, TR. It is defined to be PQ, where P denotes the price of a good and Q denotes the quantity demanded. In practice, we usually know the demand equation which provides a relationship between P and Q. This enables a formula for TR to be written down solely in terms of Q. For example, if

$$P = 100 - 2Q$$

then

$$TR = PQ$$
$$= (100 - 2Q)Q$$
$$= 100Q - 2Q^2$$

The formula can be used to calculate the value of TR corresponding to any value of Q. Not content with this, we are also interested in the effect on TR of a change in the value of Q

from some existing level. To do this we introduce the concept of marginal revenue. The **marginal revenue**, MR, of a good is defined by

$$MR = \frac{d(TR)}{dQ}$$

> marginal revenue is the derivative of total revenue
> with respect to demand

For example, the marginal revenue function corresponding to

$$TR = 100Q - 2Q^2$$

is given by

$$\frac{d(TR)}{dQ} = 100 - 4Q$$

If the current demand is 15, say, then

$$MR = 100 - 4(15) = 40$$

You may be familiar with an alternative definition often quoted in elementary economics textbooks. Marginal revenue is sometimes taken to be the change in TR brought about by a one unit increase in Q. It is easy to check that this gives an acceptable approximation to MR although it is not quite the same as the exact value obtained by differentiation. For example, substituting $Q = 15$ into the total revenue function considered previously gives

$$TR = 100(15) - 2(15)^2 = 1050$$

An increase of one unit in the value of Q produces a total revenue

$$TR = 100(16) - 2(16)^2 = 1088$$

This is an increase of 38 which, according to the non-calculus definition, is the value of MR when Q is 15. This compares with the exact value of 40 obtained by differentiation.

It is instructive to give a graphical interpretation of these two approaches. In Figure 4.13 the point A lies on the TR curve corresponding to a quantity Q_0. The exact value of MR at this point is equal to the derivative

$$\frac{d(TR)}{dQ}$$

and so is given by the slope of the tangent at A. The point B also lies on the curve but corresponds to a one unit increase in Q. The vertical distance from A to B therefore equals the change in TR when Q increases by one unit. The slope of the chord joining A and B is

$$\frac{\Delta(TR)}{\Delta Q} = \frac{\Delta(TR)}{1} = \Delta(TR)$$

In other words, the slope of the chord is equal to the value of MR obtained from the

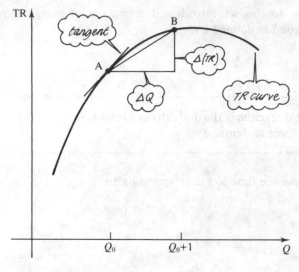

Figure 4.13

non-calculus definition. Inspection of the diagram reveals that the slope of the tangent is approximately the same as that of the chord joining A and B. In this case the slope of the tangent is slightly the larger of the two but there is not much in it. We therefore see that the one-unit-increase approach produces a reasonable approximation to the exact value of MR given by

$$\frac{d(TR)}{dQ}$$

PROBLEM

1   If the demand function is

$$P = 60 - Q$$

find an expression for TR in terms of Q.

(1)   Differentiate TR with respect to Q to find a general expression for MR in terms of Q. Hence write down the exact value of MR at $Q = 50$.

(2)   Calculate the value of TR when

(a) $Q = 50$ (b) $Q = 51$

and hence confirm that the one-unit-increase approach gives a reasonable approximation to the exact value of MR obtained in part (1).

The approximation indicated by Figure 4.13 holds for any value of ΔQ. The slope of the tangent at A is the marginal revenue, MR. The slope of the chord joining A and B is

$\Delta(TR)/\Delta Q$. It follows that

$$MR \simeq \frac{\Delta(TR)}{\Delta Q}$$

This equation can be transposed to give

$$\Delta(TR) \simeq MR \times \Delta Q$$

multiply both sides by ΔQ

that is

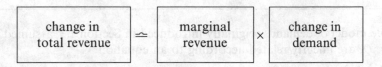

| change in total revenue | $\simeq$ | marginal revenue | $\times$ | change in demand |

Moreover, Figure 4.13 shows that the smaller the value of ΔQ the better the approximation becomes. This, of course, is similar to the argument used at the end of Section 4.1 when we discussed the formal definition of a derivative as a limit.

EXAMPLE

If the total revenue function of a good is given by

$$100Q - Q^2$$

write down an expression for the marginal revenue function. If the current demand is 60 estimate the change in the value of TR due to a two unit increase in Q.

Solution

If

$$TR = 100Q - Q^2$$

then

$$MR = \frac{d(TR)}{dQ}$$

$$= 100 - 2Q$$

When $Q = 60$

$$MR = 100 - 2(60) = -20$$

If Q increases by two units, $\Delta Q = 2$ and the formula

$$\Delta(TR) \simeq MR \times \Delta Q$$

shows that the change in total revenue is approximately

$$(-20) \times 2 = -40$$

A two unit increase in Q therefore leads to a decrease in TR of about 40.

■

PROBLEM

2 If the total revenue function of a good is given by

$$1000Q - 4Q^2$$

write down an expression for the marginal revenue function. If the current demand is 30, find the approximate change in the value of TR due to a

(1) three unit increase in Q

(2) two unit decrease in Q

The simple model of demand, originally introduced in Section 1.3, assumed that price, P, and quantity, Q, are linearly related according to an equation

$$P = aQ + b$$

where the slope, a, is negative and the intercept, b, is positive. A downward sloping demand curve such as this corresponds to the case of a **monopolist**. A single firm, or possibly a group of firms forming a cartel, is assumed to be the only supplier of a particular product and so has control over the market price. As the firm raises the price so demand falls. The associated total revenue function is given by

$$TR = PQ$$

$$= (aQ + b)Q$$

$$= aQ^2 + bQ$$

An expression for marginal revenue is obtained by differentiating TR with respect to Q to get

$$MR = 2aQ + b$$

It is interesting to notice that, on the assumption of a linear demand equation, the marginal revenue is also linear with the same intercept, b, but with slope $2a$. The marginal revenue curve slopes downhill exactly twice as fast as the demand curve. This is illustrated in Figure 4.14(a).

The **average revenue**, AR, is defined by

$$AR = \frac{TR}{Q}$$

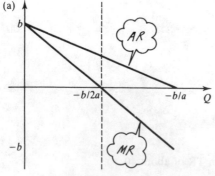

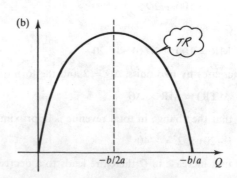

Figure 4.14

and, since TR $= PQ$, we have

$$AR = \frac{PQ}{Q} = P$$

For this reason the demand curve is labelled average revenue in Figure 4.14(a). The above derivation of the result AR $= P$ is independent of the particular demand function. Consequently, the terms average revenue curve and demand curve are synonymous.

Figure 4.14(a) shows that the marginal revenue takes both positive and negative values. This is to be expected. The total revenue function is a quadratic and its graph has the familiar parabolic shape indicated in Figure 4.14(b). To the left of $-b/2a$ the graph is uphill, corresponding to a positive value of marginal revenue, whereas to the right of this point it is downhill, giving a negative value of marginal revenue. More significantly, at the maximum point of the TR curve, the tangent is horizontal with zero slope and so MR is zero.

At the other extreme from a monopolist is the case of **perfect competition**. For this model we assume that there are a large number of firms all selling an identical product and that there are no barriers to entry into the industry. Since any individual firm produces a tiny proportion of the total output it has no control over price. The firm can sell only at the prevailing market price and, because the firm is relatively small, it can sell any number of goods at this price. If the fixed price is denoted by b then the demand function is

$$P - b$$

and the associated total revenue function is

$$TR = PQ$$
$$= bQ$$

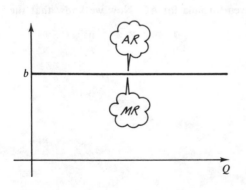

Figure 4.15

An expression for marginal revenue is obtained by differentiating TR with respect to Q and, since b is just a constant, we see that

$$MR = b$$

In the case of perfect competition, the average and marginal revenue curves are the same. They are horizontal straight lines, b units above the Q axis as shown in Figure 4.15.

So far we have concentrated on the total revenue function. Exactly the same principle can be used for other economic functions. For instance, we define the **marginal cost**, MC, by

$$MC = \frac{d(TC)}{dQ}$$

marginal cost is the derivative of total cost with respect to output

Again, using a simple geometrical argument it is easy to see that if Q changes by a small amount ΔQ then the corresponding change in TC is given by

$$\Delta(\text{TC}) \simeq \text{MC} \times \Delta Q$$

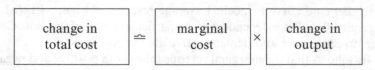

In particular, putting $\Delta Q = 1$ gives

$$\Delta(\text{TC}) \simeq \text{MC}$$

so that MC gives the approximate change in TC when Q increases by one unit.

EXAMPLE

If the average cost function of a good is

$$\text{AC} = 2Q + 6 + \frac{13}{Q}$$

find an expression for MC. If the current output is 15, estimate the effect on TC of a three unit decrease in Q.

Solution

We first need to find an expression for TC using the given formula for AC. Now we know that the average cost is just the total cost divided by Q, that is

$$\text{AC} = \frac{\text{TC}}{Q}$$

Hence

$$\text{TC} = (\text{AC})Q$$

$$= \left(2Q + 6 + \frac{13}{Q}\right)Q$$

and, after multiplying out the brackets, we get

$$\text{TC} = 2Q^2 + 6Q + 13$$

In this formula the last term, 13, is independent of Q so must denote the fixed costs. The remaining part, $2Q^2 + 6Q$, depends on Q so represents the total variable costs. Differentiating gives

$$\text{MC} = \frac{d(\text{TC})}{dQ}$$

$$= 4Q + 6$$

Notice that because the fixed costs are constant they differentiate to zero and so have no effect on the marginal cost. When $Q = 15$,

$$MC = 4(15) + 6 = 66$$

Also, if Q decreases by 3 units then $\Delta Q = -3$. Hence the change in TC is given by

$$\Delta(TC) \simeq MC \times \Delta Q$$
$$= 66 \times (-3)$$
$$= -198$$

so TC decreases by 198 units approximately.

■

PROBLEM

3 Find the marginal cost given the average cost function

$$AC = \frac{100}{Q} + 2$$

Deduce that a one unit increase in Q will always result in a two unit increase in TC, irrespective of the current level of output.

4.3.2 Production

Production functions were introduced in Section 2.3. In the simplest case output, Q, is assumed to be a function of labour, L, and capital, K. Moreover, in the short run the input K can be assumed to be fixed so Q is then only a function of one input L. (This is not a valid assumption in the long run and in general Q must be regarded as a function of at least two inputs. Methods for handling this situation are considered in the next chapter.) The variable L is usually measured in terms of the number of workers or possibly in terms of the number of worker hours. Motivated by our previous work we define the **marginal product of labour**, MP_L, by

$$MP_L = \frac{dQ}{dL}$$

> marginal product of labour is the derivative of output with respect to labour

As before, this gives the approximate change in Q that results from using one more unit of L.

EXAMPLE

If the production function is

$$Q = 300\sqrt{L} - 4L$$

where Q denotes output and L denotes the size of the workforce, calculate the value of MP_L when

(a) $L = 1$
(b) $L = 9$
(c) $L = 100$
(d) $L = 2500$

and discuss the implication of these results.

Solution

If

$$Q = 300\sqrt{L} - 4L = 300L^{1/2} - 4L$$

then

$$MP_L = \frac{dQ}{dL}$$

$$= 300(\tfrac{1}{2}L^{-1/2}) - 4$$

$$= 150L^{-1/2} - 4$$

$$= \frac{150}{\sqrt{L}} - 4$$

(a)   When $L = 1$

$$MP_L = \frac{150}{\sqrt{1}} - 4 = 146$$

(b)   When $L = 9$

$$MP_L = \frac{150}{\sqrt{9}} - 4 = 46$$

(c)   When $L = 100$

$$MP_L = \frac{150}{\sqrt{100}} - 4 = 11$$

(d)   When $L = 2500$

$$MP_L = \frac{150}{\sqrt{2500}} - 4 = -1$$

Notice that the values of MP_L decline with increasing L. Part (a) shows that if the workforce consists of only one person then to employ two people would increase output by 146 approximately. In part (b) we see that to increase the number of workers from 9 to 10 would result in about 46 additional units of output. In part (c) we see that a one unit increase in labour from a level of 100 only increases output by 11. In part (d) the situation is even worse. This indicates that to increase staff actually reduces output! The latter is a rather surprising result but it is borne out by what actually occurs in real production processes. This may be due to problems of overcrowding on the shop floor or to the need to create an elaborate administration to organize the larger workforce.

∎

This example illustrates the **law of diminishing marginal productivity** (sometimes called the **law of diminishing returns**). It states that the increase in output due to a one unit increase in labour will eventually decline. In other words, once the size of the workforce has reached a certain threshold level the marginal product of labour will get smaller. In the previous example the value of MP_L continually goes down with rising L. This is not always so. It is possible for the marginal product of labour to remain constant or to go up to begin with for small values of L. However, if it is to satisfy the law of diminishing marginal productivity then there must be some value of L above which MP_L decreases.

A typical product curve is sketched in Figure 4.16 which has slope

$$\frac{dQ}{dL} = MP_L$$

Between 0 and L_0 the curve bends upwards, becoming progressively steeper and so the slope function, MP_L, increases. Mathematically, this means that the slope of MP_L is positive, that is

$$\frac{d(MP_L)}{dQ} > 0$$

Now MP_L is itself the derivative of Q with respect to L so we can use the notation for the second derivative and write this as

$$\frac{d^2Q}{dL^2} > 0$$

Similarly, if L exceeds the threshold value of L_0, then Figure 4.16 shows that the product curve bends downwards and the slope decreases. In this region, the slope of the slope function is negative so that

$$\frac{d^2Q}{dL^2} < 0$$

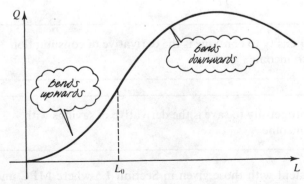

Figure 4.16

The law of diminishing returns states that this must happen eventually, that is

$$\frac{\mathrm{d}^2Q}{\mathrm{d}L^2} < 0$$

for sufficiently large L.

PROBLEM

4   A Cobb–Douglas production function is given by

$$Q = 5L^{1/2}K^{1/2}$$

Assuming that capital, K, is fixed at 100, write down a formula for Q in terms of L only. Calculate the marginal product of labour when

(a) $L = 1$ **(b)** $L = 9$ **(c)** $L = 10\,000$

Verify that the law of diminishing marginal productivity holds in this case.

4.3.3   Consumption and savings

In Chapter 1 the relationship between consumption, C, savings, S, and national income, Y, was investigated. If we assume that national income is only used up in consumption and savings then

$$Y = C + S$$

Of particular interest is the effect on C and S due to variations in Y. Expressed simply, if national income rises by a certain amount, are people more likely to go out and spend their extra income on consumer goods or will they save it? To analyse this behaviour we use the concepts **marginal propensity to consume**, MPC, and **marginal propensity to save**, MPS, which are defined by

$$\mathrm{MPC} = \frac{\mathrm{d}C}{\mathrm{d}Y} \quad \text{and} \quad \mathrm{MPS} = \frac{\mathrm{d}S}{\mathrm{d}Y}$$

> marginal propensity to consume is the derivative of consumption with respect to income

> marginal propensity to save is the derivative of savings with respect to income

These definitions are consistent with those given in Section 1.5 where MPC and MPS were taken to be the slopes of the linear consumption and savings curves respectively. At first sight it appears that, in general, we need to work out two derivatives in order to evaluate MPC and MPS. However, this is not strictly necessary. Recall that we can do whatever we like to an equation provided we do the same thing to both sides. Consequently, we can differentiate both sides of the equation

$$Y = C + S$$

with respect to Y to deduce that

$$\frac{dY}{dY} = \frac{dC}{dY} + \frac{dS}{dY}$$

$$= MPC + MPS$$

Now we are already familiar with the result that when we differentiate x with respect to x the answer is 1. In this case Y plays the role of x, so

$$\frac{dY}{dY} = 1$$

Hence

$$1 = MPC + MPS$$

This formula is identical to the result given in Section 1.5 for simple linear functions. In practice, it means that we need only work out one of the derivatives. The remaining derivative can then be calculated directly from this equation.

EXAMPLE

If the consumption function is

$$C = 0.01Y^2 + 0.2Y + 50$$

calculate MPC and MPS when $Y = 30$.

Solution

In this example the consumption function is given so we begin by finding MPC. To do this we differentiate C with respect to Y. If

$$C = 0.01Y^2 + 0.2Y + 50$$

then

$$\frac{dC}{dY} = 0.02Y + 0.2$$

so, when $Y = 30$,

$$MPC = 0.02(30) + 0.2 = 0.8$$

To find the corresponding value of MPS we use the formula

$$MPC + MPS = 1$$

which gives

$$MPS = 1 - MPC$$

$$= 1 - 0.8$$

$$= 0.2$$

This indicates that when national income increases by 1 unit (from its current level of 30) consumption rises by approximately 0.8 units, whereas savings only rise by about 0.2 units. At this level of income the nation has a greater propensity to consume than it has to save.

■

PROBLEM

5   If the savings function is given by

$$S = 0.02Y^2 - Y + 100$$

calculate the values of MPS and MPC when $Y = 40$. Give a brief interpretation of these results.

PRACTICE PROBLEMS

6   A monopolist's demand function is given by

$$P + Q = 100$$

Write down expressions for TR and MR in terms of Q and sketch their graphs. Find the value of Q which gives a marginal revenue of zero and comment on the significance of this value.

7   The fixed costs of producing a good are 100 and the variable costs are $2 + Q/10$ per unit.

(1)   Find expressions for TC and MC.
(2)   Evaluate MC at $Q = 30$ and hence estimate the change in TC brought about by a 2 unit increase in output from a current level of 30 units.
(3)   At what level of output does MC = 22?

8   A firm's production function is

$$Q = 50L - 0.01L^2$$

where L denotes the size of the workforce. Find the value of MP_L in the case when

(a) $L = 1$ (b) $L = 10$ (c) $L = 100$ (d) $L = 1000$

Does the law of diminishing marginal productivity apply to this particular function?

9   Show that the law of diminishing marginal productivity holds for the production function

$$Q = 6L^2 - 0.2L^3$$

10   If the consumption function is

$$C = 50 + 2\sqrt{Y}$$

calculate MPC and MPS when $Y = 36$ and give an interpretation of these results.

4.4 Further rules of differentiation

Objectives   At the end of this section you should be able to:

- use the chain rule to differentiate a function of a function,
- use the product rule to differentiate the product of two functions,
- use the quotient rule to differentiate the quotient of two functions,
- differentiate complicated functions using a combination of rules.

Section 4.2 introduced you to the basic rules of differentiation. Unfortunately, not all functions can be differentiated using these rules alone. For example, we are unable to differentiate the functions

$$x\sqrt{(2x-3)} \quad \text{and} \quad \frac{x}{x^2+1}$$

using just the constant, sum or difference rules. The aim of the present section is to describe three further rules which allow you to find the derivative of more complicated expressions. Indeed, the totality of all six rules will enable you to differentiate any mathematical function. Although you may find that the rules described in this section take you slightly longer to grasp than before, they are vital to any understanding of economic theory.

The first rule that we investigate is called the chain rule and it can be used to differentiate functions such as

$$y = (2x+3)^{10} \quad \text{and} \quad y = \sqrt{(1+x^2)}$$

The distinguishing feature of these expressions is that they represent a 'function of a function'. To understand what we mean by this, consider how you might evaluate

$$y = (2x+3)^{10}$$

on a calculator. You would first work out an intermediate number u, say, given by

$$u = 2x + 3$$

and then raise it to the power of 10 to get

$$y = u^{10}$$

This process is illustrated in Figure 4.17. Note how the incoming number x is first processed by the inner function, 'double and add 3'. The output u from this is then passed on to the outer function, 'raise to the power of 10', to produce the final outgoing number y.

The function

$$y = \sqrt{(1+x^2)}$$

Figure 4.17

can be viewed in the same way. To calculate y you perform the inner function, 'square and add 1', followed by the outer function, 'take square roots'.

The chain rule for differentiating a function of a function may now be stated.

Rule 4: The Chain Rule

If y is a function of u which is itself a function of x then

$$\frac{dy}{dx} = \frac{dy}{du} \times \frac{du}{dx}$$

> differentiate the outer function and multiply by the derivative of the inner function

To illustrate this rule, let us return to the function

$$y = (2x + 3)^{10}$$

in which

$$y = u^{10} \quad \text{and} \quad u = 2x + 3$$

Now

$$\frac{dy}{du} = 10u^9 = 10(2x + 3)^9$$

$$\frac{du}{dx} = 2$$

The chain rule then gives

$$\frac{dy}{dx} = \frac{dy}{du} \times \frac{du}{dx} = 10(2x + 3)^9(2) = 20(2x + 3)^9$$

With practice it is possible to perform the differentiation without explicitly introducing the variable u. To differentiate

$$y = (2x + 3)^{10}$$

we first differentiate the outer power function to get

$$10(2x + 3)^9$$

and then multiply by the derivative of the inner function, $2x + 3$, which is 2, so

$$\frac{dy}{dx} = 20(2x + 3)^9$$

EXAMPLE

Differentiate

(a) $y = (3x^2 - 5x + 2)^4$

(b) $y = \dfrac{1}{3x + 7}$

(c) $y = \sqrt{(1 + x^2)}$

Solution

(a) The chain rule shows that to differentiate $(3x^2 - 5x + 2)^4$ we first differentiate the outer power function to get

$$4(3x^2 - 5x + 2)^3$$

and then multiply by the derivative of the inner function, $3x^2 - 5x + 2$, which is $6x - 5$. Hence if

$$y = (3x^2 - 5x + 2)^4 \quad \text{then} \quad \frac{dy}{dx} = 4(3x^2 - 5x + 2)^3(6x - 5)$$

(b) To use the chain rule to differentiate

$$y = \frac{1}{3x + 7}$$

recall that reciprocals are denoted by negative powers so that

$$y = (3x + 7)^{-1}$$

The outer power function differentiates to get

$$-(3x + 7)^{-2}$$

and the inner function, $3x + 7$, differentiates to get 3. By the chain rule we just multiply these together to deduce that if

$$y = \frac{1}{3x + 7} \quad \text{then} \quad \frac{dy}{dx} = -(3x + 7)^{-2}(3) = \frac{-3}{(3x + 7)^2}$$

(c) To use the chain rule to differentiate

$$y = \sqrt{(1 + x^2)}$$

recall that roots are denoted by fractional powers so that

$$y = (1 + x^2)^{1/2}$$

The outer power function differentiates to get

$$\frac{1}{2}(1 + x^2)^{-1/2}$$

and the inner function, $1 + x^2$, differentiates to get $2x$. By the chain rule we just multiply these together to deduce that if

$$y = \sqrt{(1 + x^2)} \quad \text{then} \quad \frac{dy}{dx} = \frac{1}{2}(1 + x^2)^{-1/2}(2x) = \frac{x}{\sqrt{(1 + x^2)}}$$

■

PROBLEM

1 Differentiate

(a) $y = (3x - 4)^5$ **(b)** $y = (x^2 + 3x + 5)^3$ **(c)** $y = \dfrac{1}{2x - 3}$ **(d)** $y = \sqrt{(4x - 3)}$

The next rule is used to differentiate the product of two functions, $f(x)g(x)$. In order to give a clear statement of this rule we write

$$u = f(x) \quad \text{and} \quad v = g(x)$$

Rule 5: The Product Rule

If

$$y = uv \quad \text{then} \quad \frac{dy}{dx} = u\frac{dv}{dx} + v\frac{du}{dx}$$

This rule tells you how to differentiate the product of two functions.

> multiply each function by the derivative of the other and add

EXAMPLE

Differentiate

(a) $y = x^2(2x + 1)^3$

(b) $y = \dfrac{x}{1 + x}$

Solution

(a)   The function $x^2(2x + 1)^3$ involves the product of two simpler functions, namely x^2 and $(2x + 1)^3$ which we denote by u and v respectively. (It does not matter which function we label u and which we label v. The same answer is obtained if u is $(2x + 1)^3$ and v is x^2. You might like to check this for yourself later.) Now if

$$u = x^2 \quad \text{and} \quad v = (2x + 1)^3$$

then

$$\frac{du}{dx} = 2x \quad \text{and} \quad \frac{dv}{dx} = 6(2x + 1)^2$$

where we have used the chain rule to find dv/dx. By the product rule

$$\frac{dy}{dx} = u\frac{dv}{dx} + v\frac{du}{dx}$$

$$= x^2[6(2x + 1)^2] + (2x + 1)^3(2x)$$

The first term is obtained by leaving u alone and multiplying it by the derivative of v. Similarly, the second term is obtained by leaving v alone and multiplying it by the derivative of u.

If desired, the final answer may be simplified by taking out a common factor of $2x(2x + 1)^2$. This factor goes into the first term $3x$ times and into the second $2x + 1$ times. Hence

$$\frac{dy}{dx} = 2x(2x + 1)^2[3x + (2x + 1)]$$

$$= 2x(2x + 1)^2(5x + 1)$$

(b)   At first sight it is hard to see how we can use the product rule to differentiate

$$\frac{x}{1 + x}$$

since it appears to be the quotient and not the product of two functions. However, if we recall that reciprocals are equivalent to negative powers we may rewrite it as

$$x(1 + x)^{-1}$$

It follows that we can put

$$u = x \quad \text{and} \quad v = (1 + x)^{-1}$$

which gives

$$\frac{du}{dx} = 1 \quad \text{and} \quad \frac{dv}{dx} = -(1 + x)^{-2}$$

where we have used the chain rule to find dv/dx. By the product rule

$$\frac{dy}{dx} = u\frac{dv}{dx} + v\frac{du}{dx}$$

$$\frac{dy}{dx} = x[-(1 + x)^{-2}] + (1 + x)^{-1}(1)$$

$$= \frac{-x}{(1 + x)^2} + \frac{1}{1 + x}$$

If desired, this can be simplified by putting the second term over a common denominator

$$(1 + x)^2$$

To do this we multiply the top and bottom of the second term by $1 + x$ to get

$$\frac{1 + x}{(1 + x)^2}$$

Hence

$$\frac{dy}{dx} = \frac{-x}{(1 + x)^2} + \frac{1 + x}{(1 + x)^2}$$

$$= \frac{-x + (1 + x)}{(1 + x)^2}$$

$$= \frac{1}{(1 + x)^2}$$

∎

PROBLEM

2 Differentiate

(**a**) $y = x(3x - 1)^6$ (**b**) $y = x^3\sqrt{(2x + 3)}$ (**c**) $y = \dfrac{x}{x - 2}$

You may have found the product rule the hardest of the rules so far. This may have been due to the algebraic manipulation that is required to simplify the final expression. If this is the case, do not worry about it at this stage. The important thing is that you can use the product rule to obtain some sort of an answer even if you cannot tidy it up at the end. This is not to say that the simplification of an expression is pointless. If the result of differentiation is to be used in a subsequent piece of theory, it may well save time in the long run if it is simplified first.

One of the most difficult parts of Problem 2 is part (c) since this involves algebraic fractions. For this function, it is necessary to manipulate negative indices and to put two individual fractions over a common denominator. You may feel that you are unable to do either of these processes with confidence. For this reason we conclude this section with a rule which is specifically designed to differentiate this type of function. The rule itself is quite complicated. However, as will become apparent, it does the algebra for you, so you may prefer to use it rather than the product rule when differentiating algebraic fractions.

Rule 6: The Quotient Rule

If

$$y = \frac{u}{v} \qquad \text{then} \qquad \frac{dy}{dx} = \frac{v\,du/dx - u\,dv/dx}{v^2}$$

This rule tells you how to differentiate the quotient of two functions. Unfortunately, it is not at all easy to state this rule in words. However, it turns out to be rather more straightforward to use than you might at first think.

EXAMPLE

Differentiate

(a) $y = \dfrac{x}{1 + x}$

(b) $y = \dfrac{1 + x^2}{2 - x^3}$

Solution

(a)   In the quotient rule, u is used as the label for the numerator and v is used for the denominator, so to differentiate

$$\frac{x}{1 + x}$$

we must take

$$u = x \quad \text{and} \quad v = 1 + x$$

for which

$$\frac{du}{dx} = 1 \quad \text{and} \quad \frac{dv}{dx} = 1$$

By the quotient rule

$$\frac{dy}{dx} = \frac{v \, du/dx - u \, dv/dx}{v^2}$$

$$= \frac{(1 + x)(1) - x(1)}{(1 + x)^2}$$

$$= \frac{1 + x - x}{(1 + x)^2}$$

$$= \frac{1}{(1 + x)^2}$$

Notice how the quotient rule automatically puts the final expression over a common denominator. Compare this with the algebra required to obtain the same answer using the product rule in part (c) of the previous example.

(b)   The numerator of the algebraic fraction

$$\frac{1 + x^2}{2 - x^3}$$

is $1 + x^2$ and the denominator is $2 - x^3$ so we take

$$u = 1 + x^2 \quad \text{and} \quad v = 2 - x^3$$

for which

$$\frac{du}{dx} = 2x \qquad \text{and} \qquad \frac{dv}{dx} = -3x^2$$

By the quotient rule

$$\frac{dy}{dx} = \frac{v\,du/dx - u\,dv/dx}{v^2}$$

$$= \frac{(2 - x^3)(2x) - (1 + x^2)(-3x^2)}{(2 - x^3)^2}$$

$$= \frac{4x - 2x^4 + 3x^2 + 3x^4}{(2 - x^3)^2}$$

$$= \frac{x^4 + 3x^2 + 4x}{(2 - x^3)^2}$$

■

PROBLEM

3   Differentiate

(a) $y = \dfrac{x}{x - 2}$ (b) $y = \dfrac{x - 1}{x + 1}$

[You might like to check that your answer to part (a) is the same as that obtained in Problem 2(c).]

The product and quotient rules give alternative methods for the differentiation of algebraic fractions. It does not matter which rule you go for; use whichever rule is easiest for you. Problems 4 and 5 at the end of this section should give you further practice at 'technique bashing' if you feel you need it.

As usual, the concluding problems which follow are designed to give you an opportunity to practise the skills that you have acquired in this section. Problems 6, 7 and 8 show how the chain, product and quotient rules are used in economics and serve to revise the applications described in Section 4.3.

PRACTICE PROBLEMS

4   Use the chain rule to differentiate

(a) $y = (2x + 1)^{10}$ (b) $y = (x^2 + 3x - 5)^3$ (c) $y = \dfrac{1}{7x - 3}$ (d) $y = \dfrac{1}{x^2 + 1}$

(e) $y = \sqrt{(8x - 1)}$

5   Differentiate

(a) $y = x(x - 3)^4$ (b) $y = x\sqrt{(2x - 3)}$ (c) $y = \dfrac{x}{x + 5}$ (d) $y = \dfrac{x}{x^2 + 1}$

6 Find expressions for marginal revenue in the case when the demand equation is given by

    (a) $P = \sqrt{(100 - 2Q)}$ **(b)** $P = \dfrac{1000}{\sqrt{(2 + Q)}}$

7 If the consumption function is

$$C = \frac{300 + 2Y^2}{1 + Y}$$

calculate MPC and MPS when $Y = 36$ and give an interpretation of these results.

4.5   Elasticity

Objectives   At the end of this section you should be able to:

- calculate price elasticity averaged along an arc,

- calculate price elasticity evaluated at a point,

- decide whether supply and demand is inelastic, unit elastic or elastic,

- understand the relationship between price elasticity of demand and revenue,

- determine the price elasticity for general linear demand functions.

One important problem in business is to determine the effect on revenue of a change in the price of a good. Let us suppose that a firm's demand curve is downward sloping. If the firm lowers the price then it will receive less for each item but the number of items sold increases. The formula for total revenue is

    $\text{TR} = PQ$

and it is not immediately obvious what the net effect on TR will be as P decreases and Q increases. The crucial factor here is not the absolute changes in P and Q but rather the proportional or percentage changes. Intuitively, we expect that if the percentage rise in Q is greater than the percentage fall in P then the firm experiences an increase in revenue. Under these circumstances we say that demand is **elastic** since the demand is relatively sensitive to changes in price. Similarly, demand is said to be **inelastic** if demand is relatively insensitive to price changes. In this case, the percentage change in quantity is less than the percentage change in price. A firm can then increase revenue by raising the price of the good. Although demand falls as a result, the increase in price more than compensates for the reduced volume of sales and revenue rises. Of course, it could happen that the percentage changes in price and quantity are equal leaving revenue unchanged. We use the term **unit elastic** to describe this situation.

We quantify the responsiveness of demand to price change by defining the **price elasticity of demand** to be

$$E = \frac{\text{percentage change in demand}}{\text{percentage change in price}}$$

Notice that because the demand curve slopes downwards, a positive change in price leads to a negative change in quantity and vice versa. Consequently, the value of E is always negative. It is conventional to avoid this by deliberately changing the sign and taking

$$E = -\frac{\text{percentage change in demand}}{\text{percentage change in price}}$$

which makes E positive. The previous classification of demand functions can now be restated more succinctly in terms of E.

Demand is said to be

- inelastic if $E < 1$
- unit elastic if $E = 1$
- elastic if $E > 1$

As usual, we denote the changes in P and Q by ΔP and ΔQ respectively, and seek a formula for E in terms of these symbols. To motivate this, suppose that the price of a good is \$12 and that it rises to \$18. A moment's thought should convince you that the percentage change in price is then 50%. You can probably work this out in your head without thinking too hard. However, it is worthwhile identifying the mathematical process involved. To obtain this figure we first express the change

$$18 - 12 = 6$$

as a fraction of the original to get

$$\frac{6}{12} = 0.5$$

and then multiply by 100 to express it as a percentage. This simple example gives us a clue as to how we might find a formula for E. In general, the percentage change in price is

change in price expressed as a fraction of the original price ⟶ $\dfrac{\Delta P}{P} \times 100$ ⟵ *multiply by 100 to convert fractions into percentages*

Similarly, the percentage change in quantity is

$$\frac{\Delta Q}{Q} \times 100$$

Hence

$$E = -\left(\frac{\Delta Q}{Q} \times 100\right) \div \left(\frac{\Delta P}{P} \times 100\right)$$

Now when we divide two fractions we turn the denominator upside down and multiply, so

$$E = -\left(\frac{\Delta Q}{Q} \times \cancel{100}\right) \times \left(\frac{P}{\cancel{100} \times \Delta P}\right)$$

$$= -\frac{P}{Q} \times \frac{\Delta Q}{\Delta P}$$

A typical demand curve is illustrated in Figure 4.18 in which a price fall from P_1 to P_2 causes an increase in demand from Q_1 to Q_2.

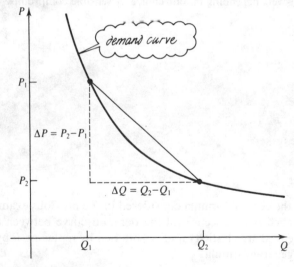

Figure 4.18

EXAMPLE

Determine the elasticity of demand when the price falls from 136 to 119, given the demand function

$$P = 200 - Q^2$$

Solution

In the notation of Figure 4.18 we are given that

$$P_1 = 136 \qquad \text{and} \qquad P_2 = 119$$

The corresponding values of Q_1 and Q_2 are obtained from the demand equation

$$P = 200 - Q^2$$

by substituting $P = 136$ and 119 respectively and solving for Q. For example, if $P = 136$ then

$$136 = 200 - Q^2$$

which rearranges to give

$$Q^2 = 200 - 136 = 64$$

This has solution $Q = \pm 8$ and, since we can obviously ignore the negative quantity, we have $Q_1 = 8$. Similarly, setting $P = 119$ gives $Q_2 = 9$. The elasticity formula is

$$E = -\frac{P}{Q} \times \frac{\Delta Q}{\Delta P}$$

and the values of ΔP and ΔQ are easily worked out to be

$$\Delta P = 119 - 136 = -17$$

$$\Delta Q = 9 - 8 = 1$$

However, it is not at all clear what to take for P and Q. Do we take P to be 136 or 119? Clearly we are going to get two different answers depending on our choice. A sensible compromise is to use their average and take

$$P = \tfrac{1}{2}(136 + 119) = 127.5$$

Similarly, averaging the Q values gives

$$Q = \tfrac{1}{2}(8 + 9) = 8.5$$

Hence

$$E = -\frac{127.5}{8.5} \times \left(\frac{1}{-17}\right) = 0.88$$

∎

The particular application of the general formula considered in the previous example provides an estimate of elasticity averaged over a section of the demand curve between (Q_1, P_1) and (Q_2, P_2). For this reason it is called **arc elasticity** and is obtained by replacing P by $\tfrac{1}{2}(P_1 + P_2)$ and Q by $\tfrac{1}{2}(Q_1 + Q_2)$ in the general formula.

PROBLEM

1   Given the demand function

$$P = 1000 - 2Q$$

calculate the arc elasticity as P falls from 210 to 200.

A disappointing feature of the previous example is the need to compromise and calculate the elasticity averaged along an arc rather than calculate the exact value at a point. Such a formula can easily be deduced from

$$E = -\frac{P}{Q} \times \frac{\Delta Q}{\Delta P}$$

by considering the limit as ΔQ and ΔP tend to zero in Figure 4.18. All that happens is that the arc shrinks to a point and the ratio $\Delta Q/\Delta P$ tends to dQ/dP. The price elasticity at a point may therefore be found from

$$E = -\frac{P}{Q} \times \frac{dQ}{dP}$$

EXAMPLE

Given the demand function

$$P = 50 - 2Q$$

find the elasticity when the price is 30. Is demand inelastic, unit elastic or elastic at this price?

Solution

To find dQ/dP we need to differentiate Q with respect to P. However, we are actually given a formula for P in terms of Q, so we need to transpose

$$P = 50 - 2Q$$

for Q. Adding $2Q$ to both sides gives

$$P + 2Q = 50$$

and if we subtract P then

$$2Q = 50 - P$$

Finally, dividing through by 2 gives

$$Q = 25 - \tfrac{1}{2}P$$

Hence

$$\frac{dQ}{dP} = -\tfrac{1}{2}$$

We are given that $P = 30$ so, at this price, demand is

$$Q = 25 - \tfrac{1}{2}(30) = 10$$

These values can now be substituted into

$$E = -\frac{P}{Q} \times \frac{dQ}{dP}$$

to get

$$E = -\frac{30}{10} \times \left(-\frac{1}{2}\right) = 1.5$$

Moreover, since $1.5 > 1$, demand is elastic at this price.

PROBLEM

2 Given the demand function

$$P = 100 - Q$$

calculate the price elasticity of demand when the price is

(a) 10   **(b)** 50   **(c)** 90

Is the demand inelastic, unit elastic or elastic at these prices?

It is quite common in economics to be given the demand function in the form

$$P = f(Q)$$

where P is a function of Q. In order to evaluate elasticity it is necessary to find

$$\frac{dQ}{dP}$$

which assumes that Q is actually given as a function of P. Consequently, we may have to transpose the demand equation and find an expression for Q in terms of P before we perform the differentiation. This was the approach taken in the previous example. Unfortunately, if $f(Q)$ is a complicated expression, it may be difficult, if not impossible, to carry out the initial rearrangement to extract Q. An alternative approach is based on the fact that

$$\frac{dQ}{dP} = \frac{1}{dP/dQ}$$

A proof of this can be obtained via the chain rule although we omit the details. This result shows that we can find dQ/dP by just differentiating the original demand function to get dP/dQ and reciprocating.

EXAMPLE

Given the demand function

$$P = -Q^2 - 4Q + 96$$

find the price elasticity of demand when $P = 51$. If this price rises by 2% calculate the corresponding percentage change in demand.

Solution

We are given that $P = 51$ so to find the corresponding demand we need to solve the quadratic equation

$$-Q^2 - 4Q + 96 = 51$$

that is

$$-Q^2 - 4Q + 45 = 0$$

To do this we use the standard formula

$$\frac{-b \pm \sqrt{(b^2 - 4ac)}}{2a}$$

discussed in Section 2.1 which gives

$$Q = \frac{-(-4) \pm \sqrt{((-4)^2 - 4(-1)(45))}}{2(-1)}$$

$$= \frac{4 \pm \sqrt{196}}{-2}$$

$$= \frac{4 \pm 14}{-2}$$

The two solutions are -9 and 5. As usual, the negative value can be ignored since it does not make sense to have a negative quantity so $Q = 5$.

To find the value of E we also need to calculate

$$\frac{dQ}{dP}$$

from the demand equation, $P = -Q^2 - 4Q + 96$. It is not at all easy to transpose this for Q. Indeed, we would have to use the formula for solving a quadratic, as above, replacing the number 51 by the letter P. Unfortunately this expression involves square roots and the subsequent differentiation is quite messy. (You might like to have a go at this yourself!) However, it is easy to differentiate the given expression with respect to Q to get

$$\frac{dP}{dQ} = -2Q - 4$$

and so

$$\frac{dQ}{dP} = \frac{1}{dP/dQ} = \frac{1}{-2Q - 4}$$

Finally, putting $Q = 5$ gives

$$\frac{dQ}{dP} = -\frac{1}{14}$$

The price elasticity of demand is given by

$$E = -\frac{P}{Q} \times \frac{dQ}{dP}$$

and if we substitute $P = 51$, $Q = 5$ and $dQ/dP = -1/14$ we get

$$E = -\frac{51}{5} \times \left(-\frac{1}{14}\right) = 0.73$$

To discover the effect on Q due to a 2% rise in P we return to the original definition

$$E = -\frac{\text{percentage change in demand}}{\text{percentage change in price}}$$

We know that $E = 0.73$ and that the percentage change in price is 2 so

$$0.73 = -\frac{\text{percentage change in demand}}{2}$$

which shows that demand changes by

$$-0.73 \times 2 = -1.46\%$$

A 2% rise in price therefore leads to a fall in demand of 1.46%.

■

PROBLEM

3 Given the demand equation

$$P = -Q^2 - 10Q + 150$$

find the price elasticity of demand when $Q = 4$. Estimate the percentage change in price needed to increase demand by 10%.

The **price elasticity of supply** is defined in an analogous way to that of demand. We define

$$E = \frac{\text{percentage change in supply}}{\text{percentage change in price}}$$

This time, however, there is no need to fiddle the sign. An increase in price leads to an increase in supply so E is automatically positive. In symbols

$$E = \frac{P}{Q} \times \frac{\Delta Q}{\Delta P}$$

If (Q_1, P_1) and (Q_2, P_2) denote two points on the supply curve then arc elasticity is obtained, as before, by setting

$$\Delta P = P_2 - P_1$$
$$\Delta Q = Q_2 - Q_1$$
$$P = \tfrac{1}{2}(P_1 + P_2)$$
$$Q = \tfrac{1}{2}(Q_1 + Q_2)$$

The corresponding formula for point elasticity is

$$E = \frac{P}{Q} \times \frac{\mathrm{d}Q}{\mathrm{d}P}$$

PROBLEM

4 If the supply equation is

$$Q = 150 + 5P + 0.1P^2$$

calculate the price elasticity of supply

(a) averaged along an arc between $P = 9$ and $P = 11$,
(b) at the point $P = 10$.

The concept of elasticity can be applied to more general functions and we consider some of these in the next chapter. For the moment we investigate the theoretical properties of demand elasticity. The following material is more difficult to understand than the foregoing so you may prefer to just concentrate on the conclusions and skip the intermediate derivations. We begin by analysing the relationship between elasticity and marginal revenue. Marginal revenue, MR, is given by

$$MR = \frac{d(TR)}{dQ}$$

Now TR is equal to the product PQ, so we can apply the product rule to differentiate it. If

$$u = P \quad \text{and} \quad v = Q$$

then

$$\frac{du}{dQ} = \frac{dP}{dQ} \quad \text{and} \quad \frac{dv}{dQ} = \frac{dQ}{dQ} = 1$$

By the product rule

$$MR = u\frac{dv}{dQ} + v\frac{du}{dQ}$$

$$= P + Q \times \frac{dP}{dQ}$$

$$= P\left(1 + \frac{Q}{P} \times \frac{dP}{dQ}\right)$$

check this by multiplying out the brackets

Now

$$-\frac{P}{Q} \times \frac{dQ}{dP} = E$$

so

$$\frac{Q}{P} \times \frac{dP}{dQ} = -\frac{1}{E}$$

turn both sides upside down and multiply by -1

This can be substituted into the expression for MR to get

$$MR = P\left(1 - \frac{1}{E}\right)$$

The connection between marginal revenue and demand elasticity is now complete and this formula can be used to justify the intuitive argument that we gave at the beginning of this section concerning revenue and elasticity. Observe that if $E < 1$ then $1/E > 1$ so MR is negative for any value of P. It follows that the revenue function is decreasing in regions where demand is inelastic because MR determines the slope of the revenue curve. Similarly, if $E > 1$ then $1/E < 1$ so MR is positive for any price, P, and the revenue curve is uphill. In other words, the revenue function is increasing in regions where demand is elastic. Finally, if $E = 1$ then MR is zero and so the slope of the revenue curve is horizontal at points where demand is unit elastic.

Throughout this section we have taken specific functions and evaluated the elasticity at particular points. It is more instructive to consider general functions and to deduce general expressions for elasticity. Consider the standard linear downward sloping demand function

$$P = aQ + b$$

where $a < 0$ and $b > 0$. As noted in Section 4.3, this typifies the demand function faced by a monopolist. To transpose this equation for Q, we subtract b from both sides to get

$$aQ = P - b$$

and then divide through by a to get

$$Q = \frac{1}{a}(P - b)$$

Hence

$$\frac{dQ}{dP} = \frac{1}{a}$$

The formula for elasticity of demand is

$$E = -\frac{P}{Q} \times \frac{dQ}{dP}$$

so replacing Q by $(1/a)(P - b)$ and dQ/dP by $1/a$ gives

$$E = \frac{-P}{(1/a)(P - b)} \times \frac{1}{a}$$

$$= \frac{-P}{P - b}$$

$$= \frac{P}{b - P}$$

multiply top and bottom by −1

Notice that this formula involves P and b but not a. Elasticity is therefore independent of the slope of linear demand curves. In particular, this shows that, corresponding to any price P, the elasticities of the two demand functions sketched in Figure 4.19 are identical. This is perhaps a rather surprising result. We might have expected demand to be more elastic at point A than at point B since A is on the steeper curve. However, the mathematics shows that this is not the case. (Can you explain, in economic terms, why this is so?)

Another interesting feature of the result

$$E = \frac{P}{b - P}$$

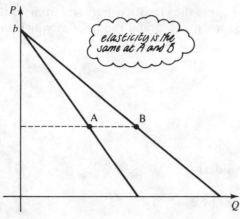

Figure 4.19

is the fact that b occurs in the denominator of this fraction, so that corresponding to any price, P, the larger the value of the intercept, b, the smaller the elasticity. In Figure 4.20, elasticity at C is smaller than that at D because C lies on the curve with the larger intercept.

The dependence of E on P is also worthy of note. It shows that elasticity varies along a linear demand curve. This is illustrated in Figure 4.21. At the left-hand end, $P = b$, so

$$E = \frac{b}{b - b} = \frac{b}{0} = \infty \qquad \text{(read 'infinity')}$$

At the right-hand end, $P = 0$, so

$$E = \frac{0}{b - 0} = \frac{0}{b} = 0$$

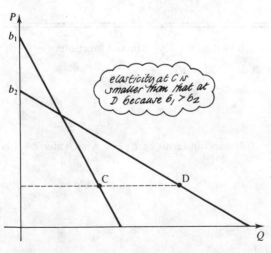

Figure 4.20

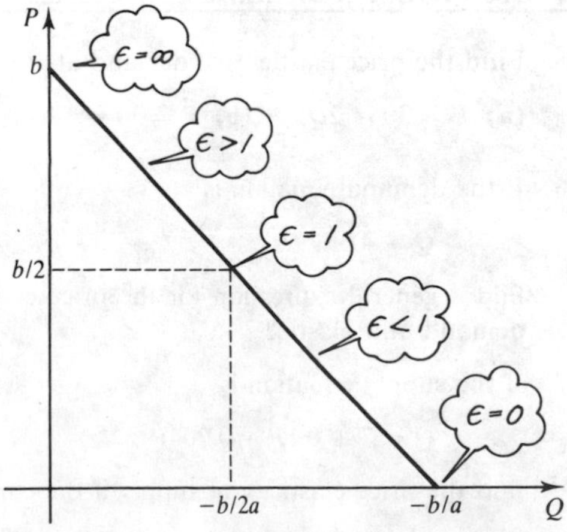

Figure 4.21

As you move down the demand curve the elasticity decreases from ∞ to 0 taking all possible values. Demand is unit elastic when $E = 1$ and the price at which this occurs can be found by solving

$$\frac{P}{b - P} = 1$$

for P:

$\qquad P = b - P \qquad$ (multiply both sides by $b - P$)

$\qquad 2P = b \qquad\qquad$ (add P to both sides)

$\qquad P = \dfrac{b}{2} \qquad\qquad$ (divide both sides by 2)

The corresponding quantity can be found by substituting $P = b/2$ into the transposed demand equation to get

$$Q = \frac{1}{a}\left(\frac{b}{2} - b\right) = -\frac{b}{2a}$$

Demand is unit elastic exactly halfway along the demand curve. To the left of this point $E > 1$ and demand is elastic, whereas to the right $E < 1$ and demand is inelastic.

In our discussion of general demand functions we have concentrated on those which are represented by straight lines since these are commonly used in simple economic models. There are other possibilities and Problem 8 investigates a class of functions which have constant elasticity.

PRACTICE PROBLEMS

5   Find the price elasticity of demand at $P = 6$ for each of the following demand functions:

(a) $P = 30 - 2Q$ (b) $P = 30 - 12Q$ (c) $P = \sqrt{(100 - 2Q)}$

6   If the demand equation is

$\qquad Q + 4P = 60$

find a general expression for the price elasticity of demand in terms of P. For what value of P is demand unit elastic?

7   If the supply equation is

$\qquad Q = 7 + 0.1P + 0.004P^2$

find the price elasticity of supply if the current price is 80.

(1)   Is supply elastic, inelastic or unit elastic at this price?
(2)   Estimate the percentage change in supply if the price rises by 5%.

8   Show that the price elasticity of demand is constant for the demand functions

$$P = \frac{A}{Q^n}$$

where A and n are positive constants.

4.6   Optimization of economic functions

Objectives   At the end of this section you should be able to:

- use the first-order derivative to find the stationary points of a function,

- use the second-order derivative to classify the stationary points of a function,

- find the maximum and minimum points of an economic function,

- use stationary points to sketch graphs of economic functions.

In Section 2.1 a simple three-step strategy was described for sketching graphs of quadratic functions of the form

$$f(x) = ax^2 + bx + c$$

The basic idea is to solve the corresponding equation

$$ax^2 + bx + c = 0$$

to find where the graph crosses the x axis. Provided that the quadratic equation has at least one solution, it is then possible to deduce the coordinates of the maximum or minimum point of the parabola. For example, if there are two solutions, then by symmetry the graph turns round at the point exactly halfway between these solutions. Unfortunately, if the quadratic equation has no solution then only a limited sketch can be obtained using this approach.

In this section we show how the techniques of calculus can be used to find the coordinates of the turning point of a parabola. The beauty of this approach is that it can be used to locate the maximum and minimum points of any economic function, not just those represented by quadratics. Look at the graph sketched in Figure 4.22. Points B, C, D, E, F and G are referred to as the **stationary points** (sometimes called **critical points**, **turning points** or **extrema**) of the function. At a stationary point the tangent to the graph is horizontal and so has zero

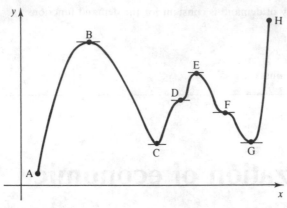

Figure 4.22

slope. Consequently, at a stationary point of a function $f(x)$,

$$f'(x) = 0$$

The reason for using the word stationary is historical. Calculus was originally used by astronomers to predict planetary motion. If a graph of the distance travelled by an object is sketched against time then the speed of the object is given by the slope, since this represents the rate of change of distance with respect to time. It follows that if the graph is horizontal at some point then the speed is zero and the object is instantaneously at rest, that is stationary.

Stationary points are classified into one of three types: local maxima, local minima and stationary points of inflection.

At a **local maximum** (sometimes called a **relative maximum**) the graph falls away on both sides. Points B and E are the local maxima for the function sketched in Figure 4.22. The word 'local' is used to highlight the fact that although these are the maximum points relative to their locality or neighbourhood they may not be the overall or global maximum. In Figure 4.22 the highest point on the graph actually occurs at the right-hand end, H, which is not a stationary point since the slope is not zero at H.

At a **local minimum** (sometimes called a **relative minimum**) the graph rises on both sides. Points C and G are the local minima in Figure 4.22. Again, it is not necessary for the global minimum to be one of the local minima. In Figure 4.22 the lowest point on the graph occurs at the left-hand end, A, which is not a stationary point.

At a **stationary point of inflection** the graph rises on one side and falls on the other. The stationary points of inflection in Figure 4.22 are labelled D and F. These points are of little value in economics although they do sometimes assist in sketching graphs of economic functions. Maxima and minima, on the other hand, are important. The calculation of the maximum points of the revenue and profit functions is clearly worthwhile. Likewise, it is useful to be able to find the minimum points of average cost functions.

For most examples in economics the local maximum and minimum points coincide with the global maximum and minimum. For this reason we shall drop the word local when describing stationary points. However, it should always be borne in mind that the global maximum and minimum could actually be attained at an end point and this possibility may need to be checked. This can be done by comparing the function values at the end points with those of the stationary points and then deciding which of them gives rise to the largest or smallest values.

Two obvious questions remain. How do we find the stationary points of any given function and how do we classify them? The first question is easily answered. As we mentioned earlier, stationary points satisfy the equation

$$f'(x) = 0$$

so all we need do is to differentiate the function, to equate to zero and to solve the resulting algebraic equation. The classification is equally straightforward. It can be shown that if a function has a stationary point at $x = a$ then if

- $f''(a) > 0$ then $f(x)$ has a minimum at $x = a$.
- $f''(a) < 0$ then $f(x)$ has a maximum at $x = a$.

Therefore, all we need do is to differentiate the function a second time and to evaluate this second-order derivative at each point. A point is a minimum if this value is positive and a maximum if this value is negative. There is, of course, a third possibility, namely $f''(a) = 0$. Sadly, when this happens it provides no information whatsoever about the stationary point. The point $x = a$ could be a maximum, minimum or inflection. This situation is illustrated in Problem 7 at the end of this section. If you are unlucky enough to encounter this case you can always classify the point by tabulating the function values in the vicinity and use these to produce a local sketch.

To summarize, the method for finding and classifying stationary points of a function, $f(x)$, is as follows:

Step 1   Solve the equation

$$f'(x) = 0$$

to find the stationary points, $x = a$.

Step 2   If

- $f''(a) > 0$ then the function has a minimum at $x = a$.
- $f''(a) < 0$ then the function has a maximum at $x = a$.
- $f''(a) = 0$ then the point cannot be classified using the available information.

EXAMPLE _____

Find and classify the stationary points of the following functions. Hence sketch their graphs.

(a) $f(x) = x^2 - 4x + 5$
(b) $f(x) = 2x^3 + 3x^2 - 12x + 4$

Solution

(a)   In order to use steps 1 and 2 we need to find the first- and second-order derivatives of the function

$$f(x) = x^2 - 4x + 5$$

Differentiating once gives

$$f'(x) = 2x - 4$$

and differentiating a second time gives

$$f''(x) = 2$$

Step 1   The stationary points are the solutions of the equation

$$f'(x) = 0$$

so we need to solve

$$2x - 4 = 0$$

This is a linear equation so has just one solution. Adding 4 to both sides gives

$$2x = 4$$

and dividing through by 2 shows that the stationary point occurs at

$$x = 2$$

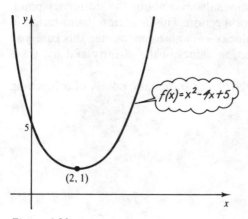

Figure 4.23

Step 2   To classify this point we need to evaluate

$$f''(2)$$

In this case

$$f''(x) = 2$$

for all values of x so in particular

$$f''(2) = 2$$

This number is positive so the function has a minimum at $x = 2$.

We have shown that the minimum point occurs at $x = 2$. The corresponding value of y is easily found by substituting this number into the function to get

$$y = (2)^2 - 4(2) + 5 = 1$$

so the minimum point has coordinates (2, 1). A graph of $f(x)$ is shown in Figure 4.23.

(b)   In order to use steps 1 and 2 we need to find the first- and second-order derivatives of the function

$$f(x) = 2x^3 + 3x^2 - 12x + 4$$

Differentiating once gives

$$f'(x) = 6x^2 + 6x - 12$$

and differentiating a second time gives

$$f''(x) = 12x + 6$$

Step 1   The stationary points are the solutions of the equation

$$f'(x) = 0$$

so we need to solve

$$6x^2 + 6x - 12 = 0$$

This is a quadratic equation and so can be solved using 'the formula'. However, before doing so, it is a good idea to divide both sides by 6 to avoid large numbers. The resulting equation

$$x^2 + x - 2 = 0$$

has solution

$$x = \frac{-1 \pm \sqrt{(1^2 - 4(1)(-2))}}{2(1)}$$

$$= \frac{-1 \pm \sqrt{9}}{2}$$

$$= \frac{-1 \pm 3}{2}$$

$$= -2, 1$$

In general, whenever $f(x)$ is a cubic function the stationary points are the solutions of a quadratic equation, $f'(x) = 0$. Moreover, we know from Section 2.1 that such an equation can have two, one or no solutions. It follows that a cubic equation can have two, one or no stationary points. In this particular example we have seen that there are two stationary points at $x = -2$ and $x = 1$.

Step 2   To classify these points we need to evaluate $f''(-2)$ and $f''(1)$. Now

$$f''(-2) = 12(-2) + 6 = -18$$

This is negative so there is a maximum at $x = -2$. When $x = -2$,

$$y = 2(-2)^3 + 3(-2)^2 - 12(-2) + 4 = 24$$

so the maximum point has coordinates $(-2, 24)$. Now

$$f''(1) = 12(1) + 6 = 18$$

This is positive so there is a minimum at $x = 1$. When $x = 1$,

$$y = 2(1)^3 + 3(1)^2 - 12(1) + 4 = -3$$

so the minimum point has coordinates $(1, -3)$.

This information enables a partial sketch to be drawn as shown in Figure 4.24. Before we can be confident about the complete picture it is useful to plot a few more points such as those below.

x	-10	0	10
y	-1816	4	2184

This table indicates that when x is positive the graph falls steeply downwards from a great height. Similarly, when x is negative the graph quickly disappears off the bottom of the page. The curve cannot wiggle and turn round except at the two stationary points already plotted (otherwise it would have more stationary points which we know is not the case). We now have enough information to join up the pieces and so sketch a complete picture as shown in Figure 4.25.

In an ideal world it would be nice to calculate the three points at which the graph crosses the x axis. These are the solutions of

$$2x^3 + 3x^2 - 12x + 4 = 0$$

There is a formula for solving cubic equations, just as there is for quadratic equations, but it is extremely complicated and is beyond the scope of this book.

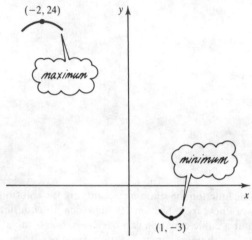

Figure 4.24

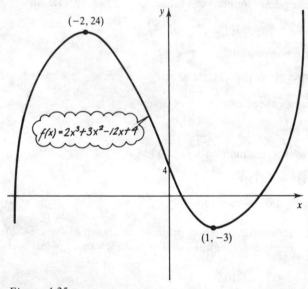

Figure 4.25

∎

PROBLEM

1 Find and classify the stationary points of the following functions. Hence sketch their graphs.

(a) $y = 3x^2 + 12x - 35$ (b) $y = -2x^3 + 15x^2 - 36x + 27$

The task of finding the maximum and minimum values of a function is referred to as **optimization**. This is an important topic in mathematical economics. It provides a rich source of examination questions and we devote the remaining part of this section and the whole of the next to applications of it. In this section we demonstrate the use of stationary points by working through four 'examination-type' problems in detail. These problems involve the optimization of specific revenue, cost, profit and production functions. They are not intended to exhaust all possibilities although they are fairly typical. The next section describes how the mathematics of optimization can be used to derive general theoretical results.

EXAMPLE

A firm's short-run production function is given by

$$Q = 6L^2 - 0.2L^3$$

where L denotes the number of workers.

(1) Find the size of the workforce which maximizes output and hence sketch a graph of this production function.

(2) Find the size of the workforce which maximizes the average product of labour. Calculate MP_L and AP_L at this value of L. What do you observe?

Solution

(1) In the first part of this example we want to find the value of L which maximizes

$$Q = 6L^2 - 0.2L^3$$

Step 1 At a stationary point

$$\frac{dQ}{dL} = 12L - 0.6L^2 = 0$$

This is a quadratic equation and so we could use 'the formula' to find L. However, this is not really necessary in this case because both terms have a common factor of L and the equation may be written as

$$L(12 - 0.6L) = 0$$

It follows that either

$$L = 0 \quad \text{or} \quad 12 - 0.6L = 0$$

that is, the equation has solutions

$$L = 0 \quad \text{and} \quad L = 12/0.6 = 20$$

Step 2 It is obvious on economic grounds that $L = 0$ is a minimum and presumably $L = 20$ is the maximum. We can, of course, check this by differentiating a second time to get

$$\frac{d^2Q}{dL^2} = 12 - 1.2L$$

When $L = 0$,

$$\frac{d^2Q}{dL^2} = 12 > 0$$

which confirms that $L = 0$ is a minimum. The corresponding output is given by

$$Q = 6(0)^2 - 0.2(0)^3 = 0$$

as expected. When $L = 20$,

$$\frac{d^2Q}{dL^2} = -12 < 0$$

which confirms that $L = 20$ is a maximum.

The firm should therefore employ 20 workers to achieve a maximum output

$$Q = 6(20)^2 - 0.2(20)^3 = 800$$

We have shown that the minimum point on the graph has coordinates $(0, 0)$ and the maximum point has coordinates $(20, 800)$. There are no further turning points so the graph of the production function has the shape sketched in Figure 4.26.

It is possible to find the precise values of L at which the graph crosses the horizontal axis. The production function is given by

$$Q = 6L^2 - 0.2L^3$$

so we need to solve

$$6L^2 - 0.2L^3 = 0$$

We can take out a factor of L^2 to get

$$L^2(6 - 0.2L) = 0$$

Hence, either

$$L^2 = 0 \qquad \text{or} \qquad 6 - 0.2L = 0$$

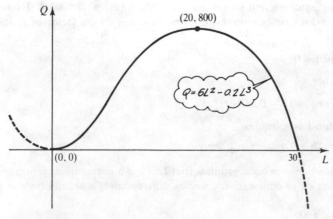

Figure 4.26

The first of these merely confirms the fact that the curve passes through the origin whereas the second shows that the curve intersects the L axis at $L = 6/0.2 = 30$.

(2) In the second part of this example we want to find the value of L which maximizes the average product of labour. This is a concept that we have not met before in this book although it is not difficult to guess how it might be defined.

The **average product of labour**, AP_L, is taken to be total output divided by labour so that in symbols

$$AP_L = \frac{Q}{L}$$

This is sometimes called **labour productivity** since it measures the average output per worker. In this example,

$$AP_L = \frac{6L^2 - 0.2L^3}{L}$$

$$= 6L - 0.2L^2$$

Step 1 At a stationary point

$$\frac{d(AP_L)}{dL} = 0$$

so

$$6 - 0.4L = 0$$

which has solution $L = 6/0.4 = 15$.

Step 2 To classify this stationary point we differentiate a second time to get

$$\frac{d^2(AP_L)}{dL^2} = -0.4 < 0$$

which shows that it is a maximum.

The labour productivity is therefore greatest when the firm employs 15 workers. In fact, the corresponding labour productivity, AP_L, is

$$6(15) - 0.2(15)^2 = 45$$

In other words, the largest number of goods produced per worker is 45.

Finally, we are invited to calculate the value of MP_L at this point. To find an expression for MP_L we need to differentiate Q with respect to L to get

$$MP_L = 12L - 0.6L^2$$

When $L = 15$,

$$MP_L = 12(15) - 0.6(15)^2 = 45$$

We observe that at $L = 15$ the values of MP_L and AP_L are equal.

■

In this particular example we discovered that at the point of maximum average product of labour

| marginal product of labour | = | average product of labour |

There is nothing special about this example and in the next section we show that this result holds for any production function.

PROBLEM

2 A firm's short-run production function is given by

$$Q = 300L^2 - L^4$$

where L denotes the number of workers. Find the size of the workforce which maximizes the average product of labour and verify that at this value of L

$$MP_L = AP_L$$

EXAMPLE

The demand equation of a good is

$$P + Q = 30$$

and the total cost function is

$$TC = \tfrac{1}{2}Q^2 + 6Q + 7$$

(1) Find the level of output which maximizes total revenue.
(2) Find the level of output which maximizes profit. Calculate MR and MC at this value of Q. What do you observe?

Solution

(1) In the first part of this example we want to find the value of Q which maximizes total revenue. To do this we use the given demand equation to find an expression for TR and then apply the theory of stationary points in the usual way.

     The total revenue is defined by

$$TR = PQ$$

We seek the value of Q which maximizes TR so we express TR in terms of the variable Q only. The demand equation

$$P + Q = 30$$

can be rearranged to get

$$P = 30 - Q$$

Hence

$$TR = (30 - Q)Q$$
$$= 30Q - Q^2$$

Step 1 At a stationary point

$$\frac{d(TR)}{dQ} = 0$$

so

$$30 - 2Q = 0$$

which has solution $Q = 30/2 = 15$.

Step 2 To classify this point we differentiate a second time to get

$$\frac{d^2(TR)}{dQ^2} = -2$$

This is negative so TR has a maximum at $Q = 15$.

(2)   In the second part of this example we want to find the value of Q which maximizes profit. To do this we begin by determining an expression for profit in terms of Q. Once this has been done it is then a simple matter to work out the first- and second-order derivatives and so to find and classify the stationary points of the profit function.

The profit function is defined by

$$\pi = TR - TC$$

From part (1)

$$TR = 30Q - Q^2$$

We are given the total cost function

$$TC = \tfrac{1}{2}Q^2 + 6Q + 7$$

Hence

$$\pi = (30Q - Q^2) - (\tfrac{1}{2}Q^2 + 6Q + 7)$$
$$= 30Q - Q^2 - \tfrac{1}{2}Q^2 - 6Q - 7$$
$$= -\tfrac{3}{2}Q^2 + 24Q - 7$$

Step 1 At a stationary point

$$\frac{d\pi}{dQ} = 0$$

so

$$-3Q + 24 = 0$$

which has solution $Q = 24/3 = 8$.

Step 2   To classify this point we differentiate a second time to get

$$\frac{d^2\pi}{dQ^2} = -3$$

This is negative so π has a maximum at $Q = 8$. In fact, the corresponding maximum profit is

$$\pi = -\tfrac{3}{2}(8)^2 + 24(8) - 7 = 89$$

Finally, we are invited to calculate the marginal revenue and marginal cost at this particular value of Q. To find expressions for MR and MC we need only differentiate TR and TC respectively.

If

$$TR = 30Q - Q^2$$

then

$$MR = \frac{d(TR)}{dQ}$$

$$= 30 - 2Q$$

so when $Q = 8$,

$$MR = 30 - 2(8) = 14$$

If

$$TC = \tfrac{1}{2}Q^2 + 6Q + 7$$

then

$$MC = \frac{d(TC)}{dQ}$$

$$= Q + 6$$

so when $Q = 8$,

$$MC = 8 + 6 = 14$$

We observe that at $Q = 8$, the values of MR and MC are equal.

∎

In this particular example we discovered that at the point of maximum profit,

$$\boxed{\text{marginal revenue}} = \boxed{\text{marginal cost}}$$

There is nothing special about this example and in the next section we show that this result holds for any profit function.

PROBLEM

3 The demand equation of a good is given by

$$P + 2Q = 20$$

and the total cost function is

$$Q^3 - 8Q^2 + 20Q + 2$$

(1) Find the level of output which maximizes total revenue.

(2) Find the maximum profit and the value of Q at which it is achieved. Verify that, at this value of Q, MR = MC.

EXAMPLE

The cost of building an office block, x floors high, is made up of three components:

(1) $10 million for the land
(2) $\frac{1}{4}$ million per floor
(3)   specialized costs of $10,000$x$ per floor

How many floors should the block contain if the average cost per floor is to be minimized?

Solution

The $10 million for the land is a fixed cost because it is independent of the number of floors. Each floor costs $\frac{1}{4}$ million so if the building has x floors altogether then the cost will be

$$250\,000x$$

In addition there are specialized costs of $10\,000x$ per floor so if there are x floors this will be

$$(10\,000x)x = 10\,000x^2$$

Notice the square term here which means that the specialized costs rise dramatically with increasing x. This is to be expected since a tall building requires a more complicated design. It may also be necessary to use more expensive materials.

The total cost, TC, is the sum of the three components, that is

$$TC = 10\,000\,000 + 250\,000x + 10\,000x^2$$

The average cost per floor, AC, is found by dividing the total cost by the number of floors, that is

$$AC = \frac{TC}{x}$$

$$= \frac{10\,000\,000 + 250\,000x + 10\,000x^2}{x}$$

$$= \frac{10\,000\,000}{x} + 250\,000 + 10\,000x$$

$$= 10\,000\,000x^{-1} + 250\,000 + 10\,000x$$

Step 1   At a stationary point

$$\frac{d(AC)}{dx} = 0$$

In this case

$$\frac{d(AC)}{dx} = -10\,000\,000x^{-2} + 10\,000$$

$$= \frac{-10\,000\,000}{x^2} + 10\,000$$

so we need to solve

$$10\,000 = \frac{10\,000\,000}{x^2}$$

or equivalently

$$10\,000x^2 = 10\,000\,000$$

Hence

$$x^2 = \frac{10\,000\,000}{10\,000} = 1000$$

This has solution

$$x = \pm\sqrt{1000} = \pm31.6$$

We can obviously ignore the negative value because it does not make sense to build an office block with a negative number of floors so we can deduce that $x = 31.6$.

Step 2   To confirm that this is a minimum we need to differentiate a second time. Now

$$\frac{d(AC)}{dx} = -10\,000\,000x^{-2} + 10\,000$$

so

$$\frac{d^2(AC)}{dx^2} = -2(-10\,000\,000)x^{-3}$$

$$= \frac{20\,000\,000}{x^3}$$

When $x = 31.6$ we see that

$$\frac{d^2(AC)}{dx^2} = \frac{20\,000\,000}{(31.6)^3} = 633.8$$

It follows that $x = 31.6$ is indeed a minimum because the second-order derivative is a positive number.

At this stage it is tempting to state that the answer is 31.6. This is mathematically correct but is a physical impossibility since x must be a whole number. To decide whether to take x to be 31 or 32 we simply evaluate AC for these two values of x and choose the one which produces the lower average cost.

When $x = 31$

$$AC = \frac{10\,000\,000}{31} + 250\,000 + 10\,000(31) = \$882,581$$

When $x = 32$

$$AC = \frac{10\,000\,000}{32} + 250\,000 + 10\,000(32) = \$882,500$$

Therefore an office block 32 floors high produces the lowest average cost per floor.

■

PROBLEM

4 The total cost function of a good is given by

$$TC = Q^2 + 3Q + 36$$

Calculate the level of output which minimizes average cost. Find AC and MC at this value of Q. What do you observe?

EXAMPLE

The supply and demand equations of a good are given by

$$P = Q_S + 8$$

and

$$P = -3Q_D + 80$$

respectively.

The government decides to impose a tax, t, per unit. Find the value of t which maximizes the government's total tax revenue on the assumption that equilibrium conditions prevail in the market.

Solution

The idea of taxation was first introduced in Chapter 1. In Section 1.3 the equilibrium price and quantity were calculated from a given value of t. In this example t is unknown but the analysis is exactly the same. All we need to do is to carry the letter t through the usual calculations and then to choose t at the end so as to maximize the total tax revenue.

To take account of the tax we replace P by $P - t$ in the supply equation. This is because the price that the supplier actually receives is the price, P, that the consumer pays less the tax, t, deducted by the government. The new supply equation is then

$$P - t = Q_S + 8$$

so that

$$P = Q_S + 8 + t$$

In equilibrium

$$Q_S = Q_D$$

If this common value is denoted by Q then the supply and demand equations become

$$P = Q + 8 + t$$

$$P = -3Q + 80$$

Hence

$$Q + 8 + t = -3Q + 80$$

since both sides are equal to P. This can be rearranged to give

$Q = -3Q + 72 - t$ (subtract $8 + t$ from both sides)

$4Q = 72 - t$ (add $3Q$ to both sides)

$Q = 18 - \frac{1}{4}t$ (divide both sides by 4)

Now if the number of goods sold is Q and the government raises t per good then the total tax revenue, T, is given by

$$T = tQ$$

$$= t(18 - \tfrac{1}{4}t)$$

$$= 18t - \tfrac{1}{4}t^2$$

This then is the expression that we wish to maximize.

Step 1   At a stationary point

$$\frac{dT}{dt} = 0$$

so

$$18 - \tfrac{1}{2}t = 0$$

which has solution

$$t = 36$$

Step 2   To classify this point we differentiate a second time to get

$$\frac{d^2T}{dt^2} = -\frac{1}{2} < 0$$

which confirms that it is a maximum.

Hence the government should impose a tax of \$36 on each good.   ∎

PROBLEM

5   The supply and demand equations of a good are given by

$$P = \tfrac{1}{2}Q_s + 25$$

and

$$P = -2Q_D + 50$$

respectively.

The government decides to impose a tax, t, per unit. Find the value of t which maximizes the government's total tax revenue on the assumption that equilibrium conditions prevail in the market.

PRACTICE PROBLEMS

6 Find and classify the stationary points of the following functions. Hence give a rough sketch of their graphs.

(a) $y = -x^2 + x + 1$ (b) $y = x^2 - 4x + 4$
(c) $y = x^2 - 20x + 105$ (d) $y = -x^3 + 3x$

7 Show that all of the following functions have a stationary point at $x = 0$. Verify in each case that $f''(0) = 0$. Classify these points by producing a rough sketch of each function.

(a) $f(x) = x^3$ (b) $f(x) = x^4$ (c) $f(x) = -x^6$

8 If the fixed costs are 13 and the variable costs are $Q + 2$ per unit show that the average cost function is

$$AC = \frac{13}{Q} + Q + 2$$

(1) Calculate the values of AC when $Q = 1, 2, 3, \ldots, 6$. Plot these points on graph paper and hence produce an accurate graph of AC against Q.
(2) Use your graph to estimate the minimum average cost.
(3) Use differentiation to confirm your estimate obtained in part (2).

9 An electronic components firm launches a new product on 1st January. During the following year a rough estimate of the number of orders, S, received t days after the launch is given by

$$S = t^2 - 0.002t^3$$

(1) What is the maximum number of orders received on any one day of the year?
(2) After how many days does the firm experience the greatest increase in orders?

10 If the demand equation of a good is

$$P = \sqrt{(1000 - 4Q)}$$

find the value of Q which maximizes total revenue.

11 The demand and total cost functions of a good are

$$4P + Q - 16 = 0$$

and

$$TC = 4 + 2Q - \frac{3Q^2}{10} + \frac{Q^3}{20}$$

respectively.

(1)   Find expressions for TR, π, MR and MC in terms of Q.

(2)   Solve the equation

$$\frac{d\pi}{dQ} = 0$$

and hence determine the value of Q which maximizes profit.

(3)   Verify that, at the point of maximum profit,

$$MR = MC$$

12   The supply and demand equations of a good are given by

$$3P - Q_S = 3$$

and

$$2P + Q_D = 14$$

respectively.

The government decides to impose a tax, t, per unit. Find the value of t which maximizes the government's total tax revenue on the assumption that equilibrium conditions prevail in the market.

4.7   Further optimization of economic functions

Objectives   At the end of this section you should be able to:

•   show that, at the point of maximum profit, marginal revenue equals marginal cost,

•   show that, at the point of maximum profit, the slope of the marginal revenue curve is less than that of marginal cost,

•   maximize profits of a firm with and without price discrimination in different markets,

•   show that, at the point of maximum average product of labour, average product of labour equals marginal product of labour.

The previous section demonstrated how mathematics can be used to optimize particular economic functions. Those examples suggested two important results:

(1)   if a firm maximizes profit then MR = MC;

(2)   if a firm maximizes average product of labour then $AP_L = MP_L$.

Although these results were found to hold for all of the examples considered in Section 4.6, it does not necessarily follow that the results are always true. The aim of this section is to prove these assertions without reference to specific functions and hence to demonstrate their generality.

Justification of result (1) turns out to be really quite easy. Profit, π, is defined to be the difference between total revenue, TR, and total cost, TC, that is

$$\pi = TR - TC$$

To find the stationary points of π we differentiate with respect to Q and equate to zero, that is

$$\frac{d\pi}{dQ} = \frac{d(TR)}{dQ} - \frac{d(TC)}{dQ} = 0$$

where we have used the difference rule to differentiate the right-hand side. In Section 4.3 we defined

$$MR = \frac{d(TR)}{dQ} \quad \text{and} \quad MC = \frac{d(TC)}{dQ}$$

so the above equation is equivalent to

$$MR - MC = 0$$

and so MR = MC as required.

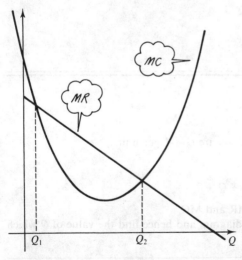

Figure 4.27

The stationary points of the profit function can therefore be found by sketching the MR and MC curves on the same diagram and inspecting the points of intersection. Figure 4.27 shows typical marginal revenue and marginal cost curves. The result

$$MR = MC$$

holds for any stationary point. Consequently, if this equation has more than one solution then we need some further information before we can decide on the profit maximizing level of output. In Figure 4.27 there are two points of intersection, Q_1 and Q_2, and it turns out (as you discovered in Problems 3 and 11 in the last section) that one of these is a maximum while the other is a minimum. Obviously, in any actual example, we can classify these points by evaluating second-order derivatives. However, it would be nice to make this decision just by inspecting the graphs of marginal revenue and marginal cost. To see how this can be done let us return to the equation

$$\frac{d\pi}{dQ} = MR - MC$$

and differentiate again with respect to Q to get

$$\frac{d^2\pi}{dQ^2} = \frac{d(MR)}{dQ} - \frac{d(MC)}{dQ}$$

Now if $d^2\pi/dQ^2 < 0$ then the profit is a maximum. This will be so when

$$\frac{d(MR)}{dQ} < \frac{d(MC)}{dQ}$$

that is when the slope of the marginal revenue curve is less than the slope of the marginal cost curve.

Looking at Figure 4.27 we deduce that this criterion is true at Q_2 so this must be the desired level of output needed to maximize profit. Note also from Figure 4.27 that the statement 'the slope of the marginal revenue curve is less than the slope of the marginal cost curve' is equivalent to saying that 'the marginal cost curve cuts the marginal revenue curve from below'. It is this latter form that is often quoted in economics textbooks. A similar argument shows that, at a minimum point, the marginal cost curve cuts the marginal revenue curve from above and so we can deduce that profit is a minimum at Q_1 in Figure 4.27. In practice, the task of sketching the graphs of MR and MC and reading off the coordinates of the points of intersection is not an attractive one, particularly if MR and MC are complicated functions. However, it might turn out that MR and MC are both linear in which case a graphical approach is feasible.

PROBLEM

1 A monopolist's demand function is

$$P = 25 - 0.5Q$$

The fixed costs of production are 7 and the variable costs are $Q + 1$ per unit.

(1) Show that

$$TR = 25Q - 0.5Q^2 \quad \text{and} \quad TC = Q^2 + Q + 7$$

and deduce the corresponding expressions for MR and MC.

(2) Sketch the graphs of MR and MC on the same diagram and hence find the value of Q which maximizes profit.

Quite often a firm identifies more than one market in which it wishes to sell its goods. For example, a firm might decide to export goods to several countries and demand conditions are likely to be different in each one. The firm may be able to take advantage of this and increase overall profit by charging different prices in each country. The theoretical result 'marginal revenue equals marginal cost' can be applied in each market separately to find the optimal pricing policy.

EXAMPLE

A firm is allowed to charge different prices for its domestic and industrial customers. If P_1 and Q_1 denote the price and demand for the domestic market then the demand equation is

$$P_1 + Q_1 = 500$$

If P_2 and Q_2 denote the price and demand for the industrial market then the demand equation is

$$2P_2 + 3Q_2 = 720$$

The total cost function is

$$TC = 50\,000 + 20Q$$

where $Q = Q_1 + Q_2$.
Determine the prices that the firm should charge to maximize profits

(a) with price discrimination
(b) without price discrimination

Compare the profits obtained in parts (a) and (b).

Solution

(a) The important thing to notice is that the total cost function is independent of the market and so marginal costs are the same in each case. In fact, since

$$TC = 50\,000 + 20Q$$

we have MC = 20. All we have to do to maximize profits is to find an expression for the marginal revenue for each market and to equate this to the constant value of marginal cost.

Domestic market The demand equation

$$P_1 + Q_1 = 500$$

rearranges to give

$$P_1 = 500 - Q_1$$

so the total revenue function for this market is

$$TR_1 = (500 - Q_1)Q_1 = 500Q_1 - Q_1^2$$

Hence

$$MR_1 = \frac{d(TR_1)}{dQ_1} = 500 - 2Q_1$$

For maximum profit

$$MR_1 = MC$$

so

$$500 - 2Q_1 = 20$$

which has solution $Q_1 = 240$. The corresponding price is found by substituting this value into the demand equation to get

$$P_1 = 500 - 240 = \$260$$

To maximize profit the firm should charge its domestic customers $260 per good.

Industrial market   The demand equation

$$2P_2 + 3Q_2 = 720$$

rearranges to give

$$P_2 = 360 - \tfrac{3}{2}Q_2$$

so the total revenue function for this market is

$$\text{TR}_2 = (360 - \tfrac{3}{2}Q_2)Q_2 = 360Q_2 - \tfrac{3}{2}Q_2^2$$

Hence

$$\text{MR}_2 = \frac{d(\text{TR}_2)}{dQ_2} = 360 - 3Q_2$$

For maximum profit

$$\text{MR}_2 = \text{MC}$$

so

$$360 - 3Q_2 = 20$$

which has solution $Q_2 = 340/3$. The corresponding price is obtained by substituting this value into the demand equation to get

$$P_2 = 360 - \frac{3}{2}\left(\frac{340}{3}\right) = \$190$$

To maximize profits the firm should charge its industrial customers $190 per good, which is lower than the price charged to its domestic customers.

(b)   If there is no price discrimination then $P_1 = P_2 = P$, say, and the demand functions for the domestic and industrial markets become

$$P + Q_1 = 500$$

and

$$2P + 3Q_2 = 720$$

respectively. We can use these to deduce a single demand equation for the combined market. We need to relate the price, P, of each good to the total demand, $Q = Q_1 + Q_2$.

This can be done by rearranging the given demand equations for Q_1 and Q_2 and then adding. For the domestic market

$$Q_1 = 500 - P$$

and for the industrial market

$$Q_2 = 240 - \tfrac{2}{3}P$$

Hence

$$Q = Q_1 + Q_2 = 740 - \tfrac{5}{3}P$$

The demand equation for the combined market is therefore

$$Q + \tfrac{5}{3}P = 740$$

The usual procedure for profit maximization can now be applied. This demand equation rearranges to give

$$P = 444 - \tfrac{3}{5}Q$$

enabling the total revenue function to be written down as

$$TR = \left(444 - \frac{3}{5}Q \right)Q = 444Q - \frac{3Q^2}{5}$$

Hence

$$MR = \frac{d(TR)}{dQ} = 444 - \frac{6}{5}Q$$

For maximum profit

$$MR = MC$$

so

$$444 - \tfrac{6}{5}Q = 20$$

which has solution $Q = 1060/3$. The corresponding price is found by substituting this value into the demand equation to get

$$P = 444 - \frac{3}{5}\left(\frac{1060}{3} \right) = \$232$$

To maximize profit without discrimination the firm needs to charge a uniform price of $232 for each good. Notice that this price lies between the prices charged to its domestic and industrial customers with discrimination.

To evaluate the profit under each policy we need to work out the total revenue and subtract the total cost. In part (a) the firm sells 240 goods at $260 each in the domestic market and sells 340/3 goods at $190 each in the industrial market, so the total revenue received is

$$240 \times 260 + \frac{340}{3} \times 190 = \$83,933.33$$

The total number of goods produced is

$$240 + \frac{340}{3} = \frac{1060}{3}$$

so the total cost is

$$50\,000 + 20 \times \frac{1060}{3} = \$57,066.67$$

Therefore the profit with price discrimination is

$$83\,933.33 - 57\,066.67 = \$26{,}866.67$$

In part (b) the firm sells 1060/3 goods at \$232 each so total revenue is

$$\frac{1060}{3} \times 232 = \$81{,}973.33$$

Now the total number of goods produced under both pricing policies is the same, that is 1060/3. Consequently, the total cost of production in part (b) must be the same as part (a), that is

$$TC = \$57{,}066.67$$

The profit without price discrimination is

$$81\,973.33 - 57\,066.67 = \$24{,}906.66$$

As expected, the profits are higher with discrimination than without.

■

PROBLEM

2 A firm has the possibility of charging different prices in its domestic and foreign markets. The corresponding demand equations are given by

$$Q_1 = 300 - P_1$$

$$Q_2 = 400 - 2P_2$$

The total cost function is

$$TC = 5000 + 100Q$$

where $Q = Q_1 + Q_2$.

Determine the prices that the firm should charge to maximize profits

(a) with price discrimination
(b) without price discrimination

Compare the profits obtained in parts (a) and (b).

In the previous example and in Problem 2 we assumed that the marginal costs were the same in each market. The level of output that maximizes profit with price discrimination was found by equating marginal revenue to this common value of marginal cost. It follows that the marginal revenue must be the same in each market. In symbols

$$MR_1 = MC \qquad \text{and} \qquad MR_2 = MC$$

so

$$MR_1 = MR_2$$

This fact is obvious on economic grounds. If it were not true then the firm's policy would be to increase sales in the market where marginal revenue is higher and to decrease sales by the same amount in the market where the marginal revenue is lower. The effect would be to increase revenue while keeping costs fixed, thereby raising profit. This property leads to an interesting result connecting price, P, with elasticity of demand, E. In Section 4.5 we derived the formula

$$MR = P\left(1 - \frac{1}{E}\right)$$

If we let the price elasticity of demand in two markets be denoted by E_1 and E_2 corresponding to prices P_1 and P_2 then the equation

$$MR_1 = MR_2$$

becomes

$$P_1\left(1 - \frac{1}{E_1}\right) = P_2\left(1 - \frac{1}{E_2}\right)$$

This equation holds whenever a firm chooses its prices P_1 and P_2 to maximize profits in each market. Note that if $E_1 < E_2$ then this equation can only be true if $P_1 > P_2$. In other words, the firm charges the higher price in the market with the lower elasticity of demand.

PROBLEM

3   Calculate the price elasticity of demand at the point of maximum profit for each of the demand functions given in Problem 2 with price discrimination. Verify that the firm charges the higher price in the market with the lower elasticity of demand.

The previous discussion concentrated on profit. We now turn our attention to average product of labour and prove result (2) stated at the beginning of this section. This concept is defined by

$$AP_L = \frac{Q}{L}$$

where Q is output and L is labour. The maximization of AP_L is a little more complicated than before since it is necessary to use the quotient rule to differentiate this function. In the notation of Section 4.4 we write

$$u = Q \quad \text{and} \quad v = L$$

so

$$\frac{du}{dL} = \frac{dQ}{dL} = MP_L \quad \text{and} \quad \frac{dv}{dL} = \frac{dL}{dL} = 1$$

where we have used the fact that the derivative of output with respect to labour is the marginal product of labour.

The quotient rule gives

$$\frac{d(AP_L)}{dL} = \frac{v\,du/dL - u\,dv/dL}{v^2}$$

$$= \frac{L(MP_L) - Q(1)}{L^2}$$

$$= \frac{MP_L - Q/L}{L} \qquad \left(\substack{\textit{divide top and} \\ \textit{bottom by } L} \right)$$

$$= \frac{MP_L - AP_L}{L} \qquad \left(\substack{\textit{by definition,} \\ AP_L = \frac{Q}{L}} \right)$$

At a stationary point

$$\frac{d(AP_L)}{dL} = 0$$

so

$$\frac{MP_L - AP_L}{L} = 0$$

Hence

$$MP_L = AP_L$$

as required.

This analysis shows that, at a stationary point of the average product of labour function, the marginal product of labour equals the average product of labour. The above argument provides a formal proof that this result is true for any average product of labour function. Figure 4.28 shows typical average and marginal product functions. Note that the two curves intersect at the peak of the AP_L curve. To the left of this point the AP_L function is increasing so that

$$\frac{d(AP_L)}{dL} > 0$$

Now we have just seen that

$$\frac{d(AP_L)}{dL} = \frac{MP_L - AP_L}{L}$$

so we deduce that, to the left of the maximum, $MP_L > AP_L$. In other words, in this region the graph of marginal product of labour lies above that of average product of labour. Similarly, to the right of the maximum, AP_L is decreasing so that

$$\frac{d(AP_L)}{dL} < 0$$

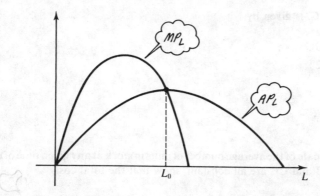

Figure 4.28

and hence $MP_L < AP_L$. The graph of marginal product of labour therefore lies below that of average product of labour in this region.

We deduce that if the stationary point is a maximum then the MP_L curve cuts the AP_L curve from above. A similar argument can be used for any average function. The particular case of the average cost function is investigated in Problem 8.

PRACTICE PROBLEMS

4   Show that if the marginal cost curve cuts the marginal revenue curve from above then profit is a minimum.

5   **(1)**   In Section 4.5 the following relationship between marginal revenue, MR, and price elasticity of demand, E, was derived

$$MR = P\left(1 - \frac{1}{E}\right)$$

Use this result to show that at the point of maximum total revenue, $E = 1$.

(2)   Verify the result of part (1) for the demand function

$$2P + 3Q = 60$$

6   The economic order quantity, EOQ, is used in cost accounting to minimize the total cost, TC, to order and carry a firm's stock over the period of a year.
The annual cost of placing orders, ACO, is given by

$$ACO = \frac{(ARU)(CO)}{EOQ}$$

where

ARU = annual required units

CO = cost per order

The annual carrying cost, ACC, is given by

$$\text{ACC} = (\text{CU})(\text{CC}) \frac{(\text{EOQ})}{2}$$

where

CU = cost per unit

CC = carrying cost

and (EOQ)/2 provides an estimate of the average number of units in stock at any given time of the year. Assuming that ARU, CO, CU and CC are all constant, show that the total cost

$$\text{TC} = \text{ACO} + \text{ACC}$$

is minimized when

$$\text{EOQ} = \sqrt{\frac{2(\text{ARU})(\text{CO})}{(\text{CU})(\text{CC})}}$$

7 The demand functions for a firm's domestic and foreign markets are

$$P_1 = 50 - 5Q_1$$

$$P_2 = 30 - 4Q_2$$

and the total cost function is

$$\text{TC} = 10 + 10Q$$

where $Q = Q_1 + Q_2$. Determine the prices needed to maximize profit

(a) with price discrimination
(b) without price discrimination

Compare the profits obtained in parts (a) and (b).

8 (1) Show that, at a stationary point of an average cost function, average cost equals marginal cost.
   (2) Show that if the marginal cost curve cuts the average cost curve from below then average cost is a minimum.

4.8 The exponential function

Objectives   At the end of this section you should be able to:

● understand how the number e is defined,

● appreciate the use of the exponential function in economic modelling,

● sketch graphs of functions involving the exponential function,

● differentiate the exponential and natural logarithm functions.

Of considerable importance in economic modelling is the exponential function. This was first introduced in Chapter 3 in the context of continuous compounding, although it is not necessary for you to have worked through that material to understand this function. In this section we review its basic properties. In particular, we describe how to differentiate the exponential function and illustrate its use in economics.

To begin with, consider the function

$$f(x) = 2^x$$

As we pointed out in Section 2.3, a number such as 2^x is said to be in exponential form. The number 2 is called the base and x is called the exponent. Values of this function are easily found either by pressing the power key $\boxed{x^y}$ on a calculator or by using the definition of b^n given in Section 2.3. A selection of these are given in the following table:

x	-3	-2	-1	0	1	2	3	4	5
2^x	0.125	0.25	0.5	1	2	4	8	16	32

A graph of $f(x)$ based on this table is sketched in Figure 4.29. Notice that the graph approaches the x axis for large negative values of x and it rises rapidly as x increases.

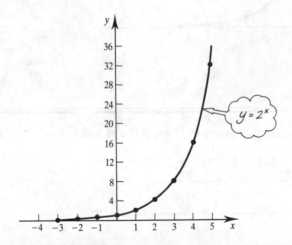

$y = 2^x$

Figure 4.29

A related function is the negative exponential

$$g(x) = 2^{-x}$$

which has values

x	-5	-4	-3	-2	-1	0	1	2	3
2^{-x}	32	16	8	4	2	1	0.5	0.25	0.125

This function is sketched in Figure 4.30. It is worth noticing that the numbers appearing in the table of 2^{-x} are the same as those of 2^x but arranged in reverse order. Hence the graph of 2^{-x} is obtained by reflecting the graph of 2^x in the y axis. Figure 4.29 displays the graph of a particular exponential function, 2^x. Quite generally, the graph of any exponential function

$$f(x) = b^x$$

has the same basic shape provided $b > 1$. The only difference is that larger values of b produce steeper curves. A similar comment applies to the negative exponential, b^{-x}.

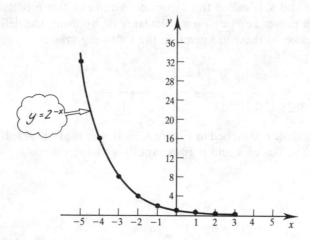

Figure 4.30

PROBLEM

1   Complete the following table of function values of 3^x and 3^{-x} and hence sketch their graphs.

x	-3	-2	-1	0	1	2	3
3^x							
3^{-x}							

Obviously there is a whole class of functions, each corresponding to a different base, b. Of particular interest is the case when b takes the value

2.718 281 828 459...

This number is written as e and the function

$$f(x) = e^x$$

is referred to as *the* exponential function. In fact, it is not necessary for you to understand where this number comes from. All scientific calculators have an $\boxed{e^x}$ button and you may simply wish to accept the results of using it. However, it might help your confidence if you have some appreciation of how it is defined. To this end consider the expression

$$\left(1 + \frac{1}{m}\right)^{m}$$

and see what happens when we evaluate it using ever increasing values of m. For example, putting $m = 1, 10, 100$ and 1000 gives

$$\left(1 + \frac{1}{1}\right)^{1} = 2^{1} = 2$$

$$\left(1 + \frac{1}{10}\right)^{10} = (1.1)^{10} = 2.593\,742\,460$$

$$\left(1 + \frac{1}{100}\right)^{100} = (1.01)^{100} = 2.704\,813\,829$$

$$\left(1 + \frac{1}{1000}\right)^{1000} = (1.001)^{1000} = 2.716\,923\,932$$

PROBLEM

2   **(1)**   Use the power key $\boxed{x^y}$ on your calculator to evaluate

$$\left(1 + \frac{1}{m}\right)^{m}$$

where $m = 10\,000, 100\,000$ and $1\,000\,000$.

(2)   Use your calculator to evaluate e^1 and compare with your answer to part (1).

Hopefully, the results of Problem 2 should convince you that as m gets larger, the value of

$$\left(1 + \frac{1}{m}\right)^{m}$$

approaches a limiting value of $2.718\,281\,828\ldots$, which we choose to denote by the letter e. In symbols we write

$$e = \lim_{m \to \infty}\left(1 + \frac{1}{m}\right)^{m}$$

In fact, using this definition, we can actually prove the formula for continuous compounding given in Chapter 3. This justification can be found in Problem 10 at the end of this section. The main reason why this particular base is so important is a quite remarkable property involving its derivative, which we shall investigate in a moment. However, before we do this it will be instructive to consider some preliminary examples. These should give you practice in using the $\boxed{e^x}$ button on your calculator and will give you some idea how this function can be used in economic modelling.

EXAMPLE

An economy is forecast to grow continuously at an annual rate of 2% so that the gross national product (GNP), measured in billions of dollars, after t years is given by

$$GNP = 80e^{0.02t}$$

(1)   Calculate the current value of GNP and its future value in three years' time.
(2)   After how many years is GNP forecast to be $88 billion?

Solution

(1)   To find the current value of GNP we substitute $t = 0$ into the formula

$$GNP = 80e^{0.02t}$$

to get

$$GNP = 80e^0 = \$80 \text{ billion}$$

$e^0 = 1$

To find the value after three years we substitute $t = 3$ to get

$$GNP = 80e^{0.06} = \$85 \text{ billion}$$

to the nearest billion. There is little point in calculating GNP more accurately since the equation only provides a forecast of GNP over time.

(2)   In this part of the question we are told the value of GNP and want to find the value of t. In other words, we need to solve

$$88 = 80e^{0.02t}$$

for t. Dividing through by 80 gives

$$1.1 = e^{0.02t}$$

Given that the unknown appears as a power we can solve this equation by taking logarithms as described in Section 2.3. This could be done by taking logarithms to base 10. However, it is easier to use logarithms to base e, which are called natural logarithms. Using the definition of logarithms given in Section 2.3 we know that

$$\text{if} \quad M = e^n \quad \text{then} \quad n = \ln M$$

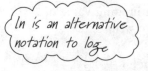

ln is an alternative notation to log$_e$

If we apply this definition to the equation

$$1.1 = e^{0.02t}$$

we deduce that

$$0.02t = \ln 1.1 = 0.095\,31\ldots$$

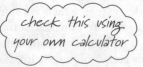

check this using your own calculator

so

$$t = \frac{0.095\,31}{0.02} = 4.77$$

We therefore deduce that GNP reaches a level of $88 billion after five years.

■

PROBLEM

3   During a recession a firm's revenue declines continuously at an annual rate of 15% so that the revenue, TR (measured in millions of dollars), in t years' time is modelled by

$$TR = 5e^{-0.15t}$$

(1)   Calculate the current revenue and also the revenue in two years' time.

(2)   After how many years will the revenue decline to $2.7 million?

EXAMPLE

The percentage, y, of households possessing refrigerators, t years after they have been introduced in a developed country, is modelled by

$$y = 100 - 95e^{-0.15t}$$

(1)   Find the percentage of households that have refrigerators

(a)   at their launch
(b)   after 1 year
(c)   after 10 years
(d)   after 20 years

(2)   What is the market saturation level?

(3)   Sketch a graph of y against t and hence give a qualitative description of the growth of refrigerator ownership over time.

Solution

(1)   To calculate the percentage of households possessing refrigerators now and in 1, 10 and 20 years' time we substitute $t = 0$, 1, 10 and 20 into the formula

$$y = 100 - 95e^{-0.15t}$$

to get

(a) $y(0) = 100 - 95e^{0} = 5\%$
(b) $y(1) = 100 - 95e^{-0.15} = 18\%$
(c) $y(10) = 100 - 95e^{-1.5} = 79\%$
(d) $y(20) = 100 - 95e^{-3.0} = 95\%$

(2)   To find the saturation level we need to investigate what happens to y as t gets ever larger. We know that the graph of a negative exponential function has the basic shape shown in

Figure 4.30. Consequently the value of $e^{-0.15t}$ will eventually approach zero as t increases. The market saturation level is therefore given by

$$y = 100 - 95(0) = 100\%$$

(3)   A graph of y against t, based on the information obtained in parts (1) and (2), is sketched in Figure 4.31.

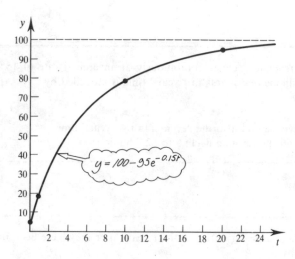

Figure 4.31

This shows that y grows rapidly to begin with but slows down as the market approaches saturation level. A saturation level of 100% indicates that eventually all households are expected to possess refrigerators, which is not surprising given the nature of the product.

■

PROBLEM

4   The percentage, y, of households possessing camcorders t years after they have been launched is modelled by

$$y = \frac{55}{1 + 800e^{-0.3t}}$$

(1)   Find the percentage of households that have camcorders

  (a)   at their launch
  (b)   after 10 years
  (c)   after 20 years
  (d)   after 30 years

(2)   What is the market saturation level?

(3)   Sketch a graph of y against t and hence give a qualitative description of the growth of camcorder ownership over time.

We now investigate the derived functions associated with the exponential and natural logarithm functions, e^x and $\ln x$. The approach that we adopt is similar to that used in Section 4.1. The derivative of a function determines the slope of the graph of a function. Consequently, to discover how to differentiate an unfamiliar function we first produce an accurate sketch and then measure the slopes of the tangents at selected points.

EXAMPLE

Complete the following table of function values and hence sketch a graph of $f(x) = e^x$.

x	-2.0	-1.5	-1.0	-0.5	0.0	0.5	1.0	1.5
$f(x)$								

Draw tangents to the graph at $x = -1$, 0 and 1. Hence estimate the values of $f'(-1)$, $f'(0)$ and $f'(1)$. Suggest a general formula for the derived function $f'(x)$.

Solution

Using a calculator we obtain

x	-2.0	-1.5	-1.0	-0.5	0.0	0.5	1.0	1.5
$f(x)$	0.14	0.22	0.37	0.61	1.00	1.65	2.72	4.48

The corresponding graph of the exponential function is sketched in Figure 4.32. From the graph we see that the slopes of the tangents are

$$f'(-1) = \frac{0.20}{0.50} = 0.4$$

$$f'(0) = \frac{0.50}{0.50} = 1.0$$

$$f'(1) = \frac{1.35}{0.50} = 2.7$$

These results are obtained by measurement and so are only quoted to 1 decimal place. We cannot really expect to achieve any greater accuracy using this approach.

The values of x, $f(x)$ and $f'(x)$ are summarized in the following table. The values of $f(x)$ are rounded to 1 decimal place in order to compare with the graphical estimates of $f'(x)$.

x	-1	0	1
$f(x)$	0.4	1.0	2.7
$f'(x)$	0.4	1.0	2.7

Notice that the values of $f(x)$ and $f'(x)$ are identical to within the accuracy quoted.

These results suggest that the slope of the graph at each point is the same as the function value at that point; that is, e^x differentiates to itself. Symbolically,

if $f(x) = e^x$ then $f'(x) = e^x$

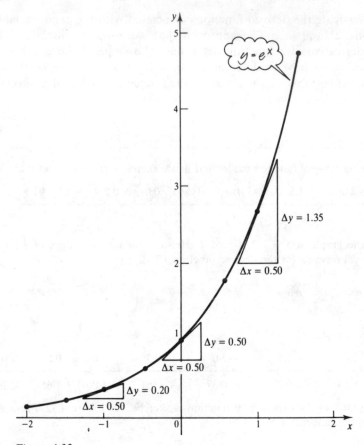

Figure 4.32

or, equivalently,

$$\text{if } y = e^x \quad \text{then} \quad \frac{dy}{dx} = e^x$$

∎

PROBLEM

5 Use your calculator to complete the following table of function values and hence sketch an accurate graph of $f(x) = \ln x$.

x	0.50	1.00	1.50	2.00	2.50	3.00	3.50	4.00
$f(x)$			0.41				1.25	

Draw the tangents to the graph at $x = 1$, 2 and 3. Hence estimate the values of $f'(1)$, $f'(2)$ and $f'(3)$. Suggest a general formula for the derived function $f'(x)$.

[Hint: for the last part you may find it helpful to rewrite your estimates of $f'(x)$ as simple fractions.]

In fact, it is possible to prove that

$$\text{if } y = e^{mx} \quad \text{then} \quad \frac{dy}{dx} = me^{mx}$$

and

$$\text{if } y = \ln mx \quad \text{then} \quad \frac{dy}{dx} = \frac{1}{x}$$

for any value of the constant m. In particular, we see by setting $m = 1$ that

   e^x differentiates to e^x

and that

   $\ln x$ differentiates to $\dfrac{1}{x}$

which agree with our practical investigations.

EXAMPLE

Differentiate

(a) $y = e^{2x}$
(b) $y = e^{-7x}$
(c) $y = \ln 5x$ $(x > 0)$
(d) $y = \ln 559x$ $(x > 0)$

Solution

(a)   Setting $m = 2$ in the general formula shows that if

$$y = e^{2x} \quad \text{then} \quad \frac{dy}{dx} = 2e^{2x}$$

Notice that when exponential functions are differentiated the power itself does not change. All that happens is that the coefficient of x comes down to the front.

(b)   Setting $m = -7$ in the general formula shows that if

$$y = e^{-7x} \quad \text{then} \quad \frac{dy}{dx} = -7e^{-7x}$$

(c)   Setting $m = 5$ in the general formula shows that if

$$y = \ln 5x \qquad \text{then} \qquad \frac{dy}{dx} = \frac{1}{x}$$

Notice the restriction $x > 0$ stated in the question. This is needed to ensure that we do not attempt to take the logarithm of a negative number which is impossible.

(d)   Setting $m = 559$ in the general formula shows that if

$$y = \ln 559x \qquad \text{then} \qquad \frac{dy}{dx} = \frac{1}{x}$$

Notice that we get the same answer as part (c). The derivative of the natural logarithm function does not depend on the coefficient of x.

■

PROBLEM

6   Differentiate

(a) $y = e^{3x}$ **(b)** $y = e^{-x}$ **(c)** $y = \ln 3x$ $(x > 0)$ **(d)** $y = \ln 51\,234x$ $(x > 0)$

The chain, product and quotient rules can be used to differentiate more complicated functions involving e^x and $\ln x$ and we illustrate this by considering some economic examples.

EXAMPLE

A firm's short-run production function is given by

$$Q = L^2 e^{-0.01L}$$

Find the value of L which maximizes the average product of labour.

Solution

The average product of labour is given by

$$AP_L = \frac{Q}{L} = \frac{L^2 e^{-0.01L}}{L} = L e^{-0.01L}$$

To maximize this function we adopt the strategy described in Section 4.6.

Step 1   At a stationary point

$$\frac{d(AP_L)}{dL} = 0$$

To differentiate $L e^{-0.01L}$, we use the product rule. If

$$u = L \qquad \text{and} \qquad v = e^{-0.01L}$$

then

$$\frac{du}{dL} = 1 \quad \text{and} \quad \frac{dv}{dL} = -0.01e^{-0.01L}$$

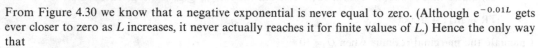

e^{mx} differentiates to me^{mx}

By the product rule

$$\frac{d(AP_L)}{dL} = u\frac{dv}{dL} + v\frac{du}{dL}$$

$$= L(-0.01e^{-0.01L}) + e^{-0.01L}$$

$$= (1 - 0.01L)e^{-0.01L} \quad (1)$$

From Figure 4.30 we know that a negative exponential is never equal to zero. (Although $e^{-0.01L}$ gets ever closer to zero as L increases, it never actually reaches it for finite values of L.) Hence the only way that

$$(1 - 0.01L)e^{-0.01L}$$

can equal zero is when

$$1 - 0.01L = 0$$

which has solution $L = 100$.

Step 2 To show that this is a maximum we need to differentiate a second time. To do this we apply the product rule to

$$(1 - 0.01L)e^{-0.01L}$$

taking

$$u = 1 - 0.01L \quad \text{and} \quad v = e^{-0.01L}$$

for which

$$\frac{du}{dL} = -0.01 \quad \text{and} \quad \frac{dv}{dL} = -0.01e^{-0.01L}$$

Hence

$$\frac{d^2(AP_L)}{dL^2} = u\frac{dv}{dL} + v\frac{du}{dL}$$

$$= (1 - 0.01L)(-0.01e^{-0.01L}) + e^{-0.01L}(-0.01)$$

$$= (-0.02 + 0.0001L)e^{-0.01L}$$

Finally, putting $L = 100$ into this gives

$$\frac{d^2(AP_L)}{dL^2} = -0.0037$$

The fact that this is negative shows that the stationary point, $L = 100$, is indeed a maximum. ∎

PROBLEM

7 The demand function of a good is given by

$$Q = 1000e^{-0.2P}$$

If fixed costs are 100 and the variable costs are 2 per unit, show that the profit function is given by

$$\pi = 1000Pe^{-0.2P} - 2000e^{-0.2P} - 100$$

Find the price needed to maximize profit.

EXAMPLE

A firm estimates that the total revenue received from the sale of Q goods is given by

$$TR = \ln(1 + 1000Q^2)$$

Calculate the marginal revenue when $Q = 10$.

Solution

The marginal revenue function is obtained by differentiating the total revenue function. To differentiate $\ln(1 + 1000Q^2)$ we use the chain rule. We first differentiate the outer log function to get

$$\frac{1}{1 + 1000Q^2}$$

natural logs differentiate to reciprocals

and then multiply by the derivative of the inner function, $1 + 1000Q^2$, to get $2000Q$. Hence

$$MR = \frac{d(TR)}{dQ} = \frac{2000Q}{1 + 1000Q^2}$$

At $Q = 10$,

$$MR = \frac{2000(10)}{1 + 1000(10)^2} = 0.2$$

PROBLEM

8   If the demand equation is

$$P = 200 - 40\ln(Q + 1)$$

calculate the price elasticity of demand when $Q = 20$.

PRACTICE PROBLEMS

9   A team of financial advisers guiding the launch of a national newspaper have modelled the future circulation of the newspaper by the equation

$$N = c(1 - e^{-kt})$$

where N is the daily circulation after t days of publication, and c and k are positive constants. Transpose this formula to show that

$$t = \frac{1}{k} \ln \left(\frac{c}{c - N} \right)$$

When the paper is launched audits show that

$$c = 700\,000 \quad \text{and} \quad k = \frac{1}{30} \ln 2$$

(1) Calculate the daily circulation after 30 days of publication.

(2) After how many days will the daily circulation first reach 525 000?

(3) What advice can you give to the newspaper proprietor if it is known that the paper will break even only if the daily circulation exceeds $\frac{3}{4}$ million?

10 If a principal, P, is invested at $r\%$ interest compounded annually then its future value, S, after n years is given by

$$S = P \left(1 + \frac{r}{100} \right)^n$$

(1) Use this formula to show that if an interest rate of $r\%$ is compounded k times a year then after t years

$$S = P \left(1 + \frac{r}{100k} \right)^{kt}$$

(2) Show that if $m = 100k/r$ then the formula given in part (1) can be written as

$$S = P \left[\left(1 + \frac{1}{m} \right)^m \right]^{rt/100}$$

(3) Use the definition

$$e = \lim_{m \to \infty} \left(1 + \frac{1}{m} \right)^m$$

to deduce that if the interest is compounded with ever increasing frequency (that is, continuously) then

$$S = Pe^{rt/100}$$

11 The number of items, N, produced each day by an assembly line worker, t days after an initial training period is modelled by

$$N = 100 - 100e^{-0.4t}$$

(1) Calculate the number of items produced daily

   (a) 1 day after the training period

   (b) 2 days after the training period

   (c) 10 days after the training period

(2) What is the worker's daily production in the long run?

(3) Sketch a graph of N against t and explain why the general shape might have been expected.

12 Use the chain rule to differentiate

   (a) $y = e^{x^2}$ (b) $y = \ln (1 + x + x^2)$

13 Use the product rule to differentiate

   (a) $y = x^4 e^{2x}$ (b) $y = x \ln x$

14 Find the output needed to maximize profit given that the total cost and total revenue functions are

$$TC = 2Q \quad \text{and} \quad TR = 100 \ln (Q + 1)$$

respectively

15 If a firm's production function is given by

$$Q = 700Le^{-0.02L}$$

find the value of L which maximizes output.

5 *Partial Differentiation*

This chapter continues the topic of calculus by describing how to differentiate functions of more than one variable. In many ways this chapter can be regarded as the climax of the whole book. It is the summit of the mathematical mountain that we have been merrily climbing. Not only are the associated mathematical ideas and techniques quite sophisticated but also partial differentiation provides a rich source of applications. In one sense there is no new material presented here. If you know how to differentiate a function of one variable then you also know how to partially differentiate a function of several variables because the rules are the same. Similarly, if you can optimize a function of one variable then you need have no fear of unconstrained and constrained optimization. Of course, if you cannot use the elementary rules of differentiation or cannot find the maximum and minimum values of a function as described in Chapter 4 then you really are fighting a lost cause. Under these circumstances you are best advised to omit this chapter entirely. There is no harm in doing this because it does not form the prerequisite for any of the later topics. However, you will miss out on one of the most elegant and useful branches of mathematics.

There are six sections. It is important that Sections 5.1 and 5.2 are read first but the remaining sections can be studied in any order. Sections 5.1 and 5.2 follow the familiar pattern. We begin by looking at the mathematical techniques and then use them to determine marginal functions and elasticities. Section 5.3 describes the multiplier concept and completes the topic of statics which you studied in Chapter 1.

The final three sections are devoted to optimization. For functions of several variables, optimization problems are split into two groups, unconstrained and constrained. Unconstrained problems, tackled in Section 5.4, involve the maximization and minimization of functions in which the variables are free to take any values whatsoever. In a constrained problem only certain combinations of the variables are examined. For example, a firm might wish to minimize costs but is constrained by the need to satisfy production quotas or an individual might want to maximize utility but is subject to a budgetary constraint and so on. There are two ways of solving constrained problems; the method of substitution and the method of Lagrange multipliers, described in Sections 5.5 and 5.6 respectively.

5.1   Functions of several variables

Objectives   At the end of this section you should be able to:

- use the function notation, $z = f(x, y)$,

- determine the first-order partial derivatives, f_x and f_y,

- determine the second-order partial derivatives, f_{xx}, f_{xy}, f_{yx} and f_{yy},

- appreciate that, for most functions, $f_{xy} = f_{yx}$,

- use the small increments formula,

- perform implicit differentiation.

Most relationships in economics involve more than two variables. The demand for a good depends not only on its own price but also on the price of substitutable and complementary goods, incomes of consumers, advertising expenditure and so on. Likewise, the output from a production process depends on a variety of inputs including land, capital and labour. To analyse general economic behaviour we must extend the concept of a function, and in particular, the differential calculus, to functions of several variables.

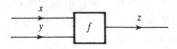

Figure 5.1

A **function, f, of two variables** is a rule which assigns to each incoming pair of numbers, (x, y), a uniquely defined outgoing number, z. This is illustrated in Figure 5.1. The 'black box' f performs some arithmetic operation on x and y to produce z. For example, the rule might be 'multiply the two numbers together and add twice the second number'. In symbols we write this either as

$$f(x, y) = xy + 2y$$

or as

$$z = xy + 2y$$

In order to be able to evaluate the function we have to specify the numerical values of both x and y. For example, substituting $x = 3$ and $y = 4$ gives

$$f(3, 4) = 3(4) + 2(4) = 20$$

and substituting $x = 4$ and $y = 3$ gives

$$f(4, 3) = 4(3) + 2(3) = 18$$

Note that, for this function, $f(3, 4)$ is not the same as $f(4, 3)$ so in general we must be careful to write down the correct ordering of the variables. We have used the labels x and y for the two incoming numbers (called the **independent** variables) and z for the outgoing number (called the **dependent** variable). We could equally well have written the function as

$$y = x_1 x_2 + 2x_2$$

say, using x_1 and x_2 to denote the independent variables and using y this time to denote the dependent variable. The use of subscripts may seem rather cumbersome but it does provide an obvious extension to functions of more than two variables. In general, a function of n variables can be written

$$y = f(x_1, x_2, \ldots, x_n)$$

PROBLEM

1 If

$$f(x, y) = 5x + xy^2 - 10$$

and

$$g(x_1, x_2, x_3) = x_1 + x_2 + x_3$$

evaluate

(a) $f(0, 0)$ **(b)** $f(1, 2)$ **(c)** $f(2, 1)$ **(d)** $g(5, 6, 10)$ **(e)** $g(0, 0, 0)$ **(f)** $g(10, 5, 6)$

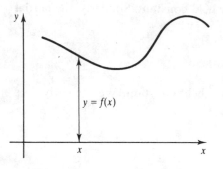

Figure 5.2

A function of one variable can be given a pictorial description using graphs which help to give an intuitive feel for its behaviour. Figure 5.2 shows the graph of a typical function

$$y = f(x)$$

in which the horizontal axis determines the incoming number, x, and the vertical axis determines the corresponding outgoing number, y. The height of the curve directly above any point on the x axis represents the value of the function at this point.

An obvious question to ask is whether there is a pictorial representation of functions of several variables. The answer is yes in the case of functions of two variables although it is not particularly easy to construct. A function

$$z = f(x, y)$$

can be thought of as a surface, rather like a mountain range, in three-dimensional space as shown in Figure 5.3. If you visualize the incoming point with coordinates (x, y) as lying in a horizontal plane then the height of the surface, z, directly above it represents the value of the function at this point. As you can probably imagine it is not an easy task to sketch the surface by hand from an equation such as

$$f(x, y) = xy^3 + 4x$$

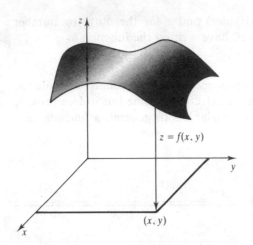

Figure 5.3

although three-dimensional graphics packages are available for most computers which can produce such a plot. Moreover, it is impossible to provide any sort of graphical interpretation for functions of more than two variables. For example, a function of, say, four variables would require five dimensions, one for each of the incoming variables and a further one for the outgoing variable! In spite of this setback we can still perform the task of differentiating functions of several variables and, as we shall see in the remaining sections of this chapter, such derivatives play a vital role in analysing economic behaviour.

Given a function of two variables,

$$z = f(x, y)$$

we can determine two first-order derivatives. The **partial derivative of f with respect to x** is written as

$$\frac{\partial z}{\partial x} \quad \text{or} \quad \frac{\partial f}{\partial x} \quad \text{or} \quad f_x$$

and is found by differentiating f with respect to x, with y held constant. Similarly, the **partial derivative of f with respect to y** is written as

$$\frac{\partial z}{\partial y} \quad \text{or} \quad \frac{\partial f}{\partial y} \quad \text{or} \quad f_y$$

and is found by differentiating f with respect to y, with x held constant. We use curly dees in the notation

$$\frac{\partial f}{\partial x}$$

read 'partial dee f by dee x'

to distinguish partial differentiation of functions of several variables from ordinary differentiation of functions of one variable. The alternative notation, f_x, is analogous to the f' notation for ordinary differentiation.

To differentiate the function

$$f(x, y) = x^2 + y^3$$

with respect to x we work as follows. By the sum rule we know that we can differentiate each part separately and add. Now, when we differentiate x^2 with respect to x we get $2x$. However, when we differentiate y^3 with respect to x we get 0. To see this, note from the definition of partial differentiation with respect to x that the variable y is held constant. Of course, if y is a constant then so is y^3 and, as we discovered in Chapter 4, constants differentiate to zero. Hence

$$\frac{\partial f}{\partial x} = 2x + 0 = 2x$$

In the same way

$$\frac{\partial f}{\partial y} = 0 + 3y^2 = 3y^2$$

This time x is held constant so x^2 goes to zero and when we differentiate y^3 with respect to y we get $3y^2$.

Now for a slightly harder example. Consider

$$f(x, y) = x^2 y$$

To find the partial derivative f_x we differentiate in the normal way taking x as the variable while pretending that y is a constant. Now, when we differentiate a constant multiple of x^2 we differentiate x^2 to get $2x$ and then multiply by the constant. For example

$$7x^2 \text{ differentiates to} \qquad 7(2x) = 14x$$
$$-100x^2 \text{ differentiates to} -100(2x) = -200x$$

and

$$cx^2 \text{ differentiates to} \qquad c(2x) = 2cx$$

for any constant c. In our case y plays the role of a constant so

$$x^2 y \text{ differentiates to } (2x)y = 2xy$$

Hence

$$f_x = 2xy$$

Similarly, to find f_y we treat y as the variable and x as a constant in the expression

$$f(x, y) = x^2 y$$

Now, when we differentiate a constant multiple of y we just get the constant so cy differentiates to c. In our case x^2 plays the role of c so $x^2 y$ differentiates to x^2. Hence

$$f_x = x^2$$

PROBLEM

2   Find expressions for the first-order partial derivatives for the functions

   (a) $f(x, y) = 5x^4 - y^2$ (b) $f(x, y) = x^2 y^3 - 10x$

In general, when we differentiate a function of two variables the thing we end up with is itself a function of two variables. This suggests the possibility of differentiating a second time. In fact there are four **second-order partial derivatives**. We write

$$\frac{\partial^2 z}{\partial x^2} \quad \text{or} \quad \frac{\partial^2 f}{\partial x^2} \quad \text{or} \quad f_{xx}$$

for the function obtained by differentiating twice with respect to x,

$$\frac{\partial^2 z}{\partial y^2} \quad \text{or} \quad \frac{\partial^2 f}{\partial y^2} \quad \text{or} \quad f_{yy}$$

for the function obtained by differentiating twice with respect to y,

$$\frac{\partial^2 z}{\partial y \, \partial x} \quad \text{or} \quad \frac{\partial^2 f}{\partial y \, \partial x} \quad \text{or} \quad f_{yx}$$

for the function obtained by differentiating first with respect to x and then with respect to y, and

$$\frac{\partial^2 z}{\partial x \, \partial y} \quad \text{or} \quad \frac{\partial^2 f}{\partial x \, \partial y} \quad \text{or} \quad f_{xy}$$

for the function obtained by differentiating first with respect to y and then with respect to x.

EXAMPLE

Find expressions for the second-order partial derivatives f_{xx}, f_{yy}, f_{yx} and f_{xy} for the functions

(a) $f(x, y) = x^2 + y^3$
(b) $f(x, y) = x^2 y$

Solution

(a)   The first-order partial derivatives of the function

$$f(x, y) = x^2 + y^3$$

have already been found and are given by

$$f_x = 2x, \quad f_y = 3y^2$$

To find f_{xx} we differentiate f_x with respect to x to get

$$f_{xx} = 2$$

To find f_{yy} we differentiate f_y with respect to y to get

$$f_{yy} = 6y$$

To find f_{yx} we differentiate f_x with respect to y to get

$$f_{yx} = 0$$

Note how f_{yx} is obtained. Starting with the original function

$$f(x, y) = x^2 + y^3$$

we first differentiate with respect to x to get $2x$ and when we differentiate this with respect to y

we keep x constant so it goes to zero. Finally, to find f_{xy} we differentiate f_y with respect to x to get

$$f_{xy} = 0$$

Note how f_{xy} is obtained. Starting with the original function

$$f(x, y) = x^2 + y^3$$

we first differentiate with respect to y to get $3y^2$ and when we differentiate this with respect to x we keep y constant so it goes to zero.

(b) The first-order partial derivatives of the function

$$f(x, y) = x^2 y$$

have already been found and are given by

$$f_x = 2xy, \quad f_y = x^2$$

Hence

$$f_{xx} = 2y, \quad f_{yy} = 0, \quad f_{yx} = 2x, \quad f_{xy} = 2x$$

∎

PROBLEM

3 Find expressions for the second-order partial derivatives of the functions

(a) $f(x, y) = 5x^4 - y^2$ **(b)** $f(x, y) = x^2 y^3 - 10x$

[Hint: you might find your answer to Problem 2 useful.]

Looking back at the expressions obtained in the previous example and Problem 3 notice that in all cases

$$\frac{\partial^2 f}{\partial y\, \partial x} = \frac{\partial^2 f}{\partial x\, \partial y}$$

$f_{yx} = f_{xy}$

It can be shown that this result holds for all functions that arise in economics. It is immaterial in which order the partial differentiation is performed. Differentiating with respect to x then y gives the same expression as differentiating with respect to y then x. (In fact, there are some weird mathematical functions for which this result is not true although they need not concern us.)

Although we have concentrated exclusively on functions of two variables it should be obvious how to work out partial derivatives of functions of more than two variables. For the general function

$$y = f(x_1, x_2, \ldots, x_n)$$

there are n first-order partial derivatives written as

$$\frac{\partial f}{\partial x_i} \quad \text{or} \quad f_i \quad (i = 1, 2, \ldots, n)$$

which are found by differentiating with respect to one variable at a time keeping the remaining $n - 1$ variables fixed. The second-order partial derivatives are determined in an analogous way. For example, suppose that

$$f(x_1, x_2, x_3) = x_1^3 + x_1 x_3^2 + 5x_2^4$$

and that we need to find

$$f_{31} = \frac{\partial^2 f}{\partial x_3 \partial x_1}$$

which denotes the function obtained by differentiating first with respect to x_1 and then with respect to x_3. Differentiating with respect to x_1 gives

$$f_1 = \frac{\partial f}{\partial x_1} = 3x_1^2 + x_3^2$$

and if we further differentiate this with respect to x_3 we get

$$f_{31} = \frac{\partial^2 f}{\partial x_3 \partial x_1} = 2x_3$$

In fact, as we have just noted for functions of two variables, we get the same answer if we differentiate in reverse order. You might like to check this for yourself.

PROBLEM

4 Find expressions for the partial derivatives f_1, f_{11} and f_{21} in the case when

$$f(x_1, x_2, x_3) = x_1 x_2 + x_1^5 - x_2^2 x_3$$

We have seen how to work out partial derivatives but have yet to give any meaning to them. To provide an interpretation of a partial derivative let us take one step back for a moment and recall the corresponding situation for functions of one variable of the form

$$y = f(x)$$

The derivative, dy/dx, gives the rate of change of y with respect to x. In other words, if x changes by a small amount Δx then the corresponding change in y satisfies

$$\Delta y \simeq \frac{dy}{dx} \Delta x$$

Moreover, the accuracy of the approximation improves as Δx becomes smaller and smaller. Given the way in which a partial derivative is found we can deduce that for a function of two variables

$$z = f(x, y)$$

if x changes by a small amount Δx and y is held fixed then the corresponding change in z satisfies

$$\Delta z \simeq \frac{\partial z}{\partial x} \Delta x$$

Similarly, if y changes by Δy and x is fixed then z changes by

$$\Delta z \simeq \frac{\partial z}{\partial y} \Delta y$$

In practice, of course, x and y may both change simultaneously. If this is the case then the net change in z will be the sum of the individual changes brought about by changes in x and y separately, so that

$$\Delta z \simeq \frac{\partial z}{\partial x} \Delta x + \frac{\partial z}{\partial y} \Delta y$$

This is referred to as the **small increments formula**. Although this is only an approximation, it can be shown that for most functions the corresponding error tends to zero as Δx and Δy both tend to zero. For this reason the formula is sometimes quoted with an equality sign and written as

$$dz = \frac{\partial z}{\partial x} dx + \frac{\partial z}{\partial y} dy$$

where the symbols dx, dy and dz are called **differentials**, and represent limiting values of Δx, Δy and Δz respectively.

EXAMPLE _____

If

$$z = x^3y - y^3x$$

evaluate

$$\frac{\partial z}{\partial x} \quad \text{and} \quad \frac{\partial z}{\partial y}$$

at the point $(1, 3)$. Hence estimate the change in z when x increases from 1 to 1.1 and y decreases from 3 to 2.8 simultaneously.

Solution

If $z = x^3 y - y^3 x$ then $\partial z / \partial x = 3x^2 y - y^3$ and $\partial z / \partial y = x^3 - 3y^2 x$ so at the point $(1, 3)$

$$\frac{\partial z}{\partial x} = 3(1)^2(3) - 3^3 = -18$$

$$\frac{\partial z}{\partial y} = 1^3 - 3(3)^2(1) = -26$$

Now, since x increases from 1 to 1.1, the change in x is

$$\Delta x = 0.1 \qquad \text{\textit{positive numbers denote increases}}$$

and, since y decreases from 3 to 2.8, the change in y is

$$\Delta y = -0.2 \qquad \text{\textit{negative numbers denote decreases}}$$

The small increments formula states that

$$\Delta z \simeq \frac{\partial z}{\partial x} \Delta x + \frac{\partial z}{\partial y} \Delta y$$

The change in z is therefore

$$\Delta z \simeq (-18)(0.1) + (-26)(-0.2) = 3.4$$

so z increases by approximately 3.4.

■

PROBLEM

5 If

$$z = xy - 5x + 2y$$

evaluate

$$\frac{\partial z}{\partial x} \quad \text{and} \quad \frac{\partial z}{\partial y}$$

at the point $(2, 6)$.

(1) Use the small increments formula to estimate the change in z as x decreases from 2 to 1.9 and y increases from 6 to 6.1.

(2) Confirm your estimate of part (1) by evaluating z at $(2, 6)$ and $(1.9, 6.1)$.

One important application of the small increments formula is to implicit differentiation. We hope by now that you are entirely happy differentiating functions of one variable such as

$$y = x^3 + 2x^2 + 5 \qquad \left(\frac{dy}{dx} = 3x^2 + 4x \right)$$

Suppose, however, that you are asked to find dy/dx given the equation

$$y^3 + 2xy^2 - x = 5$$

This is much more difficult. The reason for the difference is that in the first case y is given explicitly in terms of x whereas in the second case the functional dependence of y on x is only given implicitly. You would need to somehow rearrange this equation and to write y in terms of x before you could differentiate it. Unfortunately, this is an impossible task because of the presence of the y^3 term. The trick here is to regard the expression on the left-hand side of the equation as a function of the two variables x and y so that

$$f(x, y) = y^3 + 2xy^2 - x$$

or equivalently

$$z = y^3 + 2xy^2 - x$$

The equation

$$y^3 + 2xy^2 - x = 5$$

then reads

$$z = 5$$

In general, the differential form of the small increments formula states that

$$dz = \frac{\partial z}{\partial x} \, dx + \frac{\partial z}{\partial y} \, dy$$

In our particular case z takes the constant value of 5 so does not change. Hence $dz = 0$ and the formula reduces to

$$0 = \frac{\partial z}{\partial x} \, dx + \frac{\partial z}{\partial y} \, dy$$

which rearranges as

$$\frac{\partial z}{\partial y} \, dy = -\frac{\partial z}{\partial x} \, dx$$

that is

$$\frac{dy}{dx} = -\frac{\partial z/\partial x}{\partial z/\partial y}$$

This formula can be used to find dy/dx given any implicit function

$$f(x, y) = \text{constant}$$

that is

$$\boxed{\text{if } f(x, y) = \text{constant} \qquad \text{then} \qquad \frac{\mathrm{d}y}{\mathrm{d}x} = -\frac{f_x}{f_y}}$$

For the function

$$f(x, y) = y^3 + 2xy^2 - x$$

we have

$$f_x = 2y^2 - 1 \qquad \text{and} \qquad f_y = 3y^2 + 4xy$$

so that

$$\frac{\mathrm{d}y}{\mathrm{d}x} = -\frac{f_x}{f_y}$$

$$= -\left(\frac{2y^2 - 1}{3y^2 + 4xy}\right)$$

$$= \frac{-2y^2 + 1}{3y^2 + 4xy}$$

The technique of finding $\mathrm{d}y/\mathrm{d}x$ from $-f_x/f_y$ is called **implicit differentiation** and can be used whenever it is difficult or impossible to obtain an explicit representation for y in terms of x.

PROBLEM

6   Use implicit differentiation to find expressions for $\mathrm{d}y/\mathrm{d}x$ given that

   (a) $xy - y^3 + y = 0$ (b) $y^5 - xy^2 = 10$

PRACTICE PROBLEMS

7   If

$$f(x, y) = x^4y^5 - x^2 + y^2$$

write down expressions for the first-order partial derivatives, f_x and f_y. Hence evaluate $f_x(1, 0)$ and $f_y(1, 1)$.

8   Find expressions for all first- and second-order partial derivatives of the following functions. In each case verify that

$$\frac{\partial^2 z}{\partial y\,\partial x} = \frac{\partial^2 z}{\partial x\,\partial y}$$

   (a) $z = xy$ (b) $z = e^x y$ (c) $z = x^2 + 2x + y$ (d) $z = 16x^{1/4}y^{3/4}$ (e) $z = \dfrac{y}{x^2} + \dfrac{x}{y}$

9 Use the small increments formula to estimate the change in

$$z = x^2 y^4 - x^6 + 4y$$

when

(a) x increases from 1 to 1.1 and y remains fixed at 0
(b) x remains fixed at 1 and y decreases from 0 to -0.5
(c) x increases from 1 to 1.1 and y decreases from 0 to -0.5

10 **(1)** If

$$f(x, y) = y - x^3 + 2x$$

write down expressions for f_x and f_y. Hence use implicit differentiation to find dy/dx given that

$$y - x^3 + 2x = 1$$

(2) Confirm your answer to part (1) by rearranging the equation

$$y - x^3 + 2x = 1$$

to give y explicitly in terms of x and using ordinary differentiation.

5.2 Partial elasticity and marginal functions

Objectives At the end of this section you should be able to:

- calculate partial elasticities,

- calculate marginal utilities,

- calculate the marginal rate of commodity substitution along an indifference curve,

- calculate marginal products,

- calculate the marginal rate of technical substitution along an isoquant,

- state Euler's theorem for homogeneous production functions.

The first section of this chapter described the technique of partial differentiation. Hopefully, you have discovered that partial differentiation is no more difficult than ordinary differentiation. The only difference is that for functions of several variables you have to be clear at the outset which letter in a mathematical expression is to be the variable, and to bear in mind that all remaining letters are then just constants in disguise! Once you have done this the actual differentiation itself obeys the usual rules. In Sections 4.3 and 4.5 we considered various microeconomic applications. Given the intimate relationship between ordinary and partial differentiation you should not be too surprised to learn that we can extend these applications to functions of several variables. We concentrate on three main areas:

(1)   Elasticity of demand
(2)   Utility
(3)   Production.

We consider each of these in turn.

5.2.1   Elasticity of demand

Suppose that the demand, Q, for a certain good depends on its price, P, the price of an alternative good, P_A, and the income of consumers, Y, so that

$$Q = f(P, P_A, Y)$$

for some demand function, f.

Of particular interest is the responsiveness of demand to changes in any one of these three variables. This can be measured quantitatively using elasticity. The (**own**) **price elasticity of demand** is defined to be

$$E_P = \frac{\text{percentage change in } Q}{\text{percentage change in } P}$$

with P_A and Y held constant. This definition is identical to the one given in Section 4.5 so following the same mathematical argument presented there we deduce that

$$E_P = -\frac{P}{Q} \times \frac{\partial Q}{\partial P}$$

The partial derivative notation is used here because Q is now a function of several variables, and P_A and Y are held constant. You may recall that the introduction of the minus sign is an artificial device designed to make E_P positive.

In an analogous way we can measure the responsiveness of demand to changes in the price of the alternative good. The **cross-price elasticity of demand** is defined to be

$$E_{P_A} = \frac{\text{percentage change in } Q}{\text{percentage change in } P_A}$$

with P and Y held constant. Again, the usual mathematical argument shows that

$$E_{P_A} = \frac{P_A}{Q} \times \frac{\partial Q}{\partial P_A}$$

The sign of E_{P_A} could turn out to be positive or negative depending on the nature of the alternative good. If the alternative good is substitutable then Q increases as P_A rises because consumers buy more of the given good as it becomes relatively less expensive. Consequently,

$$\frac{\partial Q}{\partial P_A} > 0$$

and so $E_{P_A} > 0$. If the alternative good is complementary then Q decreases as P_A rises because the bundle of goods as a whole becomes more expensive. Consequently

$$\frac{\partial Q}{\partial P_A} < 0$$

and so $E_{P_A} < 0$.

Finally, the **income elasticity of demand** is defined to be

$$E_Y = \frac{\text{percentage change in } Q}{\text{percentage change in } Y}$$

and can be found from

$$E_Y = \frac{Y}{Q} \times \frac{\partial Q}{\partial Y}$$

Again, E_Y can be positive or negative. If the good is superior then demand rises as income rises and E_Y is positive. On the other hand, if the good is inferior then demand falls as income rises and E_Y is negative.

EXAMPLE

Given the demand function

$$Q = 100 - 2P + P_A + 0.1Y$$

where $P = 10$, $P_A = 12$ and $Y = 1000$, find the

(a) price elasticity of demand
(b) cross-price elasticity of demand
(c) income elasticity of demand

Is the alternative good substitutable or complementary?

Solution

We begin by calculating the value of Q when $P = 10$, $P_A = 12$ and $Y = 1000$. The demand equation gives

$$Q = 100 - 2(10) + 12 + 0.1(1000) = 192$$

(a) To find the price elasticity of demand we partially differentiate

$$Q = 100 - 2P + P_A + 0.1Y$$

with respect to P to get

$$\frac{\partial Q}{\partial P} = -2$$

Hence

$$E_P = -\frac{P}{Q} \times \frac{\partial Q}{\partial P} = -\frac{10}{192} \times (-2) = 0.10$$

(b)   To find the cross-price elasticity of demand we partially differentiate

$$Q = 100 - 2P + P_A + 0.1Y$$

with respect to P_A to get

$$\frac{\partial Q}{\partial P_A} = 1$$

Hence

$$E_{P_A} = \frac{P_A}{Q} \times \frac{\partial Q}{\partial P_A} = \frac{12}{192} \times 1 = 0.06$$

The fact that this is positive shows that the two goods are substitutable.

(c)   To find the income elasticity of demand we partially differentiate

$$Q = 100 - 2P + P_A + 0.1Y$$

with respect to Y to get

$$\frac{\partial Q}{\partial Y} = 0.1$$

Hence

$$E_Y = \frac{Y}{Q} \times \frac{\partial Q}{\partial Y} = \frac{1000}{192} \times 0.1 = 0.52$$

■

PROBLEM

1   Given the demand function

$$Q = 500 - 3P - 2P_A + 0.01Y$$

where $P = 20$, $P_A = 30$ and $Y = 5000$, find the

(a)   price elasticity of demand
(b)   cross-price elasticity of demand
(c)   income elasticity of demand

If income rises by 5% calculate the corresponding percentage change in demand. Is the good inferior or superior?

5.2.2   Utility

So far in this book we have concentrated almost exclusively on the behaviour of producers. In this case it is straightforward to identify the primary objective which is to maximize profit.

We now turn our attention to consumers. Unfortunately, it is not so easy to identify the motivation for their behaviour. One tentative suggestion is that consumers try to maximize earned income. However, if this were the case then individuals would try to work twenty-four hours a day for seven days a week, which is not so. In practice, people like to allocate a reasonable proportion of time to leisure activities. Consumers are faced with a choice of how many hours each week to spend working and how many to devote to leisure. In the same way a consumer needs to decide how many items of various goods to buy and has a preference between the options available. To analyse the behaviour of consumers quantitatively we associate with each set of options a number, U, called **utility**, which indicates the level of satisfaction. Suppose that there are two goods, G1 and G2, and that the consumer buys x_1 items of G1 and x_2 items of G2. The variable U is then a function of x_1 and x_2 which we write as

$$U = U(x_1, x_2)$$

If

$$U(3, 7) = 20 \quad \text{and} \quad U(4, 5) = 25$$

for example, then the consumer derives greater satisfaction from buying four items of G1 and five items of G2, than from buying three items of G1 and seven items of G2.

Utility is a function of two variables so we can work out two first-order partial derivatives,

$$\frac{\partial U}{\partial x_1} \quad \text{and} \quad \frac{\partial U}{\partial x_2}$$

The derivative

$$\frac{\partial U}{\partial x_i}$$

gives the rate of change of U with respect to x_i and is called the **marginal utility of x_i**. If x_i changes by a small amount Δx_i and the other variable is held fixed then the change in U satisfies

$$\Delta U \simeq \frac{\partial U}{\partial x_i} \Delta x_i$$

If x_1 and x_2 both change then the net change in U can be found from the small increments formula

$$\Delta U \simeq \frac{\partial U}{\partial x_1} \Delta x_1 + \frac{\partial U}{\partial x_2} \Delta x_2$$

EXAMPLE

Given the utility function

$$U = x_1^{1/4} x_2^{3/4}$$

determine the value of the marginal utilities

$$\frac{\partial U}{\partial x_1} \quad \text{and} \quad \frac{\partial U}{\partial x_2}$$

when $x_1 = 100$ and $x_2 = 200$. Hence estimate the change in utility when x_1 decreases from 100 to 99 and x_2 increases from 200 to 201.

Solution

If

$$U = x_1^{1/4} x_2^{3/4}$$

then

$$\frac{\partial U}{\partial x_1} = \tfrac{1}{4} x_1^{-3/4} x_2^{3/4} \quad \text{and} \quad \frac{\partial U}{\partial x_2} = \tfrac{3}{4} x_1^{1/4} x_2^{-1/4}$$

so when $x_1 = 100$ and $x_2 = 200$

$$\frac{\partial U}{\partial x_1} = \tfrac{1}{4}(100)^{-3/4}(200)^{3/4} = 0.42$$

$$\frac{\partial U}{\partial x_2} = \tfrac{3}{4}(100)^{1/4}(200)^{-1/4} = 0.63$$

Now x_1 decreases by 1 unit so

$$\Delta x_1 = -1$$

and x_2 increases by 1 unit so

$$\Delta x_2 = 1$$

The small increments formula states that

$$\Delta U \simeq \frac{\partial U}{\partial x_1} \Delta x_1 + \frac{\partial U}{\partial x_2} \Delta x_2$$

The change in utility is therefore

$$\Delta U \simeq (0.42)(-1) + (0.63)(1) = 0.21$$

■

Note that for the particular utility function

$$U = x_1^{1/4} x_2^{3/4}$$

given in this example the second-order derivatives

$$\frac{\partial^2 U}{\partial x_1^2} = \frac{-3}{16} x_1^{-7/4} x_2^{3/4} \quad \text{and} \quad \frac{\partial^2 U}{\partial x_2^2} = \frac{-3}{16} x_1^{1/4} x_2^{-5/4}$$

are both negative. Now $\partial^2 U/\partial x_1^2$ is the partial derivative of marginal utility $\partial U/\partial x_1$ with respect to x_1. The fact that this is negative means that marginal utility of x_1 decreases as x_1 rises. In other words, as the consumption of good G1 increases each additional item of G1 bought confers less utility than the previous item. A similar property holds for G2. This is known as the **law of diminishing marginal utility**. It is analogous to the law of diminishing marginal productivity for production functions which we discussed in Chapter 4.

PROBLEM

2   An individual's utility function is given by

$$U = 1000x_1 + 450x_2 + 5x_1 x_2 - 2x_1^2 - x_2^2$$

where x_1 is the amount of leisure measured in hours per week and x_2 is earned income measured in dollars per week.

Determine the value of the marginal utilities

$$\frac{\partial U}{\partial x_1} \quad \text{and} \quad \frac{\partial U}{\partial x_2}$$

when $x_1 = 138$ and $x_2 = 500$.

Hence estimate the change in U if the individual works for an extra hour which increases earned income by \$15 per week.

Does the law of diminishing marginal utility hold for this function?

It was pointed out in Section 5.1 that functions of two variables could be represented by surfaces in three dimensions. This is all very well in theory but in practice the task of sketching such a surface by hand is virtually impossible. This difficulty has been faced by geographers for years and the way they circumvent the problem is to produce a two-dimensional contour map. A contour is a curve joining all points at the same height above sea level. Exactly the same device can be used for utility functions. Rather than attempt to sketch the surface we draw an **indifference map**. This consists of **indifference curves** joining points (x_1, x_2) which give the same value of utility. Mathematically, an indifference curve is defined by an equation

$$U(x_1, x_2) = U_0$$

for some fixed value of U_0. A typical indifference map is sketched in Figure 5.4.

Points A and B both lie on the lower indifference curve, $U_0 = 20$. Point A corresponds to the case when the consumer buys a_1 units of G1 and a_2 units of G2. Likewise, point B corresponds to the case when the consumer buys b_1 units of G1 and b_2 units of G2. Both of these combinations yield the same level of satisfaction and the consumer is indifferent to choosing between them. In symbols we have

$$U(a_1, a_2) = 20 \quad \text{and} \quad U(b_1, b_2) = 20$$

Points C and D lie on indifference curves which are further away from the origin. The combinations of goods which these points represent yield higher levels of utility and so are ranked above those of A and B.

Indifference curves are usually downward sloping. If fewer purchases are made of G1 then the consumer has to compensate for this by buying more of type G2 to maintain the same level of satisfaction. Note also from Figure 5.4 that the slope of an indifference curve varies along its length, taking large negative values close to the vertical axis and becoming almost zero as the curve approaches the horizontal axis. Again this is to be expected for any function which obeys the law of diminishing marginal utility. A consumer who currently owns a large number of items of G2 and relatively few of G1 is likely to value G1 more highly. Consequently, he or she might be satisfied in sacrificing a large number of items of G2 just to gain one or two extra items of G1. In this region the marginal utility of x_1 is much greater than that of x_2 which accounts for the steepness of the curve close to the vertical axis. Similarly, as the curve approaches the horizontal axis, the situation is reversed and the curve flattens off. We quantify this exchange of goods by introducing the **marginal rate of commodity substitution**, MRCS. This is defined to be the increase in x_2 necessary to maintain a constant value of utility when x_1 decreases by 1 unit. This is illustrated in Figure 5.5.

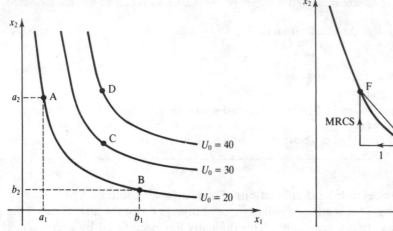

Figure 5.4   *Figure 5.5*

Starting at point E we move 1 unit to the left. The value of MRCS is then the vertical distance that we need to travel if we are to remain on the indifference curve passing through E. Now this sort of 'one-unit-change' definition is precisely the approach that we took in Section 4.3 when discussing marginal functions. In that section we actually defined the marginal function to be the derived function and we showed that the 'one-unit change' definition gave a good approximation to it. If we do the same here then we can define

$$\text{MRCS} = -\frac{dx_2}{dx_1}$$

The derivative, dx_2/dx_1, determines the slope of an indifference curve when x_1 is plotted on the horizontal axis and x_2 is plotted on the vertical axis. This is negative so we deliberately put a minus sign in front to make MRCS positive. This definition is only useful if we can find the equation of an indifference curve with x_2 given explicitly in terms of x_1. However, we may only know the utility function

$$U(x_1, x_2)$$

so that the indifference curve is determined implicitly from an equation

$$U(x_1, x_2) = U_0$$

This is precisely the situation that we discussed at the end of Section 5.1. The formula for implicit differentiation gives

$$\frac{dx_2}{dx_1} = -\frac{\partial U/\partial x_1}{\partial U/\partial x_2}$$

Hence

$$\text{MRCS} = -\frac{dx_2}{dx_1} = \frac{\partial U/\partial x_1}{\partial U/\partial x_2}$$

> marginal rate of commodity substitution is the marginal utility of x_1 divided by the marginal utility of x_2

EXAMPLE

Given the utility function

$$U = x_1^{1/2}x_2^{1/2}$$

find a general expression for MRCS in terms of x_1 and x_2.

Calculate the particular value of MRCS for the indifference curve which passes through $(300, 500)$. Hence estimate the increase in x_2 required to maintain the current level of utility when x_1 decreases by 3 units.

Solution

If

$$U = x_1^{1/2}x_2^{1/2}$$

then

$$\frac{\partial U}{\partial x_1} = \tfrac{1}{2}x_1^{-1/2}x_2^{1/2} \quad \text{and} \quad \frac{\partial U}{\partial x_2} = \tfrac{1}{2}x_1^{1/2}x_2^{-1/2}$$

Using the result

$$\text{MRCS} = \frac{\partial U/\partial x_1}{\partial U/\partial x_2}$$

we see that

$$\text{MRCS} = \frac{\tfrac{1}{2}x_1^{-1/2}x_2^{1/2}}{\tfrac{1}{2}x_1^{1/2}x_2^{-1/2}}$$

$$= x_1^{-1}x_2^1$$

rule 2 of indices;
$$6^m \div 6^n = 6^{m-n}$$

$$= \frac{x_2}{x_1}$$

$$6^1 = 6,$$
$$6^{-1} = \frac{1}{6}$$

At the point $(300, 500)$

$$\text{MRCS} = \frac{500}{300} = \frac{5}{3}$$

Now MRCS approximates the increase in x_2 required to maintain a constant level of utility when x_1 decreases by 1 unit. In this example x_1 decreases by 3 units so we multiply MRCS by 3. The approximate increase in x_2 is

$$\frac{5}{3} \times 3 = 5$$

We can check the accuracy of this approximation by evaluating U at the old point $(300, 500)$ and the new point $(297, 505)$. We get

$$U(300, 500) = (300)^{1/2}(500)^{1/2} = 387.30$$

$$U(297, 505) = (297)^{1/2}(505)^{1/2} = 387.28$$

This shows that, to all intents and purposes, the two points do indeed lie on the same indifference curve.

■

PROBLEM

3 Calculate the value of MRCS for the utility function given in Problem 2 at the point $(138, 500)$. Hence estimate the increase in earned income required to maintain the current level of utility if leisure time falls by two hours per week.

5.2.3 Production

Production functions were first introduced in Section 2.3. We assume that output, Q, depends on capital, K, and labour, L, so we can write

$$Q = f(K, L)$$

Such functions can be analysed in a similar way to that of utility functions. The partial derivative

$$\frac{\partial Q}{\partial K}$$

gives the rate of change of output with respect to capital and is called the **marginal product of capital**, MP_K. If capital changes by a small amount ΔK, with labour held constant, then the corresponding change in Q is given by

$$\Delta Q \simeq \frac{\partial Q}{\partial K} \Delta K$$

Similarly,

$$\frac{\partial Q}{\partial L}$$

gives the rate of change of output with respect to labour and is called the **marginal product of labour**, MP_L. If labour changes by a small amount ΔL, with capital held constant, then the corresponding change in Q is given by

$$\Delta Q \simeq \frac{\partial Q}{\partial L} \Delta L$$

If K and L both change simultaneously, then the net change in Q can be found from the small increments formula

$$\Delta Q \simeq \frac{\partial Q}{\partial K}\, \Delta K + \frac{\partial Q}{\partial L}\, \Delta L$$

The contours of a production function are called **isoquants**. In Greek 'iso' means 'equal' so the word isoquant literally translates as equal quantity. Points on an isoquant represent all possible combinations of inputs (K, L) which produce a constant level of output, Q_0. A typical isoquant map is sketched in Figure 5.6. Notice that we have adopted the standard convention of plotting labour on the horizontal axis and capital on the vertical axis.

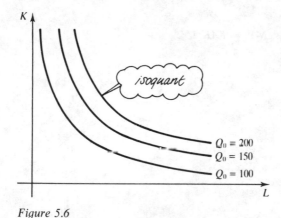

Figure 5.6

The lower curve determines the input pairs needed to output 100 units. Higher levels of output correspond to isoquants further away from the origin. Again, the general shape of the curves is to be expected. For example, as capital is reduced it is necessary to increase labour to compensate and so maintain production levels. Moreover, if capital continues to decrease, the rate of substitution of labour for capital goes up. We quantify this exchange of inputs by defining the **marginal rate of technical substitution**, MRTS, to be

$$-\frac{\mathrm{d}K}{\mathrm{d}L}$$

so that MRTS is the positive value of the slope of an isoquant. As in the case of a utility function, the formula for implicit differentiation shows that

$$\text{MRTS} = \frac{\partial Q / \partial L}{\partial Q / \partial K}$$

$$= \frac{\text{MP}_L}{\text{MP}_K}$$

> marginal rate of technical substitution is the marginal product of labour divided by the marginal product of capital

EXAMPLE

Find an expression for MRTS for the general Cobb–Douglas production function

$$Q = AK^\alpha L^\beta$$

where A, α and β are positive constants.

Solution

We begin by finding the marginal products. Partial differentiation of

$$Q = AK^\alpha L^\beta$$

with respect to K and L gives

$$MP_K = \alpha A K^{\alpha-1} L^\beta \quad \text{and} \quad MP_L = \beta A K^\alpha L^{\beta-1}$$

Hence

$$MRTS = \frac{MP_L}{MP_K}$$

$$= \frac{\beta A K^\alpha L^{\beta-1}}{\alpha A K^{\alpha-1} L^\beta}$$

$$= \frac{\beta K}{\alpha L}$$

■

PROBLEM

4 Given the production function

$$Q = K^2 + 2L^2$$

write down expressions for the marginal products

$$\frac{\partial Q}{\partial K} \quad \text{and} \quad \frac{\partial Q}{\partial L}$$

Hence show that

(a) $MRTS = \dfrac{2L}{K}$

(b) $K\dfrac{\partial Q}{\partial K} + L\dfrac{\partial Q}{\partial L} = 2Q$

In Section 2.3 a production function was described as being homogeneous of degree n if, for any number λ,

$$f(\lambda K, \lambda L) = \lambda^n f(K, L)$$

A production function is then said to display decreasing returns to scale, constant returns to scale or increasing returns to scale depending on whether $n < 1$, $n = 1$ or $n > 1$ respectively.

One useful result concerning homogeneous functions is known as **Euler's theorem** which states that

$$K \frac{\partial f}{\partial K} + L \frac{\partial f}{\partial L} = nf(K, L)$$

In fact, you have already verified this in Problem 4(b) for the particular production function

$$Q = K^2 + 2L^2$$

which is easily shown to be homogeneous of degree 2. We have no intention of proving this theorem although you are invited to confirm its validity for general Cobb–Douglas production functions in Problem 8 at the end of this section.

The special case $n = 1$ is worthy of note because the right-hand side is then simply $f(K, L)$ which is equal to the output, Q. Euler's theorem for homogeneous production functions of degree one states that

| capital times marginal product of capital | = | labour times marginal product of labour | = | total output |

If each input factor is paid an amount equal to its marginal product then each term on the left-hand side gives the total bill for that factor. For example, if each unit of labour is paid MP_L then the cost of L units of labour is $L(MP_L)$. Provided that the production function displays constant returns to scale, Euler's theorem shows that the sum of the factor payments is equal to the total output.

PRACTICE PROBLEMS

5 Given the demand function

$$Q = 200 - 2P - P_A + 0.1Y^2$$

where $P = 10$, $P_A = 15$ and $Y = 100$, find the

(a) price elasticity of demand
(b) cross-price elasticity of demand
(c) income elasticity of demand

Estimate the percentage change in demand if P_A rises by 3%. Is the alternative good substitutable or complementary?

6 Given the utility function

$$U = x_1^{1/2} x_2^{1/3}$$

determine the value of the marginal utilities

$$\frac{\partial U}{\partial x_1} \quad \text{and} \quad \frac{\partial U}{\partial x_2}$$

at the point (25, 8). Hence

(a) estimate the change in utility when x_1 and x_2 both increase by 1 unit, and

(b) find the marginal rate of commodity substitution at this point.

7 Evaluate MP_K and MP_L for the production function

$$Q = 2LK + \sqrt{L}$$

given that the current levels of K and L are 7 and 4 respectively. Hence

(a) write down the value of MRTS, and

(b) estimate the increase in capital needed to maintain the current level of output given a one unit decrease in labour.

8 Verify Euler's theorem for the Cobb–Douglas production function

$$Q = AK^{\alpha}L^{\beta}$$

[Hint: this function was shown to be homogeneous of degree $\alpha + \beta$ in Section 2.3.]

5.3 Comparative statics

Objectives At the end of this section you should be able to:

- use structural equations to derive the reduced form of macroeconomic models,

- calculate national income multipliers,

- use multipliers to give a qualitative description of economic models,

- use multipliers to give a quantitative description of economic models,

- calculate multipliers for the linear one-commodity market model.

The simplest macroeconomic model, discussed in Section 1.5, assumes that there are two sectors, households and firms, and that household consumption, C, is modelled by a linear relationship of the form

$$C = aY + b \quad (1)$$

In this equation Y denotes national income and a and b are parameters. The parameter a is the marginal propensity to consume and lies in the range $0 < a < 1$. The parameter b is the autonomous consumption and satisfies $b > 0$. In equilibrium,

$$Y = C + I \quad (2)$$

where I denotes investment which is assumed to be given by

$$I = I^* \quad (3)$$

for some constant I^*. Equations (1), (2) and (3) describe the structure of the model and as such are called **structural equations**. Substituting equations (1) and (3) into equation (2) gives

$$Y = aY + b + I^*$$

$$Y - aY = b + I^* \qquad \text{(subtract } aY \text{ from both sides)}$$

$$(1 - a)Y = b + I^* \qquad \text{(take out a common factor of } Y\text{)}$$

$$Y = \frac{b + I^*}{1 - a} \qquad \text{(divide both sides by } 1 - a\text{)}$$

This is known as the **reduced form** because it compresses the model into a single equation in which the endogenous variable, Y, is expressed in terms of the exogenous variable, I^*, and parameters, a and b. The process of analysing the equilibrium level of income in this way is referred to as **statics** because it assumes that the equilibrium state is attained instantaneously. The branch of mathematical economics which investigates time dependence is known as **dynamics** and is beyond the scope of this book.

We should like to do rather more than just to calculate the equilibrium values here. In particular, we are interested in the effect on the endogenous variables in a model brought about by changes in the exogenous variables and parameters. This is known as **comparative statics** since we seek to compare the effects obtained by varying each variable and parameter in turn. The actual mechanism for change will be ignored and it will be assumed that the system returns to equilibrium instantaneously. The equation

$$Y = \frac{b + I^*}{1 - a}$$

shows that Y is a function of three variables a, b and I^* so we can write down three partial derivatives

$$\frac{\partial Y}{\partial a} = \frac{b + I^*}{(1 - a)^2}, \quad \frac{\partial Y}{\partial b} = \frac{1}{1 - a}, \quad \frac{\partial Y}{\partial I^*} = \frac{1}{1 - a}$$

The only hard one to work out is the first and this is found using the chain rule by writing

$$Y = (b + I^*)(1 - a)^{-1}$$

which gives

$$\frac{\partial Y}{\partial a} = (b + I^*)(-1)(1 - a)^{-2}(-1) = \frac{b + I^*}{(1 - a)^2}$$

To interpret these derivatives let us suppose that the marginal propensity to consume, a, changes by Δa with b and I^* held constant. The corresponding change in Y is given by

$$\Delta Y = \frac{\partial Y}{\partial a} \Delta a$$

Strictly speaking the '=' sign should really be '$\simeq$'. However, as we have seen in the previous two sections, provided that Δa is small the approximation is reasonably accurate. In any case we could argue that the model itself is only a first approximation to what is really happening in the economy and so any further small inaccuracies which are introduced are unlikely to have any significant effect on our conclusions. The above equation shows that the change in national income is found by multiplying the change in the marginal propensity to consume by the partial derivative $\partial Y/\partial a$. For this reason the partial derivative is called the **marginal propensity to consume multiplier** for Y. In the same way $\partial Y/\partial b$ and $\partial Y/\partial I^*$ are called the **autonomous consumption multiplier** and the **investment multiplier** respectively.

Multipliers enable us to explain the behaviour of the model both qualitatively and quantitatively. The qualitative behaviour can be described simply by inspecting the multipliers as they stand, before any numerical values are assigned to the variables and parameters. It is usually possible to state whether the multipliers are positive or negative and hence whether an increase in an exogenous variable or parameter leads to an increase or decrease in the corresponding endogenous variable. In the present model it is apparent that all three multipliers for Y are positive because it is known that b and I^* are both positive and that a is less than 1. Therefore, national income rises whenever any of a, b or I^* rises. Also, we can state whether the magnitudes of the multipliers are greater than or less than 1 and hence whether the change in the endogenous variable is greater than or less than the change in the exogenous variable or parameter. For example, the denominator in the fraction

$$\frac{1}{1-a}$$

must be less than 1 because $0 < a < 1$ and so the autonomous consumption and investment multipliers both exceed one. Moreover, we see that as the marginal propensity to consume, a, increases towards 1 all three multipliers rise indefinitely because they all have a factor of $1 - a$ in their denominator.

Once the exogenous variables and parameters have been assigned specific numerical values, the behaviour of the model can be explained quantitatively. For example, if $a = 0.6$ then the investment multiplier is

$$\frac{1}{1-a} = \frac{1}{1-0.6} = \frac{1}{0.4} = 2.5$$

This means that when investment rises by, say, 4 units the change in national income is

$$2.5 \times 4 = 10$$

Of course, if a, b and I^* change by amounts Δa, Δb and ΔI^* simultaneously then the small increments formula shows that the change in Y can be found from

$$\Delta Y = \frac{\partial Y}{\partial a} \Delta a + \frac{\partial Y}{\partial b} \Delta b + \frac{\partial Y}{\partial I^*} \Delta I^*$$

PROBLEM

1 By substituting

$$Y = \frac{b + I^*}{1 - a}$$

into

$$C = aY + b$$

write down the reduced equation for C in terms of a, b and I^*.
Hence show that the investment multiplier for C is

$$\frac{a}{1 - a}$$

Deduce that an increase in investment always leads to an increase in consumption. Calculate the change in consumption when investment rises by 2 units if the marginal propensity to consume is $\frac{1}{2}$.

The following example is more difficult because it involves three sectors; households, firms and government. However, the basic strategy for analysing the model is the same. We first obtain the reduced form which is differentiated to determine the relevant multipliers. These can then be used to discuss the behaviour of national income both qualitatively and quantitatively.

EXAMPLE

Consider the three-sector model

$$Y = C + I + G \qquad (1)$$

$$C = aY_d + b \qquad (2) \qquad (0 < a < 1, b > 0)$$

$$Y_d = Y - T \qquad (3)$$

$$T = tY + T^* \qquad (4) \qquad (0 < t < 1, T^* > 0)$$

$$I = I^* \qquad (5) \qquad (I^* > 0)$$

$$G = G^* \qquad (6) \qquad (G^* > 0)$$

where G denotes government expenditure and T denotes taxation.

(1) Show that

$$Y = \frac{-aT^* + b + I^* + G^*}{1 - a + at}$$

(2) Write down the government expenditure multiplier and autonomous taxation multiplier. Deduce the direction of change in Y due to increases in G^* and T^*.

(3) If it is government policy to finance any increase in expenditure, ΔG^*, by an increase in autonomous taxation, ΔT^*, so that

$$\Delta G^* = \Delta T^*$$

show that national income rises by an amount which is less than the rise in expenditure.

(4) If $a = 0.7$, $b = 50$, $T^* = 200$, $t = 0.2$, $I^* = 100$ and $G^* = 300$ calculate the equilibrium level of national income, Y, and the change in Y due to a ten unit increase in government expenditure.

Solution

(1) We need to 'solve' equations (1)–(6) for Y. An obvious first move is to substitute equations (2), (5) and (6) into equation (1) to get

$$Y = aY_d + b + I^* + G^* \qquad (7)$$

Now from equations (3) and (4)

$$Y_d = Y - T$$
$$= Y - (tY + T^*)$$
$$= Y - tY - T^*$$

so this can be put into equation (7) to get

$$Y = a(Y - tY - T^*) + b + I^* + G^*$$
$$= aY - atY - aT^* + b + I^* + G^*$$

Collecting terms in Y on the left-hand side gives

$$(1 - a + at)Y = -aT^* + b + I^* + G^*$$

which produces the desired equation

$$Y = \frac{-aT^* + b + I^* + G^*}{1 - a + at}$$

(2) The government expenditure multiplier is

$$\frac{\partial Y}{\partial G^*} = \frac{1}{1 - a + at}$$

and the autonomous taxation multiplier is

$$\frac{\partial Y}{\partial T^*} = \frac{-a}{1 - a + at}$$

We are given that $a < 1$ so $1 - a > 0$. Also, we know that a and t are both positive so their product, at, must be positive. The expression $(1 - a) + at$ is therefore positive being the sum of two positive terms. The government expenditure multiplier is therefore positive which shows that any increase in G^* leads to an increase in Y. The autonomous taxation multiplier is negative because its numerator is negative and its denominator is positive. This shows that any increase in T^* leads to a decrease in Y.

(3) Government policy is to finance a rise in expenditure out of autonomous taxation so that

$$\Delta G^* = \Delta T^*$$

From the small increments formula

$$\Delta Y = \frac{\partial Y}{\partial G^*} \Delta G^* + \frac{\partial Y}{\partial T^*} \Delta T^*$$

we deduce that

$$\Delta Y = \left(\frac{\partial Y}{\partial G^*} + \frac{\partial Y}{\partial T^*} \right) \Delta G^*$$

$$= \left(\frac{1}{1 - a + at} + \frac{-a}{1 - a + at} \right) \Delta G^*$$

$$= \left(\frac{1 - a}{1 - a + at} \right) \Delta G^*$$

The multiplier

$$\frac{1 - a}{1 - a + at}$$

is called the **balanced budget multiplier** and is positive because the numerator and denominator are both positive. An increase in government expenditure leads to an increase in national income. However, the denominator is greater than the numerator by an amount at so that

$$\frac{1 - a}{1 - a + at} < 1$$

and $\Delta Y < \Delta G^*$ showing that the rise in national income is less than the rise in expenditure.

(4)   To solve this part of the problem we simply substitute the numerical values $a = 0.7$, $b = 50$, $T^* = 200$, $t = 0.2$, $I^* = 100$ and $G^* = 300$ into the results of parts (1) and (2). From part (1)

$$Y = \frac{-aT^* + b + I^* + G^*}{1 - a + at}$$

$$= \frac{-0.7(200) + 50 + 100 + 300}{1 - 0.7 + 0.7(0.2)}$$

$$= 704.5$$

From part (2) the government expenditure multiplier is

$$\frac{1}{1 - a + at} = \frac{1}{0.44} = 2.27$$

and we are given that $\Delta G^* = 10$ so the change in national income is

$$2.27 \times 10 = 22.7$$

∎

PROBLEM

2   Consider the four-sector model

$$Y = C + I + G + X - M$$

$$C = aY + b \qquad\qquad (0 < a < 1, b > 0)$$

$$I = I^* \qquad\qquad\qquad (I^* > 0)$$

$$G = G^* \qquad\qquad\qquad (G^* > 0)$$

$$X = X^* \qquad\qquad (X^* > 0)$$

$$M = mY + M^* \qquad\qquad (0 < m < 1, M^* > 0)$$

where X and M denote exports and imports respectively and m is the marginal propensity to import.

(1) Show that

$$Y = \frac{b + I^* + G^* + X^* - M^*}{1 - a + m}$$

(2) Write down the autonomous export multiplier

$$\frac{\partial Y}{\partial X^*}$$

and the marginal propensity to import multiplier

$$\frac{\partial Y}{\partial m}$$

Deduce the direction of change in Y due to increases in X^* and m.

(3) If $a = 0.8$, $b = 120$, $I^* = 100$, $G^* = 300$, $X^* = 150$, $m = 0.1$ and $M^* = 40$, calculate the equilibrium level of national income, Y, and the change in Y due to a ten unit increase in autonomous exports.

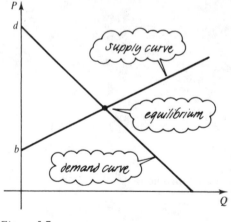

Figure 5.7

So far, all of the examples of comparative statics that we have considered have been taken from macroeconomics. The same approach can be used in microeconomics. For example, let us analyse the equilibrium price and quantity in supply and demand theory.

Figure 5.7 illustrates the simple linear one-commodity market model described in Section 1.3. The equilibrium values of price and quantity are determined from the point of inter-section of the supply and demand curves. The supply curve is a straight line with a positive slope and intercept so its equation may be written as

$$P = aQ_S + b \qquad (a > 0, b > 0)$$

The demand equation is also linear but has a negative slope and a positive intercept so its equation may be written as

$$P = -cQ_D + d \qquad (c > 0, d > 0)$$

It is apparent from Figure 5.7 that in order for these two lines to intersect in the positive quadrant it is necessary for the intercept on the demand curve to lie above that on the supply curve so we require

$$d > b$$

or equivalently

$$d - b > 0$$

In equilibrium Q_S and Q_D are equal. If we let their common value be denoted by Q then the supply and demand equations become

$$P = aQ + b$$

$$P = -cQ + d$$

and so

$$aQ + b = -cQ + d$$

since both sides are equal to P.

To solve for Q we first collect like terms which gives

$$(a + c)Q = d - b$$

and then divide by the coefficient of Q to get

$$Q = \frac{d - b}{a + c}$$

(Incidentally, this confirms the restriction $d - b > 0$. If this were not true then Q would be either zero or negative which does not make economic sense.)

Equilibrium quantity is a function of the four parameters a, b, c and d so there are four multipliers

$$\frac{\partial Q}{\partial a} = -\frac{d - b}{(a + c)^2}$$

$$\frac{\partial Q}{\partial b} = -\frac{1}{a + c}$$

$$\frac{\partial Q}{\partial c} = -\frac{d - b}{(a + c)^2}$$

$$\frac{\partial Q}{\partial d} = \frac{1}{a + c}$$

where the chain rule is used to find $\partial Q/\partial a$ and $\partial Q/\partial c$.

We noted previously that all of the parameters are positive and that $d - b > 0$ so

$$\frac{\partial Q}{\partial a} < 0, \frac{\partial Q}{\partial b} < 0, \frac{\partial Q}{\partial c} < 0 \quad \text{and} \quad \frac{\partial Q}{\partial d} > 0$$

This shows that an increase in a, b or c causes a decrease in Q whereas an increase in d causes an increase in Q. These results can also be obtained graphically. For example, from the supply equation

$$P = aQ_S + b$$

we see that a small increase in the value of the parameter a causes the supply curve to become slightly steeper as indicated by the dashed line in Figure 5.8. The effect is to shift the point of intersection to the left and so the equilibrium quantity decreases from Q_1 to Q_2. The remaining three cases can be illustrated similarly.

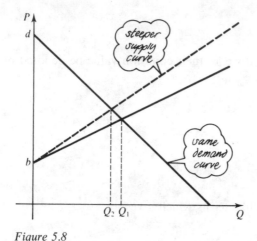

Figure 5.8

Given any pair of supply and demand equations we can easily calculate the effect on the equilibrium quantity. For example, consider the equations

$$P = Q_S + 1$$

$$P = -2Q_D + 5$$

and let us suppose that we need to calculate the change in equilibrium quantity when the coefficient of Q_S increases from 1 to 1.1. In this case we have

$$a = 1, b = 1, c = 2, d = 5$$

To find ΔQ we first evaluate the multiplier

$$\frac{\partial Q}{\partial a} = -\frac{d - b}{(a + c)^2} = -\frac{5 - 1}{(1 + 2)^2} = -0.44$$

and then multiply by 0.1 to get

$$\Delta Q = (-0.44) \times 0.1 = -0.044$$

An increase of 0.1 in the slope of the supply curve therefore produces a decrease of 0.044 in equilibrium quantity.

PROBLEM

3 Give a graphical confirmation of the sign of the multiplier

$$\frac{\partial Q}{\partial d}$$

for the linear one-commodity market model:

$$P = aQ_S + b \qquad (a > 0, b > 0)$$

$$P = -cQ_D + d \qquad (c > 0, d > 0)$$

Throughout this section all of the relations in each model have been assumed to be linear. It is possible to analyse non-linear relations in a similar way although this is beyond the scope of this book.

PRACTICE PROBLEMS

4 Consider the four-sector macroeconomic model

$$Y = C + I + G + X - M$$

$$C = aY_d + b \qquad (0 < a < 1, b > 0)$$

$$Y_d = Y - T$$

$$T = tY + T^* \qquad (0 < t < 1, T^* > 0)$$

$$I = I^* \qquad (I^* > 0)$$

$$G = G^* \qquad (G^* > 0)$$

$$X = X^* \qquad (X^* > 0)$$

$$M = mY_d + M^* \qquad (0 < m < 1, M^* > 0)$$

(1) Show that

$$Y = \frac{b + (m - a)T^* + I^* + G^* + X^* - M^*}{1 - a + at + m - mt}$$

(2) **(a)** Write down the autonomous taxation multiplier. Deduce that an increase in T^* causes a decrease in Y on the assumption that a country's marginal propensity to import, m, is less than its marginal propensity to consume, a.

   (b) Write down the government expenditure multiplier. Deduce that an increase in G^* causes an increase in Y.

(3) Let $a = 0.7, b = 150, t = 0.25, m = 0.1, T^* = 100, I^* = 100, G^* = 500, M^* = 300$ and $X^* = 160$.

   (a) Calculate the equilibrium level of national income.

   (b) Calculate the change in Y due to an 11 unit increase in G^*.

   (c) Find the increase in autonomous taxation required to restore Y to its level calculated in part (a).

5 Show that the equilibrium price for a linear one-commodity market model,

$$P = aQ_s + b \qquad (a > 0, b > 0)$$

$$P = -cQ_D + d \qquad (c > 0, d > 0)$$

where $d - b > 0$, is given by

$$P = \frac{ad + bc}{a + c}$$

Find expressions for the multipliers

$$\frac{\partial P}{\partial a}, \quad \frac{\partial P}{\partial b}, \quad \frac{\partial P}{\partial c}, \quad \frac{\partial P}{\partial d}$$

and deduce the direction of change in P due to an increase in a, b, c or d.

5.4   Unconstrained optimization

Objectives   At the end of this section you should be able to:

- use the first-order partial derivatives to find the stationary points of a function of two variables,

- use the second-order partial derivatives to classify the stationary points of a function of two variables,

- find the maximum profit of a firm which produces two goods,

- find the maximum profit of a firm which sells a single good in different markets with price discrimination.

As you might expect, methods for finding the maximum and minimum points of a function of two variables are similar to those used for functions of one variable. However, the nature of economic functions of several variables forces us to subdivide optimization problems into two types, unconstrained and constrained. To understand the distinction consider the utility function

$$U(x_1, x_2) = x_1^{1/4} x_2^{3/4}$$

The value of U measures the satisfaction gained from buying x_1 items of a good G1 and x_2 items of a good G2. The natural thing to do here is to try to pick x_1 and x_2 to make U as large as possible, thereby maximizing utility. However, a moment's thought should convince you that, as it stands, this problem does not have a finite solution. The factor $x_1^{1/4}$ can be made as large as we please by taking ever-increasing values of x_1 and likewise for the factor $x_2^{3/4}$. In other words, utility increases without bound as more and more items of goods G1 and G2 are bought. In practice, of course, this does not occur since there is a limit to the amount of money that an individual has to spend on these goods. For example, suppose that the cost of each item of G1 and G2 is $2 and $3, respectively, and that we allocate $100 for the purchase of these goods. The total cost of buying x_1 items of G1 and x_2 items of G2 is

$$2x_1 + 3x_2$$

so we require

$$2x_1 + 3x_2 = 100$$

The problem now is to maximize the utility function

$$U = x_1^{1/4} x_2^{3/4}$$

subject to the budgetary constraint

$$2x_1 + 3x_2 = 100$$

The constraint prevents us from taking ever-increasing values of x_1 and x_2 and leads to a finite solution.

We describe how to solve constrained optimization problems in the following two sections. For the moment we concentrate on the simple case of optimizing functions

$$z = f(x, y)$$

without any constraints. This is typified by the problem of profit maximization which usually has a finite solution without the need to impose constraints. In a sense the constraints are built into the profit function which is defined by

$$\pi = \text{TR} - \text{TC}$$

because there is a conflict between trying to make total revenue, TR, as large as possible while trying to make total cost, TC, as small as possible.

Let us begin by recalling how to find and classify stationary points of functions of one variable,

$$y = f(x)$$

In Section 4.6 we used the following strategy:

Step 1   Solve the equation

$$f'(x) = 0$$

to find the stationary points, $x = a$.

Step 2   If
- $f''(a) > 0$ then the function has a minimum at $x = a$.
- $f''(a) < 0$ then the function has a maximum at $x = a$.
- $f''(a) = 0$ then the point cannot be classified using the available information.

For functions of two variables,

$$z = f(x, y)$$

the stationary points are found by solving the simultaneous equations

$$\frac{\partial z}{\partial x} = 0$$

$$\frac{\partial z}{\partial y} = 0$$

that is

$$f_x(x, y) = 0$$

$$f_y(x, y) = 0$$

This is a natural extension of the one-variable case. We first write down expressions for the first-order partial derivatives and then equate to zero. This represents a system of two equations for the two unknowns x and y which we hope can be solved. Stationary points obtained in this way can be classified into one of three types: **minimum**, **maximum** and **saddle point**.

(a)   (b)   (c)

Figure 5.9

Figure 5.9(a) shows the shape of a surface in the neighbourhood of a minimum. It can be thought of as the bottom of a bowl-shaped valley. If you stand at the minimum point and walk in any direction then you are certain to start moving upwards. Mathematically, we can classify a stationary point (a, b) as a minimum provided that all three of the following conditions hold:

$$\frac{\partial^2 z}{\partial x^2} > 0, \quad \frac{\partial^2 z}{\partial y^2} > 0, \quad \left(\frac{\partial^2 z}{\partial x^2}\right)\left(\frac{\partial^2 z}{\partial y^2}\right) - \left(\frac{\partial^2 z}{\partial x \, \partial y}\right)^2 > 0$$

when $x = a$ and $y = b$, that is

$$f_{xx}(a, b) > 0, \quad f_{yy}(a, b) > 0, \quad f_{xx}(a, b)f_{yy}(a, b) - [f_{xy}(a, b)]^2 > 0$$

This triple requirement is obviously more complicated than the single condition needed in the case of a function of one variable. However, once the second-order partial derivatives have been evaluated at the stationary point the three conditions are easily checked.

Figure 5.9(b) shows the shape of a surface in the neighbourhood of a maximum. It can be thought of as the summit of a mountain. If you stand at the maximum point and walk in any direction then you are certain to start moving downwards. Mathematically, we can classify a stationary point (a, b) as a maximum provided that all three of the following conditions hold:

$$\frac{\partial^2 z}{\partial x^2} < 0, \quad \frac{\partial^2 z}{\partial y^2} < 0, \quad \left(\frac{\partial^2 z}{\partial x^2}\right)\left(\frac{\partial^2 z}{\partial y^2}\right) - \left(\frac{\partial^2 z}{\partial x \, \partial y}\right)^2 > 0$$

when $x = a$ and $y = b$, that is

$$f_{xx}(a, b) < 0, \quad f_{yy}(a, b) < 0, \quad f_{xx}(a, b)f_{yy}(a, b) - [f_{xy}(a, b)]^2 > 0$$

Of course any particular mountain range may well have lots of valleys and summits. Likewise, a function of two variables can have more than one minimum or maximum.

Figure 5.9(c) shows the shape of a surface in the neighbourhood of a saddle point. As its name suggests it can be thought of as the middle of a horse's saddle. If you sit at this point and edge towards the head or tail then you start moving upwards. On the other hand, if you edge sideways then you start moving downwards (and will probably fall off). Mathematically, we can classify a stationary point (a, b) as a saddle point provided that the following single condition holds:

$$\left(\frac{\partial^2 z}{\partial x^2}\right)\left(\frac{\partial^2 z}{\partial y^2}\right) - \left(\frac{\partial^2 z}{\partial x \, \partial y}\right)^2 < 0$$

when $x = a$ and $x = b$, that is

$$f_{xx}(a, b)f_{yy}(a, b) - [f_{xy}(a, b)]^2 < 0$$

To summarize, the method for finding and classifying stationary points of a function $f(x, y)$ is as follows:

Step 1 Solve the simultaneous equations

$$f_x(x, y) = 0$$

$$f_y(x, y) = 0$$

to find the stationary points, (a, b).

Step 2 If

- $f_{xx} > 0$, $f_{yy} > 0$ and $f_{xx}f_{yy} - f_{xy}^2 > 0$ at (a, b) then the function has a minimum at (a, b).
- $f_{xx} < 0$, $f_{yy} < 0$ and $f_{xx}f_{yy} - f_{xy}^2 > 0$ at (a, b) then the function has a maximum at (a, b).
- $f_{xx}f_{yy} - f_{xy}^2 < 0$ at (a, b) then the function has a saddle point at (a, b).

EXAMPLE

Find and classify the stationary points of the function

$$f(x, y) = x^3 - 3x + xy^2$$

Solution

In order to use steps 1 and 2 we need to find all first- and second-order partial derivatives of the function

$$f(x, y) = x^3 - 3x + xy^2$$

These are easily worked out as

$$f_x = 3x^2 - 3 + y^2$$

$$f_y = 2xy$$

$$f_{xx} = 6x$$

$$f_{xy} = 2y$$

$$f_{yy} = 2x$$

Step 1 The stationary points are the solutions of the simultaneous equations

$$f_x(x, y) = 0$$

$$f_y(x, y) = 0$$

so we need to solve

$$3x^2 - 3 + y^2 = 0$$

$$2xy = 0$$

There have been many occasions throughout this book when we have solved simultaneous equations. So far these have been linear. This time, however, we need to solve a pair of non-linear equations. Unfortunately, there is no standard method for solving such systems. We have to rely on our wits in any particular instance. The trick here is to begin with the second equation

$$2xy = 0$$

The only way that the product of three numbers can be equal to zero is when one or more of the individual numbers forming the product are zero. We know that $2 \neq 0$ so either $x = 0$ or $y = 0$. We investigate these two possibilities separately.

●   Case 1: $x = 0$. Substituting $x = 0$ into the first equation,

$$3x^2 - 3 + y^2 = 0$$

gives

$$-3 + y^2 = 0$$

that is

$$y^2 = 3$$

There are therefore two possibilities for y to go with $x = 0$, namely $y = -\sqrt{3}$ and $y = \sqrt{3}$. Hence $(0, -\sqrt{3})$ and $(0, \sqrt{3})$ are stationary points.

●   Case 2: $y = 0$. Substituting $y = 0$ into the first equation

$$3x^2 - 3 + y^2 = 0$$

gives

$$3x^2 - 3 = 0$$

that is

$$x^2 = 1$$

There are therefore two possibilities for x to go with $y = 0$, namely $x = -1$ and $x = 1$. Hence $(-1, 0)$ and $(1, 0)$ are stationary points.

These two cases indicate that there are precisely four stationary points,

$$(0, -\sqrt{3}), \quad (0, \sqrt{3}), \quad (-1, 0), \quad (1, 0)$$

Step 2   To classify these points we need to evaluate the second-order partial derivatives

$$f_{xx} = 6x, \quad f_{yy} = 2x, \quad f_{xy} = 2y$$

at each point and check the signs of

$$f_{xx}, \quad f_{yy}, \quad f_{xx}f_{yy} - f_{xy}^2$$

●   Point $(0, -\sqrt{3})$:

$$f_{xx} = 6(0) = 0, \quad f_{yy} = 2(0) = 0, \quad f_{xy} = -2\sqrt{3}$$

Hence

$$f_{xx}f_{yy} - f_{xy}^2 = 0(0) - (-2\sqrt{3})^2 = -12 < 0$$

and so $(0, -\sqrt{3})$ is a saddle point.

●   Point $(0, \sqrt{3})$:

$$f_{xx} = 6(0) = 0, \quad f_{yy} = 2(0) = 0, \quad f_{xy} = 2\sqrt{3}$$

Hence

$$f_{xx}f_{yy} - f_{xy}^2 = 0(0) - (2\sqrt{3})^2 = -12 < 0$$

and so $(0, \sqrt{3})$ is a saddle point.

- Point $(-1, 0)$:

$$f_{xx} = 6(-1) = -6, \quad f_{yy} = 2(-1) = -2, \quad f_{xy} = 2(0) = 0$$

Hence

$$f_{xx}f_{yy} - f_{xy}^2 = (-6)(-2) - 0^2 = 12 > 0$$

and so $(-1, 0)$ is not a saddle point. Moreover, since

$$f_{xx} < 0 \qquad \text{and} \qquad f_{yy} < 0$$

we deduce that $(-1, 0)$ is a maximum.

- Point $(1, 0)$:

$$f_{xx} = 6(1) = 6, \quad f_{yy} = 2(1) = 2, \quad f_{xy} = 2(0) = 0$$

Hence

$$f_{xx}f_{yy} - f_{xy}^2 = 6(2) - 0^2 = 12 > 0$$

and so $(1, 0)$ is not a saddle point. Moreover, since

$$f_{xx} > 0 \qquad \text{and} \qquad f_{yy} > 0$$

we deduce that $(1, 0)$ is a minimum.

■

PROBLEM

1 Find and classify the stationary points of the function

$$f(x, y) = x^2 + 6y - 3y^2 + 10$$

We now consider two examples from economics both involving the maximization of profit. The first considers the case of a firm producing two different goods whereas the second involves a single good sold in two different markets.

EXAMPLE

A firm is a perfectly competitive producer and sells two goods G1 and G2 at $1000 and $800 each. The total cost of producing these goods is given by

$$TC = 2Q_1^2 + 2Q_1Q_2 + Q_2^2$$

where Q_1 and Q_2 denote the output levels of G1 and G2. Find the maximum profit and the values of Q_1 and Q_2 at which this is achieved.

Solution

The fact that the firm is perfectly competitive tells us that the price of each good is fixed by the market and does not depend on Q_1 and Q_2. The actual prices are stated in the question as \$1000 and \$800. If the firm sells Q_1 items of G1 priced at \$1000 then the revenue is

$$TR_1 = 1000Q_1$$

Similarly, if the firm sells Q_2 items of G2 priced at \$800 then the revenue is

$$TR_2 = 800Q_2$$

The total revenue from the sale of both goods is then

$$TR = TR_1 + TR_2 = 1000Q_1 + 800Q_2$$

We are given that the total cost is

$$TC = 2Q_1^2 + 2Q_1Q_2 + Q_2^2$$

so the profit function is

$$\pi = TR - TC$$

$$= (1000Q_1 + 800Q_2) - (2Q_1^2 + 2Q_1Q_2 + Q_2^2)$$

$$= 1000Q_1 + 800Q_2 - 2Q_1^2 - 2Q_1Q_2 - Q_2^2$$

This is a function of two variables Q_1 and Q_2 that we wish to optimize. The first- and second-order partial derivatives are

$$\frac{\partial \pi}{\partial Q_1} = 1000 - 4Q_1 - 2Q_2$$

$$\frac{\partial \pi}{\partial Q_2} = 800 - 2Q_1 - 2Q_2$$

$$\frac{\partial^2 \pi}{\partial Q_1^2} = -4$$

$$\frac{\partial^2 \pi}{\partial Q_1 \partial Q_2} = -2$$

$$\frac{\partial^2 \pi}{\partial Q_2^2} = -2$$

The two-step strategy then gives the following:

Step 1 At a stationary point

$$\frac{\partial \pi}{\partial Q_1} = 0$$

$$\frac{\partial \pi}{\partial Q_2} = 0$$

so we need to solve the simultaneous equations

$$1000 - 4Q_1 - 2Q_2 = 0$$

$$800 - 2Q_1 - 2Q_2 = 0$$

that is

$$4Q_1 + 2Q_2 = 1000 \quad (1)$$
$$2Q_1 + 2Q_2 = 800 \quad (2)$$

The variable Q_2 can be eliminated by subtracting equation (2) from (1) to get

$$2Q_1 = 200$$

and so $Q_1 = 100$. Substituting this into either equation (1) or (2) gives $Q_2 = 300$. The profit function therefore has one stationary point at (100, 300).

Step 2   To show that the point really is a maximum we need to check that

$$\frac{\partial^2 \pi}{\partial Q_1^2} < 0, \quad \frac{\partial^2 \pi}{\partial Q_2^2} < 0, \quad \left(\frac{\partial^2 \pi}{\partial Q_1^2}\right)\left(\frac{\partial^2 \pi}{\partial Q_2^2}\right) - \left(\frac{\partial^2 \pi}{\partial Q_1 \, \partial Q_2}\right)^2 > 0$$

at this point. In this example the second-order partial derivatives are all constant. We have

$$\frac{\partial^2 \pi}{\partial Q_1^2} = -4 < 0 \quad \checkmark$$

$$\frac{\partial^2 \pi}{\partial Q_2^2} = -2 < 0 \quad \checkmark$$

$$\left(\frac{\partial^2 \pi}{\partial Q_1^2}\right)\left(\frac{\partial^2 \pi}{\partial Q_2^2}\right) - \left(\frac{\partial^2 \pi}{\partial Q_1 \, \partial Q_2}\right)^2 = (-4)(-2) - (-2)^2 = 4 > 0 \quad \checkmark$$

confirming that the firm's profit is maximized by producing 100 items of G1 and 300 items of G2.

The actual value of this profit is obtained by substituting $Q_1 = 100$ and $Q_2 = 300$ into the expression

$$\pi = 1000Q_1 + 800Q_2 - 2Q_1^2 - 2Q_1Q_2 - Q_2^2$$

to get

$$\pi = 1000(100) + 800(300) - 2(100)^2 - 2(100)(300) - (300)^2$$
$$= \$170,000$$

■

PROBLEM

2   A firm is a monopolistic producer of two goods G1 and G2. The prices are related to quantities Q_1 and Q_2 according to the demand equations

$$P_1 = 50 - Q_1$$
$$P_2 = 95 - 3Q_2$$

If the total cost function is

$$TC = Q_1^2 + 3Q_1Q_2 + Q_2^2$$

show that the firm's profit function is

$$\pi = 50Q_1 - 2Q_1^2 + 95Q_2 - 4Q_2^2 - 3Q_1Q_2$$

Hence find the values of Q_1 and Q_2 which maximize π and deduce the corresponding prices.

EXAMPLE

A firm is allowed to charge different prices for its domestic and industrial customers. If P_1 and Q_1 denote the price and demand for the domestic market then the demand equation is

$$P_1 + Q_1 = 500$$

If P_2 and Q_2 denote the price and demand for the industrial market then the demand equation is

$$2P_2 + 3Q_2 = 720$$

The total cost function is

$$TC = 50\,000 + 20Q$$

where $Q = Q_1 + Q_2$. Determine the firm's pricing policy which maximizes profit with price discrimination and calculate the value of the maximum profit.

Solution

The topic of price discrimination has already been discussed in Section 4.6. This particular problem is identical to the worked example solved in that section using ordinary differentiation. You might like to compare the details of the two approaches.

Our current aim is to find an expression for profit in terms of Q_1 and Q_2 which can then be optimized using partial differentiation. For the domestic market the demand equation is

$$P_1 + Q_1 = 500$$

which rearranges as

$$P_1 = 500 - Q_1$$

The total revenue function for this market is then

$$TR_1 = P_1Q_1 = (500 - Q_1)Q_1 = 500Q_1 - Q_1^2$$

For the industrial market the demand equation is

$$2P_2 + 3Q_2 = 720$$

which rearranges as

$$P_2 = 360 - \tfrac{3}{2}Q_2$$

The total revenue function for this market is then

$$TR_2 = P_2Q_2 = (360 - \tfrac{3}{2}Q_2)Q_2 = 360Q_2 - \tfrac{3}{2}Q_2^2$$

The total revenue received from sales in both markets is

$$TR = TR_1 + TR_2 = 500Q_1 - Q_1^2 + 360Q_2 - \tfrac{3}{2}Q_2^2$$

The total cost of producing these goods is given by

$$TC = 50\,000 + 20Q$$

and, since $Q = Q_1 + Q_2$, we can write this as

$$TC = 50\,000 + 20(Q_1 + Q_2)$$

$$= 50\,000 + 20Q_1 + 20Q_2$$

The firm's profit function is therefore

$$\pi = TR - TC$$

$$= (500Q_1 - Q_1^2 + 360Q_2 - \tfrac{3}{2}Q_2^2) - (50\,000 + 20Q_1 + 20Q_2)$$

$$= 480Q_1 - Q_1^2 + 340Q_2 - \tfrac{3}{2}Q_2^2 - 50\,000$$

This is a function of two variables, Q_1 and Q_2, that we wish to optimize. The first- and second-order partial derivatives are

$$\frac{\partial \pi}{\partial Q_1} = 480 - 2Q_1$$

$$\frac{\partial \pi}{\partial Q_2} = 340 - 3Q_2$$

$$\frac{\partial^2 \pi}{\partial Q_1^2} = -2$$

$$\frac{\partial^2 \pi}{\partial Q_1 \, \partial Q_2} = 0$$

$$\frac{\partial^2 \pi}{\partial Q_2^2} = -3$$

The two-step strategy gives the following:

Step 1   At a stationary point

$$\frac{\partial \pi}{\partial Q_1} = 0$$

$$\frac{\partial \pi}{\partial Q_2} = 0$$

so we need to solve the simultaneous equations

$$480 - 2Q_1 = 0$$

$$340 - 3Q_2 = 0$$

These are easily solved because they are 'uncoupled'. The first equation immediately gives

$$Q_1 = \frac{480}{2} = 240$$

while the second gives

$$Q_2 = \frac{340}{3}$$

Step 2   It is easy to check that the conditions for a maximum are satisfied,

$$\frac{\partial^2 \pi}{\partial Q_1^2} = -2 < 0,$$

$$\frac{\partial^2 \pi}{\partial Q_2^2} = -3 < 0$$

$$\left(\frac{\partial^2 \pi}{\partial Q_1^2}\right)\left(\frac{\partial^2 \pi}{\partial Q_2^2}\right) - \left(\frac{\partial^2 \pi}{\partial Q_1 \partial Q_2}\right)^2 = (-2)(-3) - 0^2 = 6 > 0$$

The question actually asks for the optimum prices rather than the quantities. These are found by substituting

$$Q_1 = 240 \quad \text{and} \quad Q_2 = \frac{340}{3}$$

into the corresponding demand equations. For the domestic market

$$P_1 = 500 - Q_1 = 500 - 240 = \$260$$

For the industrial market

$$P_2 = 360 - \frac{3}{2} Q_1 = 360 - \frac{3}{2}\left(\frac{340}{3}\right) = \$190$$

Finally, we substitute the values of Q_1 and Q_2 into the profit function

$$\pi = 480Q_1 - Q_1^2 + 340Q_2 - \tfrac{3}{2}Q_2^2 - 50\,000$$

to deduce that the maximum profit is \$26,866.67.

■

PROBLEM

3   A firm has the possibility of charging different prices in its domestic and foreign markets. The corresponding demand equations are given by

$$Q_1 = 300 - P_1$$
$$Q_2 = 400 - 2P_2$$

The total cost function is

$$\text{TC} = 5000 + 100Q$$

where $Q = Q_1 + Q_2$. Determine the prices that the firm should charge to maximize profit with price discrimination and calculate the value of this profit.
[You have already solved this particular example in Problem 2(a) of Section 4.7.]

As usual we conclude this section with some additional problems for you to try. Problems 4, 5 and 6 are similar to those given in the text. Problems 7 and 8 are slightly different so you may prefer to concentrate on these if you find that you do not have the time to attempt all of them.

PRACTICE PROBLEMS

4 Find and classify the stationary points of the following functions:

(a) $f(x, y) = x^3 + y^3 - 3x - 3y$ (b) $f(x, y) = x^3 + 3xy^2 - 3x^2 - 3y^2 + 10$

5 A firm is a perfectly competitive producer and sells two goods G1 and G2 at $70 and $50 each respectively. The total cost of producing these goods is given by

$$TC = Q_1^2 + Q_1Q_2 + Q_2^2$$

where Q_1 and Q_2 denote the output levels of G1 and G2. Find the maximum profit and the values of Q_1 and Q_2 at which this is achieved.

6 The demand functions for a firm's domestic and foreign markets are

$$P_1 = 50 - 5Q_1$$
$$P_2 = 30 - 4Q_2$$

and the total cost function is

$$TC = 10 + 10Q$$

where $Q = Q_1 + Q_2$. Determine the prices needed to maximize profit with price discrimination and calculate the value of the maximum profit.
[You have already solved this particular example in Problem 7(a) of Section 4.7.]

7 A firm's production function is given by

$$Q = 2L^{1/2} + 3K^{1/2}$$

where Q, L and K denote the number of units of output, labour and capital. Labour costs are $2 per unit, capital costs are $1 per unit and output sells at $8 per unit. Show that the profit function is

$$\pi = 16L^{1/2} + 24K^{1/2} - 2L - K$$

and hence find the maximum profit and the values of L and K at which it is achieved.

8 An individual's utility function is given by

$$U = 260x_1 + 310x_2 + 5x_1x_2 - 10x_1^2 - x_2^2$$

where x_1 is the amount of leisure measured in hours per week and x_2 is earned income measured in dollars per week. Find the values of x_1 and x_2 which maximize U. What is the corresponding hourly rate of pay?

5.5   Constrained optimization

Objectives   At the end of this section you should be able to:

- give a graphical interpretation of constrained optimization,

- show that when a firm maximizes output subject to a cost constraint the ratio of marginal product to price is the same for all inputs,

- show that when a consumer maximizes utility subject to a budgetary constraint the ratio of marginal utility to price is the same for all goods,

- use the method of substitution to solve constrained optimization problems in economics.

In Section 5.4 we described how to find the optimum (that is, maximum or minimum) of a function of two variables

$$z = f(x, y)$$

where the variables x and y are free to take any values. As we pointed out at the beginning of that section, this assumption is unrealistic in many economic situations. An individual wishing to maximize utility is subject to an income constraint and a firm wishing to maximize output is subject to a cost constraint.

In general, we want to optimize a function,

$$z = f(x, y)$$

called the **objective** function subject to a constraint

$$\varphi(x, y) = M$$

Here φ, the Greek letter phi, is a known function of two variables and M is a known constant. The problem is to pick the pair of numbers (x, y) which maximizes or minimizes $f(x, y)$ as before. This time, however, we limit the choice of pairs to those which satisfy

$$\varphi(x, y) = M$$

A graphical interpretation should make this clear. To be specific, let us suppose that a firm wants to maximize output and that the production function is of the form

$$Q = f(K, L)$$

Let the costs of each unit of capital and labour be P_K and P_L respectively. The cost to the firm of using as input K units of capital and L units of labour is

$$P_K K + P_L L$$

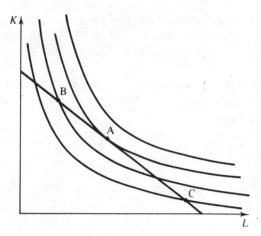

Figure 5.10

so if the firm has a fixed amount, M, to spend on these inputs then

$$P_K K + P_L L = M$$

The problem is one of trying to maximize the objective function

$$Q = f(K, L)$$

subject to the cost constraint

$$P_K K + P_L L = M$$

Sketched in Figure 5.10 is a typical isoquant map. As usual, points on any one isoquant yield the same level of output and as output rises the isoquants themselves move further away from the origin. Also sketched in Figure 5.10 is the cost constraint. This is called an **isocost** curve because it gives all combinations of K and L which can be bought for a fixed cost, M.

The fact that

$$P_K K + P_L L = M$$

is represented by a straight line should come as no surprise to you by now. We can even rewrite it in the more familiar '$y = ax + b$' form and so identify its slope and intercept. In Figure 5.10, L is plotted on the horizontal axis and K is plotted on the vertical axis so we need to rearrange

$$P_K K + P_L L = M$$

to express K in terms of L. Subtracting $P_L L$ from both sides and dividing through by P_K gives

$$K = \left(-\frac{P_L}{P_K}\right)L + \frac{M}{P_K}$$

The isocost curve is therefore a straight line with slope $-P_L/P_K$ and intercept M/P_K. Graphically, our constrained problem is to choose that point on the isocost line which maximizes output. This is given by the point labelled A in Figure 5.10. Point A certainly lies on the isocost line and it maximizes output because it also lies on the highest isoquant. Other points such as B and C also satisfy the constraint but they lie on lower isoquants and so yield smaller levels of output than A. Point A is characterized by the fact that the isocost line is tangential to an isoquant. In other words, the slope of the isocost line is the same as that of the isoquant at A.

Now we have already shown that the isocost line has slope $-P_L/P_K$. In Section 5.2 we defined the marginal rate of technical substitution, MRTS, to be minus the slope of an isoquant, so at the point A we must have

$$\frac{P_L}{P_K} = \text{MRTS}$$

We also showed that

$$\text{MRTS} = \frac{\text{MP}_L}{\text{MP}_K}$$

so

$$\frac{P_L}{P_K} = \frac{\text{MP}_L}{\text{MP}_K}$$

> the ratio of the input prices is equal to the ratio of their marginal products

This relationship can be rearranged as

$$\frac{\text{MP}_L}{P_L} = \frac{\text{MP}_K}{P_K}$$

so when output is maximized subject to a cost constraint

> the ratio of marginal product to price is the same for all inputs

The marginal product determines the change in output due to a one unit increase in input. This optimization condition therefore states that the last dollar spent on labour yields the same addition to output as the last dollar spent on capital.

The above discussion has concentrated on production functions. An analogous situation arises when we maximize utility functions

$$U = U(x_1, x_2)$$

where x_1, x_2 denote the number of items of goods G1, G2 that an individual buys. If the prices of these goods are denoted by P_1 and P_2 and the individual has a fixed budget, M, to spend on these goods then the corresponding constraint is

$$P_1 x_1 + P_2 x_2 = M$$

This budgetary constraint plays the role of the cost constraint and indifference curves are analogous to isoquants. Consequently, we analyse the problem by superimposing the budget line on an indifference map. The corresponding diagram is virtually indistinguishable from that of Figure 5.10. The only change is that the axes would be labelled x_1 and x_2 rather than L and K. Once again, the maximum point of the constrained problem occurs at the point of tangency so that, at this point, the slope of the budget line is that of an indifference curve. Hence

$$\frac{P_1}{P_2} = MRCS$$

In Section 5.2 we derived the result

$$MRCS = \frac{\partial U / \partial x_1}{\partial U / \partial x_2}$$

Writing the partial derivatives $\partial U / \partial x_i$ more concisely as U_i we can deduce that

$$\frac{P_1}{P_2} = \frac{U_1}{U_2}$$

that is

> the ratio of the prices of the goods is equal to the ratio of their marginal utilities

Again, this relationship can be rearranged into the more familiar form

$$\frac{U_1}{P_1} = \frac{U_2}{P_2}$$

so when utility is maximized subject to a budgetary constraint

> the ratio of marginal utility to price is the same for all goods consumed

If individuals allocate their budgets between goods in this way then utility is maximized when the last dollar spent on each good yields the same addition to total utility. Under these circumstances, the consumer has achieved maximum satisfaction within the constraint of a fixed budget, so there is no tendency to reallocate income between these goods. Obviously, consumer's equilibrium will be affected if there is a change in external conditions such as income or the price of any good. For example, suppose that P_1 suddenly to increase while P_2 and M remain fixed. If this happens then the equation

$$\frac{U_1}{P_1} = \frac{U_2}{P_2}$$

turns into an inequality

$$\frac{U_1}{P_1} < \frac{U_2}{P_2}$$

so equilibrium no longer holds. Given that P_1 has increased, consumers find that the last dollar spent no longer buys as many items of G1 so utility can be increased by purchasing more of G2 and less of G1. By the law of diminishing marginal utility, the effect is to increase U_1 and to decrease U_2. The process of reallocation continues until the ratio of marginal utilities to prices is again equal and equilibrium is again established.

The graphical approach provides a useful interpretation of constrained optimization. It has also enabled us to justify some familiar results in microeconomics. However, it does not give us a practical way of actually solving such problems. It is very difficult to produce an accurate isoquant or indifference map from any given production or utility function. We now describe an alternative approach, known as the **method of substitution**. To motivate the method we begin with an easy example.

EXAMPLE

Find the minimum value of the objective function

$$z = -2x^2 + y^2$$

subject to the constraint $y = 2x - 1$.

Solution

In this example we need to optimize the function

$$z = -2x^2 + y^2$$

given that x and y are related by

$$y = 2x - 1$$

The obvious thing to do is to substitute the expression for y given by the constraint directly into the function that we are trying to optimize to get

$$z = -2x^2 + (2x - 1)^2$$
$$= -2x^2 + 4x^2 - 4x + 1$$
$$= 2x^2 - 4x + 1$$

Note the wonderful effect that this has on z. Instead of z being a function of two variables, x and y, it is now just a function of the one variable x. Consequently, the minimum value of z can be found using the theory of stationary points discussed in Chapter 4.

At a stationary point,

$$\frac{dz}{dx} = 0$$

that is

$$4x - 4 = 0$$

which has solution $x = 1$. Differentiating a second time we see that

$$\frac{d^2z}{dx^2} = 4 > 0$$

confirming that the stationary point is a minimum. The value of z can be found by substituting $x = 1$ into

$$z = 2x^2 - 4x + 1$$

to get

$$z = 2(1)^2 - 4(1) + 1 = -1$$

It is also possible to find the value of y at the minimum. To do this we substitute $x = 1$ into the constraint,

$$y = 2x - 1$$

to get

$$y = 2(1) - 1 = 1$$

The constrained function therefore has a minimum value of -1 at the point $(1, 1)$.

■

The method of substitution for optimizing

$$z = f(x, y)$$

subject to

$$\varphi(x, y) = M$$

may be summarized as follows:

Step 1   Use the constraint

$$\varphi(x, y) = M$$

to express y in terms of x.

Step 2   Substitute this expression for y into the objective function,

$$z = f(x, y)$$

to write z as a function of x only.

Step 3   Use the theory of stationary points of functions of one variable to optimize z.

PROBLEM

1 Find the maximum value of the objective function

$$z = 2x^2 - 3xy + 2y + 10$$

subject to the constraint $y = x$.

The most difficult part of the three-step strategy is step 1 where we rearrange the given constraint to write y in terms of x. In the previous example and in Problem 1 this step was exceptionally easy because the constraint was linear. In both cases the constraint was even presented in the appropriate form to begin with so no extra work was required. In general, if the constraint is non-linear it may be difficult or impossible to perform the initial rearrangement. If this happens then you could try working the other way round and expressing x in terms of y, although there is no guarantee that this will be possible either. However, when step 1 can be tackled successfully, the method does provide a really quick way of solving constrained optimization problems. To illustrate this we now use the method of substitution to solve two economic problems which both involve production functions. In the first example output is maximized subject to cost constraint and in the second example cost is minimized subject to an output constraint.

EXAMPLE

A firm's unit capital and labour costs are $1 and $2 respectively. If the production function is given by

$$Q = 4LK + L^2$$

find the maximum output and the levels of K and L at which it is achieved when the total input costs are fixed at $105. Verify that the ratio of marginal product to price is the same for both inputs at the optimum.

Solution

We are told that 1 unit of capital costs $1 and that 1 unit of labour costs $2. If the firm uses K units of capital and L units of labour then the total input costs are

$$K + 2L$$

This is fixed at $105 so

$$K + 2L = 105$$

The mathematical problem is to maximize the objective function

$$Q = 4LK + L^2$$

subject to the constraint

$$K + 2L = 105$$

The three-step strategy is as follows:

Step 1 Rearranging the constraint to express K in terms of L gives

$$K = 105 - 2L$$

Step 2 Substituting this into the objective function

$$Q = 4LK + L^2$$

gives

$$Q = 4L(105 - 2L) + L^2$$
$$= 420L - 7L^2$$

and so output is now a function of the one variable, L.

Step 3 At a stationary point

$$\frac{dQ}{dL} = 0$$

that is

$$420 - 14L = 0$$

which has solution $L = 30$. Differentiating a second time gives

$$\frac{d^2Q}{dL^2} = -14 < 0$$

confirming that the stationary point is a maximum.

The maximum output is found by substituting $L = 30$ into the objective function

$$Q = 420L - 7L^2$$

to get

$$Q = 420(30) - 7(30)^2 = 6300$$

The corresponding level of capital is found by substituting $L = 30$ into the constraint

$$K = 105 - 2L$$

to get

$$K = 105 - 2(30) = 45$$

The firm should therefore use 30 units of labour and 45 units of capital to produce a maximum output of 6300.

Finally, we are asked to check that the ratio of marginal product to price is the same for both inputs. From the formula

$$Q = 4LK + L^2$$

we see that the marginal products are given by

$$\text{MP}_L = \frac{\partial Q}{\partial L} = 4K + 2L \quad \text{and} \quad \text{MP}_K = \frac{\partial Q}{\partial K} = 4L$$

so at the optimum

$$MP_L = 4(45) + 2(30) = 240$$

and

$$MP_K = 4(30) = 120$$

The ratios of marginal products to prices are then

$$\frac{MP_L}{P_L} = \frac{240}{2} = 120$$

and

$$\frac{MP_K}{P_K} = \frac{120}{1} = 120$$

which are seen to be the same.

∎

PROBLEM

2 An individual's utility function is given by

$$U = x_1 x_2$$

where x_1 and x_2 denote the number of items of two goods, G1 and G2. The prices of the goods are $2 and $10 respectively. Assuming that the individual has $400 available to spend on these goods find the utility maximizing values of x_1 and x_2. Verify that the ratio of marginal utility to price is the same for both goods at the optimum.

EXAMPLE

A firm's production function is given by

$$Q = 2K^{1/2}L^{1/2}$$

Unit capital and labour costs are $4 and $3 respectively. Find the values of K and L which minimize total input costs if the firm is contracted to provide 160 units of output.

Solution

Given that capital and labour costs are $4 and $3 per unit the total cost of using K units of capital and L units of labour is

$$TC = 4K + 3L$$

The firm's production quota is 160 so

$$2K^{1/2}L^{1/2} = 160$$

The mathematical problem is to minimize the objective function

$$TC = 4K + 3L$$

subject to the constraint

$$2K^{1/2}L^{1/2} = 160$$

Step 1   Rearranging the constraint to express L in terms of K gives

$$L^{1/2} = \frac{80}{K^{1/2}} \quad \text{(divide both sides by } 2K^{1/2}\text{)}$$

$$L = \frac{6400}{K} \quad \text{(square both sides)}$$

Step 2   Substituting this into the objective function

$$TC = 4K + 3L$$

gives

$$TC = 4K + \frac{19\,200}{K}$$

and so total cost is now a function of the one variable, K.

Step 3   At a stationary point

$$\frac{d(TC)}{dK} = 0$$

that is

$$4 - \frac{19\,200}{K^2} = 0$$

This can be written as

$$4 = \frac{19\,200}{K^2}$$

so that

$$K^2 = \frac{19\,200}{4} = 4800$$

Hence

$$K = \sqrt{4800} = 69.28$$

Differentiating a second time gives

$$\frac{d^2(TC)}{dK^2} = \frac{38\,400}{K^3} > 0 \quad \text{because} \quad K > 0$$

confirming that the stationary point is a minimum.

Finally, the value of L can be found by substituting $K = 69.28$ into the constraint

$$L = \frac{6400}{K}$$

to get

$$L = \frac{6400}{69.28} = 92.38$$

We are not asked for the minimum cost although this could easily be found by substituting the values of K and L into the objective function.

■

PROBLEM

3 A firm's total cost function is given by

$$TC = 3x_1^2 + 2x_1x_2 + 7x_2^2$$

where x_1 and x_2 denote the number of items of goods G1 and G2 that are produced. Find the values of x_1 and x_2 which minimize costs if the firm is committed to providing 40 goods of either type in total.

PRACTICE PROBLEMS

4 Find the maximum value of

$$z = 6x - 3x^2 + 2y$$

subject to the constraint

$$y - x^2 = 2$$

5 A firm's production function is given by

$$Q = 10K^{1/2}L^{1/4}$$

Unit capital and labour costs are \$4 and \$5 respectively and the firm spends a total of \$60 on these inputs. Find the values of K and L which maximize output.

6 A firm's production function is given by

$$Q = 50KL$$

Unit capital and labour costs are \$2 and \$3 respectively. Find the values of K and L which minimize total input costs if the production quota is 1200.

7 A firm's production function is given by

$$Q = 2L^{1/2} + 3K^{1/2}$$

where Q, L and K denote the number of units of output, labour and capital respectively. Labour costs are $2 per unit, capital costs are $1 per unit and output sells at $8 per unit. If the firm is prepared to spend $99 on input costs, find the maximum profit and the values of K and L at which it is achieved.

[You might like to compare your answer with the corresponding unconstrained problem which you solved in Problem 7 of Section 5.4.]

5.6   Lagrange multipliers

Objectives   At the end of this section you should be able to:

●   use the method of Lagrange multipliers to solve constrained optimization problems,

●   give an economic interpretation of Lagrange multipliers,

●   use Lagrange multipliers to maximize a Cobb–Douglas production function subject to a cost constraint,

●   use Lagrange multipliers to show that when a firm maximizes output subject to a cost constraint the ratio of marginal product to price is the same for all inputs.

We now describe the method of Lagrange multipliers for solving constrained optimization problems. This is the preferred method since it handles non-linear constraints and problems involving more than two variables with ease. It also provides some additional information which is useful when solving economic problems.

To optimize an objective function

$$f(x, y)$$

subject to a constraint

$$\varphi(x, y) = M$$

we work as follows:

Step 1   Define a new function

$$g(x, y, \lambda) = f(x, y) + \lambda[M - \varphi(x, y)]$$

Step 2   Solve the simultaneous equations

$$\frac{\partial g}{\partial x} = 0$$

$$\frac{\partial g}{\partial y} = 0$$

$$\frac{\partial g}{\partial \lambda} = 0$$

for the three unknowns, x, y and λ.

The basic steps of the method are straightforward. In step 1 we combine the objective function and constraint into a single function. To do this we first rearrange the constraint as

$$M - \varphi(x, y)$$

and multiply by the scalar, λ (the Greek letter lambda). This scalar is called the **Lagrange multiplier**. Finally, we add on the objective function to produce the new function

$$g(x, y, \lambda) = f(x, y) + \lambda[M - \varphi(x, y)]$$

This is called the **Lagrangian** function. The right-hand side involves the three letters x, y and λ so g is a function of three variables.

In step 2 we work out the three first-order partial derivatives

$$\frac{\partial g}{\partial x}, \quad \frac{\partial g}{\partial y}, \quad \frac{\partial g}{\partial \lambda}$$

and equate these to zero to produce a system of three simultaneous equations for the three unknowns x, y and λ. The point (x, y) is then the optimal solution of the constrained problem. The number λ can also be given a meaning and we consider this later. For the moment we consider a simple example to get us started.

EXAMPLE

Use Lagrange multipliers to find the optimal value of

$$x^2 - 3xy + 12x$$

subject to the constraint

$$2x + 3y = 6$$

Solution

Step 1   In this example

$$f(x, y) = x^2 - 3xy + 12x$$

$$\varphi(x, y) = 2x + 3y$$

$$M = 6$$

so the Lagrangian function is given by

$$g(x, y, \lambda) = x^2 - 3xy + 12x + \lambda(6 - 2x - 3y)$$

Step 2 Working out the three partial derivatives of g gives

$$\frac{\partial g}{\partial x} = 2x - 3y + 12 - 2\lambda$$

$$\frac{\partial g}{\partial y} = -3x - 3\lambda$$

$$\frac{\partial g}{\partial \lambda} = 6 - 2x - 3y$$

so we need to solve the simultaneous equations

$$2x - 3y + 12 - 2\lambda = 0$$

$$-3x - 3\lambda = 0$$

$$6 - 2x - 3y = 0$$

that is

$$2x - 3y - 2\lambda = -12 \quad (1)$$

$$-3x \qquad -3\lambda = \quad 0 \quad (2)$$

$$2x + 3y \qquad = \quad 6 \quad (3)$$

We can eliminate x from equation (2) by multiplying equation (1) by 3, multiplying equation (2) by 2 and adding. Similarly, x can be eliminated from equation (3) by subtracting equation (3) from (1). These operations give

$$-9y - 12\lambda = -36 \quad (4)$$

$$-6y - 2\lambda = -18 \quad (5)$$

The variable y can be eliminated by multiplying equation (4) by 6 and equation (5) by 9, and subtracting to get

$$-54\lambda = -54 \quad (6)$$

so $\lambda = 1$. Substituting this into equations (5) and (2) gives $y = 8/3$ and $x = -1$ respectively.

The optimal solution is therefore $(-1, 8/3)$ and the corresponding value of the objective function

$$x^2 - 3xy + 12x$$

is

$$(-1)^2 - 3(-1)(\tfrac{8}{3}) + 12(-1) = -3$$

∎

PROBLEM

1 Use Lagrange multipliers to optimize

$$2x^2 - xy$$

subject to

$$x + y = 12$$

Looking back at the worked example and your own solution to Problem 1 notice that the third equation in step 2 is just a restatement of the original constraint. It is easy to see that this is always the case because if

$$g(x, y, \lambda) = f(x, y) + \lambda[M - \varphi(x, y)]$$

then

$$\frac{\partial g}{\partial \lambda} = M - \varphi(x, y)$$

The equation

$$\frac{\partial g}{\partial \lambda} = 0$$

then implies the constraint

$$\varphi(x, y) = M$$

It is possible to make use of second-order partial derivatives to classify the optimal point. Unfortunately, these conditions are quite complicated and so will not be discussed in this book. In all problems that we consider there is only a single optimum and it is usually obvious on economic grounds whether it is a maximum or a minimum.

EXAMPLE

A monopolistic producer of two goods, G1 and G2, has a joint total cost function

$$TC = 10Q_1 + Q_1Q_2 + 10Q_2$$

where Q_1 and Q_2 denote the quantities of G1 and G2 respectively. If P_1 and P_2 denote the corresponding prices then the demand equations are

$$P_1 = 50 - Q_1 + Q_2$$
$$P_2 = 30 + 2Q_1 - Q_2$$

Find the maximum profit if the firm is contracted to produce a total of 15 goods of either type. Estimate the new optimal profit if the production quota rises by one unit.

Solution

The first thing that we need to do is to write down expressions for the objective function and constraint. The objective function is profit and is given by

$$\pi = TR - TC$$

The total cost function is given to be

$$TC = 10Q_1 + Q_1Q_2 + 10Q_2$$

However, we need to use the demand equations to obtain an expression for TR. Total revenue from the sale of G1 is

$$TR_1 = P_1Q_1 = (50 - Q_1 + Q_2)Q_1 = 50Q_1 - Q_1^2 + Q_2Q_1$$

and total revenue from the sale of G2 is

$$TR_2 = P_2 Q_2 = (30 + 2Q_1 - Q_2)Q_2 = 30Q_2 + 2Q_1 Q_2 - Q_2^2$$

so

$$TR = TR_1 + TR_2$$
$$= 50Q_1 - Q_1^2 + Q_2 Q_1 + 30Q_2 + 2Q_1 Q_2 - Q_2^2$$
$$= 50Q_1 - Q_1^2 + 3Q_1 Q_2 + 30Q_2 - Q_2^2$$

Hence

$$\pi = TR - TC$$
$$= (50Q_1 - Q_1^2 + 3Q_1 Q_2 + 30Q_2 - Q_2^2) - (10Q_1 + Q_1 Q_2 + 10Q_2)$$
$$= 40Q_1 - Q_1^2 + 2Q_1 Q_2 + 20Q_2 - Q_2^2$$

The constraint is more easily determined. We are told that the firm produces 15 goods in total so

$$Q_1 + Q_2 = 15$$

The mathematical problem is to maximize the objective function

$$\pi = 40Q_1 - Q_1^2 + 2Q_1 Q_2 + 20Q_2 - Q_2^2$$

subject to the constraint

$$Q_1 + Q_2 = 15$$

Step 1 The Lagrangian function is

$$g(Q_1, Q_2, \lambda) = 40Q_1 - Q_1^2 + 2Q_1 Q_2 + 20Q_2 - Q_2^2 + \lambda(15 - Q_1 - Q_2)$$

Step 2 The simultaneous equations

$$\frac{\partial g}{\partial Q_1} = 0, \quad \frac{\partial g}{\partial Q_2} = 0, \quad \frac{\partial g}{\partial \lambda} = 0$$

are

$$40 - 2Q_1 + 2Q_2 - \lambda = 0$$
$$2Q_1 + 20 - 2Q_2 - \lambda = 0$$
$$15 - Q_1 - Q_2 = 0$$

that is

$$-2Q_1 + 2Q_2 - \lambda = -40 \quad (1)$$
$$2Q_1 - 2Q_2 - \lambda = -20 \quad (2)$$
$$Q_1 + Q_2 = 15 \quad (3)$$

The obvious way of solving this system is to add equations (1) and (2) to get

$$-2\lambda = -60$$

so $\lambda = 30$. Putting this into equation (1) gives

$$-2Q_1 + 2Q_2 = -10 \quad (4)$$

Equations (3) and (4) constitute a system of two equations for the two unknowns Q_1 and Q_2. We can eliminate Q_1 by multiplying equation (3) by 2 and adding equation (4) to get

$$4Q_2 = 20$$

so $Q_2 = 5$. Substituting this into equation (3) gives

$$Q_1 = 15 - 5 = 10$$

The maximum profit is found by substituting $Q_1 = 10$ and $Q_2 = 5$ into the formula for π to get

$$\pi = 40(10) - (10)^2 + 2(10)(5) + 20(5) - 5^2 = 475$$

The final part of this example wants us to find the new optimal profit when the production quota rises by one unit. One way of doing this is just to repeat the calculations replacing the previous quota of 15 by 16 although this is extremely tedious and not strictly necessary. There is a convenient shortcut based on the value of the Lagrange multiplier λ. To understand this, let us replace the production quota, 15, by the variable M so that the Lagrangian function is

$$g(Q_1, Q_2, \lambda, M) = 40Q_1 - Q_1^2 + 2Q_1Q_2 + 20Q_2 - Q_2^2 + \lambda(M - Q_1 - Q_2)$$

The expression on the right-hand side involves Q_1, Q_2, λ and M so g is now a function of four variables. If we partially differentiate with respect to M then

$$\frac{\partial g}{\partial M} = \lambda$$

We see that λ is a multiplier not only in the mathematical but also in the economic sense. It represents the (approximate) change in g due to a one unit increase in M. Moreover, if the constraint is satisfied, then

$$Q_1 + Q_2 = M$$

and the expression for g reduces to

$$40Q_1 - Q_1^2 + 2Q_1Q_2 + 20Q_2 - Q_2^2$$

which is equal to profit. The value of the Lagrange multiplier represents the change in optimal profit brought about by a one unit increase in the production quota. In this case, $\lambda = 30$, so profit rises by 30 to become 505.

■

The interpretation placed on the value of λ in this example applies quite generally. Given an objective function

$$f(x, y)$$

and constraint

$$\varphi(x, y) = M$$

the value of λ gives the approximate change in the optimal value of f due to a one unit increase in M.

PROBLEM

2 A consumer's utility function is given by

$$U(x_1, x_2) = 2x_1x_2 + 3x_1$$

where x_1 and x_2 denote the number of items of two goods G1 and G2 that are bought. Each item costs \$1 for G1 and \$2 for G2. Use Lagrange multipliers to find the maximum value of U if the consumer's income is \$83. Estimate the new optimal utility if the consumer's income rises by \$1.

EXAMPLE

Use Lagrange multipliers to find expressions for K and L which maximize output given by a Cobb–Douglas production function

$$Q = AK^\alpha L^\beta \qquad (A, \alpha \text{ and } \beta \text{ are positive constants})$$

subject to a cost constraint

$$P_K K + P_L L = M$$

Solution

This example appears very hard at first sight because it does not involve specific numbers. However, it is easy to handle such generalized problems provided that we do not panic.

Step 1 The Lagrangian function is

$$g(K, L, \lambda) = AK^\alpha L^\beta + \lambda(M - P_K K - P_L L)$$

Step 2 The simultaneous equations

$$\frac{\partial g}{\partial K} = 0, \quad \frac{\partial g}{\partial L} = 0, \quad \frac{\partial g}{\partial \lambda} = 0$$

are

$$A\alpha K^{\alpha-1} L^\beta - \lambda P_K = 0 \qquad (1)$$

$$A\beta K^\alpha L^{\beta-1} - \lambda P_L = 0 \qquad (2)$$

$$M - P_K K - P_L L = 0 \qquad (3)$$

These equations look rather forbidding. Before we begin to solve them it pays to simplify equations (1) and (2) slightly by introducing $Q = AK^\alpha L^\beta$. Notice that

$$A\alpha K^{\alpha-1} L^\beta = \frac{\alpha(AK^\alpha L^\beta)}{K} = \frac{\alpha Q}{K}$$

$$A\beta K^\alpha L^{\beta-1} = \frac{\beta(AK^\alpha L^\beta)}{L} = \frac{\beta Q}{L}$$

so equations (1), (2) and (3) can be written

$$\frac{\alpha Q}{K} - \lambda P_K = 0 \qquad (4)$$

$$\frac{\beta Q}{L} - \lambda P_L = 0 \qquad (5)$$

$$P_K K + P_L L = M \qquad (6)$$

Equations (4) and (5) can be rearranged to give

$$\lambda = \frac{\alpha Q}{P_K K} \qquad \text{and} \qquad \lambda = \frac{\beta Q}{P_L L}$$

so that

$$\frac{\alpha Q}{P_K K} = \frac{\beta Q}{P_L L}$$

and hence

$$\frac{P_K K}{\alpha} = \frac{P_L L}{\beta} \qquad \text{(divide both sides by } Q \text{ and turn both sides upside down)}$$

that is

$$P_K K = \frac{\alpha}{\beta} P_L L \qquad (7) \qquad \text{(multiply through by } \alpha)$$

Substituting this into equation (6) gives

$$\frac{\alpha}{\beta} P_L L + P_L L = M$$

$$\alpha L + \beta L = \frac{\beta M}{P_L} \qquad \text{(multiply through by } \beta/P_L)$$

$$(\alpha + \beta) L = \frac{\beta M}{P_L} \qquad \text{(factorize)}$$

$$L = \frac{\beta M}{(\alpha + \beta) P_L} \qquad \text{(divide through by } \alpha + \beta)$$

Finally, we can put this into equation (7) to get

$$P_K K = \frac{\alpha M}{\alpha + \beta}$$

so

$$K = \frac{\alpha M}{(\alpha + \beta) P_K}$$

The values of K and L which optimize Q are therefore

$$\frac{\alpha M}{(\alpha + \beta) P_K} \qquad \text{and} \qquad \frac{\beta M}{(\alpha + \beta) P_L}$$

■

PROBLEM

3 Use Lagrange multipliers to find expressions for x_1 and x_2 which maximize the utility function

$$U = x_1^{1/2} + x_2^{1/2}$$

subject to the general budgetary constraint

$$P_1 x_1 + P_2 x_2 = M$$

The previous example illustrates the power of mathematics when solving economics problems. The main advantage of using algebra and calculus rather than just graphs and tables of numbers is its generality. In future, if we need to maximize any particular Cobb–Douglas production function subject to any particular cost constraint, then all we have to do is to quote the result of the previous example. By substituting specific values of M, α, β, P_K and P_L into the general formulas for K and L we can write down the solution in a matter of seconds. In fact, we can use mathematics to generalize still further. Rather than work with production functions of a prescribed form such as

$$Q = AK^\alpha L^\beta$$

we can obtain results pertaining to any production function

$$Q = f(K, L)$$

For instance, we can use Lagrange multipliers to justify a result that we derived graphically in Section 5.5. At the beginning of that section we showed that when output is maximized subject to a cost constraint the ratio of marginal product to price is the same for all inputs. To obtain this result using Lagrange multipliers we simply write down the Lagrangian function

$$g(K, L, \lambda) = f(K, L) + \lambda(M - P_K K - P_L L)$$

which corresponds to a production function

$$f(K, L)$$

and cost constraint

$$P_K K + P_L L = M$$

The simultaneous equations

$$\frac{\partial g}{\partial K} = 0, \quad \frac{\partial g}{\partial L} = 0, \quad \frac{\partial g}{\partial \lambda} = 0$$

are

$$\text{MP}_K - \lambda P_K = 0 \qquad (1)$$

$$\text{MP}_L - \lambda P_L = 0 \qquad (2)$$

$$M - P_K K - P_L L = 0 \qquad (3)$$

because

$$\frac{\partial f}{\partial K} = \text{MP}_K \qquad \text{and} \qquad \frac{\partial f}{\partial L} = \text{MP}_L$$

Equations (1) and (2) can be rearranged to give

$$\lambda = \frac{MP_K}{P_K} \quad \text{and} \quad \lambda = \frac{MP_L}{P_L}$$

so

$$\frac{MP_K}{P_K} = \frac{MP_L}{P_L}$$

as required.

There now follow three new practice problems for you to attempt. If you feel that you need even more practice then you are advised to rework the seven problems given in Section 5.5 using Lagrange multipliers.

PRACTICE PROBLEMS

4   A firm which manufactures speciality bicycles has a profit function

$$\pi = 5x^2 - 10xy + 3y^2 + 240x$$

where x denotes the number of frames and y denotes the number of wheels. Find the maximum profit assuming that the firm does not want any spare frames or wheels left over at the end of the production run.

5   A monopolistic producer of two goods, G1 and G2, has a total cost function

$$TC = 5Q_1 + 10Q_2$$

where Q_1 and Q_2 denote the quantities of G1 and G2 respectively. If P_1 and P_2 denote the corresponding prices then the demand equations are

$$P_1 = 50 - Q_1 - Q_2$$
$$P_2 = 100 - Q_1 - 4Q_2$$

Find the maximum profit if the firm's total costs are fixed at $100. Estimate the new optimal profit if total costs rise to $101.

6   A consumer's utility function is given by

$$U = \alpha \ln x_1 + \beta \ln x_2$$

Find the values of x_1 and x_2 which maximize U subject to the budgetary constraint

$$P_1 x_1 + P_2 x_2 = M$$

6 *Integration*

This chapter concludes the topic of calculus by considering the integration of functions of one variable. It is in two sections which should be read in the order that they appear.

Section 6.1 introduces the idea of integration as the opposite process to that of differentiation. It enables you to recover an expression for the total revenue function from any given marginal revenue function, to recover the total cost function from any marginal cost function and so on. You will no doubt be pleased to discover that no new mathematical techniques are needed for this. All that is required is for you to put your brain into reverse gear. Of course, driving backwards is a little harder to master than going forwards. However, with practice you should find integration almost as easy as differentiation.

Section 6.2 shows how integration can be used to find the area under the graph of a function. This process is called definite integration. We can apply the technique to supply and demand curves and so calculate producer's and consumer's surpluses. Definite integration can also be used to determine capital stock and to discount a continuous revenue stream.

6.1 Indefinite integration

Objectives At the end of this section you should be able to:

- recognize the notation for indefinite integration,

- write down the integrals of simple power and exponential functions,

- integrate functions of the form $af(x) + bg(x)$,

- find the total cost function given any marginal cost function,

- find the total revenue function given any marginal revenue function,

- find the consumption and savings functions given either the marginal propensity to consume or the marginal propensity to save.

Throughout mathematics there are many pairs of operations which cancel each other out and take you back to where you started. Perhaps the most obvious pair is multiplication and division. If you multiply a number by a non-zero constant, k, and then divide by k you end up with the number you first thought of. This situation is described by saying that the two operations are **inverses** of each other. In calculus, the inverse of differentiation is called **integration**.

Suppose that you are required to find a function, $F(x)$, which differentiates to

$$f(x) = 3x^2$$

Can you guess what $F(x)$ is in this case? Given such a simple function it is straightforward to write down the answer by inspection. It is

$$F(x) = x^3$$

because

$$F'(x) = 3x^2 = f(x) \quad \checkmark$$

as required.

As a second example, consider

$$f(x) = x^7$$

Can you think of a function, $F(x)$, which differentiates to this? Recall that when power functions are differentiated the power decreases by 1 so it makes sense to do the opposite here and to try

$$F(x) = x^8$$

Unfortunately, this does not quite work out because it differentiates to

$$8x^7$$

which is eight times too big! This suggests that we try

$$F(x) = \frac{1}{8} x^8$$

which does work because

$$F'(x) = \frac{8}{8} x^7 = x^7 = f(x) \quad \checkmark$$

In general, if $F'(x) = f(x)$ then $F(x)$ is said to be the **integral** (sometimes called the **antiderivative** or **primitive**) of $f(x)$ and is written

$$F(x) = \int f(x)\, dx \qquad \left(\text{read 'integral of } f \text{ of } x \text{ dee } x\text{'} \right)$$

In this notation

$$\int 3x^2\, dx = x^3$$

and

$$\int x^7 \, dx = \frac{1}{8} x^8$$

Here is a problem for you to try. Do not let the notation

$$\int dx$$

put you off. It is merely an instruction for you to think of a function which differentiates to whatever is squashed between the integral sign

$$\int$$

and dx. If you get stuck, try adding 1 on to the power as we did for x^7. Differentiate your guess and if it does not quite work out then go back and try again, adjusting the coefficient accordingly.

PROBLEM

1   Find

(a) $\displaystyle\int 2x \, dx$ **(b)** $\displaystyle\int 4x^3 \, dx$ **(c)** $\displaystyle\int 100x^{99} \, dx$ **(d)** $\displaystyle\int x^3 \, dx$ **(e)** $\displaystyle\int x^{18} \, dx$

In Problem 1(a) you probably wrote

$$\int 2x \, dx = x^2$$

However, there are other possibilities. For example, both of the functions

$$x^2 + 6 \quad \text{and} \quad x^2 - 59$$

differentiate to $2x$ because constants differentiate to zero. In fact, we can add any constant, c, to x^2 to obtain a function which differentiates to $2x$. Hence

$$\int 2x \, dx = x^2 + c$$

The arbitrary constant, c, is called the **constant of integration**. In general, if $F(x)$ is any function which differentiates to $f(x)$ then so does

$$F(x) + c$$

Hence

$$\int f(x) \, dx = F(x) + c$$

In Problem 1 you used guesswork to find various integrals. In theory most integrals can be worked out in this way. However, considerable ingenuity (and luck!) may be required when integrating complicated functions. It is possible to develop various rules similar to those of differentiation which we discussed in Chapter 4, although even then we sometimes have to resort to sheer trickery in many cases. It is not our intention to plod through each rule as we did in Chapter 4, for the simple reason that they are rarely needed in economics. However, it is worthwhile showing you a direct way of integrating simple functions such as

$$2x - 3x^2 + 10x^3 \quad \text{and} \quad x - e^{2x} + 5$$

We begin by finding general formulas for

$$\int x^n \, dx \quad \text{and} \quad \int e^{mx} \, dx$$

To integrate $f(x) = x^n$ an obvious first guess is

$$F(x) = x^{n+1}$$

This gives

$$F'(x) = (n + 1)x^n$$

which is $n + 1$ times too big. This suggests that we try again with

$$F(x) = \frac{1}{n + 1} x^{n+1}$$

which checks out because

$$F'(x) = \frac{n + 1}{n + 1} x^n = x^n = f(x) \qquad \checkmark$$

Hence

$$\boxed{\int x^n \, dx = \frac{1}{n + 1} x^{n+1} + c}$$

To integrate a power function you simply add one to the power and divide by the number you get. This formula holds whenever n is positive, negative, a whole number or a fraction. There is just one exception to the rule when $n = -1$. The formula cannot be used to integrate

$$\frac{1}{x}$$

because it is impossible to divide by zero. An alternative result is therefore required in this case. We know from Chapter 4 that the natural logarithm function

$$\ln x$$

differentiates to give

$$\frac{1}{x}$$

and so

$$\int \frac{1}{x}\, dx = \ln x + c$$

The last basic integral that we wish to determine is

$$\int e^{mx}\, dx$$

In Section 4.1 we showed that to differentiate an exponential function all we need to do is to multiply by the coefficient of x. To integrate we do exactly the opposite and divide by the coefficient of x so

$$\int e^{mx}\, dx = \frac{1}{m}\, e^{mx} + c$$

It is easy to check that this is correct because if

$$F(x) = \frac{1}{m}\, e^{mx}$$

then

$$F'(x) = \frac{m}{m}\, e^{mx} = e^{mx} \qquad \checkmark$$

EXAMPLE

Find

(a) $\displaystyle\int x^6\, dx$

(b) $\displaystyle\int \frac{1}{x^2}\, dx$

(c) $\displaystyle\int \sqrt{x}\, dx$

(d) $\displaystyle\int e^{2x}\,dx$

Solution

The formula

$$\int x^n\,dx = \frac{1}{n+1}\,x^{n+1} + c$$

can be used to find the first three integrals by substituting particular values for n.

(a) Putting $n = 6$ gives

$$\int x^6\,dx = \frac{1}{7}\,x^7 + c$$

(b) Putting $n = -2$ gives

$$\int \frac{1}{x^2}\,dx = \int x^{-2}\,dx = \frac{1}{-1}\,x^{-1} + c = -\frac{1}{x} + c$$

(c) Putting $n = \frac{1}{2}$ gives

$$\int \sqrt{x}\,dx = \int x^{1/2}\,dx = \frac{1}{3/2}\,x^{3/2} + c = \frac{2}{3}\,x^{3/2} + c$$

(d) To find

$$\int e^{2x}\,dx$$

we put $m = 2$ into the formula

$$\int e^{mx}\,dx = \frac{1}{m}\,e^{mx} + c$$

to get

$$\int e^{2x}\,dx = \frac{1}{2}\,e^{2x} + c$$

∎

PROBLEM _____

2 Find

(a) $\displaystyle\int x^4\,dx$ **(b)** $\displaystyle\int \frac{1}{x^3}\,dx$ **(c)** $\displaystyle\int x^{1/3}\,dx$ **(d)** $\displaystyle\int e^{3x}\,dx$ **(e)** $\displaystyle\int 1\,dx$

(f) $\displaystyle\int x\,dx$ **(g)** $\displaystyle\int \frac{1}{x}\,dx$

[Hint: in parts (b), (e) and (f) note that $1/x^3 = x^{-3}$, $1 = x^0$ and $x = x^1$ respectively.]

In Section 4.2 we described three rules of differentiation known as the constant, sum and difference rules. Given that integration is the inverse operation, these three rules also apply whenever we integrate a function. The integral of a constant multiple of a function is obtained by integrating the function and multiplying by the constant. The integral of the sum (or difference) of two functions is obtained by integrating the functions separately and adding (or subtracting). These three rules can be combined into the single rule:

$$\int [af(x) + bg(x)]\,\mathrm{d}x = a \int f(x)\,\mathrm{d}x + b \int g(x)\,\mathrm{d}x$$

This enables us to integrate an expression 'term by term' as the following example demonstrates.

EXAMPLE

Find

(a) $\displaystyle\int (2x^2 - 4x^6)\,\mathrm{d}x$

(b) $\displaystyle\int \left(7\mathrm{e}^{-x} + \frac{2}{x}\right)\,\mathrm{d}x$

(c) $\displaystyle\int (5x^2 + 3x + 2)\,\mathrm{d}x$

Solution

(a)

$$\int (2x^2 - 4x^6)\,\mathrm{d}x = 2 \int x^2\,\mathrm{d}x - 4 \int x^6\,\mathrm{d}x$$

Putting $n = 2$ and $n = 6$ into

$$\int x^n\,\mathrm{d}x = \frac{1}{n+1}\,x^{n+1}$$

gives

$$\int x^2\,\mathrm{d}x = \frac{1}{3}\,x^3 \qquad \text{and} \qquad \int x^6\,\mathrm{d}x = \frac{1}{7}\,x^7$$

Hence

$$\int (2x^2 - 4x^6)\,\mathrm{d}x = \frac{2}{3}\,x^3 - \frac{4}{7}\,x^7$$

Finally, we add an arbitrary constant to get

$$\int (2x^2 - 4x^6)\, dx = \frac{2}{3}x^3 - \frac{4}{7}x^7 + c$$

As a check: if

$$F(x) = \frac{2}{3}x^3 - \frac{4}{7}x^7 + c \qquad \text{then} \qquad F'(x) = 2x^2 - 4x^6 \quad \checkmark$$

(b)

$$\int \left(7e^{-x} + \frac{2}{x}\right) dx = 7 \int e^{-x}\, dx + 2 \int \frac{1}{x}\, dx$$

Now

$$\int e^{mx}\, dx = \frac{1}{m}\, e^{mx}$$

so putting $m = -1$ gives

$$\int e^{-x}\, dx = \frac{1}{-1}\, e^{-x} = -e^{-x}$$

Also, we know that the reciprocal function integrates to the natural logarithm function so

$$\int \frac{1}{x}\, dx = \ln x$$

Hence

$$\int \left(7e^{-x} + \frac{2}{x}\right) dx = -7e^{-x} + 2 \ln x$$

Finally, we add an arbitrary constant to get

$$\int \left(7e^{-x} + \frac{2}{x}\right) dx = -7e^{-x} + 2 \ln x + c$$

As a check: if

$$F(x) = -7e^{-x} + 2 \ln x + c \qquad \text{then} \qquad F'(x) = 7e^{-x} + \frac{2}{x} \quad \checkmark$$

(c)

$$\int (5x^2 + 3x + 2)\, dx = 5 \int x^2\, dx + 3 \int x\, dx + 2 \int 1\, dx$$

Putting $n = 2, 1$ and 0 into

$$\int x^n\, dx = \frac{1}{n+1}\, x^{n+1}$$

gives

$$\int x^2\, dx = \frac{1}{3}x^3, \quad \int x\, dx = \frac{1}{2}x^2, \quad \int 1\, dx = x$$

Hence

$$\int (5x^2 + 3x + 2)\, dx = \frac{5}{3} x^3 + \frac{3}{2} x^2 + 2x$$

Finally, we add an arbitrary constant to get

$$\int (5x^2 + 3x + 2)\, dx = \frac{5}{3} x^3 + \frac{3}{2} x^2 + 2x + c$$

As a check: if

$$F(x) = \frac{5}{3} x^3 + \frac{3}{2} x^2 + 2x + c \qquad \text{then} \qquad F'(x) = 5x^2 + 3x + 2 \qquad \checkmark.$$

■

We have written out the solution to this example in detail to show you exactly how integration is performed. With practice you will probably find that you can just write the answer down in a single line of working although it is always a good idea to check (at least in your head, if not on paper), by differentiating your answer, that you have not made any mistakes.

The technique of integration that we have investigated produces a function of x. In the next section a different type of integration is discussed which produces a single number as the end result. For this reason we use the word **indefinite** to describe the type of integration considered here to distinguish it from the **definite** integration in Section 6.2.

PROBLEM

3   Find the indefinite integrals

(a) $\displaystyle\int (2x - 4x^3)\, dx$ **(b)** $\displaystyle\int \left(10x^4 + \frac{5}{x^2}\right) dx$ **(c)** $\displaystyle\int (7x^2 - 3x + 2)\, dx$

In Section 4.3 we described several applications of differentiation to economics. Starting with any basic economic function we can differentiate to obtain the corresponding marginal function. Integration allows us to work backwards and to recover the original function from any marginal function. For example, by integrating a marginal cost function the total cost function is found. Likewise, given a marginal revenue function, integration enables us to determine the total revenue function which in turn can be used to find the demand function. These ideas are illustrated in the following example which also shows how the constant of integration can be given a specific numerical value in economic problems.

EXAMPLE

(1)   A firm's marginal cost function is

$$MC = Q^2 + 2Q + 4$$

Find the total cost function if the fixed costs are 100.

(2)   The marginal revenue function of a monopolistic producer is

$$MR = 10 - 4Q$$

Find the total revenue function and deduce the corresponding demand equation.

(3)   Find an expression for the consumption function if the marginal propensity to consume is given by

$$MPC = 0.5 + \frac{0.1}{\sqrt{Y}}$$

and consumption is 85 when income is 100.

Solution

(1)   We need to find the total cost from the marginal cost function

$$MC = Q^2 + 2Q + 4$$

Now

$$MC = \frac{d(TC)}{dQ}$$

so

$$TC = \int MC \, dQ$$

$$= \int (Q^2 + 2Q + 4) \, dQ$$

$$= \frac{Q^3}{3} + Q^2 + 4Q + c$$

The fixed costs are given to be 100. These are independent of the number of goods produced and represent the costs incurred when the firm does not produce any goods whatsoever. Putting $Q = 0$ into the TC function gives

$$TC = \frac{0^3}{3} + 0^2 + 4(0) + c = c$$

The constant of integration is therefore equal to the fixed costs of production, so $c = 100$. Hence

$$TC = \frac{Q^3}{3} + Q^2 + 4Q + 100$$

(2)   We need to find the total revenue from the marginal revenue function

$$MR = 10 - 4Q$$

Now

$$MR = \frac{d(TR)}{dQ}$$

so

$$TR = \int MR \, dQ$$

$$= \int (10 - 4Q) \, dQ$$

$$= 10Q - 2Q^2 + c$$

Unlike part (1) of this example we have not been given any additional information to help us to pin down the value of c. We do know, however, that when the firm produces no goods the revenue is zero so that $TR = 0$ when $Q = 0$. Putting this condition into

$$TR = 10Q - 2Q^2 + c$$

gives

$$0 = 10(0) - 2(0)^2 + c = c$$

The constant of integration is therefore equal to zero. Hence

$$TR = 10Q - 2Q^2$$

Finally, we can deduce the demand equation from this. To find an expression for total revenue from any given demand equation we normally multiply by Q because $TR = PQ$. This time we work backwards, so we divide by Q to get

$$P = \frac{TR}{Q} = \frac{10Q - 2Q^2}{Q} = 10 - 2Q$$

so the demand equation is

$$P = 10 - 2Q$$

(3) We need to find consumption given that the marginal propensity to consume is

$$MPC = 0.5 + \frac{0.1}{\sqrt{Y}}$$

Now

$$MPC = \frac{dC}{dY}$$

so

$$C = \int MPC \, dY$$

$$= \int \left(0.5 + \frac{0.1}{\sqrt{Y}} \right) dY$$

$$= 0.5Y + 0.2\sqrt{Y} + c$$

where the second term is found from

$$\int \frac{0.1}{\sqrt{Y}} \, dY = 0.1 \int Y^{-1/2} \, dY = 0.1 \left(\frac{1}{1/2} \, Y^{1/2} \right) = 0.2\sqrt{Y}$$

The constant of integration can be calculated from the additional information that $C = 85$ when $Y = 100$. Putting $Y = 100$ into the expression for C gives

$$85 = 0.5(100) + 0.2\sqrt{100} + c = 52 + c$$

and so

$$c = 85 - 52 = 33$$

Hence

$$C = 0.5Y + 0.2\sqrt{Y} + 33$$

■

PROBLEM

4 **(1)** A firm's marginal cost function is

$$MC = 2$$

Find an expression for the total cost function if the fixed costs are 500. Hence find the total cost of producing 40 goods.

(2) The marginal revenue function of a monopolistic producer is

$$MR = 100 - 6Q$$

Find the total revenue function and deduce the corresponding demand equation.

(3) Find an expression for the savings function if the marginal propensity to save is given by

$$MPS = 0.4 - 0.1Y^{-1/2}$$

and savings are zero when income is 100.

PRACTICE PROBLEMS

5 Find

(a) $\displaystyle\int 6x^5 \, dx$ **(b)** $\displaystyle\int x^4 \, dx$ **(c)** $\displaystyle\int 10e^{10x} \, dx$ **(d)** $\displaystyle\int \frac{1}{x} \, dx$

(e) $\displaystyle\int x^{3/2} \, dx$ **(f)** $\displaystyle\int (2x^3 - 6x) \, dx$ **(g)** $\displaystyle\int (x^2 - 8x + 3) \, dx$ **(h)** $\displaystyle\int (ax + b) \, dx$

(i) $\displaystyle\int \left(7x^3 + 4e^{-2x} - \frac{3}{x^2} \right) \, dx$

6 **(1)** Find the total cost if the marginal cost is

$$MC = Q + 5$$

and fixed costs are 20.

(2) Find the total cost if the marginal cost is

$$MC = 3e^{0.5Q}$$

and fixed costs are 10.

7   Find the total revenue and demand functions corresponding to each of the following marginal revenue functions.

(a) $MR = 20 - 2Q$ (b) $MR = \dfrac{6}{\sqrt{Q}}$

8   Find the consumption function if the marginal propensity to consume is 0.6 and consumption is 10 when income is 5. Deduce the corresponding savings function.

6.2   Definite integration

Objectives   At the end of this section you should be able to:

- recognize the notation for definite integration,
- evaluate definite integrals in simple cases,
- calculate the consumer's surplus,
- calculate the producer's surplus,
- calculate the capital stock formation,
- calculate the present value of a continuous revenue stream.

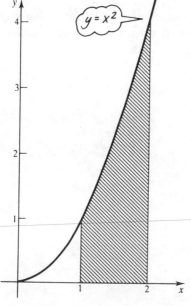

Figure 6.1

One rather tedious task that you may remember from school is that of finding areas. Sketched in Figure 6.1 is a region bounded by the curve $y = x^2$, the lines $x = 1$, $x = 2$, and the x axis. At school you may well have been asked to find the area of this region by 'counting' squares on graph paper. A much quicker and more accurate way of calculating this area is to use integration. We begin by integrating the function

$$f(x) = x^2$$

to get

$$F(x) = \frac{1}{3}x^3$$

In our case we want to find the area under the curve between $x = 1$ and $x = 2$ so we evaluate

$$F(1) = \frac{1}{3}(1)^3 = \frac{1}{3}$$

$$F(2) = \frac{1}{3}(2)^3 = \frac{8}{3}$$

Finally, we subtract $F(1)$ from $F(2)$ to get

$$F(2) - F(1) = \frac{8}{3} - \frac{1}{3} = \frac{7}{3}$$

This number is the exact value of the area of the region sketched in Figure 6.1. Given the connection with integration we write this area as

$$\int_1^2 x^2 \, dx$$

In general, the **definite integral**

$$\int_a^b f(x) \, dx$$

denotes the area under the graph of $f(x)$ between $x = a$ and $x = b$ as shown in Figure 6.2. The numbers a and b are called the **limits of integration** and it is assumed throughout this section that $a < b$ and that $f(x) \geqslant 0$ as indicated in Figure 6.2.

The technique of evaluating definite integrals is as follows. A function $F(x)$ is found which differentiates to $f(x)$. Methods of obtaining $F(x)$ have already been described in Section 6.1. The new function, $F(x)$, is then evaluated at the limits $x = a$ and $x = b$ to get $F(a)$ and $F(b)$. Finally, the second number is subtracted from the first to get the answer

$$F(b) - F(a)$$

In symbols,

$$\int_a^b f(x) \, dx = F(b) - F(a)$$

The process of evaluating a function at two distinct values of x and subtracting one from the other occurs sufficiently frequently in mathematics to warrant a special notation. We write

$$\left[F(x) \right]_a^b$$

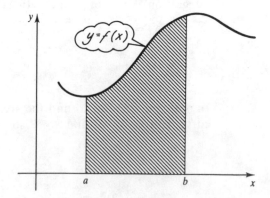

Figure 6.2

as an abbreviation for $F(b) - F(a)$ so that definite integrals are evaluated as

$$\int_a^b f(x)\,dx = \left[F(x) \right]_a^b = F(b) - F(a)$$

where $F(x)$ is the indefinite integral of $f(x)$. Using this notation the evaluation of

$$\int_1^2 x^2\,dx$$

would be written as

$$\int_1^2 x^2\,dx = \left[\frac{1}{3} x^3 \right]_1^2 = \frac{1}{3}(2)^3 - \frac{1}{3}(1)^3 = \frac{7}{3}$$

Note that it is not necessary to include the constant of integration because it cancels out when we subtract $F(a)$ from $F(b)$.

EXAMPLE

Evaluate the definite integrals

(a) $\displaystyle\int_2^6 3\,dx$

(b) $\displaystyle\int_0^2 (x + 1)\,dx$

Solution

(a) $\displaystyle\int_2^6 3\,dx = \left[3x \right]_2^6 = 3(6) - 3(2) = 12$

This value can be confirmed graphically. Figure 6.3 shows the region under the graph of $y = 3$ between $x = 2$ and $x = 6$. This is a rectangle so its area can be found from the formula

$$\text{area} = \text{base} \times \text{height}$$

which gives

$$\text{area} = 4 \times 3 = 12 \quad \checkmark$$

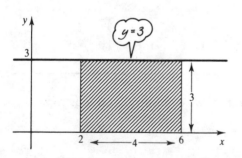

Figure 6.3

(b) $\displaystyle\int_0^2 (x + 1)\,dx = \left[\frac{x^2}{2} + x \right]_0^2 = \left(\frac{2^2}{2} + 2 \right) - \left(\frac{0^2}{2} + 0 \right) = 4$

Again this value can be confirmed graphically. Figure 6.4(a) shows the region under the graph of $y = x + 1$ between $x = 0$ and $x = 2$. This can also be regarded as one-half of the rectangle illustrated in Figure 6.4(b). This rectangle has a base of 2 units and a height of 4 units so has area

$$2 \times 4 = 8$$

The area of the region shown in Figure 6.4(a) is therefore

$$\tfrac{1}{2} \times 8 = 4 \quad \checkmark$$

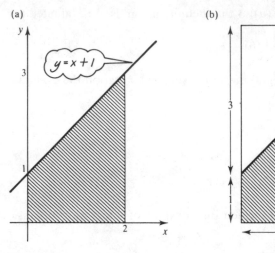

Figure 6.4

In this example we deliberately chose two very simple functions so that we could demonstrate the fact that definite integrals really do give the areas under graphs. The beauty of the integration technique, however, is that it can be used to calculate areas under quite complicated functions for which alternative methods would fail to produce the exact value.

PROBLEM

1 Evaluate the following definite integrals:

(a) $\displaystyle\int_0^1 x^3 \, dx$ **(b)** $\displaystyle\int_2^5 (2x - 1) \, dx$ **(c)** $\displaystyle\int_1^4 (x^2 - x + 1) \, dx$ **(d)** $\displaystyle\int_0^1 e^x \, dx$

To illustrate the applicability of definite integration we concentrate on four topics:

(1)   Consumer's surplus
(2)   Producer's surplus
(3)   Investment flow
(4)   Discounting.

We consider each of these in turn.

6.2.1   Consumer's surplus

The demand function, $P = f(Q)$, sketched in Figure 6.5, gives the different prices that consumers are prepared to pay for various quantities of a good. At $Q = Q_0$ the price $P = P_0$. The total amount of money spent on Q_0 goods is then $Q_0 P_0$ which is given by the area of the rectangle OABC. Now, P_0 is the price that consumers are prepared to pay for the last unit that they buy, which is the Q_0th good. For quantities up to Q_0 they would actually be

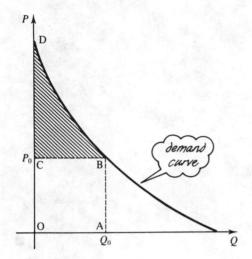

Figure 6.5

willing to pay the higher price given by the demand curve. The shaded area BCD therefore represents the benefit to the consumer of paying the fixed price of P_0 and is called the **consumer's surplus**, CS. The value of CS can be found by observing that

$$\text{area BCD} = \text{area OABD} - \text{area OABC}$$

The area OABD is the area under the demand curve, $P = f(Q)$, between $Q = 0$ and $Q = Q_0$ so is equal to

$$\int_0^{Q_0} f(Q)\, dQ$$

The region OABC is a rectangle with base Q_0 and height P_0 so

$$\text{area OABC} = Q_0 P_0$$

Hence

$$\boxed{\text{CS} = \int_0^{Q_0} f(Q)\, dQ - Q_0 P_0}$$

EXAMPLE

Find the consumer's surplus at $Q = 5$ for the demand function

$$P = 30 - 4Q$$

Solution

In this case

$$f(Q) = 30 - 4Q$$

and $Q_0 = 5$. The price is easily found by substituting $Q = 5$ into

$$P = 30 - 4Q$$

to get

$$P_0 = 30 - 4(5) = 10$$

The formula for consumer's surplus

$$CS = \int_0^{Q_0} f(Q) \, dQ - Q_0 P_0$$

gives

$$CS = \int_0^5 (30 - 4Q) \, dQ - 5(10)$$

$$= \left[30Q - 2Q^2 \right]_0^5 - 50$$

$$= [30(5) - 2(5)^2] - [30(0) - 2(0)^2] - 50$$

$$= 50$$

■

PROBLEM

2   Find the consumer's surplus at $Q = 8$ for the demand function

$$P = 100 - Q^2$$

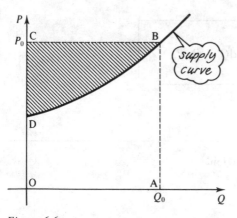

Figure 6.6

6.2.2   Producer's surplus

The supply function, $P = g(Q)$, sketched in Figure 6.6 gives the different prices at which producers are prepared to supply various quantities of a good. At $Q = Q_0$ the price $P = P_0$. Assuming that all goods are sold, the total amount of money received is then $Q_0 P_0$ which is given by the area of the rectangle OABC.

Now, P_0 is the price at which the producer is prepared to supply the last unit, which is the Q_0th good. For quantities up to Q_0 they would actually be willing to accept the lower price given by the supply curve. The shaded area BCD therefore represents the benefit to the producer of selling at the fixed price of P_0 and is called the **producer's surplus**, PS. The value of PS is found by observing that

area BCD = area OABC − area OABD

The region OABC is a rectangle with base Q_0 and height P_0 so

area OABC = $Q_0 P_0$

The area OABD is the area under the supply curve, $P = g(Q)$, between $Q = 0$ and $Q = Q_0$

so is equal to

$$\int_0^{Q_0} g(Q)\, dQ$$

Hence

$$PS = Q_0 P_0 - \int_0^{Q_0} g(Q)\, dQ$$

EXAMPLE

Given the demand function

$$P = 35 - Q_D^2$$

and supply function

$$P = 3 + Q_S^2$$

find the producer's surplus assuming pure competition.

Solution

On the assumption of pure competition the price is determined by the market. Before we can calculate the producer's surplus we therefore need to find the market equilibrium price and quantity. Denoting the common value of Q_D and Q_S by Q the demand and supply functions are

$$P = 35 - Q^2$$

and

$$P = 3 + Q^2$$

so that

$$
\begin{aligned}
35 - Q^2 &= 3 + Q^2 && \text{(both sides are equal to } P\text{)} \\
35 - 2Q^2 &= 3 && \text{(subtract } Q^2 \text{ from both sides)} \\
-2Q^2 &= -32 && \text{(subtract 35 from both sides)} \\
Q^2 &= 16 && \text{(divide both sides by } -2\text{)}
\end{aligned}
$$

which has solution $Q = \pm 4$. We can obviously ignore the negative solution because it does not make economic sense. The equilibrium quantity is therefore equal to 4. The corresponding price can be found by substituting this into either the demand or supply equation. From the demand equation we have

$$P_0 = 35 - (4)^2 = 19$$

The formula for the producer's surplus,

$$PS = Q_0 P_0 - \int_0^{Q_0} g(Q)\, dQ$$

gives

$$PS = 4(19) - \int_0^4 (3 + Q^2) \, dQ$$

$$= 76 - \left[3Q + \frac{Q^3}{3} \right]_0^4$$

$$= 76 - \{ [3(4) + \tfrac{1}{3}(4)^3] - [3(0) + \tfrac{1}{3}(0)^3] \}$$

$$= 42\tfrac{2}{3}$$

∎

PROBLEM

3   Given the demand equation

$$P = 50 - 2Q_D$$

and supply equation

$$P = 10 + 2Q_s$$

calculate

(a)   the consumer's surplus
(b)   the producer's surplus

assuming pure competition.

6.2.3   Investment flow

Net investment, I, is defined to be the rate of change of capital stock, K, so that

$$I = \frac{dK}{dt}$$

Here $I(t)$ denotes the flow of money, measured in dollars per year, and $K(t)$ is the amount of capital accumulated at time t as a result of this investment flow and is measured in dollars.

   Given a formula for capital stock in terms of time we simply differentiate to find net investment. Conversely, if we know the net investment function, then we integrate to find the capital stock. In particular, to calculate the capital formation during the time period from $t = t_1$ to $t = t_2$ we evaluate the definite integral

$$\int_{t_1}^{t_2} I(t) \, dt$$

EXAMPLE

If the investment flow is

$$I(t) = 9000\sqrt{t}$$

calculate

(a)   the capital formation from the end of the first year to the end of the fourth year

(b)   the number of years required before the capital stock exceeds $100,000.

Solution

(a)   In this part we need to calculate the capital formation from $t = 1$ to $t = 4$ so we evaluate the definite integral

$$\int_1^4 9000\sqrt{t}\ dt = 9000 \int_1^4 t^{1/2}\ dt$$

$$= 9000 \left[\frac{2}{3} t^{3/2} \right]_1^4$$

$$= 9000 \left[\frac{2}{3}(4)^{3/2} - \frac{2}{3}(1)^{3/2} \right]$$

$$= 9000 \left(\frac{16}{3} - \frac{2}{3} \right)$$

$$= \$42,000$$

(b)   In this part we need to calculate the number of years required to accumulate a total of $100,000. After T years the capital stock is

$$\int_0^T 9000\sqrt{t}\ dt = 9000 \int_0^T t^{1/2}\ dt$$

We want to find the value of T so that

$$9000 \int_0^T t^{1/2}\ dt = 100\,000$$

The integral is easily evaluated as

$$9000 \left[\frac{2}{3} t^{3/2} \right]_0^T = 9000 \left(\frac{2}{3} T^{3/2} - \frac{2}{3}(0)^{3/2} \right) = 6000 T^{3/2}$$

so T satisfies

$$6000 T^{3/2} = 100\,000$$

This non-linear equation can be solved by dividing both sides by 6000 to get

$$T^{3/2} = 16.67$$

and then raising both sides to the power of $\frac{2}{3}$ which gives

$$T = 6.5$$

The capital stock reaches the $100,000 level about halfway through the seventh year.

PROBLEM

4 If the net investment function is given by

$$I(t) = 800t^{1/3}$$

calculate

(1) the capital formation from the end of the first year to the end of the eighth year
(2) the number of years required before the capital stock exceeds $48,600.

6.2.4   Discounting

In Chapter 3 the formula

$$P = Se^{-rt/100}$$

was used to calculate the present value, P, when a single future value, S, is discounted at $r\%$ interest continuously for t years. We also discussed the idea of an annuity. This is a fund which provides a series of discrete regular payments and we showed how to calculate the original lump sum needed to secure these payments for a prescribed number of years. This amount is called the present value of the annuity. If the fund is to provide a continuous revenue stream for n years at an annual rate of S dollars per year then the present value can be found by evaluating the definite integral

$$P = \int_0^n Se^{-rt/100} \, dt$$

EXAMPLE

Calculate the present value of a continuous revenue stream for 5 years at a constant rate of $1,000 per year if the discount rate is 9%.

Solution

The present value is found from the formula

$$P = \int_0^n Se^{-rt/100} \, dt$$

with $S = 1000$, $r = 9$ and $n = 5$ so

$$P = \int_0^5 1000e^{-0.09t} \, dt$$

$$= 1000 \int_0^5 e^{-0.09t} \, dt$$

$$= 1000 \left[-\frac{1}{0.09} e^{-0.09t} \right]_0^5$$

$$= -\frac{1000}{0.09}\left[e^{-0.09t}\right]_0^5$$

$$= -\frac{1000}{0.09}(e^{-0.45} - 1)$$

$e^0 = 1$

$$= \$4,026.35$$

■

PROBLEM

5 Calculate the present value of a continuous revenue stream for 10 years at a constant rate of $5,000 per year if the discount rate is 6%.

PRACTICE PROBLEMS

6 Find the area under the graph of

$$f(x) = 4x^3 - 3x^2 + 4x + 2$$

between $x = 1$ and $x = 2$.

7 Find the consumer's surplus at $P = 5$ for the following demand functions

(a) $P = 25 - 2Q$ **(b)** $P = \dfrac{10}{\sqrt{Q}}$

8 Given the demand function

$$P = -Q_D^2 - 4Q_D + 68$$

and supply function

$$P = Q_S^2 + 2Q_S + 12$$

find

(a) the consumer's surplus
(b) the producer's surplus

assuming pure competition.

9 Find expressions for capital formation between $t = 0$ and $t = T$ for the following net investment functions

(a) $I(t) = At^\alpha$ **(b)** $I(t) = Ae^{\alpha t}$

where A and α are positive constants.

10 Calculate the present value of a continuous revenue stream of $1000 per year if the discount rate is 5% and the money is paid

(a) for 3 years   **(b)** for 10 years   **(c)** for 100 years   **(d)** in perpetuity

7 *Matrices*

The impression that you may have gained from reading this book is that mathematics consists of one main topic, calculus, and that every other topic is just a variation on this theme. This is far from the truth and in this chapter and the next we look at two refreshingly different branches of mathematics. It would be useful for you to have studied Chapter 1 although even this is not essential. There are four sections. It is essential that Sections 7.1 and 7.2 are read first but the remaining sections can be read in any order.

Section 7.1 introduces the concept of a matrix which is a convenient mathematical way of representing information displayed in a table. By defining the matrix operations of addition, subtraction and multiplication it is possible to develop an algebra of matrices. Simple economic examples are used to motivate these definitions and it is shown that the rules of matrix manipulation are almost identical to those of ordinary arithmetic. In Section 7.2 you are shown how to calculate the inverse of a matrix. This is analogous to the reciprocal of a number and enables matrix equations to be solved. In particular, inverses provide an alternative way of solving systems of simultaneous linear equations and so can be used to solve problems in statics. Section 7.3 describes Cramer's rule for solving systems of linear equations. This method is a particularly useful way of solving economic models where only a selection of endogeneous variables need to be determined.

In Section 7.4 we discuss a new economic topic known as input—output analysis and show how the matrix operations described in the first two sections can be used to determine the flow of money between firms.

7.1 Basic matrix operations

Objectives At the end of this section you should be able to:

- understand the notation and terminology of matrix algebra,

- find the transpose of a matrix,

- add and subtract matrices,

- multiply a matrix by a scalar,

- multiply matrices together,

- represent a system of linear equations in matrix notation.

Suppose that a firm produces three types of good, G1, G2 and G3 which it sells to two customers, C1 and C2. The monthly sales for these goods are given in Table 7.1. During the month the firm sells 3 items of G2 to customer C1, 6 items of G3 to customer C2, and so on. It may well be obvious from the context exactly what these numbers represent. Under these circumstances it makes sense to ignore the table headings and to write this information more concisely as

$$A = \begin{bmatrix} 7 & 3 & 4 \\ 1 & 5 & 6 \end{bmatrix}$$

which is an example of a matrix. Quite generally, any rectangular array of numbers surrounded by a pair of brackets is called a **matrix** (plural **matrices**) and the individual numbers constituting the array are called **entries** or **elements**. In this book we use square brackets although it is equally correct to use parentheses (that is, round brackets) instead. It helps to think of a matrix as being made up of rows and columns. The matrix A has two rows and three columns and is said to have order 2×3. In general, a matrix of **order** $m \times n$ has m rows and n columns. For example, the matrices

$$B = \begin{bmatrix} 2 & 1 \\ -1 & 6 \end{bmatrix} \qquad C = \begin{bmatrix} 1 & 3 & 4 & 0 \\ 1 & 2 & 1 & 1 \\ 1 & 4 & 5 & 7 \end{bmatrix}$$

have orders 2×2 and 3×4 respectively.

We denote matrices by capital letters in bold type (that is, $A, B, C, \ldots$) and their elements by the corresponding lower-case letter in ordinary type. In fact, we use a rather clever double subscript notation so that a_{ij} stands for the element of A which occurs in row i and column j. Referring to the matrices above we see that

$a_{12} = 3$ (row 1 and column 2 of A)

$b_{22} = 6$ (row 2 and column 2 of B)

Table 7.1

		Monthly sales for goods		
		G1	*G2*	*G3*
Sold to	*C1*	7	3	4
customer	*C2*	1	5	6

$c_{34} = 7$ (row 3 and column 4 of **C**)

and so on.

A general matrix **D** of order 3×2 would be written

$$\begin{bmatrix} d_{11} & d_{12} \\ d_{21} & d_{22} \\ d_{31} & d_{32} \end{bmatrix}$$

Similarly, a 3×3 matrix labelled **E** would be written

$$\begin{bmatrix} e_{11} & e_{12} & e_{13} \\ e_{21} & e_{22} & e_{23} \\ e_{31} & e_{32} & e_{33} \end{bmatrix}$$

PROBLEM

1 Let

$$\mathbf{A} = \begin{bmatrix} 1 & 2 \\ 3 & 4 \end{bmatrix} \quad \mathbf{B} = \begin{bmatrix} 1 & -1 & 0 & 6 & 2 \end{bmatrix}$$

$$\mathbf{C} = \begin{bmatrix} 1 & 0 & 2 & 3 & 1 \\ 5 & 7 & 9 & 0 & 2 \\ 3 & 4 & 6 & 7 & 8 \end{bmatrix} \quad \mathbf{D} = \begin{bmatrix} 6 \end{bmatrix}$$

(1) State the orders of the matrices **A**, **B**, **C** and **D**.

(2) Write down the values of

$$a_{11}, \quad a_{22}, \quad b_{14}, \quad c_{25}, \quad c_{33}, \quad c_{43}, \quad d_{11}$$

All we have done so far is to explain what matrices are and to provide some notation for handling them. A matrix certainly gives us a convenient shorthand to describe information presented in a table. However, we would like to go further than this and to use matrices to solve problems in economics. To do this we describe several mathematical operations which can be performed on matrices, namely

(1) Transposition
(2) Addition and subtraction
(3) Scalar multiplication
(4) Matrix multiplication.

One obvious omission from the list is matrix division. Strictly speaking it is impossible to divide one matrix by another although we can get fairly close to the idea of division by defining something called an inverse which we consider in the next section.

7.1.1   Transposition

In Table 7.1 the rows correspond to the two customers and the columns correspond to the three goods. The matrix representation of the table is then

$$\mathbf{A} = \begin{bmatrix} 7 & 3 & 4 \\ 1 & 5 & 6 \end{bmatrix}$$

The same information about monthly sales could easily have been presented the other way round as shown in Table 7.2. The matrix representation would then be

$$\mathbf{B} = \begin{bmatrix} 7 & 1 \\ 3 & 5 \\ 4 & 6 \end{bmatrix}$$

Table 7.2

		Sold to customer	
		C1	*C2*
Monthly	*G1*	7	1
sales for	*G2*	3	5
goods	*G3*	4	6

We describe this situation by saying that **A** and **B** are transposes of each other and write

$$\mathbf{A}^{\mathrm{T}} = \mathbf{B} \qquad \text{\textit{(read 'A transpose equals B)}}$$

or equivalently

$$\mathbf{B}^{\mathrm{T}} = \mathbf{A} \qquad \text{\textit{(read 'B transpose equals A)}}$$

The **transpose** of a matrix is found by replacing rows by columns so that the first row becomes the first column, the second row becomes the second column, and so on. The number of rows of **A** is then the same as the number of columns of $\mathbf{A}^{\mathrm{T}}$ and vice versa. Consequently, if **A** has order $m \times n$ then $\mathbf{A}^{\mathrm{T}}$ has order $n \times m$.

PROBLEM

2 Write down the transpose of the following matrices:

$$A = \begin{bmatrix} 1 & 4 & 0 & 1 & 2 \\ 3 & 7 & 6 & 1 & 4 \\ 2 & 1 & 3 & 5 & -1 \\ 2 & -5 & 1 & 8 & 0 \end{bmatrix}$$

$$B = \begin{bmatrix} 1 & 5 & 7 & 9 \end{bmatrix}$$

$$C = \begin{bmatrix} 1 & 2 & 3 \\ 2 & 4 & 5 \\ 3 & 5 & 6 \end{bmatrix}$$

There are two particular shapes of matrices which are given special names. A matrix which has only one row such as

$$c = \begin{bmatrix} 5 & 2 & 1 & -4 \end{bmatrix}$$

is called a **row vector** and a matrix which has only one column such as

$$d = \begin{bmatrix} -3 \\ 10 \\ 6 \\ -7 \\ 1 \\ 9 \\ 2 \end{bmatrix}$$

is called a **column vector**. It is standard practice to identify vectors using lower-case rather than upper-case letters. In books they are set in bold type. If you are writing them down by hand then you should underline the letters and put

c̲ (or possibly c̰)   and   d̲ (or possibly d̰)

This is a useful convention since it helps to distinguish scalar quantities such as x, y, a, b which denote single numbers from vector quantities such as x, y, a, b which denote matrices with one row or column. Incidentally, it is actually quite expensive to typeset column vectors in books and journals since it is wasteful on space, particularly if the number of elements is large. It is then more convenient to use the transpose notation and write the vector horizontally. For example, the 7×1 matrix d given above would be printed as

$$d = \begin{bmatrix} -3 & 10 & 6 & -7 & 1 & 9 & 2 \end{bmatrix}^T$$

where the superscript T tells us that it is the column vector that is intended.

7.1.2 Addition and subtraction

Let us suppose that, for the two-customer three-product example, the matrix

$$A = \begin{bmatrix} 7 & 3 & 4 \\ 1 & 5 & 6 \end{bmatrix}$$

gives the sales for the month of January. Similarly, the monthly sales for February might be given by

$$B = \begin{bmatrix} 6 & 2 & 1 \\ 0 & 4 & 4 \end{bmatrix}$$

This means, for example, that customer C1 buys 7 items of G1 in January and 6 items of G1 in February. Customer C1 therefore buys a total of

$$7 + 6 = 13$$

items of G1 during the two months. A similar process can be applied to the remaining goods and customers so that the matrix giving the sales for the two months is

$$C = \begin{bmatrix} 7 + 6 & 3 + 2 & 4 + 1 \\ 1 + 0 & 5 + 4 & 6 + 4 \end{bmatrix}$$

$$= \begin{bmatrix} 13 & 5 & 5 \\ 1 & 9 & 10 \end{bmatrix}$$

We describe this by saying that C is the **sum** of the two matrices A and B and we write

$$C = A + B$$

In general, to add (or subtract) two matrices of the same size, we simply add (or subtract) their corresponding elements. It is obvious from this definition that, for any two $m \times n$ matrices, A and B,

$$A + B = B + A$$

because it is immaterial which way round two numbers are added. Note that in order to combine matrices in this way it is necessary for them to have the same order. For example, it is impossible to add the matrices

$$D = \begin{bmatrix} 1 & -7 \\ 1 & 3 \end{bmatrix} \quad \text{and} \quad E = \begin{bmatrix} 1 & 2 \\ 1 & 1 \\ 3 & 5 \end{bmatrix}$$

because D has order 2×2 and E has order 3×2.

EXAMPLE

Let

$$A = \begin{bmatrix} 9 & -3 \\ 4 & 1 \\ 2 & 0 \end{bmatrix} \quad \text{and} \quad B = \begin{bmatrix} 5 & 2 \\ -1 & 6 \\ 3 & 4 \end{bmatrix}$$

Find

(a) $A + B$
(b) $A - B$
(c) $A - A$

Solution

(a)
$$A + B = \begin{bmatrix} 9 & -3 \\ 4 & 1 \\ 2 & 0 \end{bmatrix} + \begin{bmatrix} 5 & 2 \\ -1 & 6 \\ 3 & 4 \end{bmatrix} = \begin{bmatrix} 14 & -1 \\ 3 & 7 \\ 5 & 4 \end{bmatrix}$$

(b)
$$A - B = \begin{bmatrix} 9 & -3 \\ 4 & 1 \\ 2 & 0 \end{bmatrix} - \begin{bmatrix} 5 & 2 \\ -1 & 6 \\ 3 & 4 \end{bmatrix} = \begin{bmatrix} 4 & -5 \\ 5 & -5 \\ -1 & -4 \end{bmatrix}$$

(c)
$$A - A = \begin{bmatrix} 9 & -3 \\ 4 & 1 \\ 2 & 0 \end{bmatrix} - \begin{bmatrix} 9 & -3 \\ 4 & 1 \\ 2 & 0 \end{bmatrix} = \begin{bmatrix} 0 & 0 \\ 0 & 0 \\ 0 & 0 \end{bmatrix}$$

■

The result of part (c) of this example is a 3×2 matrix in which every entry is zero. Such a matrix is called a **zero matrix** and is written **0**. In fact, there are lots of zero matrices, each corresponding to a particular order. For example

$$\begin{bmatrix} 0 \end{bmatrix} \quad \begin{bmatrix} 0 & 0 \\ 0 & 0 \end{bmatrix} \quad \begin{bmatrix} 0 \\ 0 \\ 0 \\ 0 \end{bmatrix} \quad \begin{bmatrix} 0 & 0 & 0 & 0 & 0 & 0 \\ 0 & 0 & 0 & 0 & 0 & 0 \\ 0 & 0 & 0 & 0 & 0 & 0 \\ 0 & 0 & 0 & 0 & 0 & 0 \end{bmatrix}$$

are the 1×1, 2×2, 4×1 and 4×6 zero matrices respectively. However, despite this, we shall use the single symbol **0** for all of these since it is usually clear in any actual example what the order is and hence which particular zero matrix is being used. It follows from the definition of addition and subtraction that, for any matrix **A**,

$$A - A = 0$$

$$A + 0 = A$$

The role played by the matrix **0** in matrix algebra is therefore similar to that of the number 0 in ordinary arithmetic.

PROBLEM

3 Let

$$A = \begin{bmatrix} 7 & 5 \\ 2 & 1 \end{bmatrix} \quad B = \begin{bmatrix} 5 \\ 4 \end{bmatrix} \quad C = \begin{bmatrix} 2 \\ 2 \end{bmatrix} \quad D = \begin{bmatrix} -6 & 2 \\ 1 & -9 \end{bmatrix} \quad 0 = \begin{bmatrix} 0 \\ 0 \end{bmatrix}$$

Find (where possible)

(a) A + D   **(b) A + C**   **(c) B − C**   **(d) C − 0**   **(e) D − D**

7.1.3 Scalar multiplication

Returning to the two-customer three-product example, let us suppose that the sales are the same each month and are given by

$$A = \begin{bmatrix} 7 & 3 & 4 \\ 1 & 5 & 6 \end{bmatrix}$$

This means, for example, that customer C1 buys 7 items of G1 every month so in a whole year C1 buys

$$12 \times 7 = 84$$

items of G1. A similar process applies to the remaining goods and customers and the matrix giving the annual sales is

$$B = \begin{bmatrix} 12 \times 7 & 12 \times 3 & 12 \times 4 \\ 12 \times 1 & 12 \times 5 & 12 \times 6 \end{bmatrix}$$

$$= \begin{bmatrix} 84 & 36 & 48 \\ 12 & 60 & 72 \end{bmatrix}$$

Matrix **B** is found by scaling each element in **A** by 12 and we write

$$B = 12A$$

In general, to multiply a matrix **A** by a scalar k we simply multiply each element of **A** by k. The number k can be positive, negative or zero, so if

$$A = \begin{bmatrix} 1 & 2 & 3 \\ 4 & 5 & 6 \\ 7 & 8 & 9 \end{bmatrix}$$

then

$$2A = \begin{bmatrix} 2 & 4 & 6 \\ 8 & 10 & 12 \\ 14 & 16 & 18 \end{bmatrix}$$

$$-\mathbf{A} = (-1)\mathbf{A} = \begin{bmatrix} -1 & -2 & -3 \\ -4 & -5 & -6 \\ -7 & -8 & -9 \end{bmatrix}$$

$$0\mathbf{A} = \begin{bmatrix} 0 & 0 & 0 \\ 0 & 0 & 0 \\ 0 & 0 & 0 \end{bmatrix} = \mathbf{0}$$

In ordinary arithmetic we know that

$$a(b + c) = ab + ac$$

for any three numbers a, b and c. It follows from our definitions of matrix addition and scalar multiplication that

$$k(\mathbf{A} + \mathbf{B}) = k\mathbf{A} + k\mathbf{B}$$

for any $m \times n$ matrices $\mathbf{A}$ and $\mathbf{B}$, and scalar k.

Another property of matrices is

$$k(l\mathbf{A}) = (kl)\mathbf{A}$$

for scalars k and l. Again this follows from the comparable property

$$a(bc) = (ab)c$$

for ordinary numbers.

You are invited to check these two matrix properties for yourself in the following problem.

PROBLEM

4 Let

$$\mathbf{A} = \begin{bmatrix} 1 & -2 \\ 3 & 5 \\ 0 & 4 \end{bmatrix} \quad \text{and} \quad \mathbf{B} = \begin{bmatrix} 0 & -1 \\ 2 & 7 \\ 1 & 6 \end{bmatrix}$$

(1) Find

(a) 2A   **(b)** 2B   **(c)** A + B   **(d)** 2(A + B)

Hence verify that

$$2(\mathbf{A} + \mathbf{B}) = 2\mathbf{A} + 2\mathbf{B}$$

(2) Find

(a) 3A   **(b)** −6A

Hence verify that

$$-2(3\mathbf{A}) = -6\mathbf{A}$$

7.1.4   Matrix multiplication

I hope that you have found the matrix operations considered so far in this section easy to understand. We now turn our attention to matrix multiplication. If you have never multiplied matrices before, you may find that it requires a bit more effort to grasp and you should allow yourself extra time to work through the problems. There is no need to worry. Once you have performed a dozen or so matrix multiplications you will find that the technique becomes second nature, although the process may appear rather strange and complicated at first sight. We begin by showing you how to multiply a row vector by a column vector. To motivate this let us suppose that goods G1, G2 and G3 sell at \$50, \$30 and \$20 respectively, and let us introduce the row vector

$$\mathbf{p} = [50 \quad 30 \quad 20]$$

If the firm sells a total of 100, 200 and 175 goods of type G1, G2 and G3 respectively, then we can write this information as the column vector

$$\mathbf{q} = \begin{bmatrix} 100 \\ 200 \\ 175 \end{bmatrix}$$

The total revenue received from the sale of G1 is found by multiplying the price, \$50, by the quantity, 100, to get

$$\$50 \times 100 = \$5{,}000$$

Similarly, the revenue from G2 and G3 is

$$\$30 \times 200 = \$6{,}000$$

and

$$\$20 \times 175 = \$3{,}500$$

respectively. The total revenue of the firm is therefore

$$\text{TR} = \$5{,}000 + \$6{,}000 + \$3{,}500 = \$14{,}500$$

The value of TR is a single number and can be regarded as a 1×1 matrix, that is

$$[14\,500]$$

This 1×1 matrix is obtained by multiplying together the price vector, **p**, and the quantity vector, **q**, to get

$$[50 \quad 30 \quad 20] \begin{bmatrix} 100 \\ 200 \\ 175 \end{bmatrix} = [14\,500]$$

The value 14 500 is found by multiplying the corresponding elements of **p** and **q** and then adding together, that is

$$[50 \quad 30 \quad 20] \begin{bmatrix} 100 \\ 200 \\ 175 \end{bmatrix} = [5000 + 6000 + 3500]$$

$$= [14\,500]$$

In general, if **a** is the row vector

$$[a_{11} \quad a_{12} \quad a_{13} \quad \ldots \quad a_{1s}]$$

and **b** is the column vector

$$\begin{bmatrix} b_{11} \\ b_{21} \\ b_{31} \\ \vdots \\ b_{s1} \end{bmatrix}$$

then we define the matrix product

$$\mathbf{ab} = [a_{11} \quad a_{12} \quad a_{13} \quad \ldots \quad a_{1s}] \begin{bmatrix} b_{11} \\ b_{21} \\ b_{31} \\ \vdots \\ b_{s1} \end{bmatrix}$$

to be the 1×1 matrix

$$[a_{11}b_{11} + a_{12}b_{21} + a_{13}b_{31} + \ldots + a_{1s}b_{s1}]$$

It is important to notice that the single element in the 1×1 matrix **ab** is found by multiplying each element of **a** by the corresponding element of **b**. Consequently, it is essential that both vectors have the same number of elements. In other words, if **a** has order $1 \times s$ and **b** has order $t \times 1$ then it is only possible to form the product **ab** when $s = t$.

EXAMPLE

If

$$\mathbf{a} = [1 \quad 2 \quad 3 \quad 4], \quad \mathbf{b} = \begin{bmatrix} 2 \\ 5 \\ -1 \\ 0 \end{bmatrix} \quad \text{and} \quad \mathbf{c} = \begin{bmatrix} 6 \\ 9 \\ 2 \end{bmatrix}$$

find **ab** and **ac**.

Solution

Using the definition of the multiplication of a row vector by a column vector we have

$$\mathbf{ab} = \begin{bmatrix} 1 & 2 & 3 & 4 \end{bmatrix} \begin{bmatrix} 2 \\ 5 \\ -1 \\ 0 \end{bmatrix} = [1(2) + 2(5) + 3(-1) + 4(0)] = [9]$$

We have set out the calculations in this way so that you can see how the value, 9, is obtained. There is no need for you to indicate this in your own answers and you may simply write

$$\begin{bmatrix} 1 & 2 & 3 & 4 \end{bmatrix} \begin{bmatrix} 2 \\ 5 \\ -1 \\ 0 \end{bmatrix} = [9]$$

without bothering to insert any intermediate steps.

It is impossible to multiply **a** and **c** because **a** has four elements and **c** has only three elements. You can see the problem if you actually try to perform the calculations since there is no entry in **c** with which to multiply the 4 in **a**.

$$\begin{bmatrix} 1 & 2 & 3 & 4 \end{bmatrix} \begin{bmatrix} 6 \\ 9 \\ 2 \end{bmatrix} = [1(6) + 2(9) + 3(2) + 4(?)]$$

∎

PROBLEM

5 Let

$$\mathbf{a} = \begin{bmatrix} 1 & -1 & 0 & 3 & 2 \end{bmatrix} \quad \mathbf{b} = \begin{bmatrix} 1 & 2 & 9 \end{bmatrix} \quad \mathbf{c} = \begin{bmatrix} 0 \\ -1 \\ 1 \\ 1 \\ 2 \end{bmatrix}$$

and

$$\mathbf{d} = \begin{bmatrix} -2 \\ 1 \\ 0 \end{bmatrix}$$

Find (where possible)

(a) ac   **(b) bd**   **(c) ad**

We now turn our attention to general matrix multiplication which is defined as follows. If **A** is an $m \times s$ matrix and **B** is an $s \times n$ matrix then

$$\mathbf{C} = \mathbf{AB}$$

is an $m \times n$ matrix and c_{ij} is found by multiplying the ith row of **A** into the jth column of **b**.

There are three things to notice about this definition. Firstly, the number of columns of **A** is the same as the number of rows of **B**. Unless this condition is satisfied it is impossible to form the product **AB**. Secondly, the matrix **C** has order $m \times n$ where m is the number of rows of **A** and n is the number of columns of **B**. Finally, the elements of **C** are found by multiplying row vectors by column vectors. The best way of understanding this definition is to consider an example.

EXAMPLE

Find **AB** in the case when

$$\mathbf{A} = \begin{bmatrix} 2 & 1 & 0 \\ 1 & 0 & 4 \end{bmatrix} \quad \text{and} \quad \mathbf{B} = \begin{bmatrix} 3 & 1 & 2 & 1 \\ 1 & 0 & 1 & 2 \\ 5 & 4 & 1 & 1 \end{bmatrix}$$

Solution

It is a good idea to check before you begin any detailed calculations that it is possible to multiply these matrices and also to identify the order of the resulting matrix. In this case

A is a 2×3 matrix and **B** is a 3×4 matrix

Matrix **A** has three columns and **B** has the same number of rows so it *is* possible to find **AB**. Moreover, **AB** must have order 2×4 because **A** has two rows and **B** has four columns. Hence

$$\begin{bmatrix} 2 & 1 & 0 \\ 1 & 0 & 4 \end{bmatrix} \begin{bmatrix} 3 & 1 & 2 & 1 \\ 1 & 0 & 1 & 2 \\ 5 & 4 & 1 & 1 \end{bmatrix} = \begin{bmatrix} c_{11} & c_{12} & c_{13} & c_{14} \\ c_{21} & c_{22} & c_{23} & c_{24} \end{bmatrix}$$

All that remains for us to do is to calculate the eight numbers c_{ij}.

The number c_{11} in the top left-hand corner lies in the first row and first column, so to find its value we multiply the first row of **A** into the first column of **B** to get

$$\begin{bmatrix} \boxed{2 \quad 1 \quad 0} \\ 1 \quad 0 \quad 4 \end{bmatrix} \begin{bmatrix} \boxed{\begin{matrix} 3 \\ 1 \\ 5 \end{matrix}} & 1 & 2 & 1 \\ & 0 & 1 & 2 \\ & 4 & 1 & 1 \end{bmatrix} = \begin{bmatrix} \boxed{7} & c_{12} & c_{13} & c_{14} \\ c_{21} & c_{22} & c_{23} & c_{24} \end{bmatrix}$$

because $2(3) + 1(1) + 0(5) = 7$.

The number c_{12} lies in the first row and second column so to find its value we multiply the first row of **A** into the second column of **B** to get

$$\begin{bmatrix} \boxed{2 \quad 1 \quad 0} \\ 1 \quad 0 \quad 4 \end{bmatrix} \begin{bmatrix} 3 & \boxed{1} & 2 & 1 \\ 1 & \boxed{0} & 1 & 2 \\ 5 & \boxed{4} & 1 & 1 \end{bmatrix} = \begin{bmatrix} 7 & \boxed{2} & c_{13} & c_{14} \\ c_{21} & c_{22} & c_{23} & c_{24} \end{bmatrix}$$

because $2(1) + 1(0) + 0(4) = 2$.

The values of c_{13} and c_{14} are then found in a similar way by multiplying the first row of **A** into the third and fourth columns of **B** respectively, to get

$$\begin{bmatrix} \boxed{2 \quad 1 \quad 0} \\ 1 \quad 0 \quad 4 \end{bmatrix} \begin{bmatrix} 3 & 1 & \boxed{2} & \boxed{1} \\ 1 & 0 & \boxed{1} & \boxed{2} \\ 5 & 4 & \boxed{1} & \boxed{1} \end{bmatrix} = \begin{bmatrix} 7 & 2 & \boxed{5} & \boxed{4} \\ c_{21} & c_{22} & c_{23} & c_{24} \end{bmatrix}$$

because $2(2) + 1(1) + 0(1) = 5$ and $2(1) + 1(2) + 0(1) = 4$.

Finally, we repeat the whole procedure along the second row of **C**. The elements c_{21}, c_{22}, c_{23} and c_{24} are calculated by multiplying the second row of **A** into the four columns of **B** in succession to get

$$\begin{bmatrix} 2 \quad 1 \quad 0 \\ \boxed{1 \quad 0 \quad 4} \end{bmatrix} \begin{bmatrix} \boxed{3} & \boxed{1} & \boxed{2} & \boxed{1} \\ \boxed{1} & \boxed{0} & \boxed{1} & \boxed{2} \\ \boxed{5} & \boxed{4} & \boxed{1} & \boxed{1} \end{bmatrix} = \begin{bmatrix} 7 & 2 & 5 & 4 \\ \boxed{23} & \boxed{17} & \boxed{6} & \boxed{5} \end{bmatrix}$$

because

$$1(3) + 0(1) + 4(5) = 23$$
$$1(1) + 0(0) + 4(4) = 17$$
$$1(2) + 0(1) + 4(1) = 6$$
$$1(1) + 0(2) + 4(1) = 5$$

∎

In this example we have indicated how to build up the matrix **C** in a step-by-step manner and have used boxes to show you how the calculations are performed. This approach has been adopted merely as a teaching device. There is no need for you to set your calculations out in this way and you are encouraged to write down your answer in a single line of working. However, please take the trouble to check before you begin that it is possible to form the matrix product and to anticipate the order of the end result. This can be done by jotting down the orders of the original matrices side by side. The product exists if the inner numbers are the same and the order of the answer is given by the outer numbers, that is

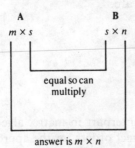

For example, if **A**, **B** and **C** have orders 3×5, 5×2 and 3×4 respectively, then **AB** exists and has order 3×2 because

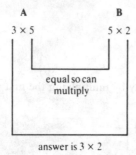

but it is impossible to form **AC** because

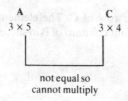

PROBLEM

6 Write down the order of the matrices

$$\mathbf{A} = \begin{bmatrix} 1 & 2 \\ 0 & 1 \\ 3 & 1 \end{bmatrix} \quad \text{and} \quad \mathbf{B} = \begin{bmatrix} 1 & 2 \\ 3 & 4 \end{bmatrix}$$

Hence verify that it is possible to form the matrix product

$$\mathbf{C} = \mathbf{AB}$$

and write down the order of **C**. Calculate all of the elements of **C**.

We have already noted that matrix operations have similar properties to those of ordinary arithmetic. Some particular rules of arithmetic are:

$a(b + c) = ab + ac$ (distributive law)

$(a + b)c = ac + bc$ (distributive law)

$a(bc) = (ab)c$ (associative law)

$ab = ba$ (commutative law)

An obvious question to ask is whether they have a counterpart in matrix algebra. It turns out that provided the matrices **A**, **B** and **C** have the correct orders for the appropriate sums and products to exist then

$$A(B + C) = AB + AC$$

$$(A + B)C = AC + BC$$

$$A(BC) = (AB)C$$

However, although it is true that

$$ab = ba$$

for numbers, this result does **not** extend to matrices. Even if **AB** and **BA** both exist it is not necessarily true that

$$AB = BA$$

To see this consider

$$A = \begin{bmatrix} 1 & -1 \\ 2 & 1 \end{bmatrix} \qquad B = \begin{bmatrix} 1 & 3 \\ 1 & 2 \end{bmatrix}$$

It is easy to check that it is possible to form both products **AB** and **BA** and that they both have order 2×2. In fact

$$AB = \begin{bmatrix} 1 & -1 \\ 2 & 1 \end{bmatrix}\begin{bmatrix} 1 & 3 \\ 1 & 2 \end{bmatrix} = \begin{bmatrix} 0 & 1 \\ 3 & 8 \end{bmatrix}$$

$$BA = \begin{bmatrix} 1 & 3 \\ 1 & 2 \end{bmatrix}\begin{bmatrix} 1 & -1 \\ 2 & 1 \end{bmatrix} = \begin{bmatrix} 7 & 2 \\ 5 & 1 \end{bmatrix}$$

so $AB \neq BA$. There are certain pairs of matrices which do commute (that is for which $AB = BA$) and we shall investigate some of these in the next section. However, these are very much the exception. We therefore have the 'non-property' that in general

$$AB \neq BA$$

PROBLEMS

7 Let

$$A = \begin{bmatrix} 2 & 1 & 1 \\ 5 & 1 & 0 \\ -1 & 1 & 4 \end{bmatrix} \qquad B = \begin{bmatrix} 1 \\ 2 \\ 1 \end{bmatrix} \qquad C = \begin{bmatrix} 1 & 2 \\ 3 & 1 \end{bmatrix}$$

$$D = \begin{bmatrix} 1 & 1 \\ -1 & 1 \\ 2 & 1 \end{bmatrix} \qquad \text{and} \qquad E = \begin{bmatrix} 1 & 2 & 3 \\ 4 & 5 & 6 \end{bmatrix}$$

Find (where possible)

(a) AB   **(b)** BA   **(c)** CD   **(d)** DC   **(e)** AE   **(f)** EA   **(g)** DE   **(h)** ED

8 Evaluate the matrix product **Ax** where

$$\mathbf{A} = \begin{bmatrix} 1 & 4 & 7 \\ 2 & 6 & 5 \\ 8 & 9 & 5 \end{bmatrix} \quad \text{and} \quad \mathbf{x} = \begin{bmatrix} x \\ y \\ z \end{bmatrix}$$

Hence show that the system of linear equations

$$x + 4y + 7z = -3$$
$$2x + 6y + 5z = 10$$
$$8x + 9y + 5z = 1$$

can be written as **Ax** = **b** where

$$\mathbf{b} = \begin{bmatrix} -3 \\ 10 \\ 1 \end{bmatrix}$$

We conclude this section by showing you how to express a familiar problem in matrix notation. Section 1.2 described the method of elimination for solving systems of simultaneous linear equations. For example, we might want to find values of x and y which satisfy

$$2x - 5y = 6$$
$$7x + 8y = -1$$

Motivated by the result of Problem 8 we write this as

$$\mathbf{Ax} = \mathbf{b}$$

where

$$\mathbf{A} = \begin{bmatrix} 2 & -5 \\ 7 & 8 \end{bmatrix} \quad \mathbf{x} = \begin{bmatrix} x \\ y \end{bmatrix} \quad \mathbf{b} = \begin{bmatrix} 6 \\ -1 \end{bmatrix}$$

It is easy to check that this is correct simply by multiplying out **Ax** to get

$$\begin{bmatrix} 2 & -5 \\ 7 & 8 \end{bmatrix}\begin{bmatrix} x \\ y \end{bmatrix} = \begin{bmatrix} 2x - 5y \\ 7x + 8y \end{bmatrix}$$

and so the matrix equation **Ax** = **b** reads

$$\begin{bmatrix} 2x - 5y \\ 7x + 8y \end{bmatrix} = \begin{bmatrix} 6 \\ -1 \end{bmatrix}$$

that is

$$2x - 5y = 6$$
$$7x + 8y = -1$$

Quite generally, any system of n linear equations in n unknowns can be written as

$$\mathbf{Ax} = \mathbf{b}$$

where $\mathbf{A}$, $\mathbf{x}$ and $\mathbf{b}$ are $n \times n$, $n \times 1$ and $n \times 1$ matrices respectively. The matrix $\mathbf{A}$ consists of the coefficients, the vector $\mathbf{x}$ consists of the unknowns and the vector $\mathbf{b}$ consists of the right-hand sides. The definition of matrix multiplication allows us to write a linear system in terms of matrices, although it is not immediately obvious that there is any advantage in doing so. In the next section we introduce the concept of a matrix inverse and show you how to use this to solve systems of equations expressed in matrix form.

Throughout this section we have noted various properties which matrices satisfy. For convenience these are summarized as follows.

Summary

Provided that the indicated sums and products make sense,

$$\mathbf{A} + \mathbf{B} = \mathbf{B} + \mathbf{A}$$

$$\mathbf{A} - \mathbf{A} = \mathbf{0}$$

$$\mathbf{A} + \mathbf{0} = \mathbf{A}$$

$$k(\mathbf{A} + \mathbf{B}) = k\mathbf{A} + k\mathbf{B}$$

$$k(l\mathbf{A}) = (kl)\mathbf{A}$$

$$\mathbf{A}(\mathbf{B} + \mathbf{C}) = \mathbf{AB} + \mathbf{AC}$$

$$(\mathbf{A} + \mathbf{B})\mathbf{C} = \mathbf{AC} + \mathbf{BC}$$

$$\mathbf{A}(\mathbf{BC}) = (\mathbf{AB})\mathbf{C}$$

We also have the non-property that, in general,

$$\mathbf{AB} \neq \mathbf{BA}$$

There now follow some practice problems. If you find that you do not have time to do all of them you should at least attempt Problem 13 because the result of this problem will be used in the next section.

PRACTICE PROBLEMS

9 A firm manufactures three products P1, P2 and P3, which it sells to two customers, C1 and C2. The number of items of each product that are sold to these customers is given by

$$\mathbf{A} = \begin{array}{c} \text{C1} \\ \text{C2} \end{array} \begin{array}{ccc} \text{P1} & \text{P2} & \text{P3} \\ \begin{bmatrix} 6 & 7 & 9 \\ 2 & 1 & 2 \end{bmatrix} \end{array}$$

The firm charges both customers the same price for each product according to

$$
\begin{array}{ccc}
\text{P1} & \text{P2} & \text{P3}
\end{array}
$$
$$\mathbf{B} = \begin{bmatrix} 100 & 500 & 200 \end{bmatrix}^{\mathsf{T}}$$

To make each item of type P1, P2 and P3, the firm uses four raw materials, R1, R2, R3 and R4. The number of tonnes required per item is given by

$$
\begin{array}{ccccc}
 & \text{R1} & \text{R2} & \text{R3} & \text{R4}
\end{array}
$$
$$
\mathbf{C} = \begin{array}{c} \text{P1} \\ \text{P2} \\ \text{P3} \end{array}
\begin{bmatrix}
1 & 0 & 0 & 1 \\
1 & 1 & 2 & 1 \\
0 & 0 & 1 & 1
\end{bmatrix}
$$

The cost per tonne of raw materials is

$$
\begin{array}{cccc}
\text{R1} & \text{R2} & \text{R3} & \text{R4}
\end{array}
$$
$$\mathbf{D} = \begin{bmatrix} 20 & 10 & 15 & 15 \end{bmatrix}^{\mathsf{T}}$$

In addition, let

$$\mathbf{E} = \begin{bmatrix} 1 & 1 \end{bmatrix}$$

Find the following matrix products and give an interpretation of each one.

(a) AB   **(b) AC**   **(c) CD**   **(d) ACD**   **(e) EAB**   **(f) EACD**   **(g) EAB − EACD**

10 (1) Let

$$
\mathbf{A} = \begin{bmatrix} 1 & 2 \\ 3 & 4 \\ 5 & 6 \end{bmatrix}
\quad \text{and} \quad
\mathbf{B} = \begin{bmatrix} 1 & -1 \\ 2 & 1 \\ -3 & 4 \end{bmatrix}
$$

Find

(a) $\mathbf{A}^{\mathsf{T}}$ **(b) $\mathbf{B}^{\mathsf{T}}$**   **(c) $\mathbf{A} + \mathbf{B}$**   **(d) $(\mathbf{A} + \mathbf{B})^{\mathsf{T}}$**

Do you notice any connection between $(\mathbf{A} + \mathbf{B})^{\mathsf{T}}$, $\mathbf{A}^{\mathsf{T}}$ and $\mathbf{B}^{\mathsf{T}}$?

(2) Let

$$
\mathbf{C} = \begin{bmatrix} 1 & 4 \\ 5 & 9 \end{bmatrix}
\quad \text{and} \quad
\mathbf{D} = \begin{bmatrix} 2 & 1 & 0 \\ -1 & 0 & 1 \end{bmatrix}
$$

Find

(a) $\mathbf{C}^{\mathsf{T}}$ **(b) $\mathbf{D}^{\mathsf{T}}$**   **(c) $\mathbf{C}\mathbf{D}$**   **(d) $(\mathbf{C}\mathbf{D})^{\mathsf{T}}$**

Do you notice any connection between $(\mathbf{C}\mathbf{D})^{\mathsf{T}}$, $\mathbf{C}^{\mathsf{T}}$ and $\mathbf{D}^{\mathsf{T}}$?

11 Verify the equations

(a) $\mathbf{A}(\mathbf{B} + \mathbf{C}) = \mathbf{A}\mathbf{B} + \mathbf{A}\mathbf{C}$ **(b)** $(\mathbf{A}\mathbf{B})\mathbf{C} = \mathbf{A}(\mathbf{B}\mathbf{C})$

in the case when

$$
\mathbf{A} = \begin{bmatrix} 5 & -3 \\ 2 & 1 \end{bmatrix}
\quad
\mathbf{B} = \begin{bmatrix} 1 & 5 \\ 4 & 0 \end{bmatrix}
\quad \text{and} \quad
\mathbf{C} = \begin{bmatrix} -1 & 1 \\ 1 & 2 \end{bmatrix}
$$

12 If

$$A = [1 \quad 2 \quad -4 \quad 3] \quad \text{and} \quad B = \begin{bmatrix} 1 \\ 7 \\ 3 \\ -2 \end{bmatrix}$$

find **AB** and **BA**.

13 Let

$$A = \begin{bmatrix} a & b \\ c & d \end{bmatrix}, A^{-1} = \frac{1}{ad - bc} \begin{bmatrix} d & -b \\ -c & a \end{bmatrix} \quad (ad - bc \neq 0)$$

$$I = \begin{bmatrix} 1 & 0 \\ 0 & 1 \end{bmatrix} \quad \text{and} \quad x = \begin{bmatrix} x \\ y \end{bmatrix}$$

Show that

(a) $AI = A$ and $IA = A$ **(b)** $A^{-1}A = I$ and $AA^{-1} = I$ **(c)** $Ix = x$

7.2 Matrix inversion

Objectives At the end of this section you should be able to:

- write down the 2×2 and 3×3 identity matrices,

- detect whether a matrix is singular or non-singular,

- calculate the determinant and inverse of a 2×2 matrix,

- calculate the cofactors of a 3×3 matrix,

- use cofactors to find the determinant and inverse of a 3×3 matrix,

- use matrix inverses to solve systems of linear equations arising in economics.

In this and the following section we consider **square** matrices in which the number of rows and columns are equal. For simplicity we concentrate on 2×2 and 3×3 matrices, although the ideas and techniques apply more generally to $n \times n$ matrices of any size. We have already seen that, with one notable exception, the algebra of matrices is virtually the same as the algebra of numbers. There are, however, two important properties of numbers which we have yet to consider. The first is the existence of a number, 1, which satisfies

$$a1 = a \qquad \text{and} \qquad 1a = a$$

for any number, a. The second is the fact that corresponding to any non-zero number, a, we can find another number, a^{-1}, with the property that

$$a^{-1}a = 1 \qquad \text{and} \qquad aa^{-1} = 1 \qquad \left(a^{-1} = \frac{1}{a} \right)$$

If you have worked through Problem 13 of Section 7.1 you will know how to extend these to 2×2 matrices. In part (a) you showed that, for any 2×2 matrix, **A**,

$$\mathbf{AI} = \mathbf{A} \qquad \text{and} \qquad \mathbf{IA} = \mathbf{A}$$

where

$$\mathbf{I} = \begin{bmatrix} 1 & 0 \\ 0 & 1 \end{bmatrix}$$

The matrix **I** is called the **identity** matrix and is analogous to the number 1 in ordinary arithmetic. You also showed in part (b) of Problem 13 that corresponding to the 2×2 matrix

$$\mathbf{A} = \begin{bmatrix} a & b \\ c & d \end{bmatrix}$$

there is another matrix

$$\mathbf{A}^{-1} = \frac{1}{ad - bc} \begin{bmatrix} d & -b \\ -c & a \end{bmatrix}$$

with the property that

$$\mathbf{A}^{-1}\mathbf{A} = \mathbf{I} \qquad \text{and} \qquad \mathbf{AA}^{-1} = \mathbf{I}$$

The matrix $\mathbf{A}^{-1}$ is said to be the **inverse** of **A** and is analogous to the reciprocal of a number. The formula for $\mathbf{A}^{-1}$ looks rather complicated but the construction of $\mathbf{A}^{-1}$ is in fact very easy. Starting with some matrix

$$\mathbf{A} = \begin{bmatrix} a & b \\ c & d \end{bmatrix}$$

we first swap the two numbers on the leading diagonal (that is, the elements along the line joining the top left-hand corner to the bottom right-hand corner of **A**) to get

$$\begin{bmatrix} d & b \\ c & a \end{bmatrix} \qquad \left(\text{swap } a \text{ and } d \right)$$

Secondly, we change the sign of the 'off-diagonal' elements to get

$$\begin{bmatrix} d & -b \\ -c & a \end{bmatrix} \qquad \left(\text{change signs of } b \text{ and } c \right)$$

Finally, we multiply the matrix by the scalar

$$\frac{1}{ad - bc}$$

to get

$$\frac{1}{ad - bc} \begin{bmatrix} d & -b \\ -c & a \end{bmatrix}$$

divide each element by ad - bc

The number $ad - bc$ is called the **determinant** of **A** and is written as

$$\det(\mathbf{A}) \quad \text{or} \quad |\mathbf{A}| \quad \text{or} \quad \begin{vmatrix} a & b \\ c & d \end{vmatrix}$$

Notice that the last step in the calculation is impossible if

$$|\mathbf{A}| = 0$$

because we cannot divide by zero. We deduce that the inverse of a matrix only exists if it has a non-zero determinant. This is comparable to the situation in arithmetic where a reciprocal of a number exists provided it is non-zero. If the matrix has a non-zero determinant it is said to be **non-singular**, otherwise it is said to be **singular**.

EXAMPLE

Find the inverse of the following matrices. Are these matrices singular or non-singular?

$$\mathbf{A} = \begin{bmatrix} 1 & 2 \\ 3 & 4 \end{bmatrix} \quad \mathbf{B} = \begin{bmatrix} 2 & 5 \\ 4 & 10 \end{bmatrix}$$

Solution

We begin by calculating the determinant of

$$\mathbf{A} = \begin{bmatrix} 1 & 2 \\ 3 & 4 \end{bmatrix}$$

to see whether or not the inverse exists.

$$\det(\mathbf{A}) = \begin{vmatrix} 1 & 2 \\ 3 & 4 \end{vmatrix} = 1(4) - 2(3) = 4 - 6 = -2$$

We see that $\det(\mathbf{A}) \neq 0$ so the matrix is non-singular and the inverse exists. To find $\mathbf{A}^{-1}$ we swap the diagonal elements, 1 and 4, change the sign of the off-diagonal elements, 2 and 3, and divide by the determinant, -2. Hence

$$\mathbf{A}^{-1} = -\frac{1}{2} \begin{bmatrix} 4 & -2 \\ -3 & 1 \end{bmatrix} = \begin{bmatrix} -2 & 1 \\ 3/2 & -1/2 \end{bmatrix}$$

Of course, if $\mathbf{A}^{-1}$ really is the inverse of **A**, then $\mathbf{A}^{-1}\mathbf{A}$ and $\mathbf{A}\mathbf{A}^{-1}$ should multiply out to give **I**. As a check:

$$\mathbf{A}^{-1}\mathbf{A} = \begin{bmatrix} -2 & 1 \\ 3/2 & -1/2 \end{bmatrix}\begin{bmatrix} 1 & 2 \\ 3 & 4 \end{bmatrix} = \begin{bmatrix} 1 & 0 \\ 0 & 1 \end{bmatrix} \quad \checkmark$$

$$\mathbf{A}\mathbf{A}^{-1} = \begin{bmatrix} 1 & 2 \\ 3 & 4 \end{bmatrix}\begin{bmatrix} -2 & 1 \\ 3/2 & -1/2 \end{bmatrix} = \begin{bmatrix} 1 & 0 \\ 0 & 1 \end{bmatrix} \quad \checkmark$$

To discover whether or not the matrix

$$\mathbf{B} = \begin{bmatrix} 2 & 5 \\ 4 & 10 \end{bmatrix}$$

has an inverse we need to find its determinant.

$$\det(\mathbf{B}) = \begin{vmatrix} 2 & 5 \\ 4 & 10 \end{vmatrix} = 2(10) - 5(4) = 20 - 20 = 0$$

We see that $\det(\mathbf{B}) = 0$ so this matrix is singular and the inverse does not exist.

∎

PROBLEM

1 Find (where possible) the inverse of the following matrices. Are these matrices singular or non-singular?

$$\mathbf{A} = \begin{bmatrix} 6 & 4 \\ 1 & 2 \end{bmatrix} \qquad \mathbf{B} = \begin{bmatrix} 6 & 4 \\ 3 & 2 \end{bmatrix}$$

One reason for calculating the inverse of a matrix is that it helps us to solve matrix equations in the same way that the reciprocal of a number is used to solve algebraic equations. We have already seen in Section 7.1 how to express a system of linear equations in matrix form. Any 2×2 system

$$ax + by = e$$
$$cx + dy = f$$

can be written as

$$\mathbf{A}\mathbf{x} = \mathbf{b}$$

where

$$\mathbf{A} = \begin{bmatrix} a & b \\ c & d \end{bmatrix} \qquad \mathbf{x} = \begin{bmatrix} x \\ y \end{bmatrix} \qquad \mathbf{b} = \begin{bmatrix} e \\ f \end{bmatrix}$$

The coefficient matrix, $\mathbf{A}$, and right-hand side vector, $\mathbf{b}$, are assumed to be given and the problem is to determine the vector of unknowns, $\mathbf{x}$. Multiplying both sides of

$$\mathbf{A}\mathbf{x} = \mathbf{b}$$

by A^{-1} gives

$$A^{-1}(Ax) = A^{-1}b$$

$$(A^{-1}A)x = A^{-1}b \qquad \text{(associative property)}$$

$$Ix = A^{-1}b \qquad \text{(definition of an inverse)}$$

$$x = A^{-1}b \qquad \text{(Problem 13(c) in Section 8.1)}$$

The solution vector **x** can therefore be found simply by multiplying A^{-1} by **b**. We are assuming here that A^{-1} exists. If the coefficient matrix is singular then the inverse cannot be found and the system of linear equations fails to possess a unique solution; there are either infinitely many solutions or no solution. These special cases are dealt with using the elimination method described in Section 1.2. The following two examples illustrate the use of inverses to solve systems of linear equations. The first is taken from microeconomics and the second from macroeconomics.

EXAMPLE

The equilibrium prices P_1 and P_2 for two goods satisfy the equations

$$-4P_1 + P_2 = -13$$

$$2P_1 - 5P_2 = -7$$

Express this system in matrix form and hence find the values of P_1 and P_2.

Solution

Using the notation of matrices the simultaneous equations

$$-4P_1 + P_2 = -13$$

$$2P_1 - 5P_2 = -7$$

can be written as

$$\begin{bmatrix} -4 & 1 \\ 2 & -5 \end{bmatrix} \begin{bmatrix} P_1 \\ P_2 \end{bmatrix} = \begin{bmatrix} -13 \\ -7 \end{bmatrix}$$

that is as

$$Ax = b$$

where

$$A = \begin{bmatrix} -4 & 1 \\ 2 & -5 \end{bmatrix} \quad x = \begin{bmatrix} P_1 \\ P_2 \end{bmatrix} \quad b = \begin{bmatrix} -13 \\ -7 \end{bmatrix}$$

The matrix **A** has determinant

$$\begin{vmatrix} -4 & 1 \\ 2 & -5 \end{vmatrix} = (-4)(-5) - (1)(2) = 20 - 2 = 18$$

To find A^{-1} we swap the diagonal elements, -4 and -5, change the sign of the off-diagonal elements,

1 and 2, and divide by the determinant, 18, to get

$$\mathbf{A}^{-1} = \frac{1}{18} \begin{bmatrix} -5 & -1 \\ -2 & -4 \end{bmatrix}$$

Finally, to calculate $\mathbf{x}$ we multiply $\mathbf{A}^{-1}$ by $\mathbf{b}$ to get

$$\mathbf{x} = \mathbf{A}^{-1}\mathbf{b}$$

$$= \frac{1}{18} \begin{bmatrix} -5 & -1 \\ -2 & -4 \end{bmatrix} \begin{bmatrix} -13 \\ -7 \end{bmatrix}$$

$$= \frac{1}{18} \begin{bmatrix} 72 \\ 54 \end{bmatrix}$$

$$= \begin{bmatrix} 4 \\ 3 \end{bmatrix}$$

Hence $P_1 = 4$ and $P_2 = 3$.

■

PROBLEM

2   The equilibrium prices P_1 and P_2 for two goods satisfy the equations

$$9P_1 + P_2 = 43$$
$$2P_1 + 7P_2 = 57$$

Express this system in matrix form and hence find the values of P_1 and P_2.
[You have already solved this particular system in Problem 5 of Section 1.3. You might like to compare the work involved in solving this system using the method of elimination described in Chapter 1 and the method based on matrix inverses considered here.]

EXAMPLE

The equilibrium levels of consumption, C, and income, Y, for the simple two-sector macroeconomic model satisfy the structural equations

$$Y = C + I^*$$
$$C = aY + b$$

where a and b are parameters in the range $0 < a < 1$ and $b > 0$, and I^* denotes investment. Express this system in matrix form and hence express Y and C in terms of a, b and I^*. Give an economic interpretation of the inverse matrix.

Solution

The reduced form of the structural equations for this simple model has already been found in Section 5.3. It is instructive to reconsider this problem using matrices. The objective is to express the endogenous variables, Y and C, in terms of the exogenous variable I^* and parameters a and b. The 'unknowns' of this problem are therefore Y and C and we begin by rearranging the structural equations so that these variables appear on the left-hand sides. Subtracting C from both sides of

$$Y = C + I^*$$

gives

$$Y - C = I^* \tag{1}$$

and if we subtract aY from both sides of

$$C = aY + b$$

we get

$$-aY + C = b \tag{2}$$

(It is convenient to put the term involving Y first so that the variables align with those of equation (1).)

In matrix form, equations (1) and (2) become

$$\begin{bmatrix} 1 & -1 \\ -a & 1 \end{bmatrix} \begin{bmatrix} Y \\ C \end{bmatrix} = \begin{bmatrix} I^* \\ b \end{bmatrix}$$

that is

$$\mathbf{Ax} = \mathbf{b}$$

where

$$\mathbf{A} = \begin{bmatrix} 1 & -1 \\ -a & 1 \end{bmatrix} \qquad \mathbf{x} = \begin{bmatrix} Y \\ C \end{bmatrix} \qquad \mathbf{b} = \begin{bmatrix} I^* \\ b \end{bmatrix}$$

The matrix $\mathbf{A}$ has determinant

$$\begin{vmatrix} 1 & -1 \\ -a & 1 \end{vmatrix} = 1(1) - (-1)(-a) = 1 - a$$

which is non-zero because $a < 1$.

To find $\mathbf{A}^{-1}$, we swap the diagonal elements, 1 and 1, change the sign of the off-diagonal elements, -1 and $-a$, and divide by the determinant, $1 - a$, to get

$$\mathbf{A}^{-1} = \frac{1}{1-a} \begin{bmatrix} 1 & 1 \\ a & 1 \end{bmatrix}$$

Finally, to determine $\mathbf{x}$ we multiply $\mathbf{A}^{-1}$ by $\mathbf{b}$ to get

$$\mathbf{x} = \mathbf{A}^{-1} \mathbf{b}$$

$$= \frac{1}{1-a} \begin{bmatrix} 1 & 1 \\ a & 1 \end{bmatrix} \begin{bmatrix} I^* \\ b \end{bmatrix}$$

$$= \frac{1}{1-a} \begin{bmatrix} I^* + b \\ aI^* + b \end{bmatrix}$$

Hence

$$Y = \frac{I^* + b}{1-a} \qquad \text{and} \qquad C = \frac{aI^* + b}{1-a}$$

The inverse matrix obviously provides a useful way of solving the structural equations of a macroeconomic model. In addition, the elements of the inverse matrix can be given an important economic interpretation.

To see this let us suppose that the investment I^* changes by an amount ΔI^* to become $I^* + \Delta I^*$, with the parameter b held fixed. The new values of Y and C are obtained by replacing I^* by $I^* + \Delta I^*$ in the expressions for Y and C and are given by

$$\frac{I^* + \Delta I^* + b}{1 - a} \quad \text{and} \quad \frac{a(I^* + \Delta I^*) + b}{1 - a}$$

respectively. The change in the value of Y is therefore

$$\Delta Y = \frac{I^* + \Delta I^* + b}{1 - a} - \frac{I^* + b}{1 - a}$$

$$= \left(\frac{1}{1 - a}\right)\Delta I^*$$

and the change in the value of C is

$$\Delta C = \frac{a(I^* + \Delta I^*) + b}{1 - a} - \frac{aI^* + b}{1 - a}$$

$$= \left(\frac{a}{1 - a}\right)\Delta I^*$$

In other words, the changes to Y and C are found by multiplying the change in I^* by

$$\frac{1}{1 - a} \quad \text{and} \quad \frac{a}{1 - a}$$

respectively. For this reason we call

$$\frac{1}{1 - a}$$

the investment multiplier for Y and

$$\frac{a}{1 - a}$$

the investment multiplier for C.

Now the inverse matrix is

$$\mathbf{A}^{-1} = \begin{bmatrix} \dfrac{1}{1 - a} & \dfrac{1}{1 - a} \\[2mm] \dfrac{a}{1 - a} & \dfrac{1}{1 - a} \end{bmatrix}$$

and we see that these multipliers are precisely the elements which appear in the first column. It is easy to show using a similar argument that the second column contains the multipliers for Y and C due to changes in the autonomous consumption, b. The four elements in the inverse matrix can thus be interpreted as follows:

$$
\begin{array}{c}
\qquad\qquad I^* \qquad\qquad\qquad\qquad\qquad\qquad b \\
\begin{array}{c} Y \\ C \end{array}
\begin{bmatrix}
\text{investment multiplier for } Y & \text{autonomous consumption multiplier for } Y \\
\text{investment multiplier for } C & \text{autonomous consumption multiplier for } C
\end{bmatrix}
\end{array}
$$

■

PROBLEM

3   The general linear supply and demand equations for a one commodity market model are given by

$$P = aQ_S + b \qquad (a > 0, \quad b > 0)$$

$$P = -cQ_D + d \qquad (c > 0, \quad d > 0)$$

Show that in matrix notation the equilibrium price, P, and quantity, Q, satisfy

$$\begin{bmatrix} 1 & -a \\ 1 & c \end{bmatrix} \begin{bmatrix} P \\ Q \end{bmatrix} = \begin{bmatrix} b \\ d \end{bmatrix}$$

Solve this system to express P and Q in terms of a, b, c and d. Write down the multiplier for Q due to changes in b and deduce that an increase in b leads to a decrease in Q.

The concepts of determinant, inverse and identity matrices apply equally well to 3×3 matrices. The identity matrix is easily dealt with. It can be shown that the 3×3 identity matrix is

$$\mathbf{I} = \begin{bmatrix} 1 & 0 & 0 \\ 0 & 1 & 0 \\ 0 & 0 & 1 \end{bmatrix}$$

You are invited to check that, for any 3×3 matrix $\mathbf{A}$,

$$\mathbf{AI} = \mathbf{A} \qquad \text{and} \qquad \mathbf{IA} = \mathbf{A}$$

Before we can discuss the determinant and inverse of a 3×3 matrix we need to introduce an additional concept known as a **cofactor**. Corresponding to each element a_{ij} of a matrix $\mathbf{A}$, there is a cofactor, A_{ij}. A 3×3 matrix has nine elements so there are nine cofactors to be computed. The cofactor, A_{ij}, is defined to be the determinant of the 2×2 matrix obtained by deleting row i and column j of $\mathbf{A}$, prefixed by a '$+$' or '$-$' sign according to the following pattern:

$$\begin{bmatrix} + & - & + \\ - & + & - \\ + & - & + \end{bmatrix}$$

For example, suppose we wish to calculate A_{23} which is the cofactor associated with a_{23} in the matrix

$$\mathbf{A} = \begin{bmatrix} a_{11} & a_{12} & a_{13} \\ a_{21} & a_{22} & a_{23} \\ a_{31} & a_{32} & a_{33} \end{bmatrix}$$

The element a_{23} lies in the second row and third column. Consequently, we delete the second row and third column to produce the 2×3 matrix

$$
\begin{bmatrix}
a_{11} & a_{12} & a_{13} \\
a_{21} & a_{22} & a_{23} \\
a_{31} & a_{32} & a_{33}
\end{bmatrix}
$$

The cofactor, A_{23}, is the determinant of this 2×2 matrix prefixed by a '$-$' sign because from the pattern

$$
\begin{bmatrix}
+ & - & + \\
- & + & \boxed{-} \\
+ & - & +
\end{bmatrix}
$$

we see that a_{23} is in a minus position. In other words,

$$
\begin{aligned}
\mathbf{A}_{23} &= - \begin{vmatrix} a_{11} & a_{12} \\ a_{31} & a_{32} \end{vmatrix} \\
&= -(a_{11}a_{32} - a_{12}a_{31}) \\
&= -a_{11}a_{32} + a_{12}a_{31}
\end{aligned}
$$

EXAMPLE

Find all the cofactors of the matrix

$$
\mathbf{A} = \begin{bmatrix}
2 & 4 & 1 \\
4 & 3 & 7 \\
2 & 1 & 3
\end{bmatrix}
$$

Solution

Let us start in the top left-hand corner and work row by row. For cofactor A_{11}, the element $a_{11} = 2$ lies in the first row and first column so we delete this row and column to produce the 2×2 matrix

$$
\begin{bmatrix}
2 & 4 & 1 \\
4 & 3 & 7 \\
2 & 1 & 3
\end{bmatrix}
$$

Cofactor A_{11} is the determinant of this 2×2 matrix, prefixed by a '$+$' sign because from the pattern

$$
\begin{bmatrix}
\boxed{+} & - & + \\
- & + & - \\
+ & - & +
\end{bmatrix}
$$

we see that a_{11} is in a plus position. Hence

$$A_{11} = + \begin{vmatrix} 3 & 7 \\ 1 & 3 \end{vmatrix}$$

$$= +(3(3) - 7(1))$$

$$= 9 - 7$$

$$= 2$$

For cofactor A_{12}, the element $a_{12} = 4$ lies in the first row and second column so we delete this row and column to produce the 2×2 matrix

$$\begin{bmatrix} 2 & 4 & 1 \\ 4 & 3 & 7 \\ 2 & 1 & 3 \end{bmatrix}$$

Cofactor A_{12} is the determinant of this 2×2 matrix, prefixed by a ' $-$ ' sign because from the pattern

$$\begin{bmatrix} + & \boxed{-} & + \\ - & + & - \\ + & - & + \end{bmatrix}$$

we see that a_{12} is in a minus position. Hence

$$A_{12} = - \begin{vmatrix} 4 & 7 \\ 2 & 3 \end{vmatrix}$$

$$= -(4(3) - 7(2))$$

$$= -(12 - 14)$$

$$= 2$$

We can continue in this way to find the remaining cofactors

$$A_{13} = + \begin{vmatrix} 4 & 3 \\ 2 & 1 \end{vmatrix} = -2$$

$$A_{21} = - \begin{vmatrix} 4 & 1 \\ 1 & 3 \end{vmatrix} = -11$$

$$A_{22} = + \begin{vmatrix} 2 & 1 \\ 2 & 3 \end{vmatrix} = 4$$

$$A_{23} = - \begin{vmatrix} 2 & 4 \\ 2 & 1 \end{vmatrix} = 6$$

$$A_{31} = + \begin{vmatrix} 4 & 1 \\ 3 & 7 \end{vmatrix} = 25$$

$$A_{32} = - \begin{vmatrix} 2 & 1 \\ 4 & 7 \end{vmatrix} = -10$$

$$A_{33} = + \begin{vmatrix} 2 & 4 \\ 4 & 3 \end{vmatrix} = -10$$

■

PROBLEM

4 Find all the cofactors of the matrix

$$A = \begin{bmatrix} 1 & 3 & 3 \\ 1 & 4 & 3 \\ 1 & 3 & 4 \end{bmatrix}$$

We are now in a position to describe how to calculate the determinant and inverse of a 3×3 matrix. The determinant is found by multiplying the elements in any one row or column by their corresponding cofactors and adding together. It does not matter which row or column is chosen; exactly the same answer is obtained in each case. If we expand along the first row of the matrix

$$A = \begin{bmatrix} a_{11} & a_{12} & a_{13} \\ a_{21} & a_{22} & a_{23} \\ a_{31} & a_{32} & a_{33} \end{bmatrix}$$

we get

$$\det(A) = a_{11}A_{11} + a_{12}A_{12} + a_{13}A_{13}$$

Similarly, if we expand down the second column we get

$$\det(A) = a_{12}A_{12} + a_{22}A_{22} + a_{32}A_{32}$$

The fact that we get the same answer irrespective of the row and column that we use for expansion is an extremely useful property. It provides us with an obvious check on our calculations. Also, there are occasions when it is more convenient to expand along certain rows or columns than others.

EXAMPLE

Find the determinants of the following matrices

$$A = \begin{bmatrix} 2 & 4 & 1 \\ 4 & 3 & 7 \\ 2 & 1 & 3 \end{bmatrix} \quad \text{and} \quad B = \begin{bmatrix} 10 & 7 & 5 \\ 0 & 2 & 0 \\ 2 & 7 & 3 \end{bmatrix}$$

Solution

We have already calculated all nine cofactors of the matrix

$$A = \begin{bmatrix} 2 & 4 & 1 \\ 4 & 3 & 7 \\ 2 & 1 & 3 \end{bmatrix}$$

in the previous example. It is immaterial which row or column we use. Let us choose the second row.

The cofactors corresponding to the three elements 4, 3, 7 in the second row were found to be -11, 4, 6 respectively. Consequently, if we expand along this row we get

$$\begin{vmatrix} 2 & 4 & 1 \\ 4 & 3 & 7 \\ 2 & 1 & 3 \end{vmatrix} = 4(-11) + 3(4) + 7(6) = 10$$

As a check, let us also expand down the third column. The elements in this column are 1, 7, 3 with cofactors, -2, 6, -10 respectively. Hence, if we multiply each element by its cofactor and add we get

$$1(-2) + 7(6) + 3(-10) = 10$$

which is the same as before. If you are interested you might like to confirm for yourself that the value of 10 is also obtained when expanding along rows 1 and 3, and down columns 1 and 2.

The matrix

$$\mathbf{B} = \begin{bmatrix} 10 & 7 & 5 \\ 0 & 2 & 0 \\ 2 & 7 & 3 \end{bmatrix}$$

is entirely new to us so we have no prior knowledge about its cofactors. In general, we need to evaluate all three cofactors in any one row or column to find the determinant of a 3×3 matrix. In this case, however, we can be much lazier. Observe that all but one of the elements in the second row are zero so when we expand along this row we get

$$\det(\mathbf{B}) = b_{21}B_{21} + b_{22}B_{22} + b_{23}B_{23}$$

$$= 0B_{21} + 2B_{22} + 0B_{23}$$

$$= 2B_{22}$$

Hence B_{22} is the only cofactor that we need to find. This corresponds to the element in the second row and second column so we delete this row and column to produce the 2×2 matrix

$$\begin{bmatrix} 10 & 7 & 5 \\ 0 & 2 & 0 \\ 2 & 7 & 3 \end{bmatrix}$$

The element b_{22} is in a plus position so

$$B_{22} = + \begin{vmatrix} 10 & 5 \\ 2 & 3 \end{vmatrix} = 20$$

Hence,

$$\det(\mathbf{B}) = 2B_{22} = 2 \times 20 = 40$$

PROBLEM

5 Find the determinant of

$$
\mathbf{A} = \begin{bmatrix} 1 & 3 & 3 \\ 1 & 4 & 3 \\ 1 & 3 & 4 \end{bmatrix} \quad \text{and} \quad \mathbf{B} = \begin{bmatrix} 270 & -372 & 0 \\ 552 & 201 & 0 \\ 999 & 413 & 0 \end{bmatrix}
$$

[Hint: you might find your answer to Problem 4 useful when calculating the determinant of **A.**]

The inverse of the 3×3 matrix

$$
\mathbf{A} = \begin{bmatrix} a_{11} & a_{12} & a_{13} \\ a_{21} & a_{22} & a_{23} \\ a_{31} & a_{32} & a_{33} \end{bmatrix}
$$

is given by

$$
\mathbf{A}^{-1} = \frac{1}{|\mathbf{A}|} \begin{bmatrix} A_{11} & A_{21} & A_{31} \\ A_{12} & A_{22} & A_{32} \\ A_{13} & A_{23} & A_{33} \end{bmatrix}
$$

Once the cofactors of **A** have been found it is easy to construct $\mathbf{A}^{-1}$. We first stack the cofactors in their natural positions

$$
\begin{bmatrix} A_{11} & A_{12} & A_{13} \\ A_{21} & A_{22} & A_{23} \\ A_{31} & A_{32} & A_{33} \end{bmatrix}
$$

called the adjugate matrix

Secondly, we take the transpose to get

$$
\begin{bmatrix} A_{11} & A_{21} & A_{31} \\ A_{12} & A_{22} & A_{32} \\ A_{13} & A_{23} & A_{33} \end{bmatrix}
$$

called the adjoint matrix

Finally, we multiply by the scalar

$$
\frac{1}{|\mathbf{A}|}
$$

to get

$$
\mathbf{A}^{-1} = \frac{1}{|\mathbf{A}|} \begin{bmatrix} A_{11} & A_{21} & A_{31} \\ A_{12} & A_{22} & A_{32} \\ A_{13} & A_{23} & A_{33} \end{bmatrix}
$$

divide each element by the determinant

The last step is impossible if

$$
|\mathbf{A}| = 0
$$

because we cannot divide by zero. Under these circumstances the inverse does not exist and the matrix is singular. As usual it is a good idea to check that no mistakes have been made by verifying that

$$\mathbf{A}^{-1}\mathbf{A} = \mathbf{I} \quad \text{and} \quad \mathbf{A}\mathbf{A}^{-1} = \mathbf{I}$$

EXAMPLE

Find the inverse of

$$\mathbf{A} = \begin{bmatrix} 2 & 4 & 1 \\ 4 & 3 & 7 \\ 2 & 1 & 3 \end{bmatrix}$$

Solution

The cofactors of this particular matrix have already been calculated as

$$A_{11} = 2, \qquad A_{12} = 2, \qquad A_{13} = -2$$
$$A_{21} = -11, \qquad A_{22} = 4, \qquad A_{23} = 6$$
$$A_{31} - 25, \qquad A_{32} = -10, \qquad A_{33} = -10$$

Stacking these numbers in their natural positions gives the adjygate matrix

$$\begin{bmatrix} 2 & 2 & -2 \\ -11 & 4 & 6 \\ 25 & -10 & -10 \end{bmatrix}$$

The adjoint matrix is found by transposing this to get

$$\begin{bmatrix} 2 & -11 & 25 \\ 2 & 4 & -10 \\ -2 & 6 & -10 \end{bmatrix}$$

In the previous example the determinant was found to be 10 so

$$\mathbf{A}^{-1} = \frac{1}{10}\begin{bmatrix} 2 & -11 & 25 \\ 2 & 4 & -10 \\ -2 & 6 & -10 \end{bmatrix} = \begin{bmatrix} 1/5 & -11/10 & 5/2 \\ 1/5 & 2/5 & -1 \\ -1/5 & 3/5 & -1 \end{bmatrix}$$

As a check:

$$\mathbf{A}^{-1}\mathbf{A} = \begin{bmatrix} 1/5 & -11/10 & 5/2 \\ 1/5 & 2/5 & -1 \\ -1/5 & 3/5 & -1 \end{bmatrix}\begin{bmatrix} 2 & 4 & 1 \\ 4 & 3 & 7 \\ 2 & 1 & 3 \end{bmatrix} = \begin{bmatrix} 1 & 0 & 0 \\ 0 & 1 & 0 \\ 0 & 0 & 1 \end{bmatrix} = \mathbf{I} \quad \checkmark$$

$$\mathbf{A}\mathbf{A}^{-1} = \begin{bmatrix} 2 & 4 & 1 \\ 4 & 3 & 7 \\ 2 & 1 & 3 \end{bmatrix}\begin{bmatrix} 1/5 & -11/10 & 5/2 \\ 1/5 & 2/5 & -1 \\ -1/5 & 3/5 & -1 \end{bmatrix} = \begin{bmatrix} 1 & 0 & 0 \\ 0 & 1 & 0 \\ 0 & 0 & 1 \end{bmatrix} = \mathbf{I} \quad \checkmark$$

∎

PROBLEM

6 Find (where possible) the inverses of

$$A = \begin{bmatrix} 1 & 3 & 3 \\ 1 & 4 & 3 \\ 1 & 3 & 4 \end{bmatrix} \quad \text{and} \quad B = \begin{bmatrix} 270 & -372 & 0 \\ 552 & 201 & 0 \\ 999 & 413 & 0 \end{bmatrix}$$

[Hint: you might find your answers to Problems 4 and 5 useful.]

Inverses of 3×3 matrices can be used to solve systems of three linear equations in three unknowns. The general system

$$a_{11}x + a_{12}y + a_{13}z = b_1$$

$$a_{21}x + a_{22}y + a_{23}z = b_2$$

$$a_{31}x + a_{32}y + a_{33}z = b_3$$

can be written as

$$Ax = b$$

where

$$A = \begin{bmatrix} a_{11} & a_{12} & a_{13} \\ a_{21} & a_{22} & a_{23} \\ a_{31} & a_{32} & a_{33} \end{bmatrix} \quad x = \begin{bmatrix} x \\ y \\ z \end{bmatrix} \quad b = \begin{bmatrix} b_1 \\ b_2 \\ b_3 \end{bmatrix}$$

The vector of unknowns, x, can be found by inverting the coefficient matrix, A, and multiplying by the right-hand side vector, b, to get

$$x = A^{-1}b$$

EXAMPLE

Determine the equilibrium prices of three interdependent commodities which satisfy

$$2P_1 + 4P_2 + P_3 = 77$$

$$4P_1 + 3P_2 + 7P_3 = 114$$

$$2P_1 + P_2 + 3P_3 = 48$$

Solution

In matrix notation this system of equations can be written as

$$Ax = b$$

where

$$A = \begin{bmatrix} 2 & 4 & 1 \\ 4 & 3 & 7 \\ 2 & 1 & 3 \end{bmatrix} \quad x = \begin{bmatrix} P_1 \\ P_2 \\ P_3 \end{bmatrix} \quad b = \begin{bmatrix} 77 \\ 114 \\ 48 \end{bmatrix}$$

The inverse of the coefficient matrix has already been found in the previous example and is

$$\mathbf{A}^{-1} = \begin{bmatrix} 1/5 & -11/10 & 5/2 \\ 1/5 & 2/5 & -1 \\ -1/5 & 3/5 & -1 \end{bmatrix}$$

so

$$\begin{bmatrix} P_1 \\ P_2 \\ P_3 \end{bmatrix} = \begin{bmatrix} 1/5 & -11/10 & 5/2 \\ 1/5 & 2/5 & -1 \\ -1/5 & 3/5 & -1 \end{bmatrix} \begin{bmatrix} 77 \\ 114 \\ 48 \end{bmatrix} = \begin{bmatrix} 10 \\ 13 \\ 5 \end{bmatrix}$$

The equilibrium prices are therefore given by

$$P_1 = 10, \ P_2 = 13, \ P_3 = 5$$

■

PROBLEM

7 Determine the equilibrium prices of three interdependent commodities which satisfy

$$P_1 + 3P_2 + 3P_3 = 32$$
$$P_1 + 4P_2 + 3P_3 = 37$$
$$P_1 + 3P_2 + 4P_3 = 35$$

[Hint: you might find your answer to Problem 6 useful.]

PRACTICE PROBLEMS

8 Let

$$\mathbf{A} = \begin{bmatrix} 2 & 1 \\ 5 & 1 \end{bmatrix} \quad \text{and} \quad \mathbf{B} = \begin{bmatrix} 1 & 0 \\ 2 & 4 \end{bmatrix}$$

(1) Find

(a) $|\mathbf{A}|$ **(b)** $|\mathbf{B}|$ **(c)** $|\mathbf{AB}|$

Do you notice any connection between $|\mathbf{A}|$, $|\mathbf{B}|$ and $|\mathbf{AB}|$?

(2) Find

(a) $\mathbf{A}^{-1}$ **(b)** $\mathbf{B}^{-1}$ **(c)** $(\mathbf{AB})^{-1}$

Do you notice any connection between $\mathbf{A}^{-1}$, $\mathbf{B}^{-1}$ and $(\mathbf{AB})^{-1}$?

9 Calculate the inverse of

$$\begin{bmatrix} -3 & 1 \\ 2 & -9 \end{bmatrix}$$

Hence find the equilibrium prices in the two-commodity market model given in Problem 9 of Section 1.3.

10   For the commodity market

$$C = aY + b \qquad (0 < a < 1, b > 0)$$

$$I = cr + d \qquad (c < 0, d > 0)$$

For the money market

$$M_S = M_S^*$$

$$M_D = k_1 Y + k_2 r + k_3 \qquad (k_1, k_3 > 0, k_2 < 0)$$

Show that when the commodity and money markets are both in equilibrium, the income, Y, and interest rate, r, satisfy the matrix equation

$$\begin{bmatrix} 1 - a & -c \\ k_1 & k_2 \end{bmatrix} \begin{bmatrix} Y \\ r \end{bmatrix} = \begin{bmatrix} b + d \\ M_S^* - k_3 \end{bmatrix}$$

and solve this system for Y and r. Write down the multiplier for r due to changes in M_S^* and deduce that interest rates fall as the money supply grows.

11   Find (where possible) the inverse of the matrices

$$\mathbf{A} = \begin{bmatrix} 2 & 1 & -1 \\ 1 & 3 & 2 \\ -1 & 2 & 1 \end{bmatrix} \qquad \mathbf{B} = \begin{bmatrix} 1 & 4 & 5 \\ 2 & 1 & 3 \\ -1 & 3 & 2 \end{bmatrix}$$

Are these matrices singular or non-singular?

12   Find the inverse of

$$\begin{bmatrix} -2 & 2 & 1 \\ 1 & -5 & -1 \\ 2 & -1 & -6 \end{bmatrix}$$

Hence find the equilibrium prices of the three-commodity market model given in Problem 10 of Section 1.3.

7.3   Cramer's rule

Objectives   At the end of this section you should be able to:

- appreciate the limitations of using inverses to solve systems of linear equations,

- use Cramer's rule to solve systems of linear equations,

- apply Cramer's rule to analyse static macroeconomic models,

- apply Cramer's rule to solve two country trading models.

In Section 7.2 we described the mechanics of calculating the determinant and inverse of 2×2 and 3×3 matrices. These concepts can be extended to larger systems in an obvious way although the amount of effort needed rises dramatically as the size of the matrix increases. For example, consider the work involved in solving the system

$$\begin{bmatrix} 1 & 0 & 2 & 3 \\ -1 & 5 & 4 & 1 \\ 0 & 7 & -3 & 6 \\ 2 & 4 & 5 & 1 \end{bmatrix} \begin{bmatrix} x_1 \\ x_2 \\ x_3 \\ x_4 \end{bmatrix} = \begin{bmatrix} -1 \\ 1 \\ -24 \\ 15 \end{bmatrix}$$

using the method of matrix inversion. In this case the coefficient matrix has order 4×4 and so has 16 elements. Corresponding to each of these elements there is a cofactor. This is defined to be the 3×3 determinant obtained by deleting the row and column containing the element, prefixed by a '+' or '−' according to the following pattern

$$\begin{bmatrix} + & - & + & - \\ - & + & - & + \\ + & - & + & - \\ - & + & - & + \end{bmatrix}$$

Determinants are found by expanding along any one row or column and inverses are found by stacking cofactors as before. However, given that there are 16 cofactors to be calculated, even the most enthusiastic student is likely to view the prospect with some trepidation. To make matters worse, it frequently happens in economics that only a few of the variables x_i are actually needed. For instance, it could be that the variable x_3 is the only one of interest. Under these circumstances it is clearly wasteful expending a large amount of effort calculating the inverse matrix, particularly since the values of the remaining variables, x_1, x_2 and x_4 are not required.

In this section we describe an alternative method which finds the value of one variable at a time. This new method requires less effort if only a selection of the variables are required. It is known as Cramer's rule and makes use of matrix determinants. **Cramer's rule** for solving any $n \times n$ system, $\mathbf{Ax} = \mathbf{b}$, states that the ith variable, x_i, can be found from

$$x_i = \frac{\det(\mathbf{A}_i)}{\det(\mathbf{A})}$$

where $\mathbf{A}_i$ is the $n \times n$ matrix found by replacing the ith column of $\mathbf{A}$ by the right-hand side vector $\mathbf{b}$. To understand this, consider the simple 2×2 system

$$\begin{bmatrix} 7 & 2 \\ 4 & 5 \end{bmatrix} \begin{bmatrix} x_1 \\ x_2 \end{bmatrix} = \begin{bmatrix} -6 \\ 12 \end{bmatrix}$$

and suppose that we need to find the value of the second variable, x_2, say. According to Cramer's rule this is given by

$$x_2 = \frac{\det(\mathbf{A}_2)}{\det(\mathbf{A})}$$

where

$$A = \begin{bmatrix} 7 & 2 \\ 4 & 5 \end{bmatrix} \quad \text{and} \quad A_2 = \begin{bmatrix} 7 & -6 \\ 4 & 12 \end{bmatrix}$$

Notice that x_2 is given by the quotient of two determinants. The one on the bottom is that of the original coefficient matrix A. The one on the top is that of the matrix found from A by replacing the second column (since we are trying to find the second variable) by the right-hand side vector

$$\begin{bmatrix} -6 \\ 12 \end{bmatrix}$$

In this case the determinants are easily worked out to get

$$\det(A_2) = \begin{vmatrix} 7 & -6 \\ 4 & 12 \end{vmatrix} = 7(12) - (-6)(4) = 108$$

$$\det(A) = \begin{vmatrix} 7 & 2 \\ 4 & 5 \end{vmatrix} = 7(5) - 2(4) = 27$$

Hence

$$x_2 = \frac{108}{27} = 4$$

EXAMPLE

Solve the system of equations

$$\begin{bmatrix} 1 & 2 & 3 \\ -4 & 1 & 6 \\ 2 & 7 & 5 \end{bmatrix} \begin{bmatrix} x_1 \\ x_2 \\ x_3 \end{bmatrix} = \begin{bmatrix} 9 \\ -9 \\ 13 \end{bmatrix}$$

using Cramer's rule to find x_1.

Solution

Cramer's rule gives

$$x_1 = \frac{\det(A_1)}{\det(A)}$$

where A is the coefficient matrix

$$\begin{bmatrix} 1 & 2 & 3 \\ -4 & 1 & 6 \\ 2 & 7 & 5 \end{bmatrix}$$

and $\mathbf{A}_1$ is constructed by replacing the first column of $\mathbf{A}$ by the right-hand side vector

$$\begin{bmatrix} 9 \\ -9 \\ 13 \end{bmatrix}$$

which gives

$$\mathbf{A}_1 = \begin{bmatrix} 9 & 2 & 3 \\ -9 & 1 & 6 \\ 13 & 7 & 5 \end{bmatrix}$$

If we expand each of these determinants along the top row we get

$$\det(\mathbf{A}_1) = \begin{vmatrix} 9 & 2 & 3 \\ -9 & 1 & 6 \\ 13 & 7 & 5 \end{vmatrix}$$

$$= 9 \begin{vmatrix} 1 & 6 \\ 7 & 5 \end{vmatrix} - 2 \begin{vmatrix} -9 & 6 \\ 13 & 5 \end{vmatrix} + 3 \begin{vmatrix} -9 & 1 \\ 13 & 7 \end{vmatrix}$$

$$= 9(-37) - 2(-123) + 3(-76)$$

$$= -315$$

and

$$\det(\mathbf{A}) = \begin{vmatrix} 1 & 2 & 3 \\ -4 & 1 & 6 \\ 2 & 7 & 5 \end{vmatrix}$$

$$= 1 \begin{vmatrix} 1 & 6 \\ 7 & 5 \end{vmatrix} - 2 \begin{vmatrix} -4 & 6 \\ 2 & 5 \end{vmatrix} + 3 \begin{vmatrix} -4 & 1 \\ 2 & 7 \end{vmatrix}$$

$$= 1(-37) - 2(-32) + 3(-30)$$

$$= -63$$

Hence

$$x_1 = \frac{\det(\mathbf{A}_1)}{\det(\mathbf{A})} = \frac{-315}{-63} = 5$$

■

PROBLEM

1 (a)   Solve the system of equations

$$2x_1 + 4x_2 = 16$$

$$3x_1 - 5x_2 = -9$$

using Cramer's rule to find x_2.

(b) Solve the system of equations

$$4x_1 + x_2 + 3x_3 = 8$$

$$-2x_1 + 5x_2 + x_3 = 4$$

$$3x_1 + 2x_2 + 4x_3 = 9$$

using Cramer's rule to find x_3.

We now illustrate the use of Cramer's rule to analyse economic models. We begin by considering the three-sector macroeconomic model involving government activity. The incorporation of government expenditure and taxation into the model has already been considered in Section 5.3 and you might like to compare the working involved in the two approaches.

EXAMPLE

The equilibrium levels of income, Y, disposable income, Y_d and taxation, T, for a three-sector macroeconomic model satisfy the structural equations

$$Y = C + I^* + G^*$$

$$C = aY_d + b \qquad (0 < a < 1, \quad b > 0)$$

$$Y_d = Y - T$$

$$T = tY + T^* \qquad (0 < t < 1, \quad T^* > 0)$$

Show that this system can be written as $\mathbf{Ax} = \mathbf{b}$, where

$$\mathbf{A} = \begin{bmatrix} 1 & -1 & 0 & 0 \\ 0 & 1 & -a & 0 \\ -1 & 0 & 1 & 1 \\ -t & 0 & 0 & 1 \end{bmatrix} \quad \mathbf{x} = \begin{bmatrix} Y \\ C \\ Y_d \\ T \end{bmatrix} \quad \text{and} \quad \mathbf{b} = \begin{bmatrix} I^* + G^* \\ b \\ 0 \\ T^* \end{bmatrix}$$

Use Cramer's rule to solve this system for Y.

Solution

In this model the endogeneous variables are Y, C, Y_d and T so we begin by manipulating the equations so that these variables appear on the left-hand sides. Moreover, since the vector of 'unknowns', $\mathbf{x}$ is given to be

$$\begin{bmatrix} Y \\ C \\ Y_d \\ T \end{bmatrix}$$

we need to arrange the equations so that the variables appear in the order Y, C, Y_d, T. For example, in the case of the third equation

$$Y_d = Y - T$$

we first subtract Y and add T to both sides to get

$$Y_d - Y + T = 0$$

but then reorder the terms to obtain

$$-Y + Y_d + T = 0$$

Performing a similar process with the remaining equations gives

$$
\begin{aligned}
Y - C & & & = I^* + G^* \\
C - aY_d & & & = b \\
-Y & + Y_d + T & & = 0 \\
-tY & + T & & = T^*
\end{aligned}
$$

so that in matrix form they become

$$
\begin{bmatrix}
1 & -1 & 0 & 0 \\
0 & 1 & -a & 0 \\
-1 & 0 & 1 & 1 \\
-t & 0 & 0 & 1
\end{bmatrix}
\begin{bmatrix}
Y \\ C \\ Y_d \\ T
\end{bmatrix}
=
\begin{bmatrix}
I^* + G^* \\ b \\ 0 \\ T^*
\end{bmatrix}
$$

The variable Y is the first so Cramer's rule gives

$$Y = \frac{\det(\mathbf{A}_1)}{\det(\mathbf{A})}$$

where

$$
\mathbf{A}_1 =
\begin{bmatrix}
I^* + G^* & -1 & 0 & 0 \\
b & 1 & -a & 0 \\
0 & 0 & 1 & 1 \\
T^* & 0 & 0 & 1
\end{bmatrix}
$$

and

$$
\mathbf{A} =
\begin{bmatrix}
1 & -1 & 0 & 0 \\
0 & 1 & -a & 0 \\
-1 & 0 & 1 & 1 \\
-t & 0 & 0 & 1
\end{bmatrix}
$$

The calculations are fairly easy to perform, in spite of the fact that both matrices are 4×4, because they contain a high proportion of zeros. Expanding $\mathbf{A}_1$ along the first row gives

$$
\det(\mathbf{A}_1) = (I^* + G^*)
\begin{vmatrix}
1 & -a & 0 \\
0 & 1 & 1 \\
0 & 0 & 1
\end{vmatrix}
- (-1)
\begin{vmatrix}
b & -a & 0 \\
0 & 1 & 1 \\
T^* & 0 & 1
\end{vmatrix}
$$

along the first row the pattern is + − + −

Notice that there is no point in evaluating the last two cofactors in the first row since the corresponding elements are both zero.

For the first of these 3×3 determinants we choose to expand down the first column since this column only has one non-zero element. This gives

$$\begin{vmatrix} 1 & -a & 0 \\ 0 & 1 & 1 \\ 0 & 0 & 1 \end{vmatrix} = (1)\begin{vmatrix} 1 & 1 \\ 0 & 1 \end{vmatrix} = 1$$

It is immaterial which row or column we choose for the second 3×3 determinant since they all contain two non-zero elements. Working along the first row gives

$$\begin{vmatrix} b & -a & 0 \\ 0 & 1 & 1 \\ T^* & 0 & 1 \end{vmatrix} = b\begin{vmatrix} 1 & 1 \\ 0 & 1 \end{vmatrix} - (-a)\begin{vmatrix} 0 & 1 \\ T^* & 1 \end{vmatrix} = b - aT^*$$

Hence

$$\det(\mathbf{A}_1) = (I^* + G^*)(1) - (-1)(b - aT^*) = I^* + G^* + b - aT^*$$

A similar process can be applied to matrix **A**. Expanding along the top row gives

$$\det(\mathbf{A}) = (1)\begin{vmatrix} 1 & -a & 0 \\ 0 & 1 & 1 \\ 0 & 0 & 1 \end{vmatrix} - (-1)\begin{vmatrix} 0 & -a & 0 \\ -1 & 1 & 1 \\ -t & 0 & 1 \end{vmatrix}$$

The first of these 3×3 determinants has already been found to be 1 in our previous calculations. The second 3×3 determinant is new and if we expand this along the first row we get

$$\begin{vmatrix} 0 & -a & 0 \\ -1 & 1 & 1 \\ -t & 0 & 1 \end{vmatrix} = -(-a)\begin{vmatrix} -1 & 1 \\ -t & 1 \end{vmatrix} = a(-1 + t)$$

Hence

$$\det(\mathbf{A}) = (1)(1) - (-1)a(-1 + t) = 1 - a + at$$

Finally we use Cramer's rule to deduce that

$$Y = \frac{I^* + G^* + b - aT^*}{1 - a + at} \qquad \blacksquare$$

PROBLEM

2 Use Cramer's rule to solve the following system of equations for Y_d.

$$\begin{bmatrix} 1 & -1 & 0 & 0 \\ 0 & 1 & -a & 0 \\ -1 & 0 & 1 & 1 \\ -t & 0 & 0 & 1 \end{bmatrix}\begin{bmatrix} Y \\ C \\ Y_d \\ T \end{bmatrix} = \begin{bmatrix} I^* + G^* \\ b \\ 0 \\ T^* \end{bmatrix}$$

[Hint: the determinant of the coefficient matrix has already been evaluated in the previous worked example.]

We conclude this section by introducing foreign trade into our model. In all of our previous macroeconomic models we have implicitly assumed that the behaviour of different countries has no effect on the national income of each other. In reality this is clearly not the case and we now investigate how the economies of trading nations interact. To simplify the situation we shall ignore all government activity and suppose that there are just two countries, labelled 1 and 2, trading with each other, but not with any other country. We shall use an obvious subscript notation so that Y_1 denotes the national income of country 1, C_2 denotes the consumption of country 2 and so on. In the absence of government activity the equation defining equilibrium in country i is

$$Y_i = C_i + I_i + X_i - M_i$$

where I_i is the investment of country i, X_i is the exports of country i and M_i is the imports of country i. As usual, we shall assume that I_i is determined exogenously and takes a known value I_i^*.

Given that there are only two countries, which trade between themselves, the exports of one country must be the same as the imports of the other. In symbols we write

$$X_1 = M_2 \quad \text{and} \quad X_2 = M_1$$

We shall assume that imports are a fraction of national income so that

$$M_i = m_i Y_i$$

where the marginal propensity to import, m_i, satisfies $0 < m_i < 1$.

Once expressions for C_i and M_i are given we can derive a system of two simultaneous equations for the two unknowns, Y_1 and Y_2, which can be solved either by using Cramer's rule or by using matrix inverses.

EXAMPLE

The equations defining a model of two trading nations are given by

$$Y_1 = C_1 + I_1^* + X_1 - M_1; \qquad Y_2 = C_2 + I_2^* + X_2 - M_2$$

$$C_1 = 0.8Y_1 + 200; \qquad C_2 = 0.9Y_2 + 100$$

$$M_1 = 0.2Y_1; \qquad M_2 = 0.1Y_2$$

Express this system in matrix form and hence write Y_1 in terms of I_1^* and I_2^*.

Write down the multiplier for Y_1 due to changes in I_2^* and hence describe the effect on the national income of country 1 due to changes in the investment in country 2.

Solution

In this problem there are six equations for six endogenous variables, Y_1, C_1, M_1 and Y_2, C_2, M_2. However, rather than working with a 6×6 matrix, we perform some preliminary algebra to reduce it to only two equations in two unknowns. To do this we substitute the expressions for C_1 and M_1 into the first equation to get

$$Y_1 = 0.8Y_1 + 200 + I_1^* + X_1 - 0.2Y_1$$

Also, since $X_1 = M_2 = 0.1Y_2$, this becomes

$$Y_1 = 0.8Y_1 + 200 + I_1^* + 0.1Y_2 - 0.2Y_1$$

which rearranges as

$$0.4Y_1 - 0.1Y_2 = 200 + I_1^*$$

A similar procedure applied to the second set of equations for country 2 gives

$$-0.2Y_1 + 0.2Y_2 = 100 + I_2^*$$

In matrix form this pair of equations can be written as

$$\begin{bmatrix} 0.4 & -0.1 \\ -0.2 & 0.2 \end{bmatrix} \begin{bmatrix} Y_1 \\ Y_2 \end{bmatrix} = \begin{bmatrix} 200 + I_1^* \\ 100 + I_2^* \end{bmatrix}$$

Cramer's rule gives

$$Y_1 = \frac{\begin{vmatrix} 200 + I_1^* & -0.1 \\ 100 + I_2^* & 0.2 \end{vmatrix}}{\begin{vmatrix} 0.4 & -0.1 \\ -0.2 & 0.2 \end{vmatrix}} = \frac{50 + 0.2I_1^* + 0.1I_2^*}{0.06}$$

To find the multiplier for Y_1 due to changes in I_2^* we consider what happens to Y_1 when I_2^* changes by an amount ΔI_2^*. The new value of Y_1 is obtained by replacing I_2^* by $I_2^* + \Delta I_2^*$ to get

$$\frac{50 + 0.2I_1^* + 0.1(I_2^* + \Delta I_2^*)}{0.06}$$

so the corresponding change in Y_1 is

$$\Delta Y_1 = \frac{50 + 0.2I_1^* + 0.1(I_2^* + \Delta I_2^*)}{0.06} - \frac{50 + 0.2I_1^* + 0.1I_2^*}{0.06}$$

$$= \frac{0.1}{0.06}\Delta I_2^* = \frac{5}{3}\Delta I_2^*$$

We deduce that any increase in investment in country 2 leads to an increase in the national income in country 1. Moreover, because $\frac{5}{3} > 1$, the increase in national income is greater than the increase in investment.

■

PROBLEM

3   The equations defining a model of two trading nations are given by

$$Y_1 = C_1 + I_1^* + X_1 - M_1; \qquad Y_2 = C_2 + I_2^* + X_2 - M_2$$

$$C_1 = 0.7Y_1 + 50; \qquad C_2 = 0.8Y_2 + 100$$

$$I_1^* = 200; \qquad I_2^* = 300$$

$$M_1 = 0.3Y_1; \qquad M_2 = 0.1Y_2$$

Express this system in matrix form and hence find the values of Y_1 and Y_2. Calculate the balance of payments between these countries.

PRACTICE PROBLEMS

4 Use Cramer's rule to solve

(a) $\begin{bmatrix} 4 & -1 \\ -2 & 5 \end{bmatrix} \begin{bmatrix} x_1 \\ x_2 \end{bmatrix} = \begin{bmatrix} 13 \\ 7 \end{bmatrix}$

for x_1

(b) $\begin{bmatrix} 3 & 2 & -2 \\ 4 & 3 & 3 \\ 2 & -1 & 1 \end{bmatrix} \begin{bmatrix} x_1 \\ x_2 \\ x_3 \end{bmatrix} = \begin{bmatrix} -5 \\ 17 \\ -1 \end{bmatrix}$

for x_2

(c) $\begin{bmatrix} 1 & 0 & 2 & 3 \\ -1 & 5 & 4 & 1 \\ 0 & 7 & -3 & 6 \\ 2 & 4 & 5 & 1 \end{bmatrix} \begin{bmatrix} x_1 \\ x_2 \\ x_3 \\ x_4 \end{bmatrix} = \begin{bmatrix} -1 \\ 1 \\ -24 \\ 15 \end{bmatrix}$

for x_4

5 Consider the macroeconomic model defined by

national income: $Y = C + I + G^*$ $(G^* > 0)$

consumption: $C = aY + b$ $(0 < a < 1, \ b > 0)$

investment: $I = cr + d$ $(c < 0, \ d > 0)$

money supply: $M_S^* = k_1 Y + k_2 r$ $(k_1 > 0, \ k_2 < 0, \ M_S^* > 0)$

Show that this system can be written as $\mathbf{Ax} = \mathbf{b}$, where

$$\mathbf{A} = \begin{bmatrix} 1 & -1 & -1 & 0 \\ -a & 1 & 0 & 0 \\ 0 & 0 & 1 & -c \\ k_1 & 0 & 0 & k_2 \end{bmatrix} \quad \mathbf{x} = \begin{bmatrix} Y \\ C \\ I \\ r \end{bmatrix} \quad \mathbf{b} = \begin{bmatrix} G^* \\ b \\ d \\ M_S^* \end{bmatrix}$$

Use Cramer's rule to show that

$$r = \frac{M_S^*(1 - a) - k_1(b + d + G^*)}{k_2(1 - a) + ck_1}$$

Write down the government expenditure multiplier for r and deduce that the interest rate, r, increases as government expenditure, G^*, increases.

6 The equations defining a model of two trading nations are given by

$$Y_1 = C_1 + I_1^* + X_1 - M_1; \qquad Y_2 = C_2 + I_2^* + X_2 - M_2$$

$$C_1 = 0.6Y_1 + 50; \qquad\qquad C_2 = 0.8Y_2 + 80$$

$$M_1 = 0.2Y_1; \qquad\qquad\quad M_2 = 0.1Y_2$$

If $I_2^* = 70$, find the value of I_1^* if the balance of payments is zero.

[Hint: construct a system of three equations for the three unknowns, Y_1, Y_2 and I_1^*.]

7 The equations defining a general model of two trading countries are given by

$$Y_1 = C_1 + I_1^* + X_1 - M_1; \qquad Y_2 = C_2 + I_2^* + X_2 - M_2$$

$$C_1 = a_1Y_1 + b_1; \qquad\qquad C_2 = a_2Y_2 + b_2$$

$$M_1 = m_1Y_1; \qquad\qquad\quad M_2 = m_2Y_2$$

where $0 < a_i < 1$, $b_i > 0$ and $0 < m_i < 1$ (i = 1, 2).

Express this system in matrix form and use Cramer's rule to solve this system for Y_1. Write down the multiplier for Y_1 due to changes in I_2^* and hence give a general description of the effect on the national income of one country due to a change in investment in the other.

7.4 Input–output analysis

Objectives At the end of this section you should be able to:

● understand what is meant by a matrix of technical coefficients,

● calculate the final demand vector given the total output vector,

● calculate the total output vector given the final demand vector,

● calculate the multipliers in simple input–output models.

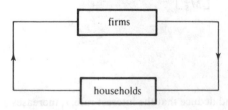

Figure 7.1

The simplest model of the macroeconomy assumes that there are only two sectors, households and firms. The flow of money between these sectors is illustrated in Figure 7.1.

The 'black box' labelled firms belies a considerable amount of economic activity. Firms exchange goods and services between themselves as well as providing them for external consumption by households. For example, the steel industry uses raw materials such as iron ore and coal to produce steel. This, in turn, is bought by mechanical engineering firms to produce machine tools. These tools are then used by other firms, including those in the steel industry. It is even possible for some businesses to use as input some of their own output. For example, in the agricultural sector, a farm might use arable land to produce grain, some of which is recycled as animal foodstuffs. Output destined for households is called **final** (or **external**) **demand**. Output which is used as input by another (or the same) firm is called **intermediate output**. The problem of identifying individual firms and goods, and of tracking down the flow of money between firms for these goods, is known as **input–output analysis**.

Suppose that there are just two industries, I1 and I2, and that $1 worth of output of I1 requires as input 10 cents worth of I1 and 30 cents worth of I2. The corresponding figures for I2 are 50 cents and 20 cents respectively. This information can be displayed in tabular form as shown in Table 7.3.

Table 7.3

		Output	
		I1	I2
Input	I1	0.1	0.5
	I2	0.3	0.2

The matrix obtained by stripping away the headings in Table 7.3 is

$$A = \begin{bmatrix} 0.1 & 0.5 \\ 0.3 & 0.2 \end{bmatrix}$$

and is called the **matrix of technical coefficients** (sometimes called the **technology matrix**). The columns of A give the inputs needed to produce $1 worth of output. In general, if there are n industries then the matrix of technical coefficients has order $n \times n$. Element a_{ij} gives the input needed from the ith industry to produce $1 worth of output for the jth industry.

We shall make the important assumption that the production functions for each industry in the model exhibit constant returns to scale. This means that the technical coefficients can be thought of as proportions which are independent of the level of output. For example, suppose that we wish to produce 500 monetary units of output of I1 instead of just one unit. The first column of A shows that the input requirements are

$0.1 \times 500 = 50$ units of I1

$0.3 \times 500 = 150$ units of I2

Similarly, if we produce 400 units of I2 then the second column of A shows that we use

$0.5 \times 400 = 200$ units of I1

$0.2 \times 400 = 80$ units of I2

In this situation, of the 500 units of I1 that are produced, 50 go back into I1 and 200 are used in I2. This means that there are 250 units left which are available for external demand. Similarly, of the 400 units of I2 that are produced, 230 are used as intermediate output leaving

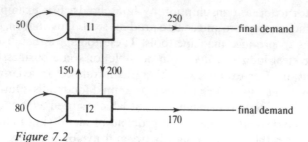

Figure 7.2

170 units to satisfy external demand. The flow of money for this simple input–output model is illustrated in Figure 7.2.

For the general case of n industries we would like to be able to use the matrix of technical coefficients to provide answers to the following questions.

Question 1 How much output is available for final demand given the total output level?

Question 2 How much total output is required to satisfy a given level of final demand?

Question 3 What changes need to be made to total output when final demand changes by a given amount?

It turns out that all three questions can be answered using one basic matrix equation which we now derive. We begin by returning to the simple two-industry model with matrix of technical coefficients

$$\mathbf{A} = \begin{bmatrix} 0.1 & 0.5 \\ 0.3 & 0.2 \end{bmatrix}$$

Let us denote the final demand for I1 and I2 by d_1 and d_2 respectively, and denote the total outputs by x_1 and x_2. Total output from I1 gets used up in three different ways. Firstly, some of the output from I1 gets used up as input to I1. The precise proportion is given by the element

$$a_{11} = 0.1$$

so I1 uses $0.1x_1$ units of its own output. Secondly, some of the output from I1 gets used as input to I2. The element

$$a_{12} = 0.5$$

gives the amount of I1 that is used to make 1 unit of I2. We make a total of x_2 units of I2 so we use up $0.5x_2$ units of I1 in this way. Finally, some of the output of I1 satisfies final demand which we denote by d_1. The total amount of I1 that is used is therefore

$$0.1x_1 + 0.5x_2 + d_1$$

If we assume that the total output from I1 is just sufficient to meet these requirements then

$$x_1 = 0.1x_1 + 0.5x_2 + d_1$$

Similarly, if I2 produces output to satisfy the input requirements of the two industries as well as final demand then

$$x_2 = 0.3x_1 + 0.2x_2 + d_2$$

In matrix notation these two equations can be written as

$$\begin{bmatrix} x_1 \\ x_2 \end{bmatrix} = \begin{bmatrix} 0.1 & 0.5 \\ 0.3 & 0.2 \end{bmatrix} \begin{bmatrix} x_1 \\ x_2 \end{bmatrix} + \begin{bmatrix} d_1 \\ d_2 \end{bmatrix}$$

that is

$$\mathbf{x} = \mathbf{Ax} + \mathbf{d}$$

where $\mathbf{x}$ is the total output vector

$$\begin{bmatrix} x_1 \\ x_2 \end{bmatrix}$$

and $\mathbf{d}$ is the final demand vector

$$\begin{bmatrix} d_1 \\ d_2 \end{bmatrix}$$

For the general case of n industries we write x_i and d_i for the total output and final demand for the ith industry. Of the x_i units of output of industry i that are produced,

$a_{i1}x_1$ is used as input for industry 1

$a_{i2}x_2$ is used as input for industry 2

$$\vdots$$

$a_{in}x_n$ is used as input for industry n

and

d_i is used for external demand

Hence

$$x_i = a_{i1}x_1 + a_{i2}x_2 + \ldots + a_{in}x_n + d_i$$

In matrix form, the totality of equations obtained by setting $i = 1, 2, \ldots, n$, in turn, can be written as

$$\begin{bmatrix} x_1 \\ x_2 \\ \vdots \\ x_n \end{bmatrix} = \begin{bmatrix} a_{11} & a_{12} & \cdots & a_{1n} \\ a_{21} & a_{22} & \cdots & a_{2n} \\ \vdots & \vdots & & \vdots \\ a_{n1} & a_{n2} & \cdots & a_{nn} \end{bmatrix} \begin{bmatrix} x_1 \\ x_2 \\ \vdots \\ x_n \end{bmatrix} + \begin{bmatrix} d_1 \\ d_2 \\ \vdots \\ d_n \end{bmatrix}$$

that is as

$$\mathbf{x} = \mathbf{Ax} + \mathbf{d}$$

where $\mathbf{A}$ is the $n \times n$ matrix of technical coefficients, $\mathbf{x}$ is the $n \times 1$ total output vector and $\mathbf{d}$ is the $n \times 1$ final demand vector.

The three questions posed can now be answered.

Question 1 How much output is available for final demand given the total output level?

Answer 1 In this case the vector **x** is assumed to be known and we need to calculate the unknown vector **d**. The matrix equation

$$\mathbf{x} = \mathbf{Ax} + \mathbf{d}$$

immediately gives

$$\mathbf{d} = \mathbf{x} - \mathbf{Ax}$$

and the right-hand side is easily evaluated to get **d**.

EXAMPLE

The output levels of machinery, electricity and oil of a small country are 3000, 5000 and 2000 respectively.
Each unit of machinery requires inputs of 0.3 units of electricity and 0.3 units of oil.
Each unit of electricity requires inputs of 0.1 units of machinery and 0.2 units of oil.
Each unit of oil requires inputs of 0.2 units of machinery and 0.1 units of electricity.
Determine the machinery, electricity and oil available for export.

Solution

Let us denote the total output for machinery, electricity and oil by x_1, x_2 and x_3 respectively, so that

$$x_1 = 3000, \ x_2 = 5000, \ x_3 = 2000$$

The second sentence of the problem statement provides details of the input requirements for machinery. To produce 1 unit of machinery we use 0 units of machinery, 0.3 units of electricity and 0.3 units of oil. The first column of the matrix of technical coefficients is therefore

$$\begin{bmatrix} 0 \\ 0.3 \\ 0.3 \end{bmatrix}$$

Likewise, the third and fourth sentences give the input requirements for electricity and oil so the complete matrix is

$$\mathbf{A} = \begin{bmatrix} 0 & 0.1 & 0.2 \\ 0.3 & 0 & 0.1 \\ 0.3 & 0.2 & 0 \end{bmatrix}$$

From the equation

$$\mathbf{d} = \mathbf{x} - \mathbf{Ax}$$

we see that the final demand vector is

$$\begin{bmatrix} d_1 \\ d_2 \\ d_3 \end{bmatrix} = \begin{bmatrix} 3000 \\ 5000 \\ 2000 \end{bmatrix} - \begin{bmatrix} 0 & 0.1 & 0.2 \\ 0.3 & 0 & 0.1 \\ 0.3 & 0.2 & 0 \end{bmatrix} \begin{bmatrix} 3000 \\ 5000 \\ 2000 \end{bmatrix}$$

$$= \begin{bmatrix} 3000 \\ 5000 \\ 2000 \end{bmatrix} - \begin{bmatrix} 900 \\ 1100 \\ 1900 \end{bmatrix}$$

$$= \begin{bmatrix} 2100 \\ 3900 \\ 100 \end{bmatrix}$$

The country therefore has 2100, 3900 and 100 units of machinery, electricity and oil available for export. ∎

PROBLEM

1 Determine the final demand vector for three firms given the matrix of technical coefficients

$$\mathbf{A} = \begin{bmatrix} 0.2 & 0.4 & 0.2 \\ 0.1 & 0.2 & 0.1 \\ 0.1 & 0.1 & 0 \end{bmatrix}$$

and the total output vector

$$\mathbf{x} = \begin{bmatrix} 1000 \\ 300 \\ 700 \end{bmatrix}$$

Question 2 How much total output is required to satisfy a given level of final demand?

Answer 2 In this case the vector **d** is assumed to be known and we need to calculate the unknown vector **x**. The matrix equation

$$\mathbf{x} = \mathbf{Ax} + \mathbf{d}$$

rearranges to give

$$\mathbf{x} - \mathbf{Ax} = \mathbf{d}$$

or equivalently as

$$(\mathbf{I} - \mathbf{A})\mathbf{x} = \mathbf{d}$$

because

$$(\mathbf{I} - \mathbf{A})\mathbf{x} = \mathbf{Ix} - \mathbf{Ax} = \mathbf{x} - \mathbf{Ax}$$

This represents a system of linear equations in which the coefficient matrix is $\mathbf{I} - \mathbf{A}$ and the right-hand side vector is **d**. From Section 8.2 we know that we can solve this by multiplying the inverse of the coefficient matrix by the right-hand side vector to get

$$\mathbf{x} = (\mathbf{I} - \mathbf{A})^{-1}\mathbf{d}$$

In the context of input–output analysis the matrix $(\mathbf{I} - \mathbf{A})^{-1}$ is called the **Leontief inverse**.

EXAMPLE

Given the matrix of technical coefficients

$$A = \begin{bmatrix} 0.3 & 0.1 & 0.1 \\ 0.2 & 0.2 & 0.2 \\ 0.4 & 0.2 & 0.3 \end{bmatrix}$$

for three industries, I1, I2 and I3, determine the total outputs required to satisfy final demands of 49, 106 and 17 respectively.

Solution

To solve this problem we need to find the inverse of $I - A$ and then to multiply by the final demand vector. The matrix $I - A$ is

$$\begin{bmatrix} 1 & 0 & 0 \\ 0 & 1 & 0 \\ 0 & 0 & 1 \end{bmatrix} - \begin{bmatrix} 0.3 & 0.1 & 0.1 \\ 0.2 & 0.2 & 0.2 \\ 0.4 & 0.2 & 0.3 \end{bmatrix} = \begin{bmatrix} 0.7 & -0.1 & -0.1 \\ -0.2 & 0.8 & -0.2 \\ -0.4 & -0.2 & 0.7 \end{bmatrix}$$

The inverse of this matrix is then found by calculating its cofactors. If we call this matrix **B** then the cofactors, B_{ij}, corresponding to elements b_{ij} are given by

$$B_{11} = 0.52, \quad B_{12} = 0.22, \quad B_{13} = 0.36$$

$$B_{21} = 0.09, \quad B_{22} = 0.45, \quad B_{23} = 0.18$$

$$B_{31} = 0.10, \quad B_{32} = 0.16, \quad B_{33} = 0.54$$

By expanding along the first row we see that

$$|B| = 0.7(0.52) + (-0.1)(0.22) + (-0.1)(0.36) = 0.306$$

Hence

$$B^{-1} = (I - A)^{-1} = \frac{1}{0.306} \begin{bmatrix} 0.52 & 0.09 & 0.10 \\ 0.22 & 0.45 & 0.16 \\ 0.36 & 0.18 & 0.54 \end{bmatrix}$$

We are given that

$$d = \begin{bmatrix} 49 \\ 106 \\ 17 \end{bmatrix}$$

so the equation

$$x = (I - A)^{-1}d$$

gives

$$\begin{bmatrix} x_1 \\ x_2 \\ x_3 \end{bmatrix} = \frac{1}{0.306} \begin{bmatrix} 0.52 & 0.09 & 0.10 \\ 0.22 & 0.45 & 0.16 \\ 0.36 & 0.18 & 0.54 \end{bmatrix} \begin{bmatrix} 49 \\ 106 \\ 17 \end{bmatrix} = \begin{bmatrix} 120 \\ 200 \\ 150 \end{bmatrix}$$

∎

PROBLEM

2   Each unit of engineering output requires as input 0.2 units of engineering and 0.4 units of transport.
Each unit of transport output requires as input 0.2 units of engineering and 0.1 units of transport.
Determine the level of total output needed to satisfy a final demand of 760 units of engineering and 420 units of transport.

Question 3   What changes need to be made to total output when final demand changes by a given amount?

Answer 3   In this case we assume that the current total output vector, **x**, is chosen to satisfy some existing final demand vector, **d**, so that

$$\mathbf{x} = \mathbf{Ax} + \mathbf{d}$$

or equivalently

$$\mathbf{x} = (\mathbf{I} - \mathbf{A})^{-1}\mathbf{d} \qquad (1)$$

Suppose that the final demand vector changes by an amount $\Delta\mathbf{d}$ so that the new final demand vector is $\mathbf{d} + \Delta\mathbf{d}$. In order to satisfy the new requirements the total output vector, $\mathbf{x} + \Delta\mathbf{x}$, is then given by

$$\mathbf{x} + \Delta\mathbf{x} = (\mathbf{I} - \mathbf{A})^{-1}(\mathbf{d} + \Delta\mathbf{d})$$

$$= (\mathbf{I} - \mathbf{A})^{-1}\mathbf{d} + (\mathbf{I} - \mathbf{A})^{-1}\,\Delta\mathbf{d} \qquad (2)$$

where we have used the distributive law to multiply out the brackets. However, from equation (1) we know that

$$(\mathbf{I} - \mathbf{A})^{-1}\mathbf{d} = \mathbf{x}$$

so equation (2) becomes

$$\mathbf{x} + \Delta\mathbf{x} = \mathbf{x} + (\mathbf{I} - \mathbf{A})^{-1}\,\Delta\mathbf{d}$$

and if **x** is subtracted from both sides then

$$\Delta\mathbf{x} = (\mathbf{I} - \mathbf{A})^{-1}\,\Delta\mathbf{d}$$

Notice that this equation does not have **d** or **x** in it. This shows that the change in output, $\Delta\mathbf{x}$, does not depend on the existing final demand or existing total output. It only depends on the change, $\Delta\mathbf{d}$. It is also interesting to observe that the mathematics needed to solve this is the same as that for Question 2. Both require the calculation of the Leontief inverse followed by a simple matrix multiplication.

EXAMPLE

Consider the following inter-industrial flow table for two industries, I1 and I2.

| | | Output | | Final |
		I1	I2	demand
Input	I1	200	300	500
	I2	100	100	300

Assuming that the total output is just sufficient to meet the input and final demand requirements write down

(a) the total output vector, and
(b) the matrix of technical coefficients.

Hence calculate the new total output vector needed when the final demand for I1 rises by 100 units.

Solution

(a) To calculate the current total outputs for I1 and I2 all we have to do is to add together the numbers along each row of the table. The first row shows that I1 uses 200 units of I1 as input, I2 uses 300 units of I1 as input and that 500 units of I1 are used in final demand. The total number of units of I1 is then

$$200 + 300 + 500 = 1000$$

Assuming that the total output of I1 exactly matches these requirements we can deduce that

$$x_1 = 1000$$

Similarly, from the second row of the table,

$$x_2 = 100 + 100 + 300 = 500$$

Hence the total output vector is

$$\mathbf{x} = \begin{bmatrix} 1000 \\ 500 \end{bmatrix}$$

(b) The first column of the matrix of technical coefficients represents the inputs needed to produce 1 unit of I1. The first column of the inter-industrial flow table gives the inputs needed to produce the current total output of I1 which we found in part (a) to be 1000. In all input–output models we assume that production is subject to constant returns to scale, so we divide the first column of the inter-industrial flow table by 1000 to find the inputs needed to produce just 1 unit of output. In part (a) the total output for I2 was found to be 500 so the second column of the matrix of technical coefficients is calculated by dividing the second column of the inter-industrial flow table by 500. Hence

$$\mathbf{A} = \begin{bmatrix} \dfrac{200}{1000} & \dfrac{300}{500} \\ \dfrac{100}{1000} & \dfrac{100}{500} \end{bmatrix}$$

$$= \begin{bmatrix} 0.2 & 0.6 \\ 0.1 & 0.2 \end{bmatrix}$$

If the demand for I1 rises by 100 units and the demand for I2 remains constant the vector giving the change in final demand is

$$\Delta \mathbf{d} = \begin{bmatrix} 100 \\ 0 \end{bmatrix}$$

To determine the corresponding change in output we use the equation

$$\Delta \mathbf{x} = (\mathbf{I} - \mathbf{A})^{-1} \, \Delta \mathbf{d}$$

Subtracting **A** from the identity matrix gives

$$\mathbf{I} - \mathbf{A} = \begin{bmatrix} 1 & 0 \\ 0 & 1 \end{bmatrix} - \begin{bmatrix} 0.2 & 0.6 \\ 0.1 & 0.2 \end{bmatrix} = \begin{bmatrix} 0.8 & -0.6 \\ -0.1 & 0.8 \end{bmatrix}$$

which has determinant

$$|\mathbf{I} - \mathbf{A}| = (0.8)(0.8) - (-0.6)(-0.1) = 0.58$$

The inverse of $\mathbf{I} - \mathbf{A}$ is then

$$(\mathbf{I} - \mathbf{A})^{-1} = \frac{1}{0.58} \begin{bmatrix} 0.8 & 0.6 \\ 0.1 & 0.8 \end{bmatrix}$$

so

$$\Delta \mathbf{x} = \frac{1}{0.58} \begin{bmatrix} 0.8 & 0.6 \\ 0.1 & 0.8 \end{bmatrix} \begin{bmatrix} 100 \\ 0 \end{bmatrix} = \begin{bmatrix} 138 \\ 17 \end{bmatrix}$$

to the nearest unit. There is an increase in total output of I2 despite the fact that the final demand for I2 remains unchanged. This is to be expected because in order to meet the increase in final demand for I1 it is necessary to raise output of I1 which in turn requires more inputs of both I1 and I2. Any change to just one industry has a knock-on effect throughout all of the industries in the model.

From part (a) the current total output vector is

$$\mathbf{x} = \begin{bmatrix} 1000 \\ 500 \end{bmatrix}$$

so the new total output vector is

$$\mathbf{x} + \Delta \mathbf{x} = \begin{bmatrix} 1000 \\ 500 \end{bmatrix} + \begin{bmatrix} 138 \\ 17 \end{bmatrix} = \begin{bmatrix} 1138 \\ 517 \end{bmatrix}$$

∎

PROBLEMS

3   Write down the 4 × 4 matrix of technical coefficients using the information provided in the following inter-industrial flow table. You may assume that the total outputs are just sufficient to satisfy the input requirements and final demands.

		Output				Final
		I1	*I2*	*I3*	*I4*	demand
Input	*I1*	0	300	100	100	500
	I2	100	0	200	100	100
	I3	200	100	0	400	1300
	I4	300	0	100	0	600

4 Given the matrix of technical coefficients

$$\mathbf{A} = \begin{array}{c} \text{I1} \\ \text{I2} \\ \text{I3} \end{array} \begin{array}{ccc} \text{I1} & \text{I2} & \text{I3} \\ \begin{bmatrix} 0.1 & 0.2 & 0.2 \\ 0.1 & 0.1 & 0.1 \\ 0.1 & 0.3 & 0.1 \end{bmatrix} \end{array}$$

determine the changes in total output for the three industries when the final demand for I1 rises by 1000 units and the final demand for I3 falls by 800 units simultaneously.

We conclude this section with a postscript highlighting again the connection between the multiplier concept and the matrix inverse. Suppose that we have a three-industry model and that the Leontief inverse, $(\mathbf{I} - \mathbf{A})^{-1}$, is given by

$$\begin{bmatrix} b_{11} & b_{12} & b_{13} \\ b_{21} & b_{22} & b_{23} \\ b_{31} & b_{32} & b_{33} \end{bmatrix}$$

The equation

$$\mathbf{x} = (\mathbf{I} - \mathbf{A})^{-1}\mathbf{d}$$

is then

$$\begin{bmatrix} x_1 \\ x_2 \\ x_3 \end{bmatrix} = \begin{bmatrix} b_{11} & b_{12} & b_{13} \\ b_{21} & b_{22} & b_{23} \\ b_{31} & b_{32} & b_{33} \end{bmatrix} \begin{bmatrix} d_1 \\ d_2 \\ d_3 \end{bmatrix}$$

so that

$$x_1 = b_{11}d_1 + b_{12}d_2 + b_{13}d_3$$
$$x_2 = b_{21}d_1 + b_{22}d_2 + b_{23}d_3$$
$$x_3 = b_{31}d_1 + b_{32}d_2 + b_{33}d_3$$

The first equation shows that x_1 is a function of the three variables d_1, d_2 and d_3. Consequently, we can write down three partial derivatives,

$$\frac{\partial x_1}{\partial d_1} = b_{11}, \quad \frac{\partial x_1}{\partial d_2} = b_{12}, \quad \frac{\partial x_1}{\partial d_3} = b_{13}$$

In the same way the second and third equations give

$$\frac{\partial x_2}{\partial d_1} = b_{21}, \quad \frac{\partial x_2}{\partial d_2} = b_{22}, \quad \frac{\partial x_2}{\partial d_3} = b_{23}$$

$$\frac{\partial x_3}{\partial d_1} = b_{31}, \quad \frac{\partial x_3}{\partial d_2} = b_{32}, \quad \frac{\partial x_3}{\partial d_3} = b_{33}$$

Recall from Chapter 5 that partial derivatives determine the multipliers in economic models. These nine partial derivatives show that if we regard the final demands as exogenous variables and the total outputs as endogenous variables then the multipliers are the elements in the matrix $(\mathbf{I} - \mathbf{A})^{-1}$. More precisely, the multiplier of the variable x_i due to changes in d_j is the element b_{ij} which lies in the ith row and jth column of $(\mathbf{I} - \mathbf{A})^{-1}$. This result can also be seen more directly from the equation

$$\Delta \mathbf{x} = (\mathbf{I} - \mathbf{A})^{-1} \, \Delta \mathbf{d}$$

If we put $\Delta \mathbf{x} = [\Delta x_1 \ \Delta x_2 \ \Delta x_3]^{\mathrm{T}}$ and $\Delta \mathbf{d} = [\Delta d_1 \ \Delta d_2 \ \Delta d_3]^{\mathrm{T}}$ then this matrix equation leads to

$$\Delta x_1 = b_{11} \, \Delta d_1 + b_{12} \, \Delta d_2 + b_{13} \, \Delta d_3$$

$$\Delta x_2 = b_{21} \, \Delta d_1 + b_{22} \, \Delta d_2 + b_{23} \, \Delta d_3$$

$$\Delta x_3 = b_{31} \, \Delta d_1 + b_{32} \, \Delta d_2 + b_{33} \, \Delta d_3$$

We see from the ith equation that the contribution to the change Δx_i due to the change Δd_j is $b_{ij} \, \Delta d_j$. In other words, if d_j changes by Δd_j and all other final demands are fixed, then we can calculate the corresponding change in x_i by multiplying Δd_j by b_{ij}.

PRACTICE PROBLEMS

5 Calculate the available final demand for five firms if the matrix of technical coefficients is

	F1	F2	F3	F4	F5
F1	0	0.1	0.1	0	0.2
F2	0.1	0	0.2	0	0.1
F3	0	0	0	0.3	0.1
F4	0.2	0.1	0.1	0	0.1
F5	0	0.3	0	0.1	0

and the total output vector is

$$[1000 \quad 1500 \quad 2000 \quad 5000 \quad 1000]^{\mathrm{T}}$$

6 Each unit of water output requires inputs of 0.1 units of steel and 0.2 units of electricity. Each unit of steel output requires inputs of 0.1 units of water and 0.2 units of electricity. Each unit of electricity output requires inputs of 0.2 units of water and 0.1 units of steel.

(1) Determine the level of total output needed to satisfy a final demand of 750 units of water, 300 units of steel and 700 units of electricity.

(2) Write down the multiplier for water output due to changes in final demand for electricity. Hence calculate the change in water output due to a 100 unit increase in final demand for electricity.

7 Consider the following inter-industrial flow table for two industries I1 and I2.

		Output		Final
		I1	*I2*	*demand*
Input	*I1*	100	100	300
	I2	200	500	300

Assuming that the total output is just sufficient to meet the input and final demand requirements find the

(a) current total output vector, $\mathbf{x}$,
(b) matrix of technical coefficients, $\mathbf{A}$,
(c) matrix of multipliers, $(\mathbf{I} - \mathbf{A})^{-1}$,
(d) future total output vector, $\mathbf{x} + \Delta\mathbf{x}$, if final demand for I1 rises by 150 units and final demand for I2 falls by 50 units simultaneously.

8 *Linear Programming*

Several methods were described in Chapter 5 for optimizing functions of two variables subject to constraints. In economics not all relationships between variables are represented by equations and we now consider the case when the constraints are given by inequalities. Provided the function to be optimized is linear and the inequalities are all linear, the problem is said to be one of linear programming. For simplicity we concentrate on problems involving just two unknowns and describe a graphical method of solution.

There are two sections which should be read in the order that they appear. Section 8.1 describes the basic mathematical techniques and considers special cases when problems either have no solution or infinitely many solutions. Section 8.2 shows how an economic problem, initially given in words, can be expressed as a linear programming problem and hence solved.

The material in this chapter can be read at any stage since it only requires an understanding of how to sketch a straight line on graph paper.

8.1 Graphical solution of linear programming problems

Objectives At the end of this section you should be able to:

- identify the region defined by a linear inequality,

- sketch the feasible region defined by simultaneous linear inequalities,

- solve linear programming problems graphically,

- appreciate that a linear programming problem may have infinitely many solutions,

- appreciate that a linear programming problem may have no finite solution.

In this and the following section we show you how to set up and solve linear programming problems. This process falls naturally into two separate phases. The first phase concerns problem formulation; a problem, initially given in words, is expressed in mathematical symbols. The second phase involves the actual solution of such a problem. Experience indicates that students usually find the first phase to the more difficult. For this reason, we postpone consideration of problem formulation until Section 8.2 and begin by investigating techniques for their mathematical solution. You may, however, prefer to glance at one or two of the examples given in Section 8.2 now to get a feel for the type of problem which can be solved using these techniques.

Before you can consider linear programming it is essential that you know how to sketch linear inequalities. In Section 1.1 we discovered that a linear equation of the form

$$dx + ey = f$$

can be represented by a straight line on graph paper. We can give a similar graphical interpretation for linear inequalities involving two variables, when the equals sign is replaced by one of

$<$ (less than)

$\leqslant$ (less than or equal to)

$>$ (greater than)

$\geqslant$ (greater than or equal to)

To motivate this consider the simple inequality

$$y \geqslant x$$

We would like to identify those points with coordinates (x, y) for which this inequality is true. Clearly this has something to do with the straight line

$$y = x$$

sketched in Figure 8.1.

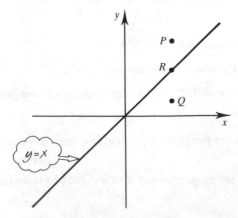

Figure 8.1

If a point P lies above the line then the y coordinate is greater than the x coordinate so that

$$y > x$$

Similarly, if a point Q lies below the line then the y coordinate is less than the x coordinate so that

$$y < x$$

Of course, the coordinates of a point R which actually lies on the line satisfy

$$y = x$$

Hence we see that the inequality

$$y \geqslant x$$

holds for any point which lies on or above the line $y = x$.

It is useful to be able to indicate this region pictorially. We do this by shading one half of the coordinate plane. There are actually two schools of thought here. Some people like to shade the region containing the points for which the inequality is true. Others prefer to shade the region for which it is false. In this book we adopt the latter approach and always shade the region that we are *not* interested in, as shown in Figure 8.2. This may seem a strange choice but the reason for making it will soon become apparent.

In general, to sketch an inequality of the form

$$dx + ey < f$$

$$dx + ey \leqslant f$$

$$dx + ey > f$$

$$dx + ey \geqslant f$$

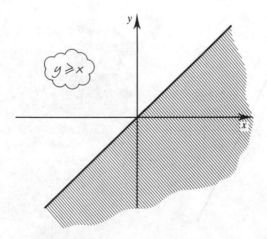

Figure 8.2

we first sketch the corresponding line

$$dx + ey = f$$

and then decide which side of the line to deal with. An easy way of doing this is to pick a 'test point', (x, y). It does not matter what point is chosen provided it does not actually lie on the line itself. The numbers x and y are then substituted into the original inequality. If the inequality is satisfied then the side containing the test point is the region of interest. If not, then we go for the region on the other side of the line.

EXAMPLE

Sketch the region

$$2x + y < 4$$

Solution

We first sketch the line

$$2x + y = 4$$

When $x = 0$ we get

$$y = 4$$

When $y = 0$ we get

$$2x = 4$$

and so $x = 4/2 = 2$.

The line passes through $(0, 4)$ and $(2, 0)$ and is shown in Figure 8.3. For a test point let us take $(3, 2)$, which lies above the line. Substituting $x = 3$ and $y = 2$ into the expression $2x + y$ gives

$$2(3) + 2 = 8$$

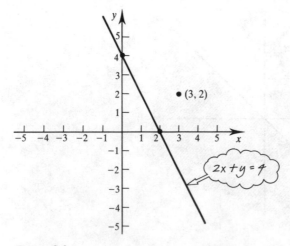

Figure 8.3

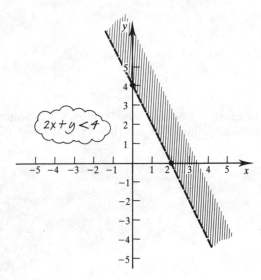

Figure 8.4

This is *not* less than 4 so the test point does not satisfy the inequality. It follows that the region of interest lies below the line. This is illustrated in Figure 8.4. In this example the symbol $<$ is used rather than $\leqslant$. Hence the points on the line itself are not included in the region of interest. We have chosen to indicate this by using a broken line for the boundary.

∎

PROBLEM

1   Sketch the straight line

$$-x + 3y = 6$$

on graph paper. By considering the test point $(1, 4)$ indicate the region

$$-x + 3y > 6$$

We now consider the region defined by simultaneous linear inequalities. This is known as a **feasible region**. It consists of those points (x, y) which satisfy several inequalities at the same time. We find it by sketching the regions defined by each inequality in turn. The feasible region is then the unshaded part of the plane corresponding to the intersection of all of the individual regions.

EXAMPLE

Sketch the feasible region

$$x + 2y \leqslant 12$$

$$-x + y \leqslant 3$$
$$x \geqslant 0$$
$$y \geqslant 0$$

Solution

In this problem the easiest inequalities to handle are the last two. These merely indicate that x and y are non-negative and so we need only consider points in the top right-hand quadrant of the plane as shown in Figure 8.5.

For the inequality

$$x + 2y \leqslant 12$$

we need to sketch the line

$$x + 2y = 12$$

When $x = 0$ we get

$$2y = 12$$

and so $y = 12/2 = 6$.

When $y = 0$ we get

$$x = 12$$

The line passes through $(0, 6)$ and $(12, 0)$.

For a test point let us take $(0, 0)$ since such a choice minimizes the amount of arithmetic that we have to do. Substituting $x = 0$ and $y = 0$ into the inequality gives

$$0 + 2(0) \leqslant 12$$

which is obviously true. Now the region containing the origin lies below the line so we shade the region which lies above it. This is indicated in Figure 8.6.

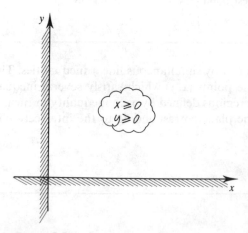

Figure 8.5

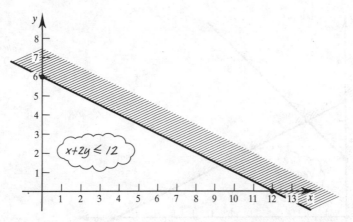

Figure 8.6

For the inequality

$$-x + y \leqslant 3$$

we need to sketch the line

$$-x + y = 3$$

When $x = 0$ we get

$$y = 3$$

When $y = 0$ we get

$$-x = 3$$

and so $x = 3/(-1) = -3$.

The line passes through $(0, 3)$ and $(-3, 0)$. Unfortunately the second point does not lie on the diagram as we have drawn it. At this stage we can either re-draw the x-axis to include -3 or we can try finding another point on the line which does fit on the graph. For example, putting $x = 5$ gives

$$-5 + y = 3$$

so $y = 3 + 5 = 8$. Hence the line passes through $(5, 8)$ which can now be plotted along with $(0, 3)$ to sketch the line. At the test point $(0, 0)$ the inequality reads

$$-0 + 0 \leqslant 3$$

which is obviously true. We are therefore interested in the region below the line since this contains the origin. As usual we indicate this by shading the region on the other side. The complete picture is shown in Figure 8.7.

Points (x, y) which satisfy all four inequalities must lie in the unshaded 'hole' in the middle. Incidentally, this explains why we did not adopt the convention of shading the region of interest. Had we done so, our task would have been to identify the most heavily shaded part of the diagram, which is not so easy.

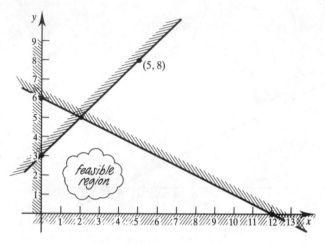

Figure 8.7

PROBLEM

2 Sketch the feasible region

$$x + 2y \leqslant 10$$
$$3x + y \leqslant 10$$
$$x \geqslant 0$$
$$y \geqslant 0$$

We are now in a position to explain exactly what we mean by a linear programming problem and how such a problem can be solved graphically. We actually intend to describe two slightly different methods of solution. One of these is fairly sophisticated and difficult to use while the other is more straightforward. The justification for bothering with the 'harder' method is that it provides the motivation for the 'easier' method. It also helps us to handle one or two trickier problems that sometimes arise. We shall introduce both methods by concentrating on a specific example:

Minimize $-2x + y$

subject to the constraints

$$x + 2y \leqslant 12$$
$$-x + y \leqslant 3$$
$$x \geqslant 0$$
$$y \geqslant 0$$

In general, there are three ingredients making up a linear programming problem. Firstly, there are several unknowns to be determined. We concentrate on the simplest case of two unknowns, x and y. (Problems with more than two unknowns are usually solved using computer packages based on the simplex algorithm and are not considered in this book.) Secondly, there is a mathematical expression of the form

$$ax + by$$

which we want to either maximize or minimize. Such an expression is called an **objective function**. In the example, $a = -2$, $b = 1$ and the problem is one of minimization. Finally, the unknowns x and y are subject to a collection of linear inequalities. Quite often (but not always) two of the inequalities are $x \geqslant 0$ and $y \geqslant 0$. These are referred to as **non-negativity constraints**. In this example there are a total of four constraints including the non-negativity constraints.

Geometrically, points (x, y) which satisfy simultaneous linear inequalities define a feasible region in the coordinate plane. In fact, for this particular problem, the feasible region has already been sketched in Figure 8.7.

The problem now is to try to identify that point inside the feasible region which minimizes the value of the objective function. One naïve way of doing this might be to use trial-and-error; that is, we could evaluate the objective function at every point within the region and choose the point which produces the smallest value. For instance, $(1, 1)$ lies in the region and when the values $x = 1$ and $y = 1$ are substituted into

$$-2x + y$$

we get

$$-2(1) + 1 = -1$$

Similarly we might try $(3.4, 2.1)$, which produces

$$-2(3.4) + 2.1 = -4.7$$

which is an improvement since $-4.7 < -1$. Here are a few more points for you to try.

PROBLEM

3 Which of the following points lie inside the feasible region shown in Figure 8.7?

$$(5, 3), \quad (-1, 5), \quad (2, 4), \quad (0, 0), \quad (14, 2), \quad (11.2, 0.2), \quad (8.6, 2.7), \quad (10.8, 9.3)$$

If the point does lie in the region calculate the corresponding value of the objective function,

$$-2x + y$$

The drawback of this approach is that there are infinitely many points inside the region, so it is going to take a very long time before we can be certain of the solution! Incidentally, can you guess, on the basis of your results obtained in Problem 3, what the answer is in this case?

A more systematic approach is to superimpose, on top of the feasible region, the family of straight lines,

$$-2x + y = c$$

for various values of the constant c. Looking back at the objective function you will notice that the number c is precisely the thing that we want to minimize. That such an equation

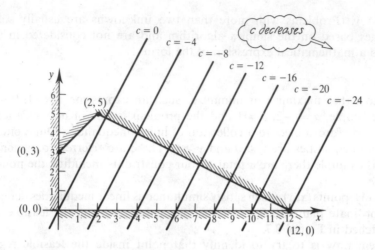

Figure 8.8

represents a straight line should come as no surprise to you by now. Indeed, we know from the rearrangement

$$y = 2x + c$$

that the line has a slope of 2 with a y-intercept of c. Consequently, all of these lines are parallel to each other, their precise location being determined from the number c.

Now when $y = 0$ the equation reads

$$0 = 2x + c$$

and so has solution $x = -c/2$. Hence the line passes through the point $(-c/2, 0)$. A selection of lines is sketched in Figure 8.8 for values of c in the range 0 to -24. These have been sketched using the information that they pass through $(-c/2, 0)$ and have a slope of 2. Note that as c decreases from 0 to -24 the lines sweep across the feasible region from left to right. Also, once c goes below -24 the lines no longer intersect this region. The minimum value of c (which, you may remember, is just the value of the objective function) is therefore -24. Moreover, when $c = -24$, the line

$$-2x + y = c$$

intersects the feasible region in exactly one point, namely $(12, 0)$. This then must be the solution of our problem. The point $(12, 0)$ lies in the feasible region as required and because it also lies on the line

$$-2x + y = -24$$

we know that the corresponding value of the objective function is -24, which is the minimum value. Other points in the feasible region also lie on lines

$$-2x + y = c$$

but with larger values of c.

PROBLEM

4 Consider the linear programming problem

Maximize $-x + y$

subject to the constraints

$$3x + 4y \leqslant 12$$

$$x \geqslant 0$$

$$y \geqslant 0$$

(1) Sketch the feasible region.

(2) Sketch, on the same diagram, the five lines

$$y = x + c$$

for $c = -4, -2, 0, 1$ and 3.

[Hint: lines of the form $y = x + c$ have a slope of 1 and pass through the points $(0, c)$ and $(-c, 0)$.]

(3) Use your answers to part (2) to solve the given linear programming problem.

In the previous example, and in Problem 4, the optimal value of the objective function is attained at one of the corners of the feasible region. This is not simply a coincidence. It can be shown that the solution of any linear programming problem always occurs at one of the corners. Consequently, the trial-and-error approach suggested earlier is not so naïve after all. The only possible candidates for the answer are the corners and so only a finite number of points need ever be examined. This method may be summarized:

Step 1 Sketch the feasible region.

Step 2 Identify the corners of the feasible region and find their coordinates.

Step 3 Evaluate the objective function at the corners and choose the one which has the maximum or minimum value.

Returning to the previous example we work as follows:

Step 1 The feasible region has already been sketched in Figure 8.7.

Step 2 There are four corners with coordinates

$$(0, 0), (0, 3), (2, 5) \text{ and } (12, 0)$$

Step 3

Corner	Objective function	
$(0, 0)$	$-2(0) + 0 =$	0
$(0, 3)$	$-2(0) + 3 =$	3
$(2, 5)$	$-2(2) + 5 =$	1
$(12, 0)$	$-2(12) + 0 =$	-24

From this we see that the minimum occurs at $(12, 0)$ at which the objective function is -24. Incidentally, if we also require the maximum then this can be deduced without further effort. From the table the maximum is 3 which occurs at $(0, 3)$.

EXAMPLE

Solve the linear programming problem

  Maximize $5x + 3y$

subject to

  $2x + 4y \leqslant 8$

  $x \geqslant 0$

  $y \geqslant 0$

Solution

Step 1 The non-negativity constraints

  $x \geqslant 0$ and $y \geqslant 0$

indicate that the region is bounded by the coordinate axes in the positive quadrant.

  The line $2x + 4y = 8$ passes through $(0, 2)$ and $(4, 0)$. Also, at the test point $(0, 0)$ the inequality

  $2x + 4y \leqslant 8$

reads

  $0 \leqslant 8$

which is true. We are therefore interested in the region below the line since this region contains the test point, $(0, 0)$. The feasible region is sketched in Figure 8.9.

Step 2 The feasible region is a triangle with three corners, $(0, 0)$, $(0, 2)$ and $(4, 0)$.

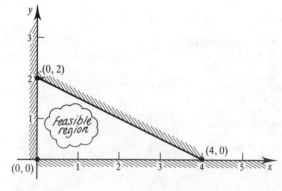

Figure 8.9

Step 3

Corner	Objective function
(0, 0)	5(0) + 3(0) = 0
(0, 2)	5(0) + 3(2) = 6
(4, 0)	5(4) + 3(0) = 20

The maximum value of the objective function is 20 which occurs when $x = 4$ and $y = 0$.

■

PROBLEMS

5 Solve the linear programming problem

   Minimize $x - y$

subject to

   $2x + y \leqslant 2$

   $x \geqslant 0$

   $y \geqslant 0$

6 Solve the linear programming problem

   Maximize $3x + 5y$

subject to

   $x + 2y \leqslant 10$

   $3x + y \leqslant 10$

   $x \geqslant 0$

   $y \geqslant 0$

[Hint: you might find your answer to Problem 2 useful.]

   In Section 1.2 we showed you how to solve a system of simultaneous linear equations. We discovered that such a system does not always have a unique solution. It is possible for a problem to have either no solution or infinitely many solutions. An analogous situation arises in linear programming. We conclude this section by considering two examples which illustrate these special cases.

EXAMPLE

Solve the linear programming problem

   Maximize $x + 2y$

subject to

$$2x + 4y \leqslant 8$$

$$x \geqslant 0$$

$$y \geqslant 0$$

Solution

Step 1   The feasible region is identical to the one sketched in Figure 8.9 for the previous worked example.

Step 2   As before, the feasible region has three corners, $(0, 0)$, $(0, 2)$ and $(4, 0)$

Step 3

Corner	Objective function
$(0, 0)$	$0 + 2(0) = 0$
$(0, 2)$	$0 + 2(2) = 4$
$(4, 0)$	$4 + 2(0) = 4$

This time, however, the maximum value is 4 which actually occurs at two corners $(0, 2)$ and $(4, 0)$. This shows that the problem does not have a unique solution. To explain what is going on here we return to the method introduced at the beginning of this section. We superimpose the family of lines obtained by setting the objective function equal to some constant, c. The parallel lines

$$x + 2y = c$$

pass through the points $(0, c/2)$ and $(c, 0)$.

A selection of lines is sketched in Figure 8.10 for values of c between 0 and 4. These particular values are chosen since they produce lines which cross the feasible region. As c increases, the lines sweep across the region from left to right. Moreover, when c goes above 4 the lines no longer intersect the region. The maximum value that c (that is, the objective function) can take is therefore 4. However, instead of the line

$$x + 2y = 4$$

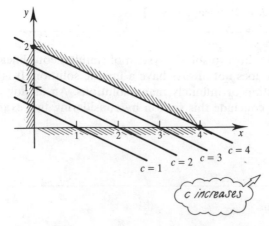

Figure 8.10

intersecting the region at only one point, it intersects along a whole line segment of points. Any point on the line joining the two corners $(0, 2)$ and $(4, 0)$ will be a solution. This follows because any point on this line segment lies in the feasible region and the corresponding value of the objective function on this line is 4 which is the maximum value.

■

This example suggests the general result. If, in Step 3, the maximum (or minimum) occurs at *two* corners then the problem has infinitely many solutions. Any point on the line segment joining these corners, including the two corners themselves, is also a solution.

EXAMPLE

Solve the linear programming problem

Maximize $3x + 2y$

subject to

$$x + 4y \geqslant 8$$
$$x + y \geqslant 5$$
$$2x + y \geqslant 6$$
$$x \geqslant 0$$
$$y \geqslant 0$$

What can you say about the solution if this problem is one of minimization rather than maximization?

Solution

Step 1   As usual the non-negativity constraints indicate that we need only consider the positive quadrant.

The line $x + 4y = 8$ passes through $(0, 2)$ and $(8, 0)$.

The line $x + y = 5$ passes through $(0, 5)$ and $(5, 0)$.

The line $2x + y = 6$ passes through $(0, 6)$ and $(3, 0)$.

Also, the test point $(0, 0)$ does not satisfy any of the corresponding constraints because the three inequality signs are all '$\geqslant$'. We are therefore interested in the region *above* all of these lines as shown in Figure 8.11.

Step 2   The feasible region has four corners, $(0, 6)$, $(1, 4)$, $(4, 1)$ and $(8, 0)$.

Step 3

Corner	Objective function
$(0, 6)$	$3(0) + 2(6) = 12$
$(1, 4)$	$3(1) + 2(4) = 11$
$(4, 1)$	$3(4) + 2(1) = 14$
$(8, 0)$	$3(8) + 2(0) = 24$

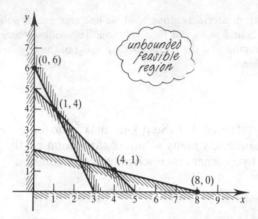

Figure 8.11

From the table the minimum and maximum values of the objective function are 11 and 24 which occur at $(1, 4)$ and $(8, 0)$ respectively. However, we do have a slightly unusual situation in that the feasible region is not enclosed on all sides. We describe this by saying that the feasible region is **unbounded**. It is open at the top and, strictly speaking, it does not make sense to talk about the corners of such a region. Are we therefore justified in applying the 'easy' method in this case? To answer this question we superimpose the family of lines

$$3x + 2y = c$$

representing the objective function as shown in Figure 8.12.

When $c = 11$ the line intersects the region at only one point $(1, 4)$. However, as c increases from this value the lines sweep across the feasible region and never leave it, no matter how large c becomes.

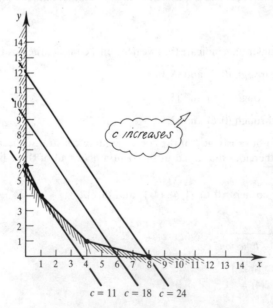

Figure 8.12

Consequently, if the problem is one of maximization we conclude that it does not have a finite solution. We can substitute huge values of x and y into $3x + 2y$ and get an ever-increasing result. On the other hand, if the problem is one of minimization then it does have a solution at the corner $(1, 4)$. This, of course, is the answer obtained previously using the 'easy' method.

■

This example shows that a linear programming problem may not have a finite solution when the feasible region is unbounded. However, when a solution does exist, it may be found simply by inspecting the corners in the normal way. In practice, linear programming problems arise from realistic economic situations. We would therefore expect the problem to possess a sensible (that is, finite) answer and so the difficulty of the non-existence of a solution rarely occurs.

PRACTICE PROBLEMS

7 Sketch the feasible regions defined by the following sets of inequalities

(a) $5x + 3y \leqslant 30$ **(b)** $2x + 5y \leqslant 20$

   $7x + 2y < 28$ $x | y \leqslant 5$

   $x \geqslant 0$ $x \geqslant 0$

   $y \geqslant 0$ $y \geqslant 0$

(c) $x - 2y \leqslant 3$

   $x - y \leqslant 4$

   $x \geqslant 1$

   $y \geqslant 0$

8 Use your answers to Problem 7 to solve the following linear programming problems

(a)   Maximize $4x + 9y$

   subject to

         $5x + 3y \leqslant 30$

         $7x + 2y \leqslant 28$

            $x \geqslant 0$

            $y \geqslant 0$

(b)   Maximize $3x + 6y$

   subject to

         $2x + 5y \leqslant 20$

         $x + y \leqslant 5$

            $x \geqslant 0$

            $y \geqslant 0$

(c)   Minimize $x + y$

subject to

$$x - 2y \leqslant 3$$
$$x - y \leqslant 4$$
$$x \geqslant 1$$
$$y \geqslant 0$$

9   What can you say about the solution to Problem 8(c) if the problem is one of maximization rather than minimization? Explain your answer by superimposing the family of lines

$$x + y = c$$

on the feasible region.

10   Solve the linear programming problem

     Minimize $6x + 2y$

subject to

$$x - y \geqslant 0$$
$$3x + y \geqslant 8$$
$$x \geqslant 0$$
$$y \geqslant 0$$

11   Show that the linear programming problem given in Problem 8(a) can be expressed in matrix notation as

     Maximize $\mathbf{c}^T\mathbf{x}$

subject to

$$\mathbf{Ax} \leqslant \mathbf{b}$$
$$\mathbf{x} \geqslant \mathbf{0}$$

where $\mathbf{c}$, $\mathbf{x}$, $\mathbf{b}$ and $\mathbf{0}$ are 2×1 matrices and $\mathbf{A}$ is a 2×2 matrix which should be stated.

8.2   Applications of linear programming

Objectives   At the end of this section you should be able to:

- identify the unknowns in a linear programming problem,

- find an expression for the objective function and decide whether it should be maximized or minimized,

- write down all of the constraints, including any obvious ones not explicitly mentioned in the problem specification,

- solve linear programming problems expressed in words, remembering to check that the answer makes sense.

The impression possibly given so far is that linear programming is a mathematical technique designed to solve rather abstract problems. This is misleading since linear programming problems do arise from concrete situations. We now put the record straight by considering three realistic examples which lead naturally to such problems. In doing so we shall develop an important skill which can loosely be called problem formulation. Here we start with information, perhaps only vaguely given in words, and try to express it using the more precise language of mathematics. Once this has been done it is a simple matter of applying mathematical techniques to produce the solution.

EXAMPLE

A small manufacturer produces two kinds of good, A and B, for which demand exceeds capacity. The production costs for A and B are $6 and $3 each, respectively, and the corresponding selling prices are $7 and $4. In addition, the transport costs are 20 cents and 30 cents for each good of type A and B, respectively. The conditions of a bank loan limit the manufacturer to maximum weekly production costs of $2,700 and maximum weekly transport costs of $120. How should the manufacturer arrange production to maximize profit?

Solution

As mentioned in Section 8.1 there are three things constituting a linear programming problem; a pair of unknowns x and y, an objective function which needs maximizing or minimizing, and some constraints. We consider each of these in turn.

The manufacturer has to decide exactly how many goods of types A and B to produce each week. These are therefore the unknowns of this problem and we denote these unknowns by the letters x and y; that is, we let

x = number of goods of type A to be made each week

y = number of goods of type B to be made each week

The final sentence of the problem states that the manufacturer should choose these quantities to maximize profit. Hence we need to find a formula for profit in terms of x and y. Now for each good of type A the production costs are $6 and the transport costs are 20 cents. The total cost is therefore $6.20. If the selling price is $7 it follows that the profit made on a single item is 80 cents. Consequently, when x goods of type A are made the total profit is x times this amount, $0.8x$. Notice that the question states that 'demand exceeds capacity' so all goods are guaranteed to be sold. Exactly the same reasoning can be applied to B. The profit is 70 cents each so when y goods of type B are made the total profit is $0.7y$. Hence the profit resulting from the production of both A and B is

$$0.8x + 0.7y$$

This then is the objective function that we want to maximize.

The next thing to do is to read through the original specification to see what restrictions are to be imposed on the production levels. We see that the total weekly production costs must not exceed $2,700. The production costs are $6 for A and $3 for B. Hence if x goods are made of type A and y goods are made of type B the total cost is

$$6x + 3y$$

so we require

$$6x + 3y \leqslant 2700$$

Similarly, the total cost of transporting the goods is

$$0.2x + 0.3y$$

and since this must not exceed $120 we need

$$0.2x + 0.3y \leqslant 120$$

On the face of it there appear to be no further constraints given in the problem. However, a moment's thought should convince you that we are missing two important constraints, namely

$$x \geqslant 0 \quad \text{and} \quad y \geqslant 0$$

Although these are not explicitly mentioned it is obvious that it is impossible to manufacture a negative number of goods.

Collecting all of the ingredients together, the linear programming problem may be stated:

Maximize $0.8x + 0.7y$

subject to

$$6x + 3y \leqslant 2700$$

$$0.2x + 0.3y \leqslant 120$$

$$x \geqslant 0$$

$$y \geqslant 0$$

The problem can now be solved using the method described in Section 8.1.

Step 1 As usual the non-negativity constraints indicate that we need only consider points in the positive quadrant.

The line $6x + 3y = 2700$ passes through $(0, 900)$ and $(450, 0)$.

The line $0.2x + 0.3y = 120$ passes through $(0, 400)$ and $(600, 0)$.

Also, using the origin as the test point reveals that the region of interest lies below both lines. It is sketched in Figure 8.13.

Step 2 The feasible region has four corners altogether, three of which have obvious coordinates $(0, 0)$, $(0, 400)$ and $(450, 0)$. Unfortunately it is not at all easy to read off from the diagram the exact coordinates of the remaining corner. This is formed by the intersection of the two lines

$$6x + 3y = 2700 \tag{1}$$

$$0.2x + 0.3y = 120 \tag{2}$$

You may have encountered this difficulty when solving Problem 8 in Section 8.1. If desired, we can always find the exact coordinates by treating the corresponding equations as a pair of simultaneous

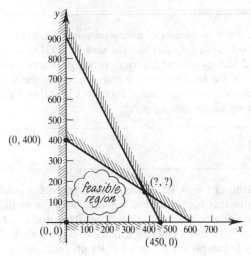

Figure 8.13

equations and solving them algebraically. The variable x can be eliminated by multiplying equation (2) by 30 and subtracting from (1) to get

$$
\begin{array}{r}
6x + 3y = 2700 \\
6x + 9y = 3600 \\
\hline
-6y = -900
\end{array}
\tag{3}
$$

Equation (3) gives $y = 150$ and if this value is substituted into either of the original equations it is easy to see that $x = 375$. The fourth corner therefore has coordinates $(375, 150)$.

Step 3

Corner	Objective function
$(0, 0)$	0
$(0, 400)$	280
$(450, 0)$	360
$(375, 150)$	405

The maximum weekly profit is $405 which occurs when 375 goods of type A and 150 goods of type B are manufactured.

∎

It is impossible to give a precise description of problem formulation. Each case has to be considered on its own merits. However the previous example does suggest the following general strategy which might be helpful:

(1) Identify the unknowns and label them x and y.
(2) Write down an expression for the objective function in terms of x and y, and decide whether it needs maximizing or minimizing.
(3) Write down all constraints on the variables x and y.

PROBLEM

1 An electronics firm decides to launch two new models of microcomputer, COM1 and COM2. The cost of producing each machine of type COM1 is $1200 and the cost for COM2 is $1600. The firm recognizes that it is a risky venture and decides to limit the total weekly production costs to $40,000. Also, due to a shortage of skilled labour, the total number of computers that the firm can produce in a week is at most 30. The profit made on each machine is $600 for COM1 and $700 for COM2. How should the firm arrange production to maximize profit?

EXAMPLE

A food producer uses two processing plants, P1 and P2. After processing, beef is graded into high, medium and low quality foodstuffs. High quality beef is sold to butchers, medium quality beef is used in supermarket ready meals and the low quality beef is used in dog food. The producer has contracted to provide 120 kg of high, 80 kg of medium and 240 kg of low quality beef each week. It costs $4000 per day to run plant P1 and $3200 per day to run plant P2. Each day P1 processes 60 kg of high quality beef, 20 kg of medium quality beef and 40 kg of low quality beef. The corresponding quantities for P2 are 20 kg, 20 kg and 120 kg, respectively. How many days each week should the plants be operated to fulfil the beef contract most economically?

Solution

The clue to the unknowns of this problem can be found in the final sentence 'How many days each week...'. We let

> x = number of days each week that plant P1 is operated

> y = number of days each week that plant P2 is operated

The objective function is harder to ascertain. The phrase 'to fulfil the contract most economically' is rather vague. It could mean that we want to maximize profit as in the previous example. Unfortunately, there is insufficient information given in the problem to determine profit since we do not know the selling prices of the three grades of meat. We are, however, given the operating cost so we take this to be the objective function which then needs to be minimized. The daily costs for plants P1 and P2 are $4000 and $3200, respectively. Consequently, if plant P1 is operated for x days and plant P2 for y days then the total weekly cost is

> $4000x + 3200y$

The remaining information is used to determine the constraints. The producer has contracted to provide 120 kg of high quality beef each week. This means that *at least* this amount must be processed to fulfil the contract. High quality beef comes from two sources. Plant P1 processes 60 kg per day whereas plant P2 processes 20 kg per day. Hence the total weekly output of high quality beef is

> $60x + 20y$

The contract is therefore satisfied provided

> $60x + 20y \geqslant 120$

A similar argument holds for both medium and low quality beef. The corresponding constraints are

> $20x + 20y \geqslant 80$

> $40x + 120y \geqslant 240$

Looking back, it is easy to check that every piece of numerical information has been used in the formulation so far. However, there are still four further constraints to write down! These are based on common sense but they do need to be built into the statement of the linear programming problem. The number of days in a week is 7 so the values of x and y must range between 0 and 7. Thus we have

$$x \geqslant 0 \quad \text{and} \quad y \geqslant 0$$
$$x \leqslant 7 \quad \text{and} \quad y \leqslant 7$$

The complete problem may now be stated:

Minimize $\quad 4000x + 3200y$

subject to

$$60x + 20y \geqslant 120$$
$$20x + 20y \geqslant 80$$
$$40x + 120y \geqslant 240$$
$$x \leqslant 7$$
$$y \leqslant 7$$
$$x \geqslant 0$$
$$y \geqslant 0$$

It can now be solved by applying the method described in Section 8.1.

Step 1   The feasible region can be sketched in the usual way. Note that the last four constraints merely indicate that the region is boxed in by the vertical and horizontal lines $x = 0$, $x = 7$, $y = 0$ and $y = 7$.

The line $60x + 20y = 120$ passes through $(0, 6)$ and $(2, 0)$.

The line $20x + 20y = 80$ passes through $(0, 4)$ and $(4, 0)$.

The line $40x + 120y = 240$ passes through $(0, 2)$ and $(6, 0)$.

Also the test point $(0, 0)$ does not satisfy any of the first three constraints so the feasible region lies above these lines, as shown in Figure 8.14.

Step 2   The feasible region has corners $(7, 0)$, $(7, 7)$, $(0, 7)$, $(1, 3)$, $(3, 1)$, $(0, 6)$ and $(6, 0)$.

Step 3

Corner	Objective function
(7, 0)	28 000
(7, 7)	50 400
(0, 7)	22 400
(0, 6)	19 200
(3, 1)	15 200
(1, 3)	13 600
(6, 0)	24 000

The minimum cost is $13,600 and is obtained by operating plant P1 for 1 day a week and plant P2 for 3 days a week.

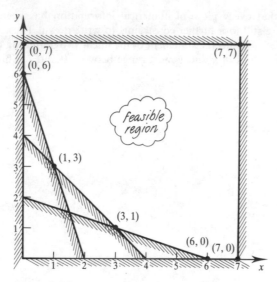

Figure 8.14

Perhaps one of the more difficult aspects of formulating linear programming problems is remembering to include the obvious constraints arising from common sense. In the previous example the last four constraints are so obvious that it is all too easy to omit them, particularly because they are not mentioned explicitly in the original specification. We might therefore include the following point in our general strategy:

(4)   Write down any obvious constraints such as the non-negativity constraints which you may have forgotten about in (3).

PROBLEM

2   A small publishing company decides to use one section of its plant to produce two textbooks called *Microeconomics* and *Macroeconomics*. The profit made on each copy is $12 for *Microeconomics* and $18 for *Macroeconomics*. Each copy of *Microeconomics* requires 12 minutes for printing and 18 minutes for binding. The corresponding figures for *Macroeconomics* are 15 and 9 minutes respectively. There are 10 hours available for printing and $10\frac{1}{2}$ hours available for binding. How many of each should be produced to maximize profit?

EXAMPLE

An insurance company employs full- and part-time staff who work 40 and 20 hours per week respectively. Full-time staff are paid $800 per week and part-time staff $320. In addition, it is company policy that the number of part-time staff should not exceed one third of the number of full-time staff.

If the number of worker hours per week required to deal with the company's work is 900, how many workers of each type should be employed in order to complete the workload at minimum cost?

Solution

If the company employs x full-time staff and y part-time staff then the company would like to choose x and y to minimize its weekly salary costs. Also, since full- and part-time staff are paid \$800 and \$320 per week, respectively, the total wage bill is then

$$800x + 320y$$

which is the objective function that needs to be minimized.

Full- and part-time staff work 40 and 20 hours per week so the total number of worker hours available is

$$40x + 20y$$

It is required that this is at least 900 so we obtain the constraint

$$40x + 20y \geqslant 900$$

A further constraint on the company arises from the fact that the number of part-time staff cannot exceed one third of the number of full-time staff. This means, for example, that if the company employs 30 full-time staff then it is not allowed to employ more than 10 part-time staff because

$$1/3 \times 30 = 10$$

In general, if x denotes the number of full-time staff then the number of part-time staff, y, cannot exceed $x/3$, that is

$$y \leqslant x/3$$

In addition we have the obvious non-negativity constraints

$$x \geqslant 0$$

$$y \geqslant 0$$

The complete problem may now be stated:

Minimize $800x + 320y$

subject to

$$40x + 20y \geqslant 900$$

$$y \leqslant x/3$$

$$x \geqslant 0$$

$$y \geqslant 0$$

It can now be solved by applying the method described in Section 8.1.

Step 1   The feasible region can be sketched in the usual way. The line $y = x/3$ passes through $(0, 0)$, $(3, 1)$, $(6, 2)$ and so on. Unfortunately, because the origin actually lies on the line, it is necessary to use some other point as a test point. For example, substituting $x = 30$, $y = 5$ into the inequality

$$y \leqslant x/3$$

gives

$$5 \leqslant (30)/3$$

This inequality is clearly true, indicating that $(30, 5)$, which lies below the line, is in the region of interest. The constraint

$$40x + 20y \geqslant 900$$

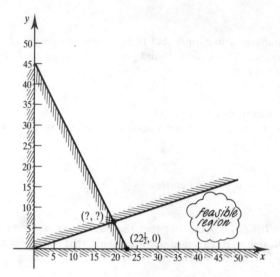

Figure 8.15

is easier to handle. The corresponding line passes through $(0, 45)$ and $(22\frac{1}{2}, 0)$, and using the origin as a test point shows that we need to shade the region below the line. The feasible region is sketched in Figure 8.15.

Step 2   The feasible region has two corners. One of these is obviously $(22\frac{1}{2}, 0)$. However, it is not possible to write down, directly from the diagram, the coordinates of the other corner. This is formed by the intersection of the two lines

$$y = x/3 \tag{1}$$

$$40x + 20y = 900 \tag{2}$$

and so we must solve this system algebraically. In this case the easiest thing to do is to substitute equation (1) into equation (2) to eliminate y immediately. This gives

$$40x + \frac{20}{3}x = 900$$

that is

$$\frac{140}{3}x = 900$$

which has solution

$$x = \frac{2700}{140} = \frac{135}{7} = 19\frac{2}{7}$$

Finally from equation (1)

$$y = \frac{1}{3}x = \frac{1}{3} \times \frac{135}{7} = \frac{45}{7} = 6\frac{3}{7}$$

The feasible region therefore has coordinates $(19\frac{2}{7}, 6\frac{3}{7})$ and $(22\frac{1}{2}, 0)$.

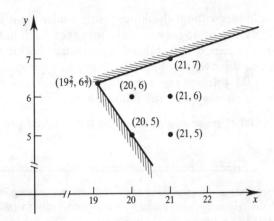

Figure 8.16

Step 3

Corner	Objective function
$(19\tfrac{2}{7}, 6\tfrac{3}{7})$	$17\,485\tfrac{5}{7}$
$(22\tfrac{1}{2}, 0)$	$18\,000$

The minimum cost is $17,485.71 which occurs when $x = 19\tfrac{2}{7}$ and $y = 6\tfrac{3}{7}$.

It might appear that this is the solution to our original problem. This is certainly mathematically correct but cannot possibly be the solution that we are looking for since it does not make sense, for example, to employ $\tfrac{2}{7}$ of a worker. We are only interested in points whose coordinates are whole numbers. A problem such as this is referred to as an **integer programming** problem. We need to find that point (x, y) inside the feasible region where both x and y are whole numbers which minimizes the objective function. A 'blow-up' picture of the feasible region near the minimum cost corner is shown in Figure 8.16 and the following table indicates that the optimal solution is (20, 5).

Corner	Objective function
(20, 5)	$17\,600$
(20, 6)	$17\,920$
(21, 5)	$18\,400$
(21, 6)	$18\,720$

Other points in the neighbourhood with whole number coordinates are (20, 6), (20, 7), (21, 5) and so on. However, all of these have either a larger value of x or a larger value of y (or both) and so must produce a larger total cost. The company should therefore employ 20 full- and 5 part-time staff to minimize its salary bill.

∎

This example highlights the need to look back at the original problem to make sure that the final answer makes sense. It is very tempting when solving linear programming problems just to write down the solution without thinking, neatly underline it and then go on to another problem. Unfortunately, it is all to easy to make mistakes, both in the problem formulation and in sketching the feasible region. Spending a few moments checking the validity of your solution may well help you to discover any blunders that you have made, as well as suggesting possible modifications to the solution procedure, as in the previous example. We might, therefore, conclude the general strategy with the following step:

(5)   Check that the final answer makes sense as a solution to the original problem.

PROBLEM

3   An individual spends 95% of earned income on essential goods and services leaving only 5% to be spent on luxury goods, which is subdivided between trendy clothes and visits to the theatre. The cost of each item of clothing is \$150 and a trip to the theatre costs \$70. The corresponding utility function is

$$U = 3x + 7y$$

where x and y denote the number of trendy clothes and theatre visits per year respectively. In order to maintain a reasonable appearance throughout the year it is vital that at least nine new items of clothing are purchased each year. Given that annual earned income is \$42,000 find the values of x and y which maximize utility.

In this section we have described how to formulate linear programming problems. The general strategy may be summarized:

(1)   Identify the unknowns and label them x and y.
(2)   Write down an expression for the objective function in terms of x and y, and decide whether it needs maximizing or minimizing.
(3)   Write down all constraints on the variables x and y.
(4)   Write down any obvious constraints such as the non-negativity constraints which you may have forgotten about in (3).
(5)   Check that the final answer makes sense as a solution to the original problem.

Obviously it is not essential that you follow this approach, although you may wish to refer to it if you get stuck.

PRACTICE PROBLEMS

4   A manufacturer produces two models of racing bikes, B and C, each of which must be processed through two machine shops. Machine shop 1 is available for 120 hours per month and machine shop 2 for 180 hours per month. The manufacture of each bike of type B takes 6 hours in shop 1 and 3 hours in shop 2. The corresponding times for C are 4 and 10 hours respectively. If the profit is \$180 and \$220 per bike of type B and C respectively, how should the manufacturer arrange production to maximize total profit?

5   A small firm manufactures and sells litre cartons of non-alcoholic cocktails, 'The Caribbean' and 'Mr Fruity' which sell for \$1 and \$1.25 respectively. Each is made by mixing fresh orange, pineapple and apple juices in different proportions. The Caribbean consists of 1 part orange, 6 parts pineapple

and 1 part apple. Mr Fruity consists of 2 parts orange, 3 parts pineapple and 1 part apple. The firm can buy up to 300 litres of orange juice, up to 1125 litres of pineapple juice and up to 195 litres of apple juice each week at a cost of $0.72, $0.64 and $0.48 per litre respectively.

Find the number of cartons of The Caribbean and Mr Fruity that the firm should produce to maximize profits. You may assume that non-alcoholic cocktails are so popular that the firm can sell all that it produces.

6 In a student's diet a meal consists of beefburgers and chips. Beefburgers have 1 unit of nutrient N1, 4 units of N2 and 125 calories per ounce. The figures for chips are $\frac{1}{2}$ unit of N1, 1 unit of N2 and 60 calories per ounce. In the interests of the student's health it is essential for the meal to contain at least 7 units of N1 and 22 units of N2.

What should the student ask for on the next visit to the refectory to satisfy the nutrient requirements and minimize the number of calories?

7 A manufacturer of outdoor clothing makes wax jackets and trousers. Each jacket requires 1 hour to make, whereas each pair of trousers takes 40 minutes. The materials for a jacket cost $32 and those for a pair of trousers cost $40. The company can devote only 34 hours per week to the production of jackets and trousers and the firm's total weekly cost for materials must not exceed $1200. The company sells the jackets at a profit of $12 each and the trousers at a profit of $14 per pair. Market research indicates that the firm can sell all of the jackets that are produced but that it can sell at most half as many pairs of trousers as jackets.

(1) How many jackets and trousers should the firm produce each week to maximize profit?

(2) Due to the changes in demand, the company has to change its profit margin on a pair of trousers. Assuming that the profit margin on a jacket remains at $12 and the manufacturing constraints are unchanged, find the minimum and maximum profit margins on a pair of trousers which the company can allow before it should change its strategy for optimum output.

Solutions to Problems

CHAPTER 1

Section 1.1

1 From Figure S1.1 note that all five points lie on a straight line.

2 (1) **(a)** -30; **(b)** 2; **(c)** -5; **(d)** 5; **(e)** 36; **(f)** -1.

(2) To enter a negative number on a calculator you first enter its positive value and then press the $\boxed{\pm}$ key to change sign. As an experiment try entering the number 6 and then repeatedly press $\boxed{\pm}$ several times to see its effect. The key sequences (working from left to right) are

(a) $\boxed{5}\ \boxed{\times}\ \boxed{6}\ \boxed{\pm}\ \boxed{=}$

(b) $\boxed{1}\ \boxed{\pm}\ \boxed{\times}\ \boxed{2}\ \boxed{\pm}\ \boxed{=}$

(c) $\boxed{5}\ \boxed{0}\ \boxed{\pm}\ \boxed{\div}\ \boxed{1}\ \boxed{0}\ \boxed{=}$

(d) $\boxed{5}\ \boxed{\pm}\ \boxed{\div}\ \boxed{1}\ \boxed{\pm}\ \boxed{=}$

(e) $\boxed{2}\ \boxed{\times}\ \boxed{1}\ \boxed{\pm}\ \boxed{\times}\ \boxed{3}$
$\boxed{\pm}\ \boxed{\times}\ \boxed{6}\ \boxed{=}$

(f) same as (e) followed by $\boxed{\div}\ \boxed{2}$

$\boxed{\pm}\ \boxed{\div}\ \boxed{3}\ \boxed{\div}\ \boxed{6}\ \boxed{=}$

3 (1) **(a)** -1; **(b)** -7; **(c)** 5; **(d)** 0; **(e)** -91; **(f)** -5.

(2) The key sequences are

(a) $\boxed{1}\ \boxed{-}\ \boxed{2}\ \boxed{=}$

(b) $\boxed{3}\ \boxed{\pm}\ \boxed{-}\ \boxed{4}\ \boxed{=}$

(c) $\boxed{1}\ \boxed{-}\ \boxed{4}\ \boxed{\pm}\ \boxed{=}$

(d) $\boxed{1}\ \boxed{\pm}\ \boxed{-}\ \boxed{1}\ \boxed{\pm}\ \boxed{=}$

(e) $\boxed{7}\ \boxed{2}\ \boxed{\pm}\ \boxed{-}\ \boxed{1}\ \boxed{9}\ \boxed{=}$

(f) $\boxed{5}\ \boxed{3}\ \boxed{\pm}\ \boxed{-}\ \boxed{4}\ \boxed{8}$
$\boxed{\pm}\ \boxed{=}$

4

Point	Check	
$(-1, 2)$	$2(-1) + 3(2) = -2 + 6 = 4$	✓
$(-4, 4)$	$2(-4) + 3(4) = -8 + 12 = 4$	✓
$(5, -2)$	$2(5) + 3(-2) = 10 - 6 = 4$	✓
$(2, 0)$	$2(2) + 3(0) = 4 + 0 = 4$	✓

The graph is sketched in Figure S1.2.

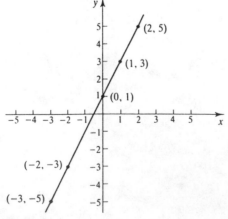

Figure S1.1

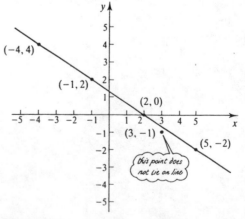

Figure S1.2

Algebraic test:

$$2(3) + 3(-1) = 6 - 3 = 3 \neq 4$$

5 $3x - 2y = 4$

$3(2) - 2y = 4$ (substitute $x = 2$)

$6 - 2y = 4$

$-2y = -2$ (subtract 6 from both sides)

$y = 1$ (divide both sides by -2)

Hence $(2, 1)$ lies on the line.

$3x - 2y = 4$

$3(-2) - 2y = 4$ (substitute $x = -2$)

$-6 - 2y = 4$

$-2y = 10$ (add 6 to both sides)

$y = -5$ (divide both sides by -2)

Hence $(-2, -5)$ lies on the line.
The line is sketched in Figure S1.3.

6 $x - 2y = 2$

$0 - 2y = 2$ (substitute $x = 0$)

$-2y = 2$

$y = -1$ (divide both sides by -2)

Hence $(0, -1)$ lies on the line.

$x - 2y = 2$

$x - 2(0) = 2$ (substitute $y = 0$)

$x - 0 = 2$

$x = 2$

Hence $(2, 0)$ lies on the line.
The graph is sketched in Figure S1.4.

7 From Figure S1.5 the point of intersection is $(1, -\frac{1}{2})$.

8 **(a)** $a = 1$, $b = 2$. The graph is sketched in Figure S1.6.

(b) $4x + 2y = 1$

$2y = 1 - 4x$ (subtract $4x$ from both sides)

$y = \frac{1}{2} - 2x$ (divide both sides by 2)

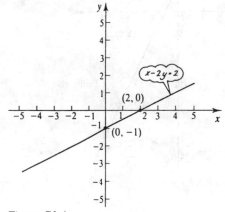

Figure S1.4

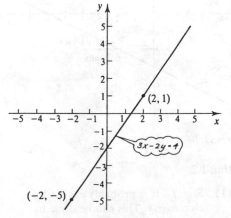

Figure S1.3

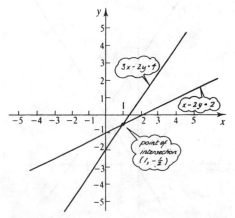

Figure S1.5

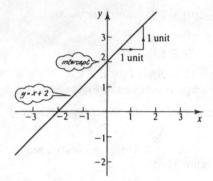

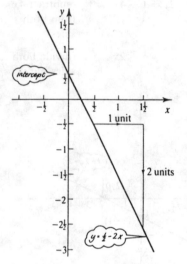

Figure S1.6

Figure S1.7

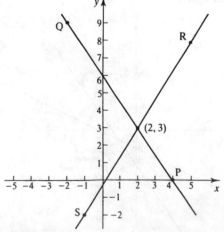

Figure S1.8

so $a = -2$, $b = \frac{1}{2}$. The graph is sketched in Figure S1.7.

9 From Figure S1.8 the point of intersection is $(2, 3)$.

10 **(a)** -20; **(b)** 3; **(c)** -4; **(d)** 1; **(e)** -1; **(f)** -3; **(g)** 11; **(h)** 0; **(i)** 18.

11 **(a)** $(-2, -2)$; **(b)** $(2, 1\frac{1}{2})$; **(c)** $(1\frac{1}{2}, 1)$; **(d)** $(10, -9)$.

12 **(a)** The graph is sketched in Figure S1.9.
   (b) The graph is sketched in Figure S1.10.

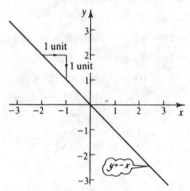

Figure S1.9

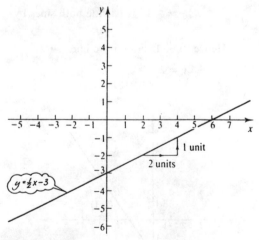

Figure S1.10

Section 1.2

1 **(1)** *Step 1* It is probably easiest to eliminate y. This can be done by subtracting the second equation from

the first:

$$3x - 2y = 4$$

$$\underline{x - 2y = 2} \quad -$$

$$2x \quad\quad = 2$$

Step 2 The equation $2x = 2$ has solution $x = 2/2 = 1$.

Step 3 If this is substituted into the first equation then

$$3(1) - 2y = 4$$

$$3 - 2y = 4$$

$$-2y = 1 \quad \text{(subtract 3 from both sides)}$$

$$y = -\tfrac{1}{2} \quad \text{(divide both sides by } -2)$$

Step 4 As a check the second equation gives

$$x - 2y = 1 - 2(-\tfrac{1}{2})$$

$$= 1 - (-1) = 2 \quad \checkmark$$

Hence the solution is $x = 1$, $y = -\tfrac{1}{2}$.

If you decide to eliminate x then the corresponding steps are as follows:

Step 1 Triple the second equation and subtract from the first:

$$3x - 2y = \quad 4$$

$$\underline{3x - 6y = \quad 6} \quad -$$

$$4y = -2$$

Step 2 The equation $4y = -2$ has solution $y = -2/4 = -\tfrac{1}{2}$.

Step 3 If this is substituted into the first equation then

$$3x - 2(-\tfrac{1}{2}) = 4$$

$$3x + 1 = 4$$

$$3x = 3$$

(subtract 1 from both sides)

$$x = 1$$

(divide both sides by 3)

(2) *Step 1* It is immaterial which variable is eliminated. To eliminate x multiply the first equation by 5, multiply the second by 3 and add:

$$15x + 25y = \quad 95$$

$$\underline{-15x + \ 6y = -33} \quad +$$

$$31y = \quad 62$$

Step 2 The equation $31y = 62$ has solution $y = 62/31 = 2$.

Step 3 If this is substituted into the first equation then

$$3x + 5(2) = 19$$

$$3x + 10 = 19$$

$$3x = \ 9$$

(subtract 10 from both sides)

$$x = \ 3$$

(divide both sides by 3)

Step 4 As a check the second equation gives

$$-5x + 2y = -5(3) + 2(2)$$

$$= -15 + 4 = -11 \quad \checkmark$$

Hence the solution is $x = 3$, $y = 2$.

2 (a) *Step 1* To eliminate x multiply the first equation by 4, multiply the second equation by 3 and add:

$$12x - 24y = \quad -8$$

$$\underline{-12x + 24y = \quad -3} \quad +$$

$$0y = -11$$

Step 2 This is impossible so there are no solutions.

(b) *Step 1* To eliminate x multiply the first equation by 2 and add to the second:

$$-10x + 2y = \quad 8$$

$$\underline{10x - 2y = -8} \quad +$$

$$0y = \quad 0$$

Step 2 This is true for any value of y so there are infinitely many solutions.

3 *Step 1* To eliminate x from the second equation multiply equation (2) by 2 and subtract from equation (1):

$$2x + 2y - 5z = -5$$
$$\underline{2x - 2y + 2z = 6} \quad -$$
$$4y - 7z = -11 \qquad (4)$$

To eliminate x from the third equation multiply equation (1) by 3, multiply equation (3) by 2 and add:

$$6x + 6y - 15z = -15$$
$$\underline{-6x + 2y + 4z = -4} \quad +$$
$$8y - 11z = -19 \qquad (5)$$

The new system is

$$2x + 2y - 5z = -5 \qquad (1)$$
$$4y - 7z = -11 \qquad (4)$$
$$8y - 11z = -19 \qquad (5)$$

Step 2 To eliminate y from the third equation multiply equation (4) by 2 and subtract equation (5)

$$8y - 14z = -22$$
$$\underline{8y - 11z = -19} \quad -$$
$$-3z = -3 \qquad (6)$$

The new system is

$$2x + 2y - 5z = -5 \qquad (1)$$
$$4y - 7z = -11 \qquad (4)$$
$$-3z = -3 \qquad (6)$$

Step 3 Equation (6) gives $z = -3/-3 = 1$. If this is substituted into equation (4) then

$$4y - 7(1) = -11$$
$$4y - 7 = -11$$
$$4y = -4 \qquad \text{(add 7 to both sides)}$$
$$y = -1 \qquad \text{(divide both sides by 4)}$$

Finally, substituting $y = -1$ and $z = 1$ into equation (1) produces

$$2x + 2(-1) - 5(1) = -5$$

$$2x - 7 = -5$$
$$2x = 2$$
$$\text{(add 7 to both sides)}$$
$$x = 1$$
$$\text{(divide both sides by 2)}$$

Step 4 As a check the original equations (1), (2) and (3) give

$$2(1) + 2(-1) - 5(1) = -5 \qquad \checkmark$$
$$1 - (-1) + 1 = 3 \qquad \checkmark$$
$$-3(1) + (-1) + 2(1) = -2 \qquad \checkmark$$

Hence the solution is $x = 1, y = -1, z = 1$.

4 (a) $x = -2, y = -2$;
(b) $x = 2, y = 3/2$;
(c) $x = 3/2, y = 1$;
(d) $x = 10, y = -9$.

5 (a) $x = 3, y = -2, z = -1$;
(b) $x = -1, y = 3, z = 4$.

6 (a) No solution.
(b) Infinitely many solutions.

Section 1.3

1 (a) 0; (b) 48; (c) 16; (d) 25;
(e) 1; (f) 17.
The function g reverses the effect of f and takes you back to where you started. For example, if 25 is put into the function f the outgoing number is 0 and when 0 is put into g the original number, 25, is produced. We describe this by saying that g is the inverse of f (and vice versa).

2 The demand curve which passes through $(0, 75)$ and $(25, 0)$ is sketched in Figure S1.11. From this diagram we see that

(a) $P = 6$ when $Q = 23$
(b) $Q = 19$ when $P = 18$

Alternatively, using algebra,

(a) substituting $Q = 23$ gives
$P = -3(23) + 75 = 6$
(b) substituting $P = 18$ gives
$18 = -3Q + 75$ with solution
$Q = 19$

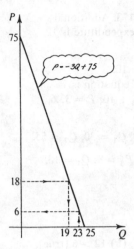

Figure S1.11

3 (a) As P_S rises, consumers are likely to switch to the good under consideration so demand for this good also rises, that is the graph shifts to the right.

(b) As P_C rises, demand for the bundle of goods as a whole is likely to fall, so the graph shifts to the left.

(c) Assuming that advertising promotes the good and is successful, demand rises and the graph shifts to the right. For some goods, such as drugs, advertising campaigns are intended to discourage consumption so the graph shifts to the left.

4 (1) In equilibrium, $Q_S = Q_D = Q$, so

$$P = -4Q + 120$$

$$P = \tfrac{1}{3}Q + 29$$

Hence

$$-4Q + 120 = \tfrac{1}{3}Q + 29$$
(since both sides equal P)

$$-4\tfrac{1}{3}Q + 120 = 29$$
(subtract $\tfrac{1}{3}Q$ from both sides)

$$-4\tfrac{1}{3}Q = -91$$
(subtract 120 from both sides)

$$Q = 21$$
(divide both sides by $-4\tfrac{1}{3}$)

Substituting this value into either the demand or supply equations gives $P = 36$.

(2) After the imposition of a $13 tax the supply equation becomes

$$P - 13 = \tfrac{1}{3}Q_S + 29$$

$$P = \tfrac{1}{3}Q_S + 42$$
(add 13 to both sides)

The demand equation remains unchanged so, in equilibrium,

$$P = -4Q + 120$$

$$P = \tfrac{1}{3}Q + 42$$

Hence

$$-4Q + 120 = \tfrac{1}{3}Q + 42$$

This equation can now be solved as before to get $Q = 18$ and the corresponding price is $P = 48$. The equilibrium price rises from $36 to $48 so the consumer pays an additional $12. The remaining $1 of the tax is paid by the firm.

5 For good 1, $Q_{D_1} = Q_{S_1} = Q_1$ in equilibrium so the demand and supply equations become

$$Q_1 = 40 - 5P_1 - P_2$$

$$Q_1 = -3 + 4P_1$$

Hence

$$40 - 5P_1 - P_2 = -3 + 4P_1$$
(since both sides equal Q_1)

$$40 - 9P_1 - P_2 = -3$$
(subtract $4P_1$ from both sides)

$$-9P_1 - P_2 = -43$$
(subtract 40 from both sides)

For good 2, $Q_{D_2} = Q_{S_2} = Q_2$ in equilibrium so the demand and supply equations become

$$Q_2 = 50 - 2P_1 - 4P_2$$

$$Q_2 = -7 + 3P_2$$

Hence

$$50 - 2P_1 - 4P_2 = -7 + 3P_2$$
(since both sides equal Q_2)

$$50 - 2P_1 - 7P_2 = -7$$
(subtract $3P_2$ from both sides)

$$-2P_1 - 7P_2 = -57$$
(subtract 50 from both sides)

The equilibrium prices therefore satisfy
the simultaneous equations

$$-9P_1 - P_2 = -43 \quad (1)$$

$$-2P_1 - 7P_2 = -57 \quad (2)$$

Step 1 Multiply equation (1) by 2 and
(2) by 9 and subtract to get

$$61P_2 = 427 \quad (3)$$

Step 2 Divide both sides of equation (3)
by 61 to get $P_2 = 7$.

Step 3 Substitute P_2 into equation (1)
to get $P_1 = 4$.

If these equilibrium prices are substituted
into either the demand or the supply
equations then $Q_1 = 13$ and $Q_2 = 14$.
The goods are complementary
because the coefficient of P_2 in the
demand equation for good 1 is negative,
and likewise for the coefficient of P_1 in
the demand equation for good 2.

6 The supply curve is sketched in Figure
S1.12.

(a) 11;

(b) 9;

(c) 0; once the price falls below 7 the firm
does not plan to produce any goods.

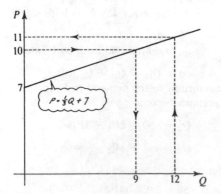

Figure S1.12

7 (1) Demand is 173. Additional
advertising expenditure is 12.

(2) Superior.

8 (1) $P = 30$, $Q = 10$.

(2) New supply equation is
$0.85P = 2Q_s + 10$; $P = 33.6$,
$Q = 9.28$.

9 $P_1 = 40$, $P_2 = 10$; $Q_1 = 30$, $Q_2 = 55$.

10 $P_1 = 20$, $P_2 = 5$, $P_3 = 8$; $Q_1 = 13$,
$Q_2 = 16$, $Q_3 = 11$.

Section 1.4

1 (a) $12 > 9$ (true); **(b)** $12 > 6$ (true);
(c) $3 > 0$ (true); **(d)** same as (c);
(e) $2 > 1$ (true); **(f)** $-24 > -12$ (false);
(g) $-6 > -3$ (false); **(h)** $-2 > -1$
(false); **(i)** $-4 > -7$ (true).

2 (a) $2x < 3x + 7$

$$-x < 7 \quad \text{(subtract } 3x \text{ from both sides)}$$

$$x > -7 \quad \text{(divide both sides by } -1 \text{ changing sense because } -1 < 0)$$

(b) $21x - 19 \geqslant 4x + 15$

$$17x - 19 \geqslant 15$$
(subtract $4x$ from both sides)

$$17x \geqslant 34$$
(add 19 to both sides)

$$x \geqslant 2$$
(divide both sides by 17 leaving
inequality unchanged because
$17 > 0$)

3 (1) (a) 8; **(b)** -12; **(c)** 14; **(d)** -1;
(e) 56; **(f)** 1. In part (f) the
innermost pair of brackets is
evaluated first.

(2) All scientific calculators have a
bracket facility. There are two keys
typically denoted by $\boxed{(\,}$ and $\boxed{)}$ for
'opening' and 'closing' brackets. It
is usually possible to have several
levels (that is, brackets within
brackets) so part (f) should
cause no additional problem.

Possible key sequences are as follows.

(a) $(\quad 1 \quad - \quad 3 \quad) \quad + \quad 1$

$0 \quad =$. Notice that when $)$ is pressed your calculator automatically evaluates the expression inside the brackets and displays the intermediate result.

(b) $1 \quad - \quad (\quad 3 \quad + \quad 1 \quad 0$ $) \quad =$.

(c) $2 \quad \times \quad (\quad 3 \quad + \quad 4 \quad)$

$=$. Note that it is essential to press the $\times$ key explicitly on most calculators.

(d) $(\quad 1 \quad 0 \quad \div \quad 5 \quad) \quad -$

$3 \quad =$.

(e) $(\quad 1 \quad 5 \quad - \quad 8 \quad) \quad \times$

$(\quad ? \quad + \quad 6 \quad) \quad =$.

(f) $(\quad (\quad 2 \quad - \quad 3 \quad) \quad +$

$7 \quad) \quad \div \quad 6 \quad)$. Notice that the effect of pressing the three $)$ keys. There is no need to press the $=$ key at the end since the expression terminates with $)$.

4 **(a)** $5z - 2z^2$
(b) $6x - 6y + 3y - 6x = -3y$
(c) $x - y + z - x^2 - x + y = z - x^2$

5 **(a)** $x^2 - 2x + 3x - 6 = x^2 + x - 6$
(b) $x^2 - xy + yx - y^2 = x^2 - y^2$
(c) $x^2 + xy + yx + y^2 = x^2 + 2xy + y^2$
(d) $5x^2 - 5xy + 5x + 2yx - 2y^2 + 2y$
$= 5x^2 - 3xy + 5x - 2y^2 + 2y$

6 **(1)** **(a)** $\dfrac{1}{2} \times \dfrac{3}{4} = \dfrac{1 \times 3}{2 \times 4} = \dfrac{3}{8}$

(b) $7 \times \dfrac{1}{14_2} = \dfrac{1}{2}$

(c) $\dfrac{2}{3} \div \dfrac{8}{9} = \dfrac{2}{3} \times \dfrac{9^3}{8_4} = \dfrac{3}{4}$

(d) $\dfrac{8}{9} \div 16 = \dfrac{8}{9} \times \dfrac{1}{16_2} = \dfrac{1}{18}$

(2) Most scientific calculators have a fractions facility typically labelled $\boxed{a^b/_c}$. To enter a number such as $3/4$ you press $3 \quad \boxed{a^b/_c} \quad 4$. Try this for yourself. The display should read something like $3 \,\square\, 4$. To enter a number such as $3\frac{5}{8}$ you press $3 \quad \boxed{a^b/_c} \quad 5 \quad \boxed{a^b/_c} \quad 8$ which then displays $3 \,\square\, 5 \,\square\, 8$. Possible key sequences for part (1) are

(a) $1 \quad \boxed{a^b/_c} \quad 2 \quad \times \quad 3 \quad \boxed{a^b/_c}$

$4 \quad =$

(b) $7 \quad \times \quad 1 \quad \boxed{a^b/_c} \quad 1 \quad 4$

$=$

(c) $2 \quad \boxed{a^b/_c} \quad 3 \quad \div \quad 8 \quad \boxed{a^b/_c}$

$9 \quad =$

(d) $8 \quad \boxed{a^b/_c} \quad 9 \quad \div \quad 1 \quad 6$

$=$

7 **(1)** **(a)** $\dfrac{3}{7} - \dfrac{1}{7} = \dfrac{2}{7}$

(b) $\dfrac{1}{3} + \dfrac{2}{5} = \dfrac{5}{15} + \dfrac{6}{15} = \dfrac{11}{15}$

(c) $\dfrac{7}{18} - \dfrac{1}{4} = \dfrac{14}{36} - \dfrac{9}{36} = \dfrac{5}{36}$

(2) The key sequences are

(a) $3 \quad \boxed{a^b/_c} \quad 7 \quad - \quad 1 \quad \boxed{a^b/_c}$

$7 \quad =$

(b) $1 \quad \boxed{a^b/_c} \quad 3 \quad + \quad 2 \quad \boxed{a^b/_c}$

$5 \quad =$

(c) $7 \quad \boxed{a^b/_c} \quad 1 \quad 8 \quad - \quad 1$

$\boxed{a^b/_c} \quad 4 \quad =$

8 **(a)** $\dfrac{5}{x-1} \times \dfrac{x-1}{x+2} = \dfrac{5}{x+2}$

(b) $\dfrac{x^2}{x+10} \div \dfrac{x}{x+1} = \dfrac{^x x^2}{x+10} \times \dfrac{x+1}{\not x}$

$$= \dfrac{x(x+1)}{x+10}$$

(c) $\dfrac{4}{x+1} + \dfrac{1}{x+1} = \dfrac{4+1}{x+1} = \dfrac{5}{x+1}$

(d) $\dfrac{2}{x+1} - \dfrac{1}{x+2}$

$$= \dfrac{2(x+2)}{(x+1)(x+2)} - \dfrac{(1)(x+1)}{(x+1)(x+2)}$$

$$= \dfrac{(2x+4) - (x+1)}{(x+1)(x+2)}$$

$$= \dfrac{x+3}{(x+1)(x+2)}$$

9 (a) $y = ax + b$

$y - ax = b$

(subtract ax from both sides)

$-ax = b - y$

(subtract y from both sides)

$x = -\dfrac{b}{a} + \dfrac{y}{a}$

(divide both sides by $-a$)

(b) $x - ay = cx + y$

$x = cx + y + ay$
(add ay to both sides)

$x - cx = y + ay$
(subtract cx from both sides)

$(1 - c)x = (1 + a)y$
(factorize both sides)

$x = \left(\dfrac{1+a}{1-c}\right)y$

(divide both sides by $1 - c$)

(c) $y = \dfrac{x-2}{x+4}$

$(x+4)y = x - 2$
(multiply both sides by $x + 4$)

$xy + 4y = x - 2$
(multiply out the brackets)

$xy = x - 2 - 4y$
(subtract $4y$ from both sides)

$xy - x = -2 - 4y$
(subtract x from both sides)

$(y - 1)x = -2 - 4y$
(factorize left-hand side)

$x = \dfrac{-2 - 4y}{y - 1}$

(divide both sides by $y - 1$)

10 (a), (d), (e), (f).

11 (a) $x > 1$; **(b)** $x \leqslant 3$; **(c)** $x \leqslant -3$;
(d) $x > 2$.

12 (a) $7x - 7y$; **(b)** $5xz - 2yz$;
(c) $-5y + 4z - 2x$;
(d) $x^2 - 7x + 10$; **(e)** $x^2 - xy + 7x$;
(f) $x^3 + 3x^2 + 2x$; **(g)** $x^2 - xy - 1 + y$.
Note: in part (f), x^3 is an abbreviation
for xxx.

13 (a) $\dfrac{5}{7}$; **(b)** $\dfrac{1}{10}$; **(c)** $\dfrac{3}{2}$; **(d)** $\dfrac{5}{48}$; **(e)** $\dfrac{8}{13}$;
(f) $\dfrac{11}{9}$; **(g)** $\dfrac{141}{35}$; **(h)** $\dfrac{34}{5}$.

14 (a) $x + 6$

(b) $\dfrac{x+1}{x}$ or equivalently $1 + \dfrac{1}{x}$

(c) $\dfrac{5}{xy}$

(d) $\dfrac{x^2 + x - 2}{x + 1}$

(e) $\dfrac{x+3}{x(x+1)}$

15 (a) $P = \dfrac{Q}{a} - \dfrac{b}{a}$ **(b)** $Y = \dfrac{b+I}{1-a}$

(c) $P = \dfrac{1}{aQ} - \dfrac{b}{a}$ **(d)** $t = \dfrac{V+1}{V-5}$

Section 1.5

1 $S = Y - C$

$= Y - (0.8Y + 25)$ (substitute
expression for C)

$= Y - 0.8Y - 25$ (multiply out brackets)

$= 0.2Y - 25$ (collect terms)

2 $Y = C + I$ (from theory)

$C = 0.8Y + 25$ (given in question)

$I = 17$ (given in question)

Substituting the given value of I into the first equation gives

$$Y = C + 17$$

and if the expression for C is substituted into this then

$$Y = 0.8Y + 42$$

$0.2Y = 42$ (subtract $0.8Y$ from both sides)

$Y = 210$ (divide both sides by 0.2)

Repeating the calculations with $I = 18$ gives $Y = 215$, so a one-unit increase in investment leads to a 5-unit increase in income. The scale factor, 5, is called the investment multiplier. In general, the investment multiplier is given by $1/(1 - a)$ where a is the marginal propensity to consume. The foregoing is a special case of this with $a = 0.8$.

3 $Y = C + I + G$ (1)

$G = 40$ (2)

$I = 55$ (3)

$C = 0.8Y_d + 25$ (4)

$T = 0.1Y + 10$ (5)

$Y_d = Y - T$ (6)

Substituting equations (2) and (3) into equation (1) gives

$$Y = C + 95   (7)$$

Substituting equation (5) into (6) gives

$$Y_d = Y - (0.1Y + 10)$$

$$= 0.9Y - 10$$

so from equation (4),

$$C = 0.8(0.9Y - 10) + 25$$

$$= 0.72Y + 17   (8)$$

Finally, substituting equation (8) into (7) gives

$$Y = 0.72Y + 112$$

which has solution $Y = 400$.

4 The commodity market is in equilibrium when

$$Y = C + I$$

so we can substitute the given expressions for consumption ($C = 0.7Y + 85$) and investment ($I = -50r + 1200$) to deduce that

$$Y = 0.7Y - 50r + 1285$$

which rearranges to give the IS schedule,

$$0.3Y + 50r = 1285   (1)$$

The money market is in equilibrium when

$$M_S = M_D$$

Now we are given that $M_S = 500$ and that total demand,

$$M_D = L_1 + L_2 = 0.2Y - 40r + 230$$

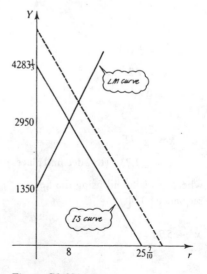

Figure S1.13

so that

$$500 = 0.2Y - 40r + 230$$

which rearranges to give the LM schedule,

$$0.2Y - 40r = 270 \qquad (2)$$

We now solve equations (1) and (2) as a pair of simultaneous equations.

Step 1 Multiply equation (1) by 0.2 and (2) by 0.3 and subtract to get

$$22r = 176$$

Step 2 Divide through by 22 to get $r = 8$.

Step 3 Substitute $r = 8$ into equation (1) to give $Y = 2950$.

The IS and LM curves shown in Figure S1.13 confirm this since the point of intersection has coordinates (8, 2950). A change in I does not affect the LM schedule. However, if the autonomous level of investment increases from its current level of 1200 then the right-hand side of the IS schedule (1) will rise. The IS curve moves upwards causing both r and Y to increase.

5 **(a)** $S = 0.1Y - 72$ **(b)** $S = \dfrac{10Y - 500}{Y + 10}$

6 **(a)** 325; **(b)** 225; **(c)** 100.

7 825.

8 $Y = 2500, r = 10$.

CHAPTER 2

Section 2.1

1 **(a)** $x^2 - 100 = 0$

$$x^2 = 100$$

$$x = \pm\sqrt{100}$$

$$x = \pm 10$$

(b) $2x^2 - 8 = 0$

$$2x^2 = 8$$

$$x^2 = 4$$

$$x = \pm\sqrt{4}$$

$$x = \pm 2$$

(c) $x^2 - 3 = 0$

$$x^2 = 3$$

$$x = \pm\sqrt{3}$$

$$x = \pm 1.73 \quad \text{(to 2 decimal places)}$$

where $\sqrt{3}$ is found using the key sequence $\boxed{3}$ $\boxed{\sqrt{}}$.

(d) $x^2 - 5.72 = 0$

$$x^2 = 5.72$$

$$x = \pm\sqrt{5.72}$$

$$x = \pm 2.39 \quad \text{(to 2 decimal places)}$$

where $\sqrt{5.72}$ is found using the key sequence $\boxed{5}$ $\boxed{.}$ $\boxed{7}$ $\boxed{2}$ $\boxed{\sqrt{}}$.

(e) $x^2 + 1 = 0$

$$x^2 = -1$$

This equation does not have a solution because the square of a number is always positive. Try using your calculator to find $\sqrt{(-1)}$ using the key sequence $\boxed{1}$ $\boxed{\pm}$ $\boxed{\sqrt{}}$. An error message should be displayed.

(f) $3x^2 + 6.21 = 0$

$$3x^2 = -6.21$$

$$x^2 = -2.07$$

This equation does not have a solution because it is impossible to find the square root of a negative number.

(g) $x^2 = 0$

This equation has exactly one solution, $x = 0$.

2 (a) $a = 2, b = -19, c = -10.$

$$x = \frac{-(-19) \pm \sqrt{((-19)^2 - 4(2)(-10))}}{2(2)}$$

$$= \frac{19 \pm \sqrt{(361 + 80)}}{4}$$

$$= \frac{19 \pm \sqrt{441}}{4}$$

$$= \frac{19 \pm 21}{4}$$

This equation has two solutions

$$x = \frac{19 + 21}{4} = 10$$

$$x = \frac{19 - 21}{4} = -\frac{1}{2}$$

(b) $a = 4, b = 12, c = 9.$

$$x = \frac{-12 \pm \sqrt{((12)^2 - 4(4)(9))}}{2(4)}$$

$$= \frac{-12 \pm \sqrt{(144 - 144)}}{8}$$

$$= \frac{-12 \pm 0}{8}$$

This equation has one solution,
$x = -\frac{3}{2}$.

(c) $a = 1, b = 1, c = 1.$

$$x = \frac{-1 \pm \sqrt{((1)^2 - 4(1)(1))}}{2(1)}$$

$$= \frac{-1 \pm \sqrt{(1 - 4)}}{2}$$

$$= \frac{-1 \pm \sqrt{(-3)}}{2}$$

This equation has no solutions
because $\sqrt{(-3)}$ does not exist.

(d) We first need to collect like terms to
convert

$$x^2 - 3x + 10 = 2x + 4$$

into the standard form

$$ax^2 + bx + c = 0$$

Subtracting $2x + 4$ from both sides
gives

$$x^2 - 5x + 6 = 0$$

$a = 1, b = -5, c = 6.$

$$x = \frac{-(-5) \pm \sqrt{((-5)^2 - 4(1)(6))}}{2(1)}$$

$$= \frac{5 \pm \sqrt{(25 - 24)}}{2}$$

$$= \frac{5 \pm \sqrt{1}}{2}$$

$$= \frac{5 \pm 1}{2}$$

This equation has two solutions

$$x = \frac{5 + 1}{2} = 3$$

$$x = \frac{5 - 1}{2} = 2$$

3 (a) If $(x - 4)(x + 3) = 0$ then either

$$x - 4 = 0 \text{ with solution } x = 4$$

or

$$x + 3 = 0 \text{ with solution } x = -3$$

This equation has two solutions,
$x = 4$ and $x = -3$.

(b) If $x(10 - 2x) = 0$ then either

$$x = 0$$

or

$$10 - 2x = 0 \text{ with solution } x = 5$$

This equation has two solutions,
$x = 0$ and $x = 5$.

(c) If $(2x - 6)(2x - 6) = 0$ then

$$2x - 6 = 0 \text{ with solution } x = 3$$

This equation has one solution, $x = 3$.

4 (a)

x		-1	0	1	2	3	4
$f(x)$		21	5	-3	-3	5	21

The graph is sketched in Figure S2.1.

(b)

x	0	1	2	3	4	5	6
$f(x)$	-9	-4	-1	0	-1	-4	-9

The graph is sketched in Figure S2.2.

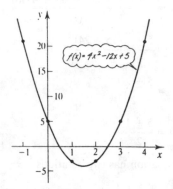

Figure S2.1

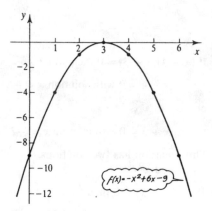

Figure S2.2

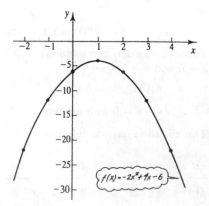

Figure S2.3

(c)

x	-2	-1	0	1	2	3	4
$f(x)$	-22	-12	-6	-4	-6	-12	-22

The graph is sketched in Figure S2.3.

5 (a) *Step 1* The coefficient of x^2 is 2 which is positive so the graph is U shaped.

Step 2 The constant term is -6 so the graph crosses the vertical axis at $y = -6$.

Step 3 The quadratic equation

$$2x^2 - 11x - 6 = 0$$

has solution

$$x = \frac{-(-11) \pm \sqrt{((-11)^2 - 4(2)(-6))}}{2(2)}$$

$$= \frac{11 \pm \sqrt{(121 + 48)}}{4}$$

$$= \frac{11 \pm \sqrt{169}}{4}$$

$$= \frac{11 \pm 13}{4}$$

so the graph crosses the horizontal axis at $x = -\frac{1}{2}$ and $x = 6$.

In fact, we can use symmetry to locate the coordinates of the turning point on the curve. The x coordinate of the minimum occurs halfway between $x = -\frac{1}{2}$ and $x = 6$ at

$$x = \frac{1}{2}\left(-\frac{1}{2} + 6\right) = \frac{11}{4}$$

The corresponding y coordinate is

$$2\left(\frac{11}{4}\right)^2 - 11\left(\frac{11}{4}\right) - 6 = -\frac{169}{8}$$

The graph is sketched in Figure S2.4.

(b) *Step 1* The coefficient of x is 1 which is positive so the graph is U shaped.

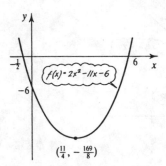

$f(x) = 2x^2 - 11x - 6$

$(\frac{11}{4}, -\frac{169}{8})$

Figure S2.4

Step 2 The constant term is 9 so the graph crosses the vertical axis at $y = 9$.

Step 3 The quadratic equation

$$x^2 - 6x + 9 = 0$$

has solution

$$x = \frac{-(-6) \pm \sqrt{((-6)^2 - 4(1)(9))}}{2(1)}$$

$$= \frac{6 \pm \sqrt{(36 - 36)}}{2}$$

$$= \frac{6 \pm \sqrt{0}}{2}$$

$$= 3$$

so the graph crosses the *x* axis at $x = 3$.

The graph is sketched in Figure S2.5.

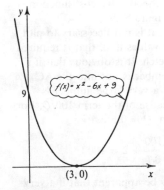

$f(x) = x^2 - 6x + 9$

$(3, 0)$

Figure S2.5

6 In equilibrium, $Q_S = Q_D = Q$ so the supply and demand equations become

$$P = 2Q^2 + 10Q + 10$$
$$P = -Q^2 - 5Q + 52$$

Hence

$$2Q^2 + 10Q + 10 = -Q^2 - 5Q + 52$$
$$3Q^2 + 15Q - 42 = 0$$
$$\text{(collecting like terms)}$$
$$Q^2 + 5Q - 14 = 0$$
$$\text{(dividing both sides by 3)}$$
$$Q = \frac{-5 \pm \sqrt{((5)^2 - 4(1)(-14))}}{2(1)}$$
$$= \frac{-5 \pm \sqrt{81}}{2}$$
$$= \frac{-5 \pm 9}{2}$$

so $Q = -7$ and $Q = 2$. Ignoring the negative solution gives $Q = 2$. From the supply equation the corresponding equilibrium price is

$$P = 2(2)^2 + 10(2) + 10 = 38$$

As a check, the demand equation gives

$$P = -(2)^2 - 5(2) + 52 = 38 \quad \checkmark$$

7 (a) $-4, 4$; (b) $0, 100$; (c) $5, 17$; (d) 9; (e) no solution.

8 The graphs are sketched in Figure S2.6.

9 $Q = 4$, $P = 36$.

Section 2.2

1 $TR = PQ = (1000 - Q)Q = 1000Q - Q^2$

Step 1 The coefficient of Q^2 is negative so the graph has an inverted U-shape.

Step 2 The constant term is zero so the graph crosses the vertical axis at the origin.

Step 3 From the factorization,

$$TR = (1000 - Q)Q$$

the graph crosses the horizontal axis at $Q = 0$ and $Q = 1000$.

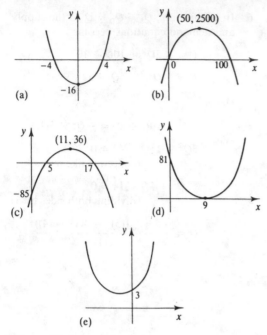

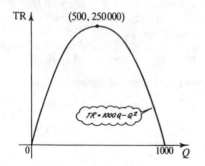

Figure S2.6

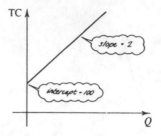

Figure S2.8

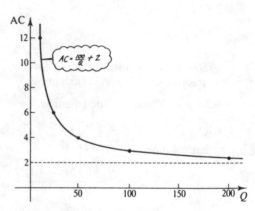

Figure S2.9

TR graph:

(500, 250 000)

$TR = 1000Q - Q^2$

1000   Q

Figure S2.7

The graph is sketched in Figure S2.7. By symmetry the parabola reaches its maximum halfway between 0 and 1000 at $Q = 500$. The corresponding value of TR is

$$TR = 1000(500) - (500)^2 = 250\,000$$

From the demand equation, when $Q = 500$,

$$P = 1000 - 500 = 500$$

2 $TC = 100 + 2Q$

$$AC = \frac{100 + 2Q}{Q} = \frac{100}{Q} + 2$$

The graph of the total cost function is sketched in Figure S2.8.

One possible table of function values for the average cost function is

Q	10	25	50	100	200
AC	12	6	4	3	2.5

The graph of the average cost function is sketched in Figure S2.9.

In fact, it is not necessary to plot the tabulated values if all that is required is a rough sketch. It is obvious that if a very small number is put into the AC function then a very large number is produced because of the term $100/Q$. For example, when $Q = 0.1$

$$AC = \frac{100}{0.1} + 2 = 1002$$

It should also be apparent that if a very large number is put into the average cost function then the term $100/Q$ is insignificant, so AC is approximately 2. For example, when $Q = 10\,000$

$$AC = \frac{100}{10\,000} + 2 = 2.01$$

The graph of AC therefore 'blows up' near $Q = 0$ but settles down to a value just greater than 2 for large Q. Consequently the general shape of the graph shown in Figure S2.9 is to be expected.

3 $TC = 25 + 2Q$

$TR = PQ = (20 - Q)Q = 20Q - Q^2$

Hence,

$$\begin{aligned}\pi &= TR - TC \\ &= (20Q - Q^2) - (25 + 2Q) \\ &= 20Q - Q^2 - 25 - 2Q \\ &= -Q^2 + 18Q - 25\end{aligned}$$

Step 1 The coefficient of Q^2 is negative so the graph has an inverted U-shape.

Step 2 The constant term is -25 so the graph crosses the vertical axis at -25.

Step 3 The quadratic equation

$$-Q^2 + 18Q - 25 = 0$$

has solutions

$$Q = \frac{-18 \pm \sqrt{(324 - 100)}}{-2}$$

$$= \frac{-18 \pm 14.97}{-2}$$

so the graph crosses the horizontal axis at $Q = 1.52$ and $Q = 16.48$.

The graph of the profit function is sketched in Figure S2.10.

(1) If $\pi = 31$ then we need to solve

$$-Q^2 + 18Q - 25 = 31$$

that is

$$-Q^2 + 18Q - 56 = 0$$

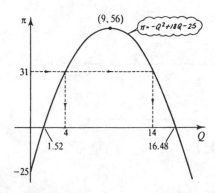

Figure S2.10

$$Q = \frac{-18 \pm \sqrt{(324 - 224)}}{-2}$$

$$= \frac{-18 \pm 10}{-2}$$

so $Q = 4$ and $Q = 14$.

These values can also be found by drawing a horizontal line $\pi = 31$ and then reading off the corresponding values of Q from the horizontal axis as shown on Figure S2.10.

(2) By symmetry the parabola reaches its maximum halfway between 1.52 and 16.48, that is at

$$Q = \tfrac{1}{2}(1.52 + 16.48) = 9$$

The corresponding profit is given by

$$\pi = -(9)^2 + 18(9) - 25 = 56$$

4 **(a)** $4Q$; **(b)** 7; **(c)** $10Q - 4Q^2$. The graphs are sketched in Figures S2.11, S2.12 and S2.13.

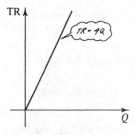

Figure S2.11

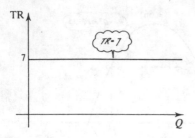

Figure S2.12

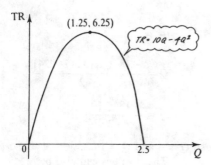

Figure S2.13

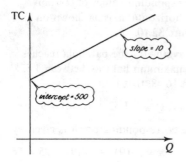

Figure S2.14

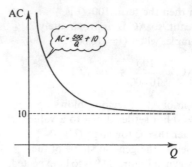

Figure S2.15

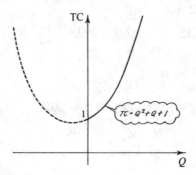

Figure S2.16

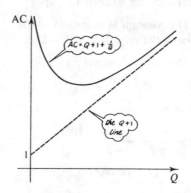

Figure S2.17

5 $TC = 500 + 10Q$; $AC = \dfrac{500}{Q} + 10$

The graphs are sketched in Figures S2.14 and S2.15.

6 $TC = Q^2 + Q + 1$; $AC = Q + 1 + \dfrac{1}{Q}$

The graphs are sketched in Figures S2.16 and S2.17.

7 $\pi = -2Q^2 + 20Q - 32$; **(a)** 2, 8; **(b)** 20; **(c)** 5.

8   The graphs of TR and TC are sketched in Figure S2.18. **(1)** 1, 5; **(2)** 3.

Section 2.3

1   **(1)**   **(a)** 100; **(b)** 10; **(c)** 1; **(d)** 1/10;
        (e) 1/100; **(f)** 1; **(g)** −1; **(h)** 1/343;
        (i) 81; **(j)** 72 101; **(k)** 1.

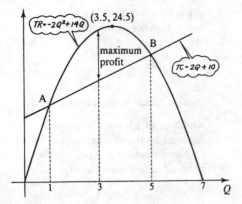

Figure S2.18

(2) To evaluate b^n on a calculator you enter the base, b, press the power key (typically denoted by $\boxed{x^y}$), enter the power, n, and finally press the $\boxed{=}$ key to get the result. For example to calculate 10^2 the key sequence is $\boxed{1}\ \boxed{0}\ \boxed{x^y}\ \boxed{2}\ \boxed{=}$.

2 (1) **(a)** 4 because $4^2 = 16$.
(b) 3 because $3^3 = 27$.
(c) 32 because $4^{5/2} = (4^{1/2})^5 = 2^5$.
(d) $\frac{1}{4}$ because
$$8^{-2/3} = (8^{1/3})^{-2} = 2^{-2} = 1/2^2.$$
(e) 1 because $1^n = 1$ for any index, n.

(2) Some calculators have a function key (typically labelled $\boxed{x^{1/y}}$) which can be used to evaluate $b^{1/n}$ directly. However, this does not result in any real reduction in the number of key presses. In practice, it is just as easy to handle fractional indices using the ordinary power key $\boxed{x^y}$. The corresponding key sequences are

(a) $\boxed{1}\ \boxed{6}\ \boxed{x^y}\ \boxed{1}\ \boxed{a^b/_c}\ \boxed{2}\ \boxed{=}$

(b) $\boxed{2}\ \boxed{7}\ \boxed{x^y}\ \boxed{1}\ \boxed{a^b/_c}\ \boxed{3}\ \boxed{=}$

(c) $\boxed{4}\ \boxed{x^y}\ \boxed{5}\ \boxed{a^b/_c}\ \boxed{2}\ \boxed{=}$

(d) $\boxed{8}\ \boxed{x^y}\ \boxed{2}\ \boxed{a^b/_c}\ \boxed{3}\ \boxed{\pm}\ \boxed{=}$

(e) $\boxed{1}\ \boxed{x^y}\ \boxed{1}\ \boxed{7}\ \boxed{a^b/_c}\ \boxed{2}\ \boxed{5}$
$\boxed{\pm}\ \boxed{=}$

3 **(a)** $(x^{3/4})^8 = x^{(3/4)\times 8} = x^6$ (rule 3)

(b) $x^2 \div x^{3/2} = x^{2-(3/2)} = x^{1/2}$ (rule 2)

(c) $(x^2 y^4)^3 = (x^2)^3 (y^4)^3$ (rule 4)

$= x^{2\times 3} y^{4\times 3}$ (rule 3)

$= x^6 y^{12}$

(d) $\sqrt{x}(x^{5/2} + y^3) = x^{1/2}(x^{5/2} + y^3)$
(definition of $b^{1/n}$)

$= x^{1/2} x^{5/2} + x^{1/2} y^3$
(multiply out the parentheses)

$= x^{(1/2)+(5/2)} + x^{1/2} y^3$
(rule 1)

$= x^3 + x^{1/2} y^3$

The term $x^{1/2} y^3$ cannot be simplified because $x^{1/2}$ and y^3 have different bases.

4 **(a)** $f(K, L) = 7KL^2$

$f(\lambda K, \lambda L) = 7(\lambda K)(\lambda L)^2$

$= 7\lambda K \lambda^2 L^2$ (rule 4)

$= (\lambda \lambda^2)(7KL^2)$

$= \lambda^3 f(K, L)$ (rule 1)

Increasing returns to scale because $3 > 1$.

(b) $f(K, L) = 50K^{1/4} L^{3/4}$

$f(\lambda K, \lambda L) = 50(\lambda K)^{1/4}(\lambda L)^{3/4}$

$= 50\lambda^{1/4} K^{1/4} \lambda^{3/4} L^{3/4}$
(rule 4)

$= (\lambda^{1/4} \lambda^{3/4})(50K^{1/4} L^{3/4})$

$= \lambda^1 f(K, L)$ (rule 1)

Constant returns to scale.

5 **(1)** **(a)** 3; **(b)** 2; **(c)** 1; **(d)** 0; **(e)** -1;
(f) -2.

(2) Same as part (1) because if $M = 10^n$ then $\log_{10} M = n$.

(3) On most calculators there are two logarithm function keys, $\log_{10}$ (possibly labelled log or $\log_{10}$) and ln (possibly labelled ln or $\log_e$). The latter is known as the natural logarithm and we introduce this function in the next chapter. This question wants you to evaluate logarithms to base 10 so we use the key $\boxed{\log}$. For example, to calculate $\log_{10} 1000$ the key sequence is $\boxed{1}\ \boxed{0}\ \boxed{0}\ \boxed{0}\ \boxed{\log}$.

Warning: there is no standard layout for the keyboard of a calculator. It may be necessary for you first to use the shift key (sometimes called the inverse function or second function key) to activate the $\log_{10}$ function.

6 (a) $\qquad 3^x = 7$

$\log(3^x) = \log 7$
    (take logarithms of both sides)

$x \log 3 = \log 7$
    (rule 3)

$x = \dfrac{\log 7}{\log 3}$
    (divide both sides by log 3)

$x = \dfrac{0.845\,098\,040}{0.477\,121\,255}$
    (using base 10 on a calculator)

$x = 1.77$
    (to 2 decimal places)

(b) $\qquad 5(2)^x = 10^x$

$\log[5(2)^x] = \log(10)^x$
    (take logarithms of both sides)

$\log 5 + \log(2^x) = \log(10)^x$
    (rule 1)

$\log 5 + x \log 2 = x \log 10$
    (rule 3)

$x(\log 10 - \log 2) = \log 5$
    (collect terms and factorize)

$x \log 5 = \log 5$
    (rule 2)

$x = 1$
    (divide both sides by log 5)

which is, of course, the obvious solution to the original equation! Did you manage to spot this for yourself *before* you started taking logs?

7 (a) 64; (b) 2; (c) 1/3; (d) 1; (e) 1; (f) 6; (g) 4; (h) 1/343.

8 (a) y^2; (b) xy^2; (c) $x^4 y^2$.

9 The functions in parts (a) and (b) are homogeneous of degree 7/12 and 2 respectively so (a) displays decreasing returns to scale and (b) displays increasing returns to scale. The function in part (c) is not homogeneous.

10 $A[b(\lambda K)^\alpha + (1-b)(\lambda L)^\alpha]^{1/\alpha}$

$= A[b\lambda^\alpha K^\alpha + (1-b)\lambda^\alpha L^\alpha]^{1/\alpha}$ (rule 4)

$= A[(\lambda^\alpha)(bK^\alpha + (1-b)L^\alpha)]^{1/\alpha}$ (factorize)

$= A(\lambda^\alpha)^{1/\alpha}[bK^\alpha + (1-b)L^\alpha]^{1/\alpha}$ (rule 4)

$= \lambda A[bK^\alpha + (1-b)L^\alpha]^{1/\alpha}$ (rule 3)

so $f(\lambda K, \lambda L) = \lambda^1 f(K, L)$ as required. This is known as the constant elasticity of substitution (CES) production function.

11 (a) 2; (b) 1; (c) 0; (d) $\frac{1}{2}$; (e) -1.

12 (a) 78.31; (b) 1.48; (c) 3; (d) 0.23.

CHAPTER 3

Section 3.1

1 $\dfrac{90}{100} \times 300\,000 = \$270,000$

2 $\dfrac{15}{100} \times 1000 = \$150$

so the consumer pays \$1,150.

3 Sales rise by 5000 which is $1/10 = 10/100$ths of the original so sales rise by 10%.

4 The calculations are summarized in Table S3.1.

Table S3.1

End of year	Interest	Investment
1	$80	$1,080
2	$86.40	$1,166.40
3	$93.31	$1,259.71
4	$100.78	$1,360.49
5	$108.84	$1,469.33
6	$117.55	$1,586.88
7	$126.95	$1,713.83
8	$137.11	$1,850.94
9	$148.08	$1,999.02
10	$159.92	$2,158.94

5   $S = 1000(1.08)^{10} = \$2,158.92$

The slight discrepancy between the two answers obtained in Problems 4 and 5 arises because the intermediate results in Problem 4 are rounded to 2 decimal places.

6   $9000(1.03)^n = 10\,000$

$$(1.03)^n = 1.11$$

$$\log(1.03)^n = \log(1.11)$$

$$n\log(1.03) = \log(1.11)$$

$$n = \frac{\log(1.11)}{\log(1.03)} = 3.53$$

so the firm makes a profit for the first time after 4 years.

7   **(1)**   **(a)** $S = 30(1.06)^2 = \$33.71$
        (b) $S = 30(1.03)^4 = \$33.77$
        (c) $S = 30(1.015)^8 = \$33.79$
        (d) $S = 30(1.005)^{24} = \$33.81$
        (e) $S = 30(1.001\,15)^{104} = \$33.82$
        (f) $S = 30(1.000\,164)^{730} = \$33.82$

    (2) $S = 30e^{0.12} = \$33.82$
        The results in part (1) are settling down at this value.

8   $4000 = 1000e^{0.1r}$

$$4 = e^{0.1r}$$

$$0.1r = \ln 4 = 1.386$$

$$r = 13.86\%$$

9   At the end of one year the future value

of a principal, P, invested at 12% compounded quarterly is

$$P(1.03)^4$$

If this is equivalent to $r\%$ compounded annually then

$$P\left(1 + \frac{r}{100}\right) = P(1.03)^4 = P(1.1255)$$

$$1 + \frac{r}{100} = 1.1255$$

$$r = 12.55\%$$

10 **(1)** $619,173.64; **(2)** 13.

11 15 years.

12 $50,000 (0.95)^3 = \$42,868.75.

13 **(a)** $13,947.94; **(b)** $14,156.59;
    (c) $14,342.45; **(d)** $14,381.03.

14 We are charged interest on the interest; 26.82%.

15 7.25%.

Section 3.2

1   The geometric ratios of (a), (c), (d) and (e) are 2, -3, $\frac{1}{2}$ and 1.07 respectively. The sequence in part (b) is not a geometric progression because to go from one number to the next we add on the fixed value of 5. Such a sequence is called an **arithmetic progression**.

2   **(1)**   The geometric ratio is 2 so the next term is $8 \times 2 = 16$.

$$1 + 2 + 4 + 8 + 16 = 31$$

For this series, $a = 1$, $r = 2$ and $n = 5$, so its value is

$$(1)\left(\frac{2^5 - 1}{2 - 1}\right) = 32 - 1 = 31$$

    (2)   For this series, $a = 100(1.07)$, $r = 1.07$ and $n = 20$ so its value is

$$100(1.07)\left(\frac{1.07^{20} - 1}{1.07 - 1}\right) = 4386.52$$

3 (1) The first $1,000 payment is invested for the full 10 years at 8% interest compounded annually so its future value is

$$1000(1.08)^{10}$$

The second $1,000 payment is invested for 9 years so its future value is

$$1000(1.08)^9$$

and so on.

The final payment of $1,000 is invested for just 1 year so its future value is

$$1000(1.08)^1$$

Total savings

$$= 1000(1.08)^{10}$$

$$+ 1000(1.08)^9$$

$$+ \ldots + 1000(1.08)$$

$$= 1000(1.08)\left(\frac{1.08^{10} - 1}{1.08 - 1}\right)$$

$$= \$15,645.49$$

(2) After n years,

$$\text{total savings} = 1000(1.08)\left(\frac{1.08^n - 1}{1.08 - 1}\right)$$

$$= 13\,500(1.08^n - 1)$$

so we need to solve

$$13\,500(1.08^n - 1) = 20\,000$$

This can be done by taking logarithms following the strategy described in Section 2.3. The corresponding value of n is 11.8 so it takes 12 years.

4 If $x denotes the monthly repayment the amount owed at the end of the first month is

$$2000(1.01) - x$$

After 2 months the amount owed is

$$[2000(1.01) - x](1.01) - x$$

$$= 2000(1.01)^2 - x(1.01) - x$$

Each month we multiply by 1.01 to add on the interest and subtract x to deduct the repayment, so after 12 months the outstanding debt is

$$2000(1.01)^{12}$$

$$- x[1.01^{11} + 1.01^{10} + \ldots + 1]$$

$$= 2253.650 - x\left(\frac{1.01^{12} - 1}{1.01 - 1}\right)$$

$$= 2253.650 - 12.683x$$

If the debt is to be cleared then

$$x = \frac{2253.650}{12.683} = \$177.69$$

5 11 463.88.

6 (a) $9,280.71; **(b)** $9,028.14.

7 $313,238.

8 $424.19; **(a)** $459.03, **(b)** $456.44.

9 $rS_n = r(a + ar + ar^2 + \ldots + ar^{n-1})$

$$= ar + ar^2 + ar^3 + \ldots + ar^n$$

which is very similar to the given expression for S_n except that the first term, a, is missing and we have the extra term, ar^n. Consequently when S_n is subtracted from rS_n the rest of the terms cancel leaving

$$rS_n - S_n = ar^n - a$$

$$(r - 1)S_n = a(r^n - 1)$$
$$\text{(factorize both sides)}$$

$$S_n = a\left(\frac{r^n - 1}{r - 1}\right)$$
$$\text{(divide through by } r - 1)$$

The expression for S_n denotes the sum of the first n terms of a geometric series because the powers of r run from 0 to $n - 1$ making n terms in total. Notice that we are not allowed to divide by zero so the last step is not valid for $r = 1$.

Section 3.3

1 (a) $P = 100\,000(1.06)^{-10} = \$55,839.48$
(b) $P = 100\,000e^{-0.6} = \$54,881.16$

2 **(a)** $\text{NPV} = \$17,000(1.15)^{-5} - \$8,000$
$= \$452$

Worthwhile since this is positive.

(b) The IRR, r, is the solution of

$$8000\left(1 + \frac{r}{100}\right)^5 = 17\,000$$

$$\left(1 + \frac{r}{100}\right)^5 = 2.125$$

(divide by 8000)

$$1 + \frac{r}{100} = 1.16$$

(take fifth roots)

$$r = 16\%$$

Worthwhile since the IRR exceeds the market rate.

3 NPV of Project A is

$$\text{NPV}_A = \$18,000(1.07)^{-2} \quad \$13,500$$
$$= \$2,221.90$$

NPV of Project B is

$$\text{NPV}_B = \$13,000(1.07)^{-2} - \$9,000$$
$$= \$2,354.70$$

Project B is to be preferred since
$$\text{NPV}_B > \text{NPV}_A$$

4 Rate of interest per month is $\frac{1}{2}\%$ so the present value, P, of $\$S$ in t months' time is

$$P = S(1.005)^{-t}$$

The total present value is

$$2000(1.005)^{-1} + 2000(1.005)^{-2}$$
$$+ \ldots + 2000(1.005)^{-120}$$

because there are 120 months in 10 years. Using the formula for a geometric series gives

$$2000(1.005)^{-1}\left(\frac{1.005^{-120} - 1}{1.005^{-1} - 1}\right)$$

$$= \$180,146.91$$

5 The formula for discounting is

$$P = S(1.15)^{-t}$$

The results are given in Table S3.2. There is very little to choose between

Table S3.2

End of year	Discounted revenue	
	Project 1	Project 2
1	$1,739.13	$869.57
2	$1,512.29	$756.14
3	$1,972.55	$1,315.03
4	$1,715.26	$3,430.52
5	$1,491.53	$1,988.71
Total	$8,430.76	$8,359.97

these two projects. Both present values are considerably less than the original expenditure of $10,000. Consequently neither project is to be recommended since the net present values are negative. The firm would be better off just investing the $10,000 at 15% interest!

6 The IRR satisfies the equation

$$12\,000 = 8000\left(1 + \frac{r}{100}\right)^{-1}$$
$$+ 2000\left(1 + \frac{r}{100}\right)^{-2}$$
$$+ 2000\left(1 + \frac{r}{100}\right)^{-3}$$
$$+ 2000\left(1 + \frac{r}{100}\right)^{-4}$$

Values of the right-hand side of this equation corresponding to $r = 5, 6, \ldots, 10$ are listed in the table below:

r	5	6	7	8	9	10
value	12 806	12 591	12 382	12 180	11 984	11 794

This shows that r is between 8 and 9. To decide which of these to go for we evaluate $r = 8\frac{1}{2}$, which gives 12 081 which is greater than 12 000 so $r = 9\%$ to the nearest percentage. This exceeds the market rate so the project is worthwhile.

7 If the yield is 7% then each year the income is $70 with the exception of the last year when it is $1,070 because the bond is redeemed for its original value.

Table S3.3

End of year	Cash flow	Present value
1	$70	$64.81
2	$70	$60.01
3	$1,070	$849.40
Total present value		$974.22

The present values of this income stream are listed in Table S3.3 and are calculated using the formula

$$P = S(1.08)^{-t}$$

8 **(a)** $5,974.43; **(b)** $5,965.01.

9 **(1)** 7%; **(2)** yes, provided there are no risks.

10 NPA$_A$=$1,595.94; NPV$_B$=$1,961.99; NPV$_C$=$1,069.00 so Project B is best.

11 **(a)** $379.08; **(b)** $1,000.

12 $61,672.67.

13 $38,887.69.

14 27%.

15 $349.15.

CHAPTER 4

Section 4.1

1 **(a)** $\dfrac{11 - 3}{3 - (-1)} = \dfrac{8}{4} = 2$

(b) $\dfrac{-2 - 3}{4 - (-1)} = \dfrac{-5}{5} = -1$

(c) $\dfrac{3 - 3}{49 - (-1)} = \dfrac{0}{50} = 0$

2 Using the power key $\boxed{x^y}$ on a calculator the values of the cube function, correct to 2 decimal places, are

x	−1.50	−1.25	−1.00	−0.75
$f(x)$	−3.38	−1.95	−1.00	−0.42

x	−0.50	−0.25	0.00	0.25	0.50
$f(x)$	−0.13	−0.02	0.00	0.02	0.13

x	0.75	1.00	1.25	1.50
$f(x)$	0.42	1.00	1.95	3.38

The graph of the cube function is sketched in Figure S4.1.

$$f'(-1) = \frac{1.5}{0.5} = 3.0$$

$f'(0) = 0$ (because the tangent is horizontal at $x = 0$)

$$f'(1) = \frac{1.5}{0.5} = 3.0$$

[Note: $f'(-1) = f'(1)$ because of the symmetry of the graph.]

3 If $n = 3$ then the general formula gives

$$f'(x) = 3x^{3-1} = 3x^2$$

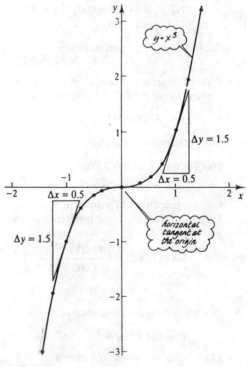

Figure S4.1

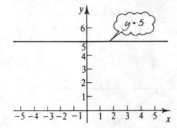

Figure S4.2

Hence

$$f'(-1) = 3(-1)^2 = 3$$

$$f'(0) = 3(0)^2 = 0$$

$$f'(1) = 3(1)^2 = 3$$

4   (a) $5x^4$; (b) $6x^5$; (c) $100x^{99}$;
   (d) $-x^{-2}$ (that is, $-1/x^2$);
   (e) $-2x^{-3}$ (that is, $-2/x^3$).

5   $-\frac{2}{3}$; downhill.

6   When $x = 0$, $y = a(0) + b = b$ ✓
   When $x = 1$, $y = a(1) + b = a + b$ ✓
   Slope $= \dfrac{(a+b) - b}{1 - 0} = a$

7   The graph of $f(x) = 5$ is sketched in
   Figure S4.2. The graph is horizontal so
   has zero slope at all values of x.

8   $7x^6$; 448.

9   (a) $8x^7$; (b) $50x^{49}$; (c) $-3x^{-4}$;
   (d) $\frac{1}{3}x^{-2/3}$.

Section 4.2

1   (a) $4(3x^2) = 12x^2$.
   (b) $-2/x^2$ because $1/x = x^{-1}$ which
   differentiates to $-x^{-2}$.

2   (a) $5x^4 + 1$; (b) $2x + 0 = 2x$.

3   (a) $2x - 3x^2$; (b) $0 - (-3x^{-4}) = \dfrac{3}{x^4}$.

4   (a) $9(5x^4) + 2(2x) = 45x^4 + 4x$.
   (b) $5(8x^7) - 3(-1)x^{-2} = 40x^7 + 3/x^2$.
   (c) $2x + 6(1) + 0 = 2x + 6$.
   (d) $2(4x^3) + 12(3x^2) - 4(2x) + 7(1) - 0$
   $= 8x^3 + 36x^2 - 8x + 7$.

5   $f'(x) = 4(3x^2) - 5(2x) = 12x^2 - 10x$
   $f''(x) = 12(2x) - 10(1) = 24x - 10$
   $f''(6) = 24(6) - 10 = 134$

6   (a) $10x$; (b) $-3/x^2$; (c) 2; (d) $2x + 1$;
   (e) $2x - 3$; (f) $3 + 7/x^2$;
   (g) $6x^2 - 12x + 49$; (h) a; (i) $2ax + b$;
   (j) $2/\sqrt{x} + 3/x^2 - 14/x^3$.

7   (a) 14; (b) $6/x^4$; (c) 0.

8   (a) $2P + 1$; (b) $50 - 6Q$; (c) $-30/Q^2$;
   (d) 3; (e) $5/\sqrt{L}$; (f) $-6Q^2 + 30Q - 24$.

Section 4.3

1   TR $= PQ = (60 - Q)Q = 60Q - Q^2$

   (1)   MR $= 60 - 2Q$

   When $Q = 50$,

   $$MR = 60 - 2(50) = -40$$

   (2)   (a) TR $= 60(50) - (50)^2 = 500$
        (b) TR $= 60(51) - (51)^2 = 459$

   so TR changes by -41 which is
   approximately the same as the
   exact value obtained in part (1).

2   MR $= 1000 - 8Q$ so when $Q = 30$,

   $$MR = 1000 - 8(30) = 760$$

   (1) $\Delta(\text{TR}) \simeq \text{MR} \times \Delta Q = 760 \times 3 = 2280$
        so total revenue rises by about 2280.
   (2) $\Delta(\text{TR}) \simeq \text{MR} \times \Delta Q = 760 \times (-2)$
        $= -1520$
        so total revenue falls by about 1520.

3   TC $= (\text{AC})Q = \left(\dfrac{100}{Q} + 2\right)Q = 100 + 2Q$

   This function differentiates to give
   MC $= 2$ so a one unit increase in Q
   always leads to a two unit increase in TC
   irrespective of the level of output.

4   If $K = 100$ then
   $Q = 5L^{1/2}(100)^{1/2} = 50L^{1/2}$ because
   $\sqrt{100} = 10$. Differentiating gives

   $$MP_L = 50(\tfrac{1}{2}L^{-1/2}) = \dfrac{25}{\sqrt{L}}$$

(a) $\dfrac{25}{\sqrt{1}} = 25$; (b) $\dfrac{25}{\sqrt{9}} = \dfrac{25}{3} = 8.3$

(c) $\dfrac{25}{\sqrt{10\,000}} = \dfrac{25}{100} = 0.25$

The fact that these values decrease as L increases suggests that the law of diminishing marginal productivity holds for this function. This can be confirmed by differentiating a second time to get

$$\frac{d^2Q}{dL^2} = 25\left(-\tfrac{1}{2}L^{-3/2}\right) = \frac{-25}{2L^{3/2}}$$

which is negative for all values of L.

5 The savings function is given so we begin by finding MPS. Differentiating S with respect to Y gives

$$\text{MPS} = 0.04Y - 1$$

so when $Y = 40$,

$$\text{MPS} = 0.04(40) - 1 = 0.6$$

To find MPC we use the formula

$$\text{MPC} + \text{MPS} = 1$$

that is,

$$\text{MPC} = 1 - \text{MPS} = 1 - 0.6 = 0.4$$

This indicates that, at the current level of income, a one unit increase in national income causes a rise of about 0.6 units in savings and 0.4 units in consumption.

6 $\text{TR} = 100Q - Q^2$; $\text{MR} = 100 - 2Q$. Graphs of TR and MR are sketched in Figures S4.3 and S4.4 respectively. $\text{MR} = 0$ when $Q = 50$. This is the value of Q at which TR is a maximum.

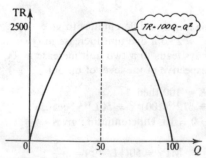

Figure S4.3

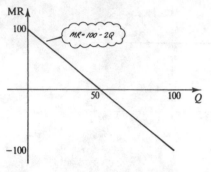

Figure S4.4

7 (1) $\text{TC} = 100 + 2Q + Q^2/10$;
        $\text{MC} = 2 + Q/5$.
   (2) $\text{MC} = 8$; $\Delta(\text{TC}) \simeq 16$.
   (3) 100.

8 (a) 49.98; (b) 49.8; (c) 48; (d) 30. Yes, because $d^2Q/dL^2 = -0.02 < 0$.

9 $\dfrac{d^2Q}{dL^2} = 12 - 1.2L < 0$ for all $L > 10$.

10 MPC $= 1/6$ and MPS $= 5/6$. If national income rises by 1 unit, the approximate increase in consumption and savings is $1/6$ and $5/6$ respectively.

Section 4.4

1 (a) The outer power function differentiates to get $5(3x - 4)^4$ and the derivative of the inner function, $3x - 4$, is 3 so

$$\frac{dy}{dx} = 5(3x - 4)^4(3) = 15(3x - 4)^4$$

   (b) The outer power function differentiates to get $3(x^2 + 3x + 5)^2$ and the derivative of the inner function, $x^2 + 3x + 5$, is $2x + 3$ so

$$\frac{dy}{dx} = 3(x^2 + 3x + 5)^2(2x + 3)$$

   (c) Note that $y = (2x - 3)^{-1}$. The outer power function differentiates to get $-(2x - 3)^{-2}$ and the derivative of the inner function, $2x - 3$, is 2 so

$$\frac{dy}{dx} = -(2x - 3)^{-2}(2) = \frac{-2}{(2x - 3)^2}$$

(d) Note that $y = (4x - 3)^{1/2}$. The outer power function differentiates to get $\frac{1}{2}(4x - 3)^{-1/2}$ and the derivative of the inner function, $4x - 3$, is 4 so

$$\frac{dy}{dx} = \frac{1}{2}(4x - 3)^{-1/2}(4) = \frac{2}{\sqrt{(4x - 3)}}$$

2 (a) $u = x$ $v = (3x - 1)^6$

$$\frac{du}{dx} = 1 \qquad \frac{dv}{dx} = 6(3x - 1)^5(3)$$

So

$$\frac{dy}{dx} = 18x(3x - 1)^5 + (3x - 1)^6$$

$$= (3x - 1)^5[18x + (3x - 1)]$$

$$= (3x - 1)^5(21x - 1)$$

(b) $u = x^3$ $v = (2x + 3)^{1/2}$

$$\frac{du}{dx} = 3x^2 \quad \frac{dv}{dx} = \frac{1}{2}(2x + 3)^{-1/2}(2)$$

$$= \frac{1}{\sqrt{(2x + 3)}}$$

So

$$\frac{dy}{dx} = \frac{x^3}{\sqrt{(2x + 3)}} + 3x^2\sqrt{(2x + 3)}$$

(c) $u = x$ $v = (x - 2)^{-1}$

$$\frac{du}{dx} = 1 \qquad \frac{dv}{dx} = -(x - 2)^{-2}$$

So

$$\frac{dy}{dx} = \frac{-x}{(x - 2)^2} + \frac{1}{x - 2}$$

$$= \frac{-x + (x - 2)}{(x - 2)^2}$$

$$= \frac{-2}{(x - 2)^2}$$

3 (a) $u = x$ $v = x - 2$

$$\frac{du}{dx} = 1 \qquad \frac{dv}{dx} = 1$$

So

$$\frac{dy}{dx} = \frac{(x - 2) - x}{(x - 2)^2}$$

$$= \frac{-2}{(x - 2)^2}$$

(b) $u = x - 1$ $v = x + 1$

$$\frac{du}{dx} = 1 \qquad \frac{dv}{dx} = 1$$

So

$$\frac{dy}{dx} = \frac{(x + 1) - (x - 1)}{(x + 1)^2}$$

$$= \frac{2}{(x + 1)^2}$$

4 **(a)** $20(2x + 1)^9$;
(b) $3(x^2 + 3x - 5)^2(2x + 3)$;
(c) $-7/(7x - 3)^2$; **(d)** $-2x/(x^2 + 1)^2$;
(e) $4/\sqrt{(8x - 1)}$.

5 **(a)** $4x(x - 3)^3 + (x - 3)^4 = (x - 3)^3(5x - 3)$

(b) $\dfrac{x}{\sqrt{(2x - 3)}} + \sqrt{(2x - 3)} = \dfrac{3x - 3}{\sqrt{(2x - 3)}}$

(c) $\dfrac{5}{(x + 5)^2}$

(d) $\dfrac{1 - x^2}{(x^2 + 1)^2}$

6 **(a)** $\dfrac{100 - 3Q}{\sqrt{(100 - 2Q)}}$

(b) $\dfrac{1000(2 + Q)^{1/2} - 500Q(2 + Q)^{-1/2}}{(2 + Q)}$

$$= \frac{2000 + 500Q}{(2 + Q)^{3/2}}$$

7 MPC = 1.8, MPS = -0.8. If national income rises by 1 unit, consumption rises by 1.8 units whereas savings actually fall by 0.8 units.

Section 4.5

1 We are given that $P_1 = 210$ and $P_2 = 200$. Substituting $P = 210$ into the demand equation gives

$$1000 - 2Q_1 = 210$$
$$-2Q_1 = -790$$
$$Q_1 = 395$$

Similarly, putting $P = 200$ gives $Q_2 = 400$. Hence

$$\Delta P = 200 - 210 = -10$$
$$\Delta Q = 400 - 395 = 5$$

Averaging the P values gives $P = \frac{1}{2}(210 + 200) = 205$. Averaging the Q values gives $Q = \frac{1}{2}(395 + 400) = 397.5$. Hence, arc elasticity is

$$-\left(\frac{205}{397.5}\right) \times \left(\frac{5}{-10}\right) = 0.26$$

2 The quickest way of solving this problem is to find a general expression for E in terms of P and then just to replace P by 10, 50 and 90 in turn. The equation

$$P = 100 - Q$$

rearranges as

$$Q = 100 - P$$

so

$$\frac{dQ}{dP} = -1$$

Hence

$$E = -\frac{P}{Q} \times \frac{dQ}{dP} = \frac{-P}{100 - P} \times (-1)$$
$$= \frac{P}{100 - P}$$

(a) If $P = 10$ then $E = 1/9 < 1$ so inelastic.
(b) If $P = 50$ then $E = 1$ so unit elastic.
(c) If $P = 90$ then $E = 9$ so elastic.

At the end of Section 4.5 it is shown quite generally that the price elasticity of demand for a linear function

$$P = aQ + b$$

is given by

$$E = \frac{P}{b - P}$$

The above is a special case of this with $b = 100$.

3 Substituting $Q = 4$ into the demand equation gives

$$P = -(4)^2 - 10(4) + 150 = 94$$

Differentiating the demand equation with respect to Q gives

$$\frac{dP}{dQ} = -2Q - 10$$

so

$$\frac{dQ}{dP} = \frac{1}{-2Q - 10}$$

When $Q = 4$, $\dfrac{dQ}{dP} = -\dfrac{1}{18}$

The price elasticity of demand is then

$$-\left(\frac{94}{4}\right) \times \left(-\frac{1}{18}\right) = \frac{47}{36}$$

From the definition,

$$E = -\frac{\text{percentage change in demand}}{\text{percentage change in price}}$$

we have

$$\frac{47}{36} = -\frac{10}{\text{percentage change in price}}$$

Hence the percentage change in price is $-10 \times 36/47 = -7.7\%$, that is the firm must decrease prices by 7.7% to achieve a 10% increase in demand.

4 (a) Putting $P = 9$ and 11 directly into the supply equation gives $Q = 203.1$ and 217.1 respectively, so

$$\Delta P = 11 - 9 = 2$$
$$\Delta Q = 217.1 - 203.1 = 14$$

Averaging the P values gives $P = \frac{1}{2}(9 + 11) = 10$. Averaging the Q

values gives
$Q = \frac{1}{2}(203.1 + 217.1) = 210.1$. Arc
elasticity is

$$\frac{10}{210.1} \times \frac{14}{2} = 0.333\,175$$

(b) Putting $P = 10$ directly into the
supply equation, we get $Q = 210$.
Differentiating the supply equation
immediately gives

$$\frac{dQ}{dP} = 5 + 0.2P$$

so when $P = 10$, $dQ/dP = 7$. Hence

$$E = \frac{10}{210} \times 7 = \frac{1}{3}$$

Note that, as expected, the results in parts
(a) and (b) are similar. They are not
identical because in part (a) the elasticity
is 'averaged' over the arc from $P = 9$ to
$P = 11$, whereas in part (b) the elasticity is
evaluated exactly at the midpoint, $P = 10$.

5 **(a)** 1/4; **(b)** 1/4; **(c)** 9/8.

6 $4P/(60 - 4P)$; 7.5.

7 1.46; **(1)** elastic; **(2)** 7.3%.

8 If $P = AQ^{-n}$ then

$$\frac{dP}{dQ} = -nAQ^{-(n+1)}$$

so

$$\frac{dQ}{dP} = \frac{1}{-nAQ^{-(n+1)}}$$

Hence

$$E = -\frac{P}{Q} \times \frac{dQ}{dP}$$

$$= -\left(\frac{AQ^{-n}}{Q}\right) \times \left(\frac{1}{-nAQ^{-(n+1)}}\right)$$

$$= -Q^{-n} \times \left(\frac{1}{-nQ^{-n}}\right) = \frac{1}{n}$$

which is a constant.

Section 4.6

1 **(a)** *Step 1*

$$\frac{dy}{dx} = 6x + 12 = 0$$

has solution $x = -2$.

Step 2

$$\frac{d^2y}{dx^2} = 6 > 0$$

so minimum.

Finally, note that when $x = -2$,
$y = -47$ so the minimum point has
coordinates $(-2, -47)$. A graph is
sketched in Figure S4.5.

(b) *Step 1*

$$\frac{dy}{dx} = -6x^2 + 30x - 36 = 0$$

has solutions $x = 2$ and $x = 3$.

Step 2

$$\frac{d^2y}{dx^2} = -12x + 30$$

which takes the values 6 and -6 at
$x = 2$ and $x = 3$ respectively. Hence
minimum at $x = 2$ and maximum at
$x = 3$.

A graph is sketched in Figure S4.6

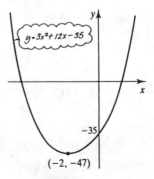

$y = 3x^2 + 12x - 35$

-35

$(-2, -47)$

Figure S4.5

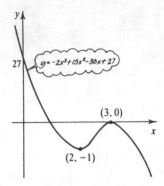

Figure S4.6

based on the following table of function values:

x	-10	0	2	3	10
$f(x)$	3887	27	-1	0	-833

2 $AP_L = \dfrac{Q}{L} = \dfrac{300L^2 - L^4}{L} = 300L - L^3$

Step 1

$$\frac{d(AP_L)}{dL} = 300 - 3L^2 = 0$$

has solution $L = \pm 10$. We can ignore -10 because it does not make sense to employ a negative number of workers.

Step 2

$$\frac{d^2(AP_L)}{dL^2} = -6L$$

which takes the value $-60 < 0$ at $L = 10$. Hence $L = 10$ is a maximum.

Now

$$MP_L = \frac{dQ}{dL} = 600L - 4L^3$$

so at $L = 10$,

$$MP_L = 600(10) - 4(10)^3 = 2000$$

$$AP_L = 300(10) - (10)^3 = 2000$$

that is $MP_L = AP_L$.

3 (1) $TR = PQ = (20 - 2Q)Q = 20Q - 2Q^2$

Step 1

$$\frac{d(TR)}{dQ} = 20 - 4Q = 0$$

has solution $Q = 5$.

Step 2

$$\frac{d^2(TR)}{dQ^2} = -2 < 0$$

so maximum.

(2) $\pi = TR - TC$

$\quad = (20Q - 2Q^2)$

$\qquad - (Q^3 - 8Q^2 + 20Q + 2)$

$\quad = -Q^3 + 6Q^2 - 2$

Step 1

$$\frac{d\pi}{dQ} = -3Q^2 + 12Q = 0$$

has solutions $Q = 0$ and $Q = 4$.

Step 2

$$\frac{d^2\pi}{dQ^2} = -6Q + 12$$

which takes the values 12 and -12 when $Q = 0$ and $Q = 4$ respectively. Hence minimum at $Q = 0$ and maximum at $Q = 4$.

Finally, evaluating π at $Q = 4$ gives the maximum profit, $\pi = 30$. Now

$$MR = \frac{d(TR)}{dQ} = 20 - 4Q$$

so at $Q = 4$, $MR = 4$

$$MC = \frac{d(TC)}{dQ} = 3Q^2 - 16Q + 20$$

so at $Q = 4$, $MC = 4$

4 $AC = Q + 3 + \dfrac{36}{Q}$

Step 1

$$\frac{d(AC)}{dQ} = 1 - \frac{36}{Q^2} = 0$$

has solution $Q = \pm 6$. A negative value of Q does not make sense so we just take $Q = 6$.

Step 2

$$\frac{d^2(AC)}{dQ^2} = \frac{72}{Q^3}$$

is positive when $Q = 6$ so it is a minimum.

Now when $Q = 6$, $AC = 15$. Also

$$MC = \frac{d(TC)}{dQ} = 2Q + 3$$

which takes the value 15 at $Q = 6$. We observe that the values of AC and MC are the same; that is, at the point of minimum average cost

average cost	=	marginal cost

There is nothing special about this example and in the next section we show that this result is true for any average cost function.

5 After tax the supply equation becomes

$$P = \tfrac{1}{2}Q_S + 25 + t$$

In equilibrium, $Q_S = Q_D = Q$ so

$$P = \tfrac{1}{2}Q + 25 + t$$

$$P = -2Q + 50$$

Hence

$$\tfrac{1}{2}Q + 25 + t = -2Q + 50$$

which rearranges to give

$$Q = 10 - \tfrac{2}{5}t$$

Hence the tax revenue, T, is

$$T = tQ = 10t - \tfrac{2}{5}t^2$$

Step 1

$$\frac{dT}{dt} = 10 - \tfrac{4}{5}t^2 = 0$$

has solution $t = 12.5$.

Step 2

$$\frac{d^2T}{dt^2} = \frac{-4}{5} < 0$$

so maximum. Government should therefore impose a tax of $12.50 per good.

6 (a) Maximum at $(1/2, 5/4)$; graph is sketched in Figure S4.7.

(b) Minimum at $(2, 0)$; graph is sketched in Figure S4.8.

(c) Minimum at $(10, 5)$; graph is sketched in Figure S4.9.

(d) Maximum at $(1, 2)$, minimum at $(-1, -2)$; graph is sketched in Figure S4.10.

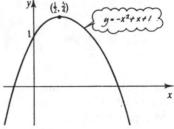

Figure S4.7

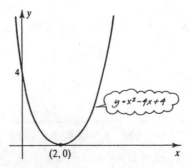

Figure S4.8

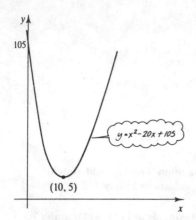

Figure S4.9

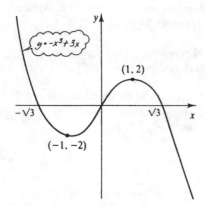

Figure S4.10

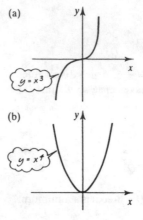

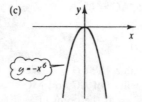

Figure S4.11

7 Graphs of the three functions are sketched in Figure S4.11 which shows that the stationary points in (a), (b) and (c) are a point of inflection, minimum and maximum respectively.

8 **(1)** $TC = 13 + (Q + 2)Q$

$= 13 + Q^2 + 2Q$

$$AC = \frac{TC}{Q} = \frac{13}{Q} + Q + 2$$

Q	1	2	3	4	5	6
AC	16	10.5	9.3	9.3	9.6	10.2

The graph of AC is sketched in Figure S4.12.

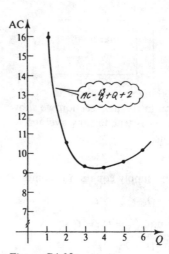

Figure S4.12

(2) From Figure S4.12 minimum average cost $\simeq 9.2$.

(3) Minimum at $Q = \sqrt{13}$ which gives $AC = 9.21$.

9 **(1)** 37 037 after 333 days.
(2) 167.

10 167.

11 (1) $\quad TR = 4Q - \dfrac{Q^2}{4}$

$$\pi = \dfrac{-Q^3}{20} + \dfrac{Q^2}{20} + 2Q - 4$$

$$MR = 4 - \dfrac{Q}{2}$$

$$MC = 2 - \dfrac{3Q}{5} + \dfrac{3Q^2}{20}$$

(2) 4.
(3) MR = 2 = MC.

12 $3.

Section 4.7

1 (1) $\quad TR = (25 - 0.5Q)Q = 25Q - 0.5Q^2$

$\quad\quad\quad TC = 7 + (Q + 1)Q = Q^2 + Q + 7$

$\quad\quad\quad MR = 25 - Q$

$\quad\quad\quad MC = 2Q + 1$

(2) From Figure S4.13 the point of intersection of the MR and MC curves occurs at $Q = 8$. The MC curve cuts the MR curve from below so this must be a maximum point.

2 MC = 100.

(a) *Domestic market* $P_1 = 300 - Q_1$

$$TR_1 = 300Q_1 - Q_1^2$$

so

$$MR_1 = 300 - 2Q_1$$

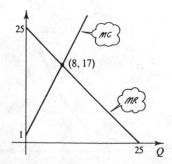

Figure S4.13

To maximize profit, $MR_1 = MC$, that is

$$300 - 2Q_1 = 100$$

which has solution $Q_1 = 100$. Corresponding price is
$P_1 = 300 - 100 = \$200$.

Foreign market $P_2 = 200 - \frac{1}{2}Q_2$

$$TR_2 = 200Q_2 - \tfrac{1}{2}Q_2^2$$

so

$$MR_2 = 200 - Q_2$$

To maximize profit, $MR_2 = MC$, that is

$$200 - Q_2 = 100$$

which has solution $Q_2 = 100$. Corresponding price is
$P_2 = 200 - \frac{1}{2}(100) = \$150$.

(b) Without discrimination, $P_1 = P_2 = P$, say, so individual demand equations become

$$Q_1 = 300 - P$$

$$Q_2 = 400 - 2P$$

Adding shows that the demand equation for combined market is

$$Q = 700 - 3P$$

where $Q = Q_1 + Q_2$.

$$TR = \dfrac{700}{3}Q - \dfrac{Q^2}{3}$$

so

$$MR = \dfrac{700}{3} - \dfrac{2Q}{3}$$

To maximize profit, $MR = MC$, that is

$$\dfrac{700}{3} - \dfrac{2Q}{3} = 100$$

which has solution $Q = 200$. Corresponding price is
$P = 700/3 - 200/3 = \$500/3$.

Total cost of producing 200 goods is

$$5000 + 100(200) = \$25,000$$

With discrimination, total revenue is

$$100 \times 200 + 100 \times 150 = \$35,000$$

so profit is $\$35,000 - \$25,000 = \$10,000$.
Without discrimination, total revenue is

$$200 \times \frac{500}{3} = \$33,333$$

so profit is $\$33,333 - \$25,000 = \$8,333$.

3 *Domestic market* From Problem 2, profit
is maximum when $P_1 = 200$, $Q_1 = 100$.
Also, since $Q_1 = 300 - P_1$ we have
$dQ_1/dP_1 = -1$. Hence

$$E_1 = -\frac{P_1}{Q_1} \times \frac{dQ_1}{dP_1}$$

$$= -\frac{200}{100} \times (-1) = 2$$

Foreign market From Problem 2, profit
is maximum when $P_2 = 150$, $Q_2 = 100$.
Also, since $Q_2 = 400 - 2P_2$ we have
$dQ_2/dP_2 = -2$. Hence

$$E_2 = -\frac{P_2}{Q_2} \times \frac{dQ_2}{dP_2}$$

$$= -\frac{150}{100} \times (-2) = 3$$

We see that the firm charges the higher
price in the domestic market which has
the lower elasticity of demand.

4 Argument is similar to that given in text
but with $<$ replaced by $>$.

5 **(1)** At the point of maximum total
revenue,

$$MR = \frac{d(TR)}{dQ} = 0$$

so $E = 1$.

(2) Maximum occurs when $Q = 10$.

6 $TC = ACO + ACC$

$$= \frac{(ARU)(CO)}{EOQ} + (CU)(CC)\frac{(EOQ)}{2}$$

At a stationary point,

$$\frac{d(TC)}{d(EOQ)} = -\frac{(ARU)(CO)}{(EOQ)^2}$$

$$+ \frac{(CU)(CC)}{2} = 0$$

which has solution

$$EOQ = \sqrt{\frac{2(ARU)(CO)}{(CU)(CC)}}$$

Also

$$\frac{d^2(TC)}{d(EOQ)^2} = \frac{2(ARU)(CO)}{(EOQ)^3} > 0$$

so minimum.

7 **(a)** $P_1 = \$30$, $P_2 = \$20$.
(b) $P = \$24.44$.

The profits in parts (a) and (b) are $\$95$
and $\$83.89$ respectively.

8 The argument is similar to that given in
the text for AP_L.

Section 4.8

1

x	-3	-2	-1	0	1	2	3
3^x	0.04	0.11	0.33	1	3	9	27
3^{-x}	27	9	3	1	0.33	0.11	0.04

The graphs of 3^x and 3^{-x} are sketched in
Figures S4.14 and S4.15, respectively.

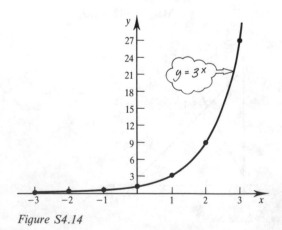

Figure S4.14

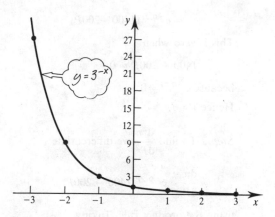

Figure S4.15

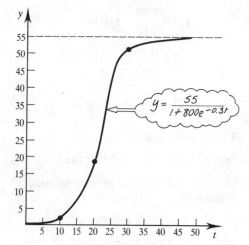

Figure S4.16

2 **(1)** 2.718 145 927, 2.718 268 237,
2.718 280 469.

 (2) values in part (1) are getting closer
to that of part (2).

3 **(1)** Putting $t = 0$ and 2 into the
expression for TR gives

$$\text{TR} = 5e^0 = \$5 \text{ million}$$

$$\text{TR} = 5e^{-0.3} = \$3.7 \text{ million}$$

 (2) To solve $5e^{-0.15t} = 2.7$ we divide by
5 to get $e^{-0.15t} = 0.54$ and then take
natural logarithms which gives

$$-0.15t = \ln(0.54) = -0.62$$

Hence $t = 4$ years.

4 **(1)** Substituting $t = 0, 10, 20$ and 30 gives

 (a) $y(0) = \dfrac{55}{1 + 800e^0} = 0.07\%$

 (b) $y(10) = \dfrac{55}{1 + 800e^{-3}} = 1.35\%$

 (c) $y(20) = \dfrac{55}{1 + 800e^{-6}} = 18.44\%$

 (d) $y(30) = \dfrac{55}{1 + 800e^{-9}} = 50.06\%$

 (2) As t increases, $e^{-0.3t}$ goes to zero so
y approaches

$$\frac{55}{1 + 800(0)} = 55\%$$

 (3) A graph of y against t, based on the
information obtained in parts (1)
and (2), is sketched in Figure S4.16.
This shows that, after a slow start,
camcorder ownership grows rapidly
between $t = 10$ and 30. However,
the rate of growth then decreases as
the market approaches its
saturation level of 55%.

5

x		0.50	1.00	1.50	2.00
$f(x)$		-0.69	0.00	0.41	0.69
x		2.50	3.00	3.50	4.00
$f(x)$		0.92	1.10	1.25	1.39

The graph of the natural logarithm
function is sketched in Figure S4.17.

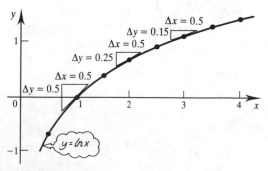

Figure S4.17

$$f'(1) = \frac{0.50}{0.50} = 1.00 \simeq 1$$

$$f'(2) = \frac{0.25}{0.50} = 0.50 \simeq \frac{1}{2}$$

$$f'(3) = \frac{0.15}{0.50} = 0.30 \simeq \frac{1}{3}$$

These results suggest that $f'(x) = 1/x$.

6 (a) $3e^{3x}$; (b) $-e^{-x}$; (c) $1/x$; (d) $1/x$.

7 In terms of P the total revenue function is given by

$$\text{TR} = PQ = 1000Pe^{-0.2P}$$

and the total cost function is

$$\text{TC} = 100 + 2Q = 100 + 2000e^{-0.2P}$$

Hence

$$\pi = \text{TR} - \text{TC} = \\ 1000Pe^{-0.2P} - 2000e^{-0.2P} - 100$$

Step 1 At a stationary point

$$\frac{d\pi}{dP} = 0$$

To differentiate the first term, $1000Pe^{-0.2P}$, we use the product rule with

$$u = 1000P \quad \text{and} \quad v = e^{-0.2P}$$

for which

$$\frac{du}{dP} = 1000 \quad \text{and} \quad \frac{dv}{dP} = -0.2e^{-0.2P}$$

Hence the derivative of $1000Pe^{-0.2P}$ is

$$u\frac{dv}{dP} + v\frac{du}{dP}$$

$$= 1000P(-0.2e^{-0.2P}) + e^{-0.2P}(1000)$$

$$= e^{-0.2P}(1000 - 200P)$$

Now

$$\pi = 1000Pe^{-0.2P} - 2000e^{-0.2P} - 100$$

so

$$\frac{d\pi}{dP} = e^{-0.2P}(1000 - 200P)$$

$$- 2000(-0.2e^{-0.2P})$$

$$= e^{-0.2P}(1400 - 200P)$$

This is zero when

$$1400 - 200P = 0$$

because $e^{-0.2P} \neq 0$.

Hence $P = 7$.

Step 2 To find $\dfrac{d^2\pi}{dP^2}$ we differentiate

$$\frac{d\pi}{dP} = e^{-0.2P}(1400 - 200P)$$

using the product rule. Taking

$$u = e^{-0.2P} \quad \text{and} \quad v = 1400 - 200P$$

gives

$$\frac{du}{dP} = -0.2e^{-0.2P} \quad \text{and} \quad \frac{dv}{dP} = -200$$

Hence

$$\frac{d^2\pi}{dP^2} = u\frac{dv}{dP} + v\frac{du}{dP}$$

$$= e^{-0.2P}(-200)$$

$$+ (1400 - 200P)(-0.2e^{-0.2P})$$

$$= e^{-0.2P}(40P - 480)$$

Putting $P = 7$ gives

$$\frac{d^2\pi}{dP^2} = -200e^{-1.4}$$

This is negative so the stationary point is a maximum.

8 To find the price elasticity of demand we need to calculate the values of P, Q and dQ/dP. We are given that $Q = 20$ and the demand equation gives

$$P = 200 - 40\ln(20 + 1) = 78.22$$

The demand equation expresses P in terms of Q so we first evaluate dP/dQ and then use the result

$$\frac{dQ}{dP} = 1 \bigg/ \frac{dP}{dQ}$$

To differentiate $\ln(Q + 1)$ by the chain rule we differentiate the outer log function to get

$$\frac{1}{Q+1}$$

and then multiply by the derivative of the inner function, $Q + 1$, to get 1. Hence the derivative of

$$\ln(Q + 1) \quad \text{is} \quad \frac{1}{Q+1}$$

and so $\dfrac{dP}{dQ} = \dfrac{-40}{Q+1}$

Putting $Q = 20$ gives $dP/dQ = -40/21$ so that $dQ/dP = -21/40$. Finally, we use the formula

$$E = -\frac{P}{Q} \times \frac{dQ}{dP}$$

to calculate the price elasticity of demand as

$$E = -\frac{78.22}{20} \times \left(\frac{-21}{40}\right) = 2.05$$

9 The equation

$$N = c(1 - e^{-kt}) = c - ce^{-kt}$$

rearranges as

$$e^{-kt} = \frac{c - N}{c}$$

Taking logarithms gives

$$-kt = \ln\left(\frac{c - N}{c}\right)$$

so

$$t = -\frac{1}{k}\ln\left(\frac{c - N}{c}\right)$$

$$= \frac{1}{k}\ln\left(\frac{c - N}{c}\right)^{-1}$$

$$= \frac{1}{k}\ln\left(\frac{c}{c - N}\right)$$

making use of the third rule of logarithms.

(1) 350 000.
(2) 60 days.
(3) Market saturation level is 700 000

which is less than the $\frac{3}{4}$ million needed to make a profit so the proprietor should sell.

10 (1) Interest is $(r/k)\%$ per period and there are kt periods in t years so

$$S = P\left(1 + \frac{r}{100k}\right)^{kt}$$

(2) If $m = \dfrac{100k}{r}$ then $\dfrac{r}{100k} = \dfrac{1}{m}$ and

$$kt = \frac{mrt}{100} \quad \text{so}$$

$$S = P\left(1 + \frac{1}{m}\right)^{rtm/100}$$

$$= P\left[\left(1 + \frac{1}{m}\right)^{m}\right]^{rt/100}$$

by the third rule of indices.

(3) Now since $m = 100k/r$ we see that if the frequency increases (i.e. if $k \to \infty$) then $m \to \infty$ causing

$$\left(1 + \frac{1}{m}\right)^{m}$$

to approach e. Substituting this into the result of part (2) gives

$$S = Pe^{rt/100}$$

11 (1) (a) 32; **(b)** 55; **(c)** 98.
(2) 100.
(3) A graph of N against t is sketched in Figure S4.18. This is known as a

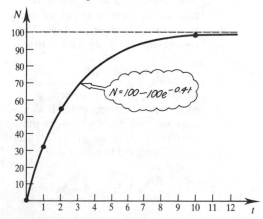

$$N = 100 - 100e^{-0.4t}$$

Figure S4.18

learning curve. It shows that
immediately after training the
worker can produce only a small
number of items. However, with
only a few days of practice, output
quickly increases to eventually
produce a daily rate of 100 items.

12 (a) $2xe^{x^2}$;   (b) $\dfrac{1 + 2x}{1 + x + x^2}$

13 (a) $(4x^3 + 2x^4)e^{2x}$;   (b) $\ln x + 1$

14 49.

15 50.

CHAPTER 5

Section 5.1

1 (a) -10; (b) -1; (c) 2; (d) 21; (e) 0;
    (f) 21. The value of g is independent
    of the ordering of the variables. Such
    a function is said to be **symmetric**.

2 (a) Differentiating $5x^4$ with respect to x
    gives $20x^3$ and, since y is held
    constant, y^2 differentiates to zero.
    Hence
    $$\frac{\partial f}{\partial x} = 20x^3 - 0 = 20x^3$$
    Differentiating $5x^4$ with respect to y
    gives zero because x is held fixed.
    Also differentiating y^2 with respect
    to y gives $2y$ so
    $$\frac{\partial f}{\partial y} = 0 - 2y = -2y$$

  (b) To differentiate the first term, x^2y^3,
    with respect to x we regard it as a
    constant multiple of x^2 (where the
    constant is y^3) so we get $2xy^3$. The
    second term obviously gives -10 so
    $$\frac{\partial f}{\partial x} = 2xy^3 - 10$$
    To differentiate the first term, x^2y^3,
    with respect to y we regard it as a
    constant multiple of y^3 (where the
    constant is x^2) so we get $3x^2y^2$. The
    second term is a constant and goes
    to zero so
    $$\frac{\partial f}{\partial y} = 3x^2y^2 - 0 = 3x^2y^2$$

3 (a) $f_{xx} = 60x^2$, $f_{yy} = -2$, $f_{yx} = f_{xy} = 0$.

  (b) $f_{xx} = 2y^3$, $f_{yy} = 6x^2y$,
      $f_{yx} = f_{xy} = 6xy^2$.

4 $f_1 = \dfrac{\partial f}{\partial x_1} = x_2 + 5x_1^4$

  $f_{11} = \dfrac{\partial^2 f}{\partial x_1^2} = 20x_1^3$

  $f_{21} = \dfrac{\partial^2 f}{\partial x_2 \partial x_1} = 1$

5 $\dfrac{\partial z}{\partial x} = y - 5$, $\dfrac{\partial z}{\partial y} = x + 2$

  so, at $(2, 6)$,

  $$\frac{\partial z}{\partial x} = 1, \frac{\partial z}{\partial y} = 4$$

  (1) $\Delta x = -0.1$, $\Delta y = 0.1$;
      $z \simeq 1(-0.1) + 4(0.1) = 0.3$, so z
      increases by approximately 0.3.
  (2) At $(2, 6)$, $z = 14$, and at $(1.9, 6.1)$,
      $z = 14.29$, so the exact increase is
      0.29.

6 (a) $\dfrac{dy}{dx} = \dfrac{-y}{x - 3y^2 + 1}$

  (b) $\dfrac{dy}{dx} = \dfrac{y^2}{5y^4 - 2xy}$

7 $f_x = 4x^3y^5 - 2x$, $f_y = 5x^4y^4 + 2y$,
    $f_x(1, 0) = -2$, $f_y(1, 1) = 7$.

8

	f_x	f_y	f_{xx}	f_{yy}	f_{yx}	f_{xy}
(a)	y	x	0	0	1	1
(b)	$e^x y$	e^x	$e^x y$	0	e^x	e^x
(c)	$2x + 2$	1	2	0	0	0
(d)	$4x^{-3/4}y^{3/4}$	$12x^{1/4}y^{-1/4}$	$-3x^{-7/4}y^{3/4}$	$-3x^{1/4}y^{-5/4}$	$3x^{-3/4}y^{-1/4}$	$3x^{-3/4}y^{-1/4}$
(e)	$\dfrac{-2y}{x^3} + \dfrac{1}{y}$	$\dfrac{1}{x^2} - \dfrac{x}{y^2}$	$\dfrac{6y}{x^4}$	$\dfrac{2x}{y^3}$	$\dfrac{-2}{x^3} - \dfrac{1}{y^2}$	$\dfrac{-2}{x^3} - \dfrac{1}{y^2}$

9 (a) -0.6; (b) -2; (c) -2.6.

10 (1) $f_x = -3x^2 + 2$, $f_y = 1$

$$\frac{dy}{dx} = -\frac{-3x^2 + 2}{1} = 3x^2 - 2$$

(2) $y = x^3 - 2x + 1$ so

$$\frac{dy}{dx} = 3x^2 - 2 \quad \checkmark$$

Section 5.2

1 Substituting the given values of P, P_A and Y into the demand equation gives

$$Q = 500 - 3(20) - 2(30) + 0.01(5000)$$

$$= 430$$

(a) $\dfrac{\partial Q}{\partial P} = -3$ so

$$E_P = -\frac{20}{430} \times (-3) = 0.14$$

(b) $\dfrac{\partial Q}{\partial P_A} = -2$ so

$$E_{P_A} = \frac{30}{430} \times (-2) = -0.14$$

(c) $\dfrac{\partial Q}{\partial Y} = 0.01$ so

$$E_Y = \frac{5000}{430} \times 0.01 = 0.12$$

By definition,

$$E_Y = \frac{\text{percentage change in } Q}{\text{percentage change in } Y}$$

so demand rises by $0.12 \times 5 = 0.6\%$. A rise in income causes a rise in demand so good is superior.

2 $\dfrac{\partial U}{\partial x_1} = 1000 + 5x_2 - 4x_1$

$$\frac{\partial U}{\partial x_2} = 450 + 5x_1 - 2x_2 \text{ so at } (138, 500)$$

$$\frac{\partial U}{\partial x_1} = 2948 \quad \text{and} \quad \frac{\partial U}{\partial x_2} = 140$$

If working time increases by one hour then leisure time decreases by one hour so $\Delta x_1 = -1$. Also $\Delta x_2 = 15$. By the small increments formula

$$\Delta U \simeq 2948(-1) + 140(15) = -848$$

The law of diminishing marginal utility holds for both x_1 and x_2 because

$$\frac{\partial^2 U}{\partial x_1^2} = -4 < 0$$

and

$$\frac{\partial^2 U}{\partial x_2^2} = -2 < 0$$

3 Using the numerical results in Problem 2,

$$\text{MRCS} = \frac{2948}{140} = 21.06$$

This represents the increase in x_2 required to maintain the current level of utility when x_1 falls by 1 unit. Hence if x_1 falls by 2 units the increase in x_2 is approximately

$$21.06 \times 2 = \$42.12$$

4 $MP_K = 2K$ and $MP_L = 4L$

(a) $MRTS = \dfrac{MP_L}{MP_K} = \dfrac{4L}{2K} = \dfrac{2L}{K}$

(b) $K\dfrac{\partial Q}{\partial K} + L\dfrac{\partial Q}{\partial L} = K(2K) + L(4L)$

$= 2(K^2 + 2L^2) = 2Q$ ✓

5 (a) 20/1165; (b) −15/1165;
(c) 2000/1165; −0.04%; complementary.

6 $\dfrac{\partial U}{\partial x_1} = \dfrac{1}{5}$ and $\dfrac{\partial U}{\partial x_2} = \dfrac{5}{12}$

(a) 37/60; (b) 12/25.

7 $MP_K = 8$, $MP_L = 14\frac{1}{4}$; (a) $1\frac{25}{32}$; (b) $1\frac{25}{32}$.

8 $\dfrac{\partial Q}{\partial K} = \alpha A K^{\alpha-1} L^\beta$ and

$\dfrac{\partial Q}{\partial L} = \beta A K^\alpha L^{\beta-1}$ so

$K\dfrac{\partial Q}{\partial K} + L\dfrac{\partial Q}{\partial L} = \alpha A K^\alpha L^\beta + \beta A K^\alpha L^\beta$

$= (\alpha + \beta)(A K^\alpha L^\beta)$

$= (\alpha + \beta)Q$ ✓

Section 5.3

1 $C = a\left(\dfrac{b + I^*}{1 - a}\right) + b$

$\dfrac{\partial C}{\partial I^*} = \dfrac{a}{1 - a} > 0$ because $0 < a < 1$

Hence an increase in I^* leads to an increase in C. If $a = \frac{1}{2}$ then

$\dfrac{\partial C}{\partial I^*} = \dfrac{\frac{1}{2}}{1 - \frac{1}{2}} = 1$

Change in C is

$1 \times 2 = 2$

2 (1) Substitute C, I, G, X and M into the Y equation to get

$$Y = aY + b + I^* + G^* + X^* - (mY + M^*)$$

Collecting like terms gives

$$(1 - a + m)Y = b + I^* + G^* + X^* - M^*$$

so

$$Y = \frac{b + I^* + G^* + X^* - M^*}{1 - a + m}$$

(2) $\dfrac{\partial Y}{\partial X^*} = \dfrac{1}{1 - a + m}$

$\dfrac{\partial Y}{\partial m} = -\dfrac{b + I^* + G^* + X^* - M^*}{(1 - a + m)^2}$

Now $a < 1$ and $m > 0$ so $1 - a + m > 0$. The autonomous export multiplier is positive so an increase in X^* leads to an increase in Y. The marginal propensity to import multiplier is negative. To see this note from part (1) that $\partial Y/\partial m$ can be written as

$$-\frac{Y}{1 - a + m}$$

and $Y > 0$ and $1 - a + m > 0$.

(3) $Y = \dfrac{120 + 100 + 300 + 150 - 40}{1 - 0.8 + 0.1}$

$= 2100$

$\dfrac{\partial Y}{\partial X^*} = \dfrac{1}{1 - 0.8 + 0.1} = \dfrac{10}{3}$

and

$\Delta X^* = 10$

so

$\Delta Y = \dfrac{10}{3} \times 10 = \dfrac{100}{3}$

3 If d increases by a small amount then the intercept increases and the demand curve shifts upwards slightly. Figure S5.1 shows

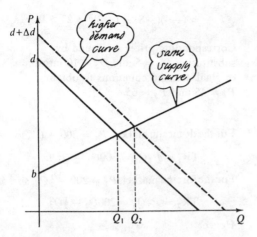

Figure S5.1

that the effect is to increase the equilibrium quantity from Q_1 to Q_2 confirming that $\partial Q/\partial d > 0$.

4 (1) From the relations

$$C = aY_d + b$$

$$Y_d = Y - T$$

$$T = tY + T^*$$

we see that
$C = a(Y - tY - T^*) + b$. Similarly
$M = m(Y - tY - T^*) + M^*$.
Substitute these together with I, G
and X into the Y equation to get the
desired result.

(2) (a)

$$\frac{\partial Y}{\partial T^*} = \frac{m - a}{1 - a + at + m - mt}$$

Numerator is negative because
$m < a$. Denominator can be
written as

$$(1 - a) + at + m(1 - t)$$

which represents the sum of
three positive numbers so is
positive. Hence the autonomous
taxation multiplier is negative.

(b)

$$\frac{\partial Y}{\partial G^*} = \frac{1}{1 - a + at + m - mt} > 0$$

(3) (a) 1000; **(b)** $\Delta Y = 20$; **(c)** $\Delta T^* = 33\frac{1}{3}$.

5 From text, equilibrium quantity is

$$\frac{d - b}{a + c}$$

Substituting this into either the supply or
demand equation gives the desired result.

$$\frac{\partial P}{\partial a} = \frac{c(d - b)}{(a + c)^2} > 0, \frac{\partial P}{\partial b} = \frac{c}{a + c} > 0$$

$$\frac{\partial P}{\partial c} = -\frac{a(d - b)}{(a + c)^2} < 0, \frac{\partial P}{\partial d} = \frac{a}{a + c} > 0$$

where the quotient rule is used to obtain
$\partial P/\partial a$ and $\partial P/\partial c$. An increase in a, b or d
leads to an increase in P whereas an
increase in c leads to a decrease in P.

Section 5.4

1 $f_x = 2x$, $f_y = 6 - 6y$, $f_{xx} = 2$, $f_{yy} = -6$,
$f_{xy} = 0$

Step 1 At a stationary point

$$2x = 0$$

$$6 - 6y = 0$$

which shows that there is just one
stationary point at $(0, 1)$.

Step 2

$$f_{xx}f_{yy} - f_{xy}^2 = 2(-6) - 0^2 = -12 < 0$$

so it is a saddle point.

2 Total revenue from the sale of G1 is

$$TR_1 = P_1 Q_1 = (50 - Q_1)Q_1$$

$$= 50Q_1 - Q_1^2$$

Total revenue from the sale of G2 is

$$TR_2 = P_2 Q_2 = (95 - 3Q_2)Q_2$$

$$= 95Q_2 - 3Q_2^2$$

Total revenue from the sale of both goods is

$$TR = TR_1 + TR_2$$

$$= 50Q_1 - Q_1^2 + 95Q_2 - 3Q_2^2$$

Profit is

$$\pi = TR - TC$$

$$= (50Q_1 - Q_1^2 + 95Q_2 - 3Q_2^2)$$

$$- (Q_1^2 + 3Q_1Q_2 + Q_2^2)$$

$$= 50Q_1 - 2Q_1^2 + 95Q_2 - 4Q_2^2$$

$$- 3Q_1Q_2$$

Now

$$\frac{\partial \pi}{\partial Q_1} = 50 - 4Q_1 - 3Q_2,$$

$$\frac{\partial \pi}{\partial Q_2} = 95 - 8Q_2 - 3Q_1$$

$$\frac{\partial^2 \pi}{\partial Q_1^2} = -4, \frac{\partial^2 \pi}{\partial Q_1 \partial Q_2} = -3,$$

$$\frac{\partial^2 \pi}{\partial Q_2^2} = -8$$

Step 1   At a stationary point

$$50 - 4Q_1 - 3Q_2 = 0$$

$$95 - 3Q_1 - 8Q_2 = 0$$

that is

$$4Q_1 + 3Q_2 = 50 \qquad (1)$$

$$3Q_1 + 8Q_2 = 95 \qquad (2)$$

Multiply equation (1) by 3, and equation (2) by 4 and subtract to get

$$23Q_2 = 230$$

so $Q_2 = 10$. Substituting this into either equation (1) or equation (2) gives $Q_1 = 5$.

Step 2   This is a maximum because

$$\frac{\partial^2 \pi}{\partial Q_1^2} = -4 < 0, \frac{\partial^2 \pi}{\partial Q_2^2} = -8 < 0$$

and

$$\left(\frac{\partial^2 \pi}{\partial Q_1^2}\right)\left(\frac{\partial^2 \pi}{\partial Q_2^2}\right) - \left(\frac{\partial^2 \pi}{\partial Q_1 \partial Q_2}\right)^2$$

$$= (-4)(-8) - (-3)^2 = 23 > 0$$

Corresponding prices are found by substituting $Q_1 = 5$ and $Q_2 = 10$ into the original demand equations to obtain $P_1 = 45$ and $P_2 = 65$.

3   For the domestic market, $P_1 = 300 - Q_1$, so

$$TR_1 = P_1Q_1 = 300Q_1 - Q_1^2$$

For the foreign market, $P_2 = 200 - \frac{1}{2}Q_2$, so

$$TR_2 = P_2Q_2 = 200Q_2 - \frac{1}{2}Q_2^2$$

Hence

$$TR = TR_1 + TR_2$$

$$= 300Q_1 - Q_1^2 + 200Q_2 - \frac{1}{2}Q_2^2$$

We are given that

$$TC = 5000 + 100(Q_1 + Q_2)$$

$$= 5000 + 100Q_1 + 100Q_2$$

so

$$\pi = TR - TC$$

$$= (300Q_1 - Q_1^2 + 200Q_2 - \frac{1}{2}Q_2^2)$$

$$- (5000 + 100Q_1 + 100Q_2)$$

$$= 200Q_1 - Q_1^2 + 100Q_2$$

$$- \frac{1}{2}Q_2^2 - 5000$$

Now

$$\frac{\partial \pi}{\partial Q_1} = 200 - 2Q_1, \frac{\partial \pi}{\partial Q_2} = 100 - Q_2$$

$$\frac{\partial^2 \pi}{\partial Q_1^2} = -2, \frac{\partial^2 \pi}{\partial Q_1 \partial Q_2} = 0, \frac{\partial^2 \pi}{\partial Q_2^2} = -1$$

Step 1   At a stationary point

$$200 - 2Q_1 = 0$$

$$100 - Q_2 = 0$$

which have solution $Q_1 = 100$, $Q_2 = 100$.

Step 2   This is a maximum because

$$\frac{\partial^2 \pi}{\partial Q_1^2} = -2 < 0, \frac{\partial^2 \pi}{\partial Q_2^2} = -1 < 0$$

and

$$\left(\frac{\partial^2 \pi}{\partial Q_1^2}\right)\left(\frac{\partial^2 \pi}{\partial Q_2^2}\right) - \left(\frac{\partial^2 \pi}{\partial Q_1\, \partial Q_2}\right)^2$$

$$= (-2)(-1) - 0^2 = 2 > 0$$

Substitute $Q_1 = 100$, $Q_2 = 100$, into the demand and profit functions to get $P_1 = 200$, $P_2 = 150$ and $\pi = 10\,000$.

4　(a)　Minimum at $(1, 1)$, maximum at $(-1, -1)$, and saddle point at $(1, -1)$ and $(-1, 1)$.

　　(b)　Minimum at $(2, 0)$, maximum at $(0, 0)$, and saddle point at $(1, 1)$ and $(1, -1)$.

5　Maximum profit is \$1300 when $Q_1 = 30$ and $Q_2 = 10$.

6　Maximum profit is \$95 when $P_1 = 30$ and $P_2 = 20$.

7　Maximum profit is \$176 when $L = 16$ and $K = 144$.

8　$x_1 = 138$, $x_2 = 500$; \$16.67 per hour.

Section 5.5

1　*Step 1*　We are given that $y = x$, so no rearrangement is necessary.

Step 2　Substituting $y = x$ into the objective function

$$z = 2x^2 - 3xy + 2y + 10$$

gives

$$z = 2x^2 - 3x^2 + 2x + 10$$

$$= -x^2 + 2x + 10$$

Step 3　At a stationary point

$$\frac{dz}{dx} = 0$$

that is

$$-2x + 2 = 0$$

which has solution $x = 1$. Differentiating a

second time gives

$$\frac{d^2z}{dx^2} = -2$$

confirming that the stationary point is a maximum.

The value of z can be found by substituting $x = 1$ into

$$z = -x^2 + 2x + 10$$

to get $z = 11$. Finally, putting $x = 1$ into the constraint $y = x$ gives $y = 1$. The constrained function therefore has a maximum value of 11 at the point $(1, 1)$.

2　We want to maximize the objective function

$$U = x_1 x_2$$

subject to the budgetary constraint

$$2x_1 + 10x_2 = 400$$

Step 1　$x_1 = 200 - 5x_2$.

Step 2　$U = 200x_2 - 5x_2^2$.

Step 3

$$\frac{dU}{dx_2} = 200 - 10x_2 = 0$$

has solution $x_2 = 20$.

$$\frac{d^2U}{dx_2^2} = -10 < 0$$

so maximum.

Putting $x_2 = 20$ into constraint gives $x_1 = 100$.

$$U_1 = \frac{\partial U}{\partial x_1} = x_2 = 20$$

and

$$U_2 = \frac{\partial U}{\partial x_2} = x_1 = 100$$

so the ratios of marginal utilities to prices are

$$\frac{U_1}{P_1} = \frac{20}{2} = 10$$

and

$$\frac{U_2}{P_2} = \frac{100}{10} = 10$$

which are the same.

3 We want to minimize the objective function

$$TC = 3x_1^2 + 2x_1x_2 + 7x_2^2$$

subject to the production constraint

$$x_1 + x_2 = 40$$

Step 1 $x_1 = 40 - x_2$.

Step 2 $TC = 3(40 - x_2)^2$

$$+ 2(40 - x_2)x_2 + 7x_2^2$$

$$= 4800 - 160x_2 + 8x_2^2$$

Step 3

$$\frac{d(TC)}{dx_2} = -160 + 16x_2 = 0$$

has solution $x_2 = 10$.

$$\frac{d^2(TC)}{dx_2^2} = 16 > 0$$

so minimum.

Finally, putting $x_2 = 10$ into constraint gives $x_1 = 30$.

4 Maximum value of z is 13 which occurs at $(3, 11)$.

5 $K = 10$ and $L = 4$.

6 $K = 6$ and $L = 4$.

7 Maximum profit is \$165 which is achieved when $K = 81$ and $L = 9$.

Section 5.6

1 *Step 1*

$$g(x, y, \lambda) = 2x^2 - xy + \lambda(12 - x - y)$$

Step 2

$$\frac{\partial g}{\partial x} = 4x - y - \lambda = 0$$

$$\frac{\partial g}{\partial y} = -x - \lambda = 0$$

$$\frac{\partial g}{\partial \lambda} = 12 - x - y = 0$$

that is

$$4x - y - \lambda = 0 \quad (1)$$

$$-x \quad - \lambda = 0 \quad (2)$$

$$x + y \quad = 12 \quad (3)$$

Multiply equation (2) by 4 and add equation (1), multiply equation (3) by 4 and subtract from equation (1) to get

$$-y - 5\lambda = 0 \quad (4)$$

$$-5y - \lambda = -48 \quad (5)$$

Multiply equation (4) by 5 and subtract equation (5) to get

$$-24\lambda = 48 \quad (6)$$

Equations (6), (5) and (1) can be solved in turn to get

$$\lambda = -2, y = 10, x = 2$$

so the optimal point has coordinates $(2, 10)$. The corresponding value of the objective function is

$$2(2)^2 - 2(10) = -12$$

2 Maximize

$$U = 2x_1x_2 + 3x_1$$

subject to

$$x_1 + 2x_2 = 83$$

Step 1

$$g(x_1, x_2, \lambda) = 2x_1x_2 + 3x_1$$
$$+ \lambda(83 - x_1 - 2x_2)$$

Step 2

$$\frac{\partial g}{\partial x_1} = 2x_2 + 3 - \lambda = 0$$

$$\frac{\partial g}{\partial x_2} = 2x_1 - 2\lambda = 0$$

$$\frac{\partial g}{\partial \lambda} = 83 - x_1 - 2x_2 = 0$$

that is

$$2x_2 - \lambda = -3 \quad (1)$$

$$2x_1 - 2\lambda = 0 \quad (2)$$

$$x_1 + 2x_2 = 83 \quad (3)$$

The easiest way of solving this system is to use equations (1) and (2) to get

$$\lambda = 2x_2 + 3 \quad \text{and} \quad \lambda = x_1$$

respectively. Hence

$$x_1 = 2x_2 + 3$$

Substituting this into equation (3) gives

$$4x_2 + 3 = 83$$

which has solution $x_2 = 20$ and so $x_1 = \lambda = 43$.

The corresponding value of U is

$$2(43)(20) + 3(43) = 1849$$

The value of λ is 43 so when income rises by 1 unit utility increases by approximately 43 to 1892.

3 *Step 1*

$$g(x_1, x_2, \lambda) = x_1^{1/2} + x_2^{1/2}$$
$$+ \lambda(M - P_1 x_1 - P_2 x_2)$$

Step 2

$$\frac{\partial g}{\partial x_1} = \frac{1}{2} x_1^{-1/2} - \lambda P_1 = 0 \quad (1)$$

$$\frac{\partial g}{\partial x_2} = \frac{1}{2} x_2^{-1/2} - \lambda P_2 = 0 \quad (2)$$

$$\frac{\partial g}{\partial \lambda} = M - P_1 x_1 - P_2 x_2 = 0 \quad (3)$$

From equations (1) and (2)

$$\lambda = \frac{1}{2x_1^{1/2} P_1} \quad \text{and} \quad \lambda = \frac{1}{2x_2^{1/2} P_2}$$

respectively. Hence

$$\frac{1}{2x_1^{1/2} P_1} = \frac{1}{2x_2^{1/2} P_2}$$

that is

$$x_1 P_1^2 = x_2 P_2^2$$

so

$$x_1 = \frac{x_2 P_2^2}{P_1^2} \quad (4)$$

Substituting this into equation (3) gives

$$M - \frac{x_2 P_2^2}{P_1} - P_2 x_2 = 0$$

which rearranges as

$$x_2 = \frac{P_1 M}{P_2(P_1 + P_2)}$$

Substitute this into equation (4) to get

$$x_1 = \frac{P_2 M}{P_1(P_1 + P_2)}$$

4 There are two wheels per frame so the constraint is $y = 2x$. Maximum profit is \$4800 at $x = 40$, $y = 80$.

5 Maximum profit is \$600 at $Q_1 = 10$, $Q_2 = 5$. Lagrange multiplier is 4 so profit rises to \$604 when total cost increases by 1 unit.

6 $x_1 = \dfrac{\alpha M}{(\alpha + \beta)P_1}$ and $x_2 = \dfrac{\beta M}{(\alpha + \beta)P_2}$

CHAPTER 6

Section 6.1

1 (a) x^2; (b) x^4; (c) x^{100}; (d) $\frac{1}{4}x^4$;

(e) $\frac{1}{19}x^{19}$.

2 (a) $\frac{1}{5}x^5 + c$; (b) $-\frac{1}{2x^2} + c$; (c) $\frac{3}{4}x^{4/3} + c$;

(d) $\frac{1}{3}e^{3x} + c$; (e) $x + c$; (f) $\frac{x^2}{2} + c$;

(g) $\ln x + c$.

3 (a) $x^2 - x^4 + c$; (b) $2x^5 - \frac{5}{x} + c$;

(c) $\frac{7}{3}x^3 - \frac{3}{2}x^2 + 2x + c$.

4 (1) $TC = \int 2 \, dQ = 2Q + c$

Fixed costs are 500 so $c = 500$. Hence

$$TC = 2Q + 500$$

Put $Q = 40$ to get $TC = 580$.

(2) $TR = \int (100 - 6Q) \, dQ$

$$= 100Q - 3Q^2 + c$$

Revenue is zero when $Q = 0$ so $c = 0$. Hence

$$TR = 100Q - 3Q^2$$

$$P = \frac{TR}{Q} = \frac{100Q - 3Q^2}{Q}$$

$$= 100 - 3Q$$

so demand equation is $P = 100 - 3Q$.

(3) $S = \int (0.4 - 0.1Y^{-1/2}) \, dY$

$$= 0.4Y - 0.2Y^{1/2} + c$$

The condition $S = 0$ when $Y = 100$

gives

$$0 = 0.4(100) - 0.2(100)^{1/2} + c$$

$$= 38 + c$$

so $c = -38$. Hence

$$S = 0.4Y - 0.2Y^{1/2} - 38$$

5 (a) $x^6 + c$; (b) $\frac{1}{5}x^5 + c$; (c) $e^{10x} + c$;

(d) $\ln x + c$; (e) $\frac{2}{5}x^{5/2} + c$;

(f) $\frac{1}{2}x^4 - 3x^2 + c$;

(g) $\frac{1}{3}x^3 - 4x^2 + 3x + c$; (h) $\frac{ax^2}{2} + bx + c$;

(i) $\frac{7}{4}x^4 - 2e^{-2x} + \frac{3}{x} + c$.

6 (1) $TC = \frac{Q^2}{2} + 5Q + 20$

(2) $TC = 6e^{0.5Q} + 4$

7 (a) $TR = 20Q - Q^2$; $P = 20 - Q$.

(b) $TR = 12\sqrt{Q}$; $P = \frac{12}{\sqrt{Q}}$.

8 $C = 0.6Y + 7$, $S = 0.4Y - 7$.

Section 6.2

1 (a) $\int_0^1 x^3 \, dx = \left[\frac{1}{4}x^4\right]_0^1$

$$= \frac{1}{4}(1)^4 - \frac{1}{4}(0)^4 = \frac{1}{4}$$

(b) $\int_2^5 (2x - 1) \, dx = \left[x^2 - x\right]_2^5$

$$= (5^2 - 5) - (2^2 - 2)$$

$$= 18$$

(c) $\displaystyle\int_1^4 (x^2 - x + 1)\,dx$

$$= \left[\frac{1}{3}x^3 - \frac{1}{2}x^2 + x\right]_1^4$$

$$= \left[\frac{1}{3}(4)^3 - \frac{1}{2}(4)^2 + 4\right]$$

$$- \left[\frac{1}{3}(1)^3 - \frac{1}{2}(1)^2 + 1\right]$$

$$= 16.5$$

(d) $\displaystyle\int_0^1 e^x\,dx = \left[e^x\right]_0^1 = e^1 - e^0$

$$= e - 1 = 1.718\,28\ldots$$

2 Substitute $Q = 8$ to get

$$P = 100 - 8^2 = 36$$

$$\text{CS} = \int_0^8 (100 - Q^2)\,dQ - 8(36)$$

$$= \left[100Q - \frac{1}{3}Q^3\right]_0^8 - 288$$

$$= \left[100(8) - \frac{1}{3}(8)^3\right]$$

$$- \left[100(0) - \frac{1}{3}(0)^2\right]$$

$$- 288$$

$$= 341.33$$

3 In equilibrium, $Q_S = Q_D = Q$ so

$$P = 50 - 2Q$$

$$P = 10 + 2Q$$

Hence

$$50 - 2Q = 10 + 2Q$$

which has solution $Q = 10$. The demand equation gives

$$P = 50 - 2(10) = 30$$

(a) $\displaystyle\text{CS} = \int_0^{10} (50 - 2Q)\,dQ - 10(30)$

$$= \left[50Q - Q^2\right]_0^{10} - 300$$

$$= [50(10) - (10)^2] - [50(0) - 0^2]$$

$$- 300$$

$$= 100$$

(b) $\displaystyle\text{PS} = 10(30) - \int_0^{10} (10 + 2Q)\,dQ$

$$= 300 - \left[10Q + Q^2\right]_0^{10}$$

$$= 300 - \{[10(10) + (10)^2]$$

$$- [10(0) + 0^2]\}$$

$$= 100$$

4 (1) $\displaystyle\int_1^8 800t^{1/3}\,dt$

$$= 800\left[\frac{3}{4}t^{4/3}\right]_1^8$$

$$= 800\left[\frac{3}{4}(8)^{4/3} - \frac{3}{4}(1)^{4/3}\right]$$

$$= 9000$$

(2) $\displaystyle\int_0^T 800t^{1/3}\,dt$

$$= 800\left[\frac{3}{4}t^{4/3}\right]_0^T$$

$$= 800\left[\frac{3}{4}T^{4/3} - \frac{3}{4}(0)^{4/3}\right]$$

$$= 600T^{4/3}$$

We need to solve

$$600T^{4/3} = 48\,600$$

that is

$$T^{4/3} = 81$$

so

$$T = 81^{3/4} = 27$$

5 $\displaystyle P = \int_0^{10} 5000e^{-0.06t}\,dt$

$$= 5000\int_0^{10} e^{-0.06t}\,dt$$

$$= 5000\left[-\frac{1}{0.06}\,e^{-0.06t}\right]_0^{10}$$

$$= -\frac{5000}{0.06}\,(e^{-0.6} - 1)$$

$$= \$37,599.03$$

6 Area is 16.

CHAPTER 7

Section 7.1

1 **(1)** 2×2, 1×5, 3×5, 1×1.
   (2) 1, 4, 6, 2, 6, ?, 6; the value of c_{43}
      does not exist because **C** only has
      three rows.

2
$$\mathbf{A}^\mathrm{T} = \begin{bmatrix} 1 & 3 & 2 & 2 \\ 4 & 7 & 1 & -5 \\ 0 & 6 & 3 & 1 \\ 1 & 1 & 5 & 8 \\ 2 & 4 & -1 & 0 \end{bmatrix} \quad \mathbf{B}^\mathrm{T} = \begin{bmatrix} 1 \\ 5 \\ 7 \\ 9 \end{bmatrix}$$

$$\mathbf{C}^\mathrm{T} = \begin{bmatrix} 1 & 2 & 3 \\ 2 & 4 & 5 \\ 3 & 5 & 6 \end{bmatrix} = \mathbf{C}$$

Matrices with the property that $\mathbf{C}^\mathrm{T} = \mathbf{C}$
are called **symmetric**. Elements in the top
right-hand corner are a mirror image of
those in the bottom left-hand corner.

3 **(a)** $\begin{bmatrix} 1 & 7 \\ 3 & -8 \end{bmatrix}$; **(c)** $\begin{bmatrix} 3 \\ 2 \end{bmatrix}$; **(d)** $\begin{bmatrix} 2 \\ 2 \end{bmatrix}$;
   (e) $\begin{bmatrix} 0 & 0 \\ 0 & 0 \end{bmatrix}$.

Part (b) is impossible because **A** and **C**
have different orders.

4 **(1)** **(a)** $\begin{bmatrix} 2 & -4 \\ 6 & 10 \\ 0 & 8 \end{bmatrix}$; **(b)** $\begin{bmatrix} 0 & -2 \\ 4 & 14 \\ 2 & 12 \end{bmatrix}$;
      (c) $\begin{bmatrix} 1 & -3 \\ 5 & 12 \\ 1 & 10 \end{bmatrix}$; **(d)** $\begin{bmatrix} 2 & -6 \\ 10 & 24 \\ 2 & 20 \end{bmatrix}$.

7 **(a)** 100; **(b)** 20.

8 **(a)** 74.67; **(b)** 58.67.

9 **(a)** $\dfrac{AT^{\alpha+1}}{\alpha+1}$; **(b)** $\dfrac{A}{\alpha}\,(e^{\alpha T} - 1)$.

10 **(a)** \$2785.84; **(b)** \$7869.39; **(c)** \$19,865.24;
   (d) \$20,000.

From (a) and (b)

$$2\mathbf{A} + 2\mathbf{B} = \begin{bmatrix} 2 & -4 \\ 6 & 10 \\ 0 & 8 \end{bmatrix} + \begin{bmatrix} 0 & -2 \\ 4 & 14 \\ 2 & 12 \end{bmatrix}$$

$$= \begin{bmatrix} 2 & -6 \\ 10 & 24 \\ 2 & 20 \end{bmatrix}$$

which is the same as (d) so

$$2(\mathbf{A} + \mathbf{B}) = 2\mathbf{A} + 2\mathbf{B}$$

   (2) **(a)** $\begin{bmatrix} 3 & -6 \\ 9 & 15 \\ 0 & 12 \end{bmatrix}$; **(b)** $\begin{bmatrix} -6 & 12 \\ -18 & -30 \\ 0 & -24 \end{bmatrix}$.

From (a),

$$-2(3\mathbf{A}) = -2\begin{bmatrix} 3 & -6 \\ 9 & 15 \\ 0 & 12 \end{bmatrix}$$

$$= \begin{bmatrix} -6 & 12 \\ -18 & -30 \\ 0 & -24 \end{bmatrix}$$

which is the same as (b) so

$$-2(3\mathbf{A}) = -6\mathbf{A}$$

5 **(a)** $[8]$ because
      $1(0) + (-1)(-1)$
      $\qquad\qquad + 0(1) + 3(1) + 2(2) = 8$.
   (b) $[0]$ because $1(-2) + 2(1) + 9(0) = 0$.
   (c) This is impossible because **a** and **d**
      have different numbers of elements.

6

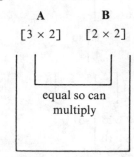

A   B

[3 × 2]   [2 × 2]

equal so can
multiply

answer is 3 × 2

$$AB = \begin{bmatrix} 1 & 2 \\ 0 & 1 \\ 3 & 1 \end{bmatrix} \begin{bmatrix} 1 & 2 \\ 3 & 4 \end{bmatrix} = \begin{bmatrix} c_{11} & c_{12} \\ c_{21} & c_{22} \\ c_{31} & c_{32} \end{bmatrix}$$

$$AB = \begin{bmatrix} \boxed{1 \quad 2} \\ 0 & 1 \\ 3 & 1 \end{bmatrix} \begin{bmatrix} \boxed{\begin{matrix}1\\3\end{matrix}} & 2 \\ & 4 \end{bmatrix} = \begin{bmatrix} \boxed{7} & c_{12} \\ c_{21} & c_{22} \\ c_{31} & c_{32} \end{bmatrix}$$

$$AB = \begin{bmatrix} \boxed{1 \quad 2} \\ 0 & 1 \\ 3 & 1 \end{bmatrix} \begin{bmatrix} 1 & \boxed{\begin{matrix}2\\4\end{matrix}} \\ 3 & \end{bmatrix} = \begin{bmatrix} 7 & \boxed{10} \\ c_{21} & c_{22} \\ c_{31} & c_{32} \end{bmatrix}$$

$$AB = \begin{bmatrix} 1 & 2 \\ \boxed{0 \quad 1} \\ 3 & 1 \end{bmatrix} \begin{bmatrix} \boxed{\begin{matrix}1\\3\end{matrix}} & 2 \\ & 4 \end{bmatrix} = \begin{bmatrix} 7 & 10 \\ \boxed{3} & c_{22} \\ c_{31} & c_{32} \end{bmatrix}$$

$$AB = \begin{bmatrix} 1 & 2 \\ \boxed{0 \quad 1} \\ 3 & 1 \end{bmatrix} \begin{bmatrix} 1 & \boxed{\begin{matrix}2\\4\end{matrix}} \\ 3 & \end{bmatrix} = \begin{bmatrix} 7 & 10 \\ 3 & \boxed{4} \\ c_{31} & c_{32} \end{bmatrix}$$

$$AB = \begin{bmatrix} 1 & 2 \\ 0 & 1 \\ \boxed{3 \quad 1} \end{bmatrix} \begin{bmatrix} \boxed{\begin{matrix}1\\3\end{matrix}} & 2 \\ & 4 \end{bmatrix} = \begin{bmatrix} 7 & 10 \\ 3 & 4 \\ \boxed{6} & c_{32} \end{bmatrix}$$

$$AB = \begin{bmatrix} 1 & 2 \\ 0 & 1 \\ \boxed{3 \quad 1} \end{bmatrix} \begin{bmatrix} 1 & \boxed{\begin{matrix}2\\4\end{matrix}} \\ 3 & \end{bmatrix} = \begin{bmatrix} 7 & 10 \\ 3 & 4 \\ 6 & \boxed{10} \end{bmatrix}$$

7 (a) $\begin{bmatrix} 5 \\ 7 \\ 5 \end{bmatrix}$; **(d)** $\begin{bmatrix} 4 & 3 \\ 2 & -1 \\ 5 & 5 \end{bmatrix}$;

(f) $\begin{bmatrix} 9 & 6 & 13 \\ 27 & 15 & 28 \end{bmatrix}$; **(g)** $\begin{bmatrix} 5 & 7 & 9 \\ 3 & 3 & 3 \\ 6 & 9 & 12 \end{bmatrix}$;

(h) $\begin{bmatrix} 5 & 6 \\ 11 & 15 \end{bmatrix}$.

Parts (b), (c), (e) are impossible because,
in each case, the number of columns in
the first matrix is not equal to the
number of rows in the second.

8   Ax is the 3 × 1 matrix

$$\begin{bmatrix} x + 4y + 7z \\ 2x + 6y + 5z \\ 8x + 9y + 5z \end{bmatrix}$$

However, $x + 4y + 7z = -3$,
$2x + 6y + 5z = 10$ and $8x + 9y + 5z = 1$
so this matrix is just

$$\begin{bmatrix} -3 \\ 10 \\ 1 \end{bmatrix}$$

which is **b**. Hence **Ax = b**.

9 (a) $\begin{bmatrix} 5900 \\ 1100 \end{bmatrix}$

Total cost charged to each customer.

(b) $\begin{bmatrix} 13 & 7 & 23 & 22 \\ 3 & 1 & 4 & 5 \end{bmatrix}$

Amount of raw materials used to
manufacture each customer's goods.

(c) $\begin{bmatrix} 35 \\ 75 \\ 30 \end{bmatrix}$

Total raw material costs to
manufacture one item of each good.

(d) $\begin{bmatrix} 1005 \\ 205 \end{bmatrix}$

Total raw material costs to
manufacture requisite number of
goods for each customer.

(e) $[7000]$

Total revenue received from customers.

(f) $[1210]$

Total cost of raw materials.

(g) $[5790]$

Profit before deduction of labour, capital and overheads.

10 (1) (a) $\begin{bmatrix} 1 & 3 & 5 \\ 2 & 4 & 6 \end{bmatrix}$;

(b) $\begin{bmatrix} 1 & 2 & -3 \\ -1 & 1 & 4 \end{bmatrix}$;

(c) $\begin{bmatrix} 2 & 1 \\ 5 & 5 \\ 2 & 10 \end{bmatrix}$;

(d) $\begin{bmatrix} 2 & 5 & 2 \\ 1 & 5 & 10 \end{bmatrix}$.

$(\mathbf{A} + \mathbf{B})^T = \mathbf{A}^T + \mathbf{B}^T$; that is, 'transpose of the sum is the sum of the transposes'.

(2) (a) $\begin{bmatrix} 1 & 5 \\ 4 & 9 \end{bmatrix}$; **(b)** $\begin{bmatrix} 2 & -1 \\ 1 & 0 \\ 0 & 1 \end{bmatrix}$;

(c) $\begin{bmatrix} -2 & 1 & 4 \\ 1 & 5 & 9 \end{bmatrix}$;

(d) $\begin{bmatrix} -2 & 1 \\ 1 & 5 \\ 4 & 9 \end{bmatrix}$.

$(\mathbf{CD})^T = \mathbf{D}^T\mathbf{C}^T$; that is 'transpose of a product is the product of the transposes multiplied in reverse order'.

11 (a) $\mathbf{B} + \mathbf{C} = \begin{bmatrix} 0 & 6 \\ 5 & 2 \end{bmatrix}$

so $\mathbf{A}(\mathbf{B} + \mathbf{C}) = \begin{bmatrix} -15 & 24 \\ 5 & 14 \end{bmatrix}$

$\mathbf{AB} = \begin{bmatrix} -7 & 25 \\ 6 & 10 \end{bmatrix}$ and

$\mathbf{AC} = \begin{bmatrix} -8 & -1 \\ -1 & 4 \end{bmatrix}$ so

$\mathbf{AB} + \mathbf{AC} = \begin{bmatrix} -15 & 24 \\ 5 & 14 \end{bmatrix}$

(b) $\mathbf{AB} = \begin{bmatrix} -7 & 25 \\ 6 & 10 \end{bmatrix}$ so

$(\mathbf{AB})\mathbf{C} = \begin{bmatrix} 32 & 43 \\ 4 & 26 \end{bmatrix}$

$\mathbf{BC} = \begin{bmatrix} 4 & 11 \\ -4 & 4 \end{bmatrix}$ so

$\mathbf{A}(\mathbf{BC}) = \begin{bmatrix} 32 & 43 \\ 4 & 26 \end{bmatrix}$

12 $\mathbf{AB} = [-3]$; $\mathbf{BA} = \begin{bmatrix} 1 & 2 & -4 & 3 \\ 7 & 14 & -28 & 21 \\ 3 & 6 & -12 & 9 \\ -2 & -4 & 8 & -6 \end{bmatrix}$

13 (a) $\mathbf{AI} = \begin{bmatrix} a & b \\ c & d \end{bmatrix}\begin{bmatrix} 1 & 0 \\ 0 & 1 \end{bmatrix} = \begin{bmatrix} a & b \\ c & d \end{bmatrix} = \mathbf{A}$

Similarly, $\mathbf{IA} = \mathbf{A}$.

(b) $\mathbf{A}^{-1}\mathbf{A}$

$= \dfrac{1}{ad - bc}\begin{bmatrix} d & -b \\ -c & a \end{bmatrix}\begin{bmatrix} a & b \\ c & d \end{bmatrix}$

$= \dfrac{1}{ad - bc}\begin{bmatrix} da - bc & db - bd \\ -ca + ac & -cb + ad \end{bmatrix}$

$= \dfrac{1}{ad - bc}\begin{bmatrix} ad - bc & 0 \\ 0 & ad - bc \end{bmatrix}$

$= \begin{bmatrix} 1 & 0 \\ 0 & 1 \end{bmatrix}$

Similarly, $\mathbf{AA}^{-1} = \mathbf{I}$.

(c) $\mathbf{Ix} = \begin{bmatrix} 1 & 0 \\ 0 & 1 \end{bmatrix}\begin{bmatrix} x \\ y \end{bmatrix} = \begin{bmatrix} x \\ y \end{bmatrix} = \mathbf{x}$

Section 7.2

1 $|A| = 6(2) - 4(1) = 8 \neq 0$

so **A** is non-singular and its inverse is given by

$$\frac{1}{8}\begin{bmatrix} 2 & -4 \\ -1 & 6 \end{bmatrix} = \begin{bmatrix} 1/4 & -1/2 \\ -1/8 & 3/4 \end{bmatrix}$$

$$|B| = 6(2) - 4(3) = 0$$

so **B** is singular and its inverse does not exist.

2 We need to solve $Ax = b$ where

$$A = \begin{bmatrix} 9 & 1 \\ 2 & 7 \end{bmatrix} \quad x = \begin{bmatrix} P_1 \\ P_2 \end{bmatrix}$$

and

$$b = \begin{bmatrix} 43 \\ 57 \end{bmatrix}$$

Now

$$A^{-1} = \frac{1}{61}\begin{bmatrix} 7 & -1 \\ -2 & 9 \end{bmatrix}$$

so

$$\begin{bmatrix} P_1 \\ P_2 \end{bmatrix} = \frac{1}{61}\begin{bmatrix} 7 & -1 \\ -2 & 9 \end{bmatrix}\begin{bmatrix} 43 \\ 57 \end{bmatrix}$$

$$= \begin{bmatrix} 4 \\ 7 \end{bmatrix}$$

3 In equilibrium, $Q_S = Q_D = Q$, say, so the supply equation becomes

$$P = aQ + b$$

Subtracting aQ from both sides gives

$$P - aQ = b \qquad (1)$$

Similarly the demand equation leads to

$$P + cQ = d \qquad (2)$$

In matrix notation equations (1) and (2) become

$$\begin{bmatrix} 1 & -a \\ 1 & c \end{bmatrix}\begin{bmatrix} P \\ Q \end{bmatrix} = \begin{bmatrix} b \\ d \end{bmatrix}$$

The coefficient matrix has an inverse,

$$\frac{1}{c+a}\begin{bmatrix} c & a \\ -1 & 1 \end{bmatrix}$$

so that

$$\begin{bmatrix} P \\ Q \end{bmatrix} = \frac{1}{c+a}\begin{bmatrix} c & a \\ -1 & 1 \end{bmatrix}\begin{bmatrix} b \\ d \end{bmatrix}$$

that is,

$$P = \frac{cb + ad}{c+a} \quad \text{and} \quad Q = \frac{-b + d}{c+a}$$

The multiplier for Q due to changes in b is given by the (2,1) element of the inverse matrix so is

$$\frac{-1}{c+a}$$

Given that c and a are both positive it follows that the multiplier is negative. Consequently an increase in b leads to a decrease in Q.

4

$$A_{11} = + \begin{vmatrix} 4 & 3 \\ 3 & 4 \end{vmatrix} = 7$$

$$A_{12} = - \begin{vmatrix} 1 & 3 \\ 1 & 4 \end{vmatrix} = -1$$

$$A_{13} = + \begin{vmatrix} 1 & 4 \\ 1 & 3 \end{vmatrix} = -1$$

$$A_{21} = - \begin{vmatrix} 3 & 3 \\ 3 & 4 \end{vmatrix} = -3$$

$$A_{22} = + \begin{vmatrix} 1 & 3 \\ 1 & 4 \end{vmatrix} = 1$$

$$A_{23} = - \begin{vmatrix} 1 & 3 \\ 1 & 3 \end{vmatrix} = 0$$

$$A_{31} = + \begin{vmatrix} 3 & 3 \\ 4 & 3 \end{vmatrix} = -3$$

$$A_{32} = - \begin{vmatrix} 1 & 3 \\ 1 & 3 \end{vmatrix} = 0$$

$$A_{33} = + \begin{vmatrix} 1 & 3 \\ 1 & 4 \end{vmatrix} = 1$$

5 Expanding along the top row of **A** gives

$$|A| = a_{11}A_{11} + a_{12}A_{12} + a_{13}A_{13}$$
$$= 1(7) + 3(-1) + 3(-1) = 1$$

using the values of A_{11}, A_{12} and A_{13} from Problem 4. Other rows and columns are treated similarly. Expanding down the last column of **B** gives

$$|B| = b_{13}B_{13} + b_{23}B_{23} + b_{33}B_{33}$$
$$= 0(B_{13}) + 0(B_{23}) + 0(B_{33}) = 0$$

6 The cofactors of **A** have already been found in Problem 4. Stacking them in their natural positions gives the adjugate matrix

$$\begin{bmatrix} 7 & -1 & -1 \\ -3 & 1 & 0 \\ -3 & 0 & 1 \end{bmatrix}$$

Transposing gives the adjoint matrix

$$\begin{bmatrix} 7 & -3 & -3 \\ -1 & 1 & 0 \\ -1 & 0 & 1 \end{bmatrix}$$

The determinant of **A** has already been found in Problem 5 to be 1 so the inverse matrix is the same as the adjoint matrix.
    The determinant of **B** has already been found in Problem 5 to be zero so **B** is singular and does not have an inverse.

7 Using the inverse matrix in Problem 6

$$\begin{bmatrix} P_1 \\ P_2 \\ P_3 \end{bmatrix} = \begin{bmatrix} 7 & -3 & -3 \\ -1 & 1 & 0 \\ -1 & 0 & 1 \end{bmatrix} \begin{bmatrix} 32 \\ 37 \\ 35 \end{bmatrix} = \begin{bmatrix} 8 \\ 5 \\ 3 \end{bmatrix}$$

8 (1) (a) $|A| = -3$ (b) $|B| = 4$

(c) $AB = \begin{bmatrix} 4 & 4 \\ 7 & 4 \end{bmatrix}$

so $|AB| = -12$. These results give $|AB| = |A||B|$, that is 'determinant of a product is the product of the determinants'.

(2) (a) $A^{-1} = \begin{bmatrix} -1/3 & 1/3 \\ 5/3 & -2/3 \end{bmatrix}$

(b) $B^{-1} = \begin{bmatrix} 1 & 0 \\ -1/2 & 1/4 \end{bmatrix}$

(c) $(AB)^{-1} = \begin{bmatrix} -1/3 & 1/3 \\ 7/12 & -1/3 \end{bmatrix}$

These results give $(AB)^{-1} = B^{-1}A^{-1}$, that is 'inverse of a product is the product of the inverses multiplied in reverse order'.

9 $\dfrac{1}{25} \begin{bmatrix} -9 & -1 \\ -2 & -3 \end{bmatrix}; \begin{bmatrix} P_1 \\ P_2 \end{bmatrix} = \begin{bmatrix} 40 \\ 10 \end{bmatrix}.$

10 Commodity market is in equilibrium when $Y = C + I$ so $Y = aY + b + cr + d$ which rearranges as

$$(1 - a)Y - cr = b + d \qquad (1)$$

Money market is in equilibrium when $M_S = M_D$ so $M_S^* = k_1Y + k_2r + k_3$ which rearranges as

$$k_1Y + k_2r = M_S^* - k_3 \qquad (2)$$

In matrix notation equations (1) and (2) become

$$\begin{bmatrix} 1-a & -c \\ k_1 & k_2 \end{bmatrix} \begin{bmatrix} Y \\ r \end{bmatrix} = \begin{bmatrix} b+d \\ M_S^* - k_3 \end{bmatrix}$$

Using the inverse of the coefficient matrix,

$$\begin{bmatrix} Y \\ r \end{bmatrix} = \frac{1}{k_2(1-a) + ck_1}$$
$$\times \begin{bmatrix} k_2 & c \\ -k_1 & 1-a \end{bmatrix} \begin{bmatrix} b+d \\ M_S^* - k_3 \end{bmatrix}$$
$$Y = \frac{k_2(b+d) + c(M_S^* - k_3)}{k_2(1-a) + ck_1}$$

and

$$r = \frac{-k_1(b+d) + (1-a)(M_S^* - k_3)}{k_2(1-a) + ck_1}$$

The required multiplier is

$$\frac{\partial r}{\partial M_S^*} = \frac{1-a}{k_2(1-a) + ck_1}$$

Now $1 - a > 0$ since $a < 1$ so numerator is positive. Also $k_2 < 0$, $1 - a > 0$, gives $k_2(1 - a) < 0$ and $c < 0$, $k_1 > 0$ gives $ck_1 < 0$, so the denominator is negative.

11 The determinant of **A** is $-10 \neq 0$ so matrix is non-singular.

$$\mathbf{A}^{-1} = \begin{bmatrix} 1/10 & 3/10 & -1/2 \\ 3/10 & -1/10 & 1/2 \\ -1/2 & 1/2 & -1/2 \end{bmatrix}$$

It is interesting to notice that because the original matrix **A** is symmetric so is $\mathbf{A}^{-1}$. The determinant of **B** is zero so it is singular and does not have an inverse.

12 $$\mathbf{A}^{-1} = \frac{1}{-41} \begin{bmatrix} 29 & 11 & 3 \\ 4 & 10 & -1 \\ 9 & 2 & 8 \end{bmatrix};$$

$$\begin{bmatrix} P_1 \\ P_2 \\ P_3 \end{bmatrix} = \begin{bmatrix} 20 \\ 5 \\ 8 \end{bmatrix}$$

Section 7.3

1 (a) By Cramer's rule,

$$x_2 = \frac{\det(\mathbf{A}_2)}{\det(\mathbf{A})}$$

where

$$\det(\mathbf{A}_2) = \begin{vmatrix} 2 & 16 \\ 3 & -9 \end{vmatrix} = -66$$

$$\det(\mathbf{A}) = \begin{vmatrix} 2 & 4 \\ 3 & -5 \end{vmatrix} = -22$$

Hence

$$x_2 = \frac{-66}{-22} = 3$$

(b) By Cramer's rule,

$$x_3 = \frac{\det(\mathbf{A}_3)}{\det(\mathbf{A})}$$

where

$$\det(\mathbf{A}_3) = \begin{vmatrix} 4 & 1 & 8 \\ -2 & 5 & 4 \\ 3 & 2 & 9 \end{vmatrix}$$

$$= 4 \begin{vmatrix} 5 & 4 \\ 2 & 9 \end{vmatrix} - 1 \begin{vmatrix} -2 & 4 \\ 3 & 9 \end{vmatrix}$$
$$+ 8 \begin{vmatrix} -2 & 5 \\ 3 & 2 \end{vmatrix}$$

$$= 4(37) - 1(-30) + 8(-19)$$

$$= 26$$

and

$$\det(\mathbf{A}) = \begin{vmatrix} 4 & 1 & 3 \\ -2 & 5 & 1 \\ 3 & 2 & 4 \end{vmatrix}$$

$$= 4 \begin{vmatrix} 5 & 1 \\ 2 & 4 \end{vmatrix} - 1 \begin{vmatrix} -2 & 1 \\ 3 & 4 \end{vmatrix}$$
$$+ 3 \begin{vmatrix} -2 & 5 \\ 3 & 2 \end{vmatrix}$$

$$= 4(18) - 1(-11) + 3(-19)$$

$$= 26$$

Hence

$$x_3 = \frac{26}{26} = 1$$

2 The variable Y_d is the third so Cramer's rule gives

$$Y_d = \frac{\det(\mathbf{A}_3)}{\det(\mathbf{A})}$$

where

$$\mathbf{A}_3 = \begin{bmatrix} 1 & -1 & I^* + G^* & 0 \\ 0 & 1 & b & 0 \\ -1 & 0 & 0 & 1 \\ -t & 0 & T^* & 1 \end{bmatrix}$$

Expanding along the second row gives

$$\det(\mathbf{A}_3) = 1 \begin{vmatrix} 1 & I^* + G^* & 0 \\ -1 & 0 & 1 \\ -t & T^* & 1 \end{vmatrix}$$

$$-b\begin{vmatrix} 1 & -1 & 0 \\ -1 & 0 & 1 \\ -t & 0 & 1 \end{vmatrix}$$

since along the second row the pattern is '$-+-+$'. Now

$$\begin{vmatrix} 1 & I^*+G^* & 0 \\ -1 & 0 & 1 \\ -t & T^* & 1 \end{vmatrix} = 1\begin{vmatrix} 0 & 1 \\ T^* & 1 \end{vmatrix}$$

$$-(I^*+G^*)\begin{vmatrix} -1 & 1 \\ -t & 1 \end{vmatrix}$$

$$= -T^* - (I^*+G^*)(-1+t)$$

(expanding along the first row) and

$$\begin{vmatrix} 1 & -1 & 0 \\ -1 & 0 & 1 \\ -t & 0 & 1 \end{vmatrix} = -(-1)\begin{vmatrix} -1 & 1 \\ -t & 1 \end{vmatrix} = -1+t$$

(expanding down the second column).
Hence

$$\det(A_3) = -T^* - (I^*+G^*)(-1+t) \\ -b(-1+t)$$

From the worked example given in the text,

$$\det(A) = 1 - a + at$$

Hence

$$Y_d = \frac{-T^* - (I^*+G^*)(-1+t) - b(-1+t)}{1-a+at}$$

3 Substituting C_1, M_1 and I_1^* into the equation for Y_1 gives

$$Y_1 = 0.7Y_1 + 50 + 200 + X_1 - 0.3Y_1$$

Also, since $X_1 = M_2 = 0.1Y_2$, we get

$$Y_1 = 0.7Y_1 + 50 + 200 + 0.1Y_2 - 0.3Y_1$$

which rearranges as

$$0.6Y_1 - 0.1Y_2 = 250$$

In the same way the second set of equations leads to

$$-0.3Y_1 + 0.3Y_2 = 400$$

Hence

$$\begin{bmatrix} 0.6 & -0.1 \\ -0.3 & 0.3 \end{bmatrix}\begin{bmatrix} Y_1 \\ Y_2 \end{bmatrix} = \begin{bmatrix} 250 \\ 400 \end{bmatrix}$$

In this question both Y_1 and Y_2 are required so it is easier to solve using matrix inverses rather than Cramer's rule which gives

$$Y_1 = \frac{1}{0.15}\begin{bmatrix} 0.3 & 0.1 \\ 0.3 & 0.6 \end{bmatrix}\begin{bmatrix} 250 \\ 400 \end{bmatrix}$$

$$= \frac{1}{0.15}\begin{bmatrix} 115 \\ 315 \end{bmatrix}$$

Hence $Y_1 = 766.67$ and $Y_2 = 2100$. The balance of payments for country 1 is

$$X_1 - M_1 = M_2 - M_1 = 0.1Y_2 - 0.3Y_1 \\ = 0.1(2100) - 0.3(766.67) = -20$$

Moreover, since only two countries are involved, it follows that country 2 will have a surplus of 20.

4 **(a)** $x_1 = \dfrac{\det(A_1)}{\det(A)} = \dfrac{72}{18} = 4$

(b) $x_2 = \dfrac{\det(A_2)}{\det(A)} = \dfrac{126}{42} = 3$

(c) $x_4 = \dfrac{\det(A_4)}{\det(A)} = \dfrac{-1425}{475} = -3$

5 The multiplier is

$$\frac{-k_1}{k_2(1-a)+ck_1}$$

which is positive since the top and bottom of this fraction are both negative. To see that the bottom is negative, note that $k_2(1-a) < 0$ because $k_2 < 0$ and $a < 1$, and $ck_1 < 0$ because $c < 0$ and $k_1 > 0$.

6 The equations are

$$0.6Y_1 - 0.1Y_2 - I_1^* = 50$$

$$-0.2Y_1 + 0.3Y_2 = 150$$

$$0.2Y_1 - 0.1Y_2 = 0$$

The third equation follows from the fact

that if the balance of payments is zero then $M_1 = X_1$, or equivalently, $M_1 = M_2$. Cramer's rule gives

$$I_1^* = \frac{\det(A_3)}{\det(A)} = \frac{4}{0.04} = 100$$

7
$$\begin{bmatrix} 1-a_1+m_1 & -m_2 \\ -m_1 & 1-a_2+m_2 \end{bmatrix} \begin{bmatrix} Y_1 \\ Y_2 \end{bmatrix}$$
$$= \begin{bmatrix} b_1 + I_1^* \\ b_2 + I_2^* \end{bmatrix}$$

$$Y_1 = \frac{(b_1+I_1^*)(1-a_2+m_2) + m_2(b_2+I_2^*)}{(1-a_1+m_1)(1-a_2+m_2) - m_1 m_2}$$

The multiplier is

$$\frac{m_2}{(1-a_1+m_1)(1-a_2+m_2) - m_1 m_2}$$

which is positive since the top and bottom of the fraction are both positive. To see that the bottom is positive, note that since $a_1 < 1$, $1-a_i+m_i > m_i$ so that $(1-a_1+m_1)(1-a_2+m_2) > m_1 m_2$. Hence the national income of one country rises as the investment in the other country rises.

Section 7.4

1 $\quad d = \begin{bmatrix} 1000 \\ 300 \\ 700 \end{bmatrix} - \begin{bmatrix} 0.2 & 0.4 & 0.2 \\ 0.1 & 0.2 & 0.1 \\ 0.1 & 0.1 & 0 \end{bmatrix} \begin{bmatrix} 1000 \\ 300 \\ 700 \end{bmatrix}$

$$= \begin{bmatrix} 540 \\ 70 \\ 570 \end{bmatrix}$$

2 The matrix of technical coefficients is

$$A = \begin{bmatrix} 0.2 & 0.2 \\ 0.4 & 0.1 \end{bmatrix}$$

so

$$I - A = \begin{bmatrix} 0.8 & -0.2 \\ -0.4 & 0.9 \end{bmatrix}$$

which has inverse

$$(I-A)^{-1} = \frac{1}{0.64} \begin{bmatrix} 0.9 & 0.2 \\ 0.4 & 0.8 \end{bmatrix}$$

Hence

$$x = \frac{1}{0.64} \begin{bmatrix} 0.9 & 0.2 \\ 0.4 & 0.8 \end{bmatrix} \begin{bmatrix} 760 \\ 420 \end{bmatrix}$$

$$= \begin{bmatrix} 1200 \\ 1000 \end{bmatrix}$$

so total output is 1200 units for engineering and 1000 units for transport.

3 Total outputs for I1, I2, I3 and I4 are found by summing along each row to get 1000, 500, 2000 and 1000 respectively. Matrix of technical coefficients is obtained by dividing the columns of the inter-industrial flow table by these numbers to get

$$A = \begin{bmatrix} 0 & 0.6 & 0.05 & 0.1 \\ 0.1 & 0 & 0.1 & 0.1 \\ 0.2 & 0.2 & 0 & 0.4 \\ 0.3 & 0 & 0.05 & 0 \end{bmatrix}$$

4 $\quad I - A = \begin{bmatrix} 0.9 & -0.2 & -0.2 \\ -0.1 & 0.9 & -0.1 \\ -0.1 & -0.3 & 0.9 \end{bmatrix}$

so

$$(I-A)^{-1} = \frac{1}{0.658} \begin{bmatrix} 0.78 & 0.24 & 0.20 \\ 0.10 & 0.79 & 0.11 \\ 0.12 & 0.29 & 0.79 \end{bmatrix}$$

We are given that

$$\Delta d = \begin{bmatrix} 1000 \\ 0 \\ -800 \end{bmatrix}$$

so

$$\Delta x = \frac{1}{0.658} \begin{bmatrix} 0.78 & 0.24 & 0.20 \\ 0.10 & 0.79 & 0.11 \\ 0.12 & 0.29 & 0.79 \end{bmatrix}$$

$$\times \begin{bmatrix} 1000 \\ 0 \\ -800 \end{bmatrix} = \begin{bmatrix} 942 \\ 18 \\ -778 \end{bmatrix}$$

Hence, total outputs for I1 and I2 rise by

942 and 18 respectively, and total output for I3 falls by 778 (to the nearest whole number).

5 $[450 \quad 900 \quad 400 \quad 4350 \quad 50]^T$.

6 $A = \begin{bmatrix} 0 & 0.1 & 0.2 \\ 0.1 & 0 & 0.1 \\ 0.2 & 0.2 & 0 \end{bmatrix}$

$(I - A)^{-1} = \dfrac{1}{0.924} \begin{bmatrix} 0.98 & 0.14 & 0.21 \\ 0.12 & 0.96 & 0.12 \\ 0.22 & 0.22 & 0.99 \end{bmatrix}$

(1) 1000 units of water, 500 units of steel and 1000 units of electricity.

(2) The element in the first row and third column of $(I - A)^{-1}$ is

$$\frac{0.21}{0.924} = 0.23$$

Change in water output is $0.23 \times 100 = 23$.

7 (a) $[500 \quad 1000]^T$

(b) $\begin{bmatrix} 0.2 & 0.1 \\ 0.4 & 0.5 \end{bmatrix}$

(c) $\dfrac{1}{36} \begin{bmatrix} 0.5 & 0.1 \\ 0.4 & 0.8 \end{bmatrix}$

(d) $[694 \quad 1056]^T$

CHAPTER 8

Section 8.1

1 The line $-x + 3y = 6$ passes through $(0, 2)$ and $(-6, 0)$. Substituting $x = 1$, $y = 4$ into the equation gives

$$-1 + 3(4) = 11$$

This is greater than 6 so the test point satisfies the inequality. The corresponding region is shown in Figure S8.1.

2 The non-negativity constraints indicate that we restrict our attention to the positive quadrant.

The line $x + 2y = 10$ passes through $(0, 5)$ and $(10, 0)$

The line $3x + y = 10$ passes through $(0, 10)$ and $(\frac{10}{3}, 0)$

Also the test point $(0, 0)$ satisfies both of the corresponding inequalities so we are interested in the region below both lines as shown in Figure S8.2.

3

Point	Objective function
(5, 3)	$-2(5) + 3 = -7$
(2, 4)	$-2(2) + 4 = 0$
(0, 0)	$-2(0) + 0 = 0$
(11.2, 0.2)	$-2(11.2) + 0.2 = -22.2$

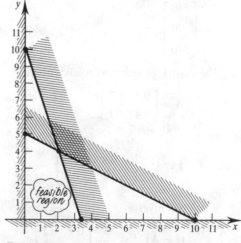

Figure S8.2

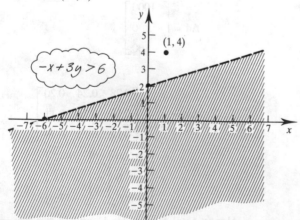

Figure S8.1

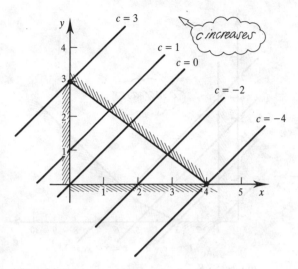

Figure S8.3

The remaining points lie outside the feasible region.

4 The answers to parts (1) and (2) are shown in Figure S8.3.
   (3) Once c becomes greater than 3 the lines no longer intersect the feasible region. The maximum value of c (that is, the objective function) is therefore 3 which occurs at the corner $(0, 3)$, when $x = 0$, $y = 3$.

5 *Step 1*   The feasible region is sketched in Figures S8.4.

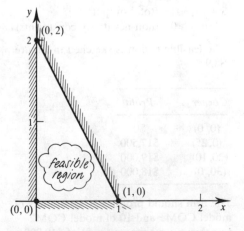

Figure S8.4

Step 2   Corners are $(0, 0)$ $(1, 0)$ and $(0, 2)$
Step 3

Corner	Objective function
$(0, 0)$	$0 - 0 = 0$
$(1, 0)$	$1 - 0 = 1$
$(0, 2)$	$0 - 2 = -2$

Minimum is -2 which occurs at $(0, 2)$.

6 *Step 1*   The feasible region is sketched in Figure S8.2.
   Step 2   Corners are $(0, 0), (0, 5), (2, 4)$ and $(\frac{10}{3}, 0)$
   Step 3

Corner	Objective function
$(0, 0)$	$3(0) + 5(0) = 0$
$(0, 5)$	$3(0) + 5(5) = 25$
$(2, 4)$	$3(2) + 5(4) = 26$
$(\frac{10}{3}, 0)$	$3(\frac{10}{3}) + 5(0) = 10$

Maximum is 26 which occurs at $(2,4)$.

7 The feasible regions for parts (a), (b) and (c) are sketched in Figures S8.5, S8.6 and S8.7 respectively.

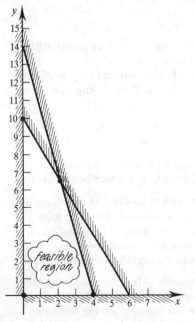

Figure S8.5

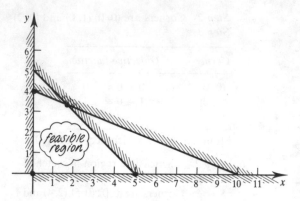

Figure S8.6

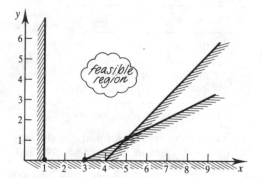

Figure S8.7

8 **(a)** Maximum is 90 which occurs at (0, 10).
  (b) Maximum is 25 which occurs at
   $(\frac{5}{3}, \frac{10}{3})$. Note that the exact coordinates
   can be found by solving the
   simultaneous equations

$$2x + 5y = 20$$
$$x + y = 5$$

   using an algebraic method.
  (c) Minimum is 1 which occurs at (1, 0).

9 Figure S8.8 shows that the problem does
  not have a finite solution. The lines
  $x+y=c$ pass through $(c, 0)$ and $(0, c)$.
  As c increases the lines move across the
  region to the right without bound.

10 Minimum is -16 which occurs at the
  two corners (2, 2) and $(\frac{8}{3}, 0)$ so any point
  on the line segment joining these two
  corners is also a solution.

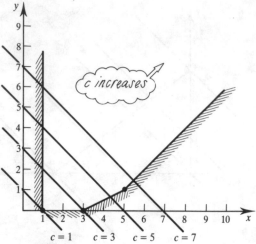

Figure S8.8

11 $\mathbf{c} = \begin{bmatrix} 4 \\ 9 \end{bmatrix}$ $\mathbf{x} = \begin{bmatrix} x \\ y \end{bmatrix}$ $\mathbf{b} = \begin{bmatrix} 30 \\ 28 \end{bmatrix}$ $\mathbf{0} = \begin{bmatrix} 0 \\ 0 \end{bmatrix}$

  and $\mathbf{A} = \begin{bmatrix} 5 & 3 \\ 7 & 2 \end{bmatrix}$

Section 8.2

1 Let x = weekly output of model COM1,
   y = weekly output of model COM2.

Maximize $600x + 700y$ (profit)

subject to

$1200x + 1600y \leqslant 40\,000$ (production costs)

$x + y \leqslant 30$ (total output)
$x \geqslant 0, \, y \geqslant 0$ (non-negativity constraints)

The feasible region is sketched in Figure
S8.9.

Corner	Profit
(0, 0)	$0
(0, 25)	$17,500
(20, 10)	$19,000
(30, 0)	$18,000

The firm should produce 20 computers of
model COM1 and 10 of model COM2
to achieve a maximum profit of $19,000.

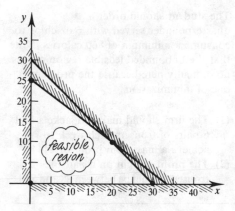

Figure S8.9

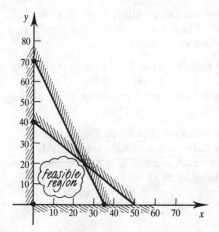

Figure S8.10

2 Let $x =$ number of copies of
Microeconomics, $y =$ number of copies of
Macroeconomics.

Maximize $12x + 18y$ (profit)

subject to

$$12x + 15y \leqslant 600 \quad \text{(printing time)}$$
$$18x + 9y \;\leqslant 630 \quad \text{(binding time)}$$
$$x \geqslant 0, \; y \geqslant 0 \quad \text{(non-negativity}$$
$$\text{constraints)}$$

The feasible region is sketched in Figure
S8.10

Corner	Profit
(0, 0)	$0
(0, 40)	$720
(25, 20)	$660
(35, 0)	$420

The publisher should produce 40 copies of
Macroeconomics and no copies of
Microeconomics to achieve a maximum
profit of $720.

3 Maximize $3x + 7y$ (utility)

subject to

$$150x + 70y \leqslant 2100 \quad \text{(cost)}$$
$$x \geqslant 9, \; y \geqslant 0$$

The feasible region is sketched in Figure
S8.11.

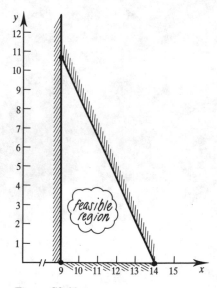

Figure S8.11

Corner	Objective function
(9, 0)	27
(14, 0)	42
$(9, \frac{75}{7})$	102

The maximum value of U occurs at $(9, \frac{75}{7})$.
However, it is impossible to visit the
theatre $\frac{75}{7}$ times. The point in the feasible
region with whole number coordinates

which maximizes utility is (9, 10) so we need to buy 9 items of clothing and visit the theatre 10 times per year.

4 The manufacturer should produce 10 bikes of type B and 15 of type C each month to achieve a maximum profit of $5100.

5 The firm should produce 720 cartons of The Caribbean and 630 cartons of Mr Fruity each week to give a maximum profit of $650.70.

6 The student should order a quarterpounder served with 6 oz chips to consume a minimum of 860 calories. Note that the unbounded feasible region causes no difficulty here because the problem is one of minimization.

7 (1) The firm should make 30 jackets and 6 pairs of trousers each week to achieve a maximum profit of $444.
(2) The profit margin on a pair of trousers should be between $8 and $14.

Index